BENCHMARK PRESS

A BREED APART

Douglas Hunter is a freelance writer, editor and graphic designer. He is the author of two books on yacht racing, *Against the Odds* and *Trials* (with co-author Jeff Boyd), as well as the bestselling and critically acclaimed *Open Ice: The Tim Horton Story*. He lives in Burlington, Ontario with his wife Debbie and their three children.

For Andrew, who stopped his share.

Goaltender for Winnipeg's
Victoria Hockey Club of 1899

A BREED APART

AN ILLUSTRATED HISTORY OF GOALTENDING

DOUGLAS HUNTER

Benchmark
PRESS

A division of Triumph Books

BENCHMARK
Distributed in the United States by Benchmark Press
601 South LaSalle Street, Suite 500
Chicago, Illinois 60605
(312) 939-3330

ISBN 1-892049-03-1

A VIKING BOOK
Published by the Penguin Group
Penguin Books Canada Ltd, 10 Alcorn Avenue, Toronto, Ontario, Canada M4V 3B2
Penguin Books Ltd, 27 Wrights Lane, London W8 5TZ, England
Penguin Putnam Inc., 375 Hudson Street Street, New York, New York 10014, U.S.A.
Penguin Books Australia Ltd, Ringwood, Victoria, Australia
Penguin Books (NZ) Ltd, cnr Rosedale and Airborne Roads, Albany, Auckland 1310, New Zealand

Penguin Books Ltd, Registered Offices: Harmondsworth, Middlesex, England

First published 1995
10 9 8 7 6 5 4 3 2 1

Copyright © Douglas Hunter, 1995

Manufactured in Italy.

ACKNOWLEDGEMENTS

This book would not exist had a lightbulb not appeared over the head of Wayne Epp, who thought it was time somebody took a good hard look at those folks behind the mask. Penguin Books Canada executive assistant Jane Cain then brought Wayne's suggestion into the publisher's editorial circle, whereupon it was flung in my direction. My thanks to both Wayne and Jane for a concept I took to with great delight.

This is the fourth book that I have written, but the first that I have also designed and illustrated. Going solo on an illustrated book can feel like starring in some cliched B-movie in which a neophyte ends up flying a 747. Keeping the machine in the air isn't the tricky part; it's *landing*. In this situation you need lots of trained professionals on the ground to talk you in, telling you what a fine job you're doing while judiciously spraying the runway with fire-retardant foam and calling in every emergency response vehicle from miles around. I'm relieved to say that the fact you are reading these words is proof I did not buzz the control-tower upside-down, at least not more than once. Profuse thanks are extended to the publishing professionals at and associated with Penguin who took turns at the mike and brought me and this project back to earth, safe and sound, if a little twitchy. They are publisher Cynthia Good, my editor, Meg Masters, freelance copy editor Jem Bates, art director Martin Gould, production director Dianne Craig and production editor Lori Ledingham. Publicity manager and confirmed hockey connoisseur Scott Sellers also weighed in with his ideas on who should be in this volume, and at times I actually listened. To all of the above, and to the rest of the Penguin staffers (Jackie, Louise, Sharon, Barb) who kept me running nearly on time and at top speed, my gratitude. My thanks also to a friend and publishing professional, Robin Brass, for his voluminous advice and occasional use of his studio.

The meat and potatoes of this book were made possible by the cooperation of two key groups: the archivists at the Hockey Hall of Fame, and the goaltenders who were so generous with their time. Craig Campbell, Jeff Davis and Phil Pritchard at the hall were full of advice and assistance. Craig (who is known to stop pucks just because he likes to) bore the brunt of my demands on their time and patience, and did a terrific job of digging up photographs that have never before been published.

For a bunch of people who are supposed to be a breed apart, the members of the goaltending fraternity were quick to welcome into their midst a total stranger. Gerry McNeil, Johnny Bower, Glenn Hall, Dave Dryden, Frank Brimsek, Emile Francis, Ed Giacomin and Chuck Rayner made it possible for me to appreciate their profession in a way I never could have from films, photographs, yellowing clippings and volumes of anecdotes and statistics alone. They learned from the greats before them, were greats themselves, and in some cases they went on to coach a new generation of greats. Collectively they provided a wonderful perspective on what has changed, and what has not, in the business of stopping pucks, and on what it has meant to be a goaltender. I must also thank several shooters—Dave Keon, Ted Kennedy and Don Rope—for their valued input.

Finally, a word of appreciation to my wife and children, for putting up for so long with a dad who seemed to spend most of his waking hours transfixed before a computer monitor in the basement, and for peeling my fingers off the joystick when everything had stopped moving.

Douglas Hunter

CONTENTS

Above: Hockey team of
Gleichen, Alberta, 1920/21

For a guide to the career chart format used in this book, see pages 16–17.

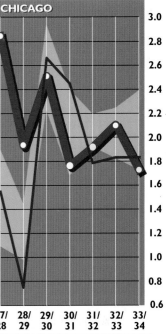

CHICAGO

	27/28	28/29	29/30	30/31	31/32	32/33	33/34
GAMES	40	44	44	44	48	48	48
SHUTOUTS	3	5	3	12	4	5	10
STANLEY CUP			QF	F	QF		W
ALL-STAR TEAM			1		1	2	1

WHAT'S IT _all about,_ ALFIE?

WHO HONOURS THE GOALTENDER MOST? OTHER GOALTENDERS, MAINLY. EVER SINCE SOMEONE FIRST STOPPED A PUCK, THEY HAVE TRULY BEEN A BREED APART

THE NEW YORK RANGERS SCORE ON MONTREAL'S BILL DURNAN, WHO HAS LOST HIS STICK, IN 1949. DURNAN WON SIX VEZINAS IN SEVEN SEASONS, BUT THE PRESSURES OF PERFORMANCE CONSUMED HIM. WHEN THE RANGERS RACED TO A 3–0 SERIES LEAD AGAINST MONTREAL IN THE 1950 SEMIFINAL, DURNAN QUIT, UNABLE TO FACE ANOTHER SHOT.

No other athlete quite measures up to hockey's goaltender. People who seek out parallels, even goaltenders themselves, tend to turn to baseball. Sometimes they select the pitcher, because, like the goaltender, his role is so distinct from that of his teammates, and because the game's outcome rides so much on his singular performance. And, like a goaltender, he can be unceremoniously yanked from the game when things aren't going well. Others cite the catcher, because of the similarity of his equipment, and of his duty to stop a hard projectile. But Eddie Giacomin, who played catcher in the off-season while starring in goal for the New York Rangers, stresses that at least the catcher knows what's coming at him, because he gives the pitcher the signal for a particular pitch.

"A baseball catcher's job is the closest thing to it," Gerry Cheevers has observed. "I mean, he alone dons the tools of ignorance and crouches behind the plate like an orangutan. But even the catcher goes up to hit like the rest of the ballplayers. So we goaltenders, alone and unloved, tend to be very proud bastards."

There really is no one else like them. Hockey's goaltenders are a breed apart, and always have been.

No role in team sport has such violence associated with it. Injury, now much less a part of goaltending with advances in equipment, is an essential part of its lore, and is still implicit, even though the goaltenders themselves have tended to downplay the risk. Terry Sawchuk, for one, insisted that defencemen bore the brunt of the game's abuse. Yet the goaltender alone dresses for the worst. He is sheathed in more paraphernalia than a medieval knight, deliberately placing himself in the path of a chunk of vulcanized rubber hurtling at more than 100 miles per hour. Sticks whack him. Skates threaten to slice him open. Opposing players bowl him right over, jab at his underbelly as he smothers a loose puck.

Few people remember particular saves by a goaltender. Rather, they remember the goals that got by them. Scarcely a spring goes by when someone in the thrall of the latest playoffs doesn't remind former Montreal goaltender Gerry McNeil of the overtime goal by Bill Barilko that won the Maple Leafs the 1950/51 Stanley Cup. And they remember the violence. The most gripping images of the goaltender are of Georges Vezina leaving the ice of the Montreal Forum for the last time in 1925, coughing up blood as tuberculosis advanced to claim him. They include Jacques Plante in 1959 leaving the ice bloodied for the umpteenth time, and returning wearing the first functional face mask. And even after the mask had become part of the game, the stitches painted onto Gerry Cheevers' mask reminded fans of the implicit hazards of the profession.

Other injuries can't be fixed with casts or stitches. Coaches humiliate you by pulling you out of the game in front of a crowd of thousands, thereby blaming you alone for a bad night by the team. You are praised routinely as the most important player on a team, but routinely overlooked when it comes to handing out major trophies or the fattest contracts.

Who honours the goaltender most? Other goaltenders, mainly. The National Hockey League's Hart Memorial Trophy, awarded to the player judged most valuable to his team, has been awarded to a goaltender only four times since its creation in 1923, and not once since 1962. The Hart voting has seen great names like Sawchuk, Bower, Hall, Giacomin, Esposito, Dryden, Cheevers and Parent, to name but a few, skate by, and has passed over every one of them. While ten goaltenders' numbers have been retired or honoured by NHL teams, the Bruins have yet to pay formal tribute to Thompson, Brimsek or Cheevers.

There is still a sense of fraternity among them. The rest of the game understands that there cannot be a game without them, but historically has shown reluctance to make their duties physically and mentally tolerable. Yet there has never been a shortage of young men—and women—determined to join this peculiar fraternity. "It's amazing the number of goaltenders that came up who were that good," says Chuck Rayner of his glory days after the Second World War, when there was no mask, the slapshot was a newly arrived terror, the crease was at its smallest size in history, and the stresses of the game were driving one star netminder after another into early retirement, only to be replaced by fresh cannon fodder of equal or greater talent.

There is a fable-like quality common to many great careers. The young hopefuls arrive as raw, eager rookies, sometimes in their teens, to replace a beloved star, sometimes drinking from the Stanley Cup in their very first tour of duty. And in time, perhaps in only a few seasons, the team's management decides that the once-sparkling rookie has given them all they can wring from him, and

they sell him or trade him. And lo and behold, another raw, eager rookie is ready to take his place on the ice and taste the champagne, just as he once did. The king is dead; long live the king.

The cycle rolls on, each generation experiencing a different game from the one they inherited. It has always changed, and continues to change. The goaltenders themselves sometimes fail to appreciate how much it has changed, to realize, irrespective of the fact that there are still six players on each team, two nets, one puck and a sheet of ice 200 feet long and 85 feet wide, that every era has made its own particular demands on the goaltender. For the first few decades of the sport, until 1917, a goaltender wasn't allowed to drop to the ice. For decades more, he was permitted to catch the puck, but not to hold it, or to smother it. It wasn't until the Second World War that goaltenders began wearing a proper catching glove, a fact that astonishes goaltenders who know stealing a goal in the palm of their hand, to be one of the position's most basic, elegant attractions. And until the mid-1960s, professional goaltenders overwhelmingly carried their teams singlehanded. Nobody would take their place in mid-game, except in the case of the most serious injury, and even then, goaltenders like Roy Worters remained in the net when they should have been on their way to the hospital for surgery.

Their lives were defined so much by their equipment—the lack of it or the quality of it—that it is equipment the retired ones cite overwhelmingly when they explain how and why their position has changed. They pay the compliments they feel the new breed deserve, but they also voice their concerns over what has happened to the craft they helped shape. They wish they could do it all over with the equipment now used. They try not to give weight to numbers of any kind, be it a goals-against average or a won-lost record or a save percentage. Goaltenders knew when they played a good game, whether they won 1–0 in double overtime or lost 9–0, and they still know that. Back in 1899, Quebec goaltender Frank Stocking stated: "It is a mistake for a goal minder to imagine that he is not doing his duty because three or four or more points have been scored against him, because the fault may, and very often does, rest upon the poor assistance he receives from his defence and forwards." Goaltenders are still nodding enthusiastically at those words.

They knew what it took to play the position well, but they had to listen to coaches and managers who thought they knew better. When they tried to tell a coach that someone had scored with a drop shot, they had to listen to that coach telling them there was no such thing. When they tried to tell an equipment manufacturer that the padding was wrong, and couldn't make them understand, they had to put up with what they were given or make the gear themselves. When a league's finer minds decided to change rules that directly affected the

HOW SWEET IT IS: MORE THAN FORTY YEARS AFTER BILL DURNAN QUIT THE GAME, MONTREAL GOALTENDER PATRICK ROY CELEBRATED THE CANADIENS' VICTORY IN THE 1992/93 STANLEY CUP.

goaltender, there was almost certainly no goaltender in the room. They took what the game fired at them, and did their best to turn it away.

They made for some of the game's best analytic minds. Emile Francis shone behind the bench and in management; Bill Durnan, Turk Broda, Clint Benedict and Gerry Cheevers, to name only a few, tried coaching, and Ken Dryden described on paper the position, and the game itself, the way it had never been described. They were able to do so because they played a role that allowed for contemplation, for seeing the entire game in motion before them and around them. They rested at the very heart of what it means to win and lose.

No other player feels the responsibility of success and failure as they do, and they can be hurt by it in ways more painful than the way a puck can hurt. They are measured by relative failure, which can make it difficult to find comfort in success when the team as a whole does not succeed. If three goals get by him and his team only produces two in response, then he has failed, even if he has not. In a nominally team sport, he stands truly apart, almost solitarily accountable, all too easy to damn when praise, in fact, is called for. And because there is such a separateness to his role, he can allow that separateness to make a team's failure his own. And if he takes the opposite tack, and turns failure back upon the team, then he is an arrogant loner and an eccentric and not a "team" player.

It is difficult to appreciate, when the team is passing around the plate of bitter pills, that the goaltender has the most difficulty choking one down, because once he has swallowed one he might as well swallow all of them. Once a goaltender concedes that the score should not have been 3–2 for the other side, then the rest of the team is off the hook. Rather than thinking that they—all twenty of them—should have come up with one more goal to tie it, they may conclude that they in fact produced all the points necessary. It was their own goaltender, one man, who gave away the goal they could not produce. After all, if it is true that a goaltender is singlehandedly capable of winning a game, then surely he is singlehandedly capable of losing one. A goaltender who believes the former is predisposed to believe the latter. He is hardwired to be both hero and goat.

Any exploration of goaltending's history is plagued by an unanswerable question: who was the greatest? The goaltenders themselves do their best to answer this, and never by suggesting themselves. But too many of the greats are no longer alive to speak for their era, and there are too many distinct eras to the game. You can compare the greats from one era or another, but you cannot measure them qualitatively against one another. You can only understand what made them special at the time they played the game.

In the modern era—that is, from the time the two-line offside was introduced in 1943 (and the slapshot soon thereafter) until the present day—three names consistently surface when excellence is the subject. They are all from the Original Six days, which ended with the NHL's expansion in 1967/68 to twelve teams: Terry Sawchuk, Jacques Plante and Glenn Hall. They are important because they had long careers at the peak of their profession, and they made contributions to the game that are still evident. You could pick Hall above all others if only because, in an evolutionary sense, he falls into a logical chain of excellence. It begins with Tiny Thompson in Boston in the 1930s, moves to Chuck Rayner in New York in the 1940s and early 1950s, is taken up by Hall in the mid-1950s and carried forward into the early 1970s, and is assumed by Tony Esposito and Ken Dryden in the 1970s. Every goaltender today who plays the ubiquitous inverted-V style owes Hall and his "butterfly" style a debt.

But in mulling over the identity of the signature goaltender, this writer cannot help thinking of a virtual unknown, a hapless minor-leaguer named Alfie Moore who was pulled off a bar stool and pressed into service as the starting goaltender for the Chicago Blackhawks in the opening game of the 1937/38 Stanley Cup. The Blackhawks starter Mike Karakas was unable to play because of a broken toe, and Moore was the best the Blackhawks could do in very convoluted circumstances (see Chapter 3). When he took to the ice of Maple Leaf Gardens that night to face down the season's champions from Toronto, he was unloved by all. The Blackhawks didn't want him, and the Leafs and their home crowd wanted him shelled without mercy. But after scoring on Moore on their first shot, the Leafs could not get another by him for the rest of the night, while Chicago put three behind Toronto's Turk Broda.

Moore was the consummate goaltender—truly alone, truly apart and truly triumphant. He lived the dream that all goaltenders dream: to show all comers and all doubters what he was made of, to snatch up the glory from the attacking player, juggle it in his glove and toss it into the corner. A rare few players on the ice, players like Orr and the Rocket and Gretzky and Lemieux, have known what it is like to be someone upon whose performance an entire game can hinge. Every goaltender in every game ever played has known that same feeling. It is the most exhilarating, intoxicating and, sometimes, destructive burden in sport.

Alfie Moore never played another game as important as the opening match of the 1937/38 Stanley Cup, but he skated off the ice of Maple Leaf Gardens with the most important prize of his profession: the respect of the man in the net at the other end of the rink. "We threw everything at him but the house," Turk Broda declared.

When you think of the greats, and what makes for great goaltending, spare a moment's consideration for Alfie. ○

ACCOLADES

In addition to their "own" trophies, the Vezina and the Jennings, NHL goaltenders are as eligible as any other player for a wide variety of awards. But as the record book shows, goaltenders are more likely to be honoured by some prizes than by others. They are regularly feted in voting for the Conn Smythe and the Calder, yet rarely win the top-player awards, the Hart and the Pearson. And goaltenders have been shut out entirely in voting for the Lady Byng, which recognizes sportsmanship and gentlemanly conduct.

HART MEMORIAL TROPHY

Awarded to the player voted "most valuable to his team" by hockey writers and broadcasters. Since its dedication in 1923, it has been won by only four goaltenders, the last, Jacques Plante, in 1961/62.

CONN SMYTHE TROPHY

Awarded to the most valuable player in the Stanley Cup playoffs in a vote by the league board of governors. The playoffs are when the best goaltenders shine, and in twenty-nine seasons the trophy has been awarded to ten netminders—including three (Roger Crozier, Glenn Hall and Ron Hextall) on the losing team.

CALDER MEMORIAL TROPHY

Awarded to the player voted the most outstanding rookie by hockey writers and broadcasters. The league's top rookie has been named since 1932/33; the actual trophy was introduced in 1937/38. It has consistently recognized the efforts of rookie goaltenders, who have won it (or been runner-up) in seventeen of sixty-three seasons.

BILL MASTERTON TROPHY

Awarded by the Professional Hockey Writers Association to "the NHL player who exemplifies the qualities of perseverance, sportsmanship and dedication to hockey." Glenn "Chico" Resch is the only goaltender to have received it.

LESTER B. PEARSON TROPHY

Awarded by the NHL Players' Association to the league's outstanding player. Mike Liut has been the lone goaltending recipient.

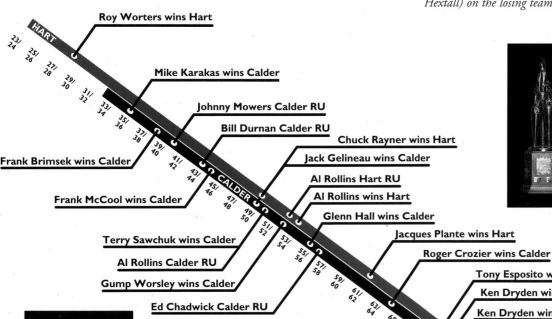

Roy Worters wins Hart
Mike Karakas wins Calder
Johnny Mowers Calder RU
Bill Durnan Calder RU
Chuck Rayner wins Hart
Jack Gelineau wins Calder
Al Rollins Hart RU
Al Rollins wins Hart
Glenn Hall wins Calder
Jacques Plante wins Hart
Roger Crozier wins Calder
Tony Esposito wins Calder
Ken Dryden wins Conn Smythe
Ken Dryden wins Calder
Rogatien Vachon Hart RU
Glenn Resch Calder RU
Tom Barrasso wins Calder
Ed Belfour wins Calder
Dominik Hasek Hart RU
Martin Brodeur wins Calder

Frank Brimsek wins Calder
Frank McCool wins Calder
Terry Sawchuk wins Calder
Al Rollins Calder RU
Gump Worsley wins Calder
Ed Chadwick Calder RU
Roger Crozier wins Conn Smythe
Glenn Hall wins Conn Smythe
Bernie Parent wins Conn Smythe
Mike Liut wins Pearson
Glenn Resch wins Masterton
Billy Smith wins Conn Smythe
Patrick Roy wins Conn Smythe
Ron Hextall wins Conn Smythe, Calder RU
Bill Ranford wins Conn Smythe
Patrick Roy wins Conn Smythe

HART
CALDER
MASTERTON
PEARSON
CONN SMYTHE

23/24 25/26 27/28 29/30 31/32 33/34 35/36 37/38 39/40 41/42 43/44 45/46 47/48 49/50 51/52 53/54 55/56 57/58 59/60 61/62 63/64 65/66 67/68 69/70 71/72 73/74 75/76 77/78 79/80 81/82 83/84 85/86 87/88 89/90 91/92 93/94

THE GREATS

A compilation of Vezina winners and other star goaltenders over the history of the National Hockey League

Player careers are shown with a red bar, with Vezina awards in gold and Jennings awards in green. If the player won both the Vezina and the Jennings in the same season, a green circle with a gold center is employed. Vezina awards are keyed to the vertical white "season" lines. Careers may include partial seasons and seasons in the World Hockey Association. Dashed red lines indicate periods of absence from the NHL or minimal appearances, WHA years excepted. H denotes induction in Hockey Hall of Fame.

The Vezina Trophy was first awarded by the NHL in 1926/27. Prior to that season, this chart shows the league-leading goals-against average as posted by a particular goaltender. From 1926/27 to 1963/64, the Vezina was awarded to the goaltender playing the most games on the team with the leading GA. Beginning in 1964/65, the Vezina was shared by all the active goaltenders on the team posting the leading GA. Where a single goaltender was the recipient, this chart shows his personal GA. Where the Vezina was shared, the team GA is used.

Since 1981/82, the Vezina has been awarded to an individual goaltender on the basis of a vote by hockey writers and broadcasters. In 1981/82, a new trophy, the William M. Jennings Award, was introduced to recognize goaltending excellence according to the old Vezina criterion. The "Jennings" average is plotted in green, and winners are indicated in the career bars with a green dot.

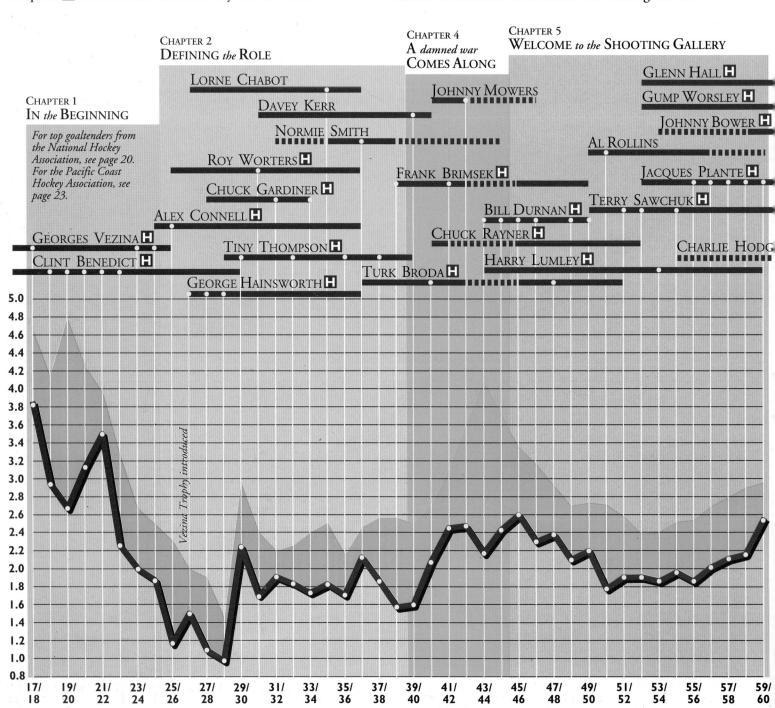

CHAPTER 10
MODERN *Times*

Eras are colour-coded according to chapters in the book.

Vezina and Jennings averages are plotted against the NHL's overall GA average (LGA), shown in blue.

CHAPTER 7
The MORE *the* MERRIER

For top goaltenders in the WHA, see page 139

CHAPTER 10
MODERN *Times*

CHAPTER 5
WELCOME *to the* SHOOTING GALLERY

BRIAN HAYWARD
DARREN JENSEN
RICK WAMSLEY
ROLAND MELANSON
AL JENSEN
REGGIE LEMELIN
PAT RIGGIN
TONY ESPOSITO H
BERNIE PARENT H
GARY SMITH
GILLES VILLEMURE
ED GIACOMIN H
ROGATIEN VACHON
BOB FROESE
GRANT FUHR
ANDY MOOG
PETE PEETERS
TOM BARRASSO
GLENN HALL H
GUMP WORSLEY H
BILLY SMITH H
JOHNNY BOWER H
RICHARD SEVIGNY
DOMINIK HASEK
DENIS HERRON
AL ROLLINS
ROGER CROZIER
DON EDWARDS
ED BELFOUR
JACQUES PLANTE H
RON HEXTALL
BOB SAUVE
TERRY SAWCHUK H
KEN DRYDEN H
JOHN VANBIESBROUCK
GERRY CHEEVERS H
PELLE LINDBERGH
CHARLIE HODGE
CHICO RESCH
HARRY LUMLEY H
MICHEL LAROCQUE
PATRICK ROY
DENIS DEJORDY

5.0
4.8
4.6
4.4
4.2
4.0
3.8
3.6
3.4
3.2
3.0
2.8
2.6
2.4
2.2
2.0
1.8
1.6
1.4
1.2
1.0
0.8

53/54 55/56 57/58 59/60 61/62 63/64 65/66 67/68 69/70 71/72 73/74 75/76 77/78 79/80 81/82 83/84 85/86 87/88 89/90 91/92 93/94

PLAYING *by* *the* NUMBERS

WHAT, IF ANYTHING, CAN A GOALTENDER'S GOALS-AGAINST AVERAGE TELL US ABOUT THE QUALITY OF THE PLAYER?

ow do you measure success by addressing failure? This has been the longstanding difficulty in qualifying empirically the performances of goaltenders. For much of hockey's history, the standard measure has been the player's average goals-against per game (GA), following the logic that the fewer pucks that get by a goaltender, the better he is at his job. Until 1981/82, the Vezina Trophy for the league's top goaltender was awarded to the one(s) on the team allowing the fewest total goals over the season, and there have been times when the Vezina's recipient has been decided by only one goal—such as in its inaugural season, 1926/27, when the Canadiens' George Hainsworth edged out the Maroons' Clint Benedict, and in the early 1950s, when Terry Sawchuk of the Red Wings twice fell short by the narrowest margin. But in 1981/82, the National Hockey League decided that raw numbers weren't telling the full story of goaltending excellence, and put the Vezina to a vote among sports writers and broadcasters. The Jennings Award was introduced to recognize goaltending excellence along the old GA criteria.

If the award system had not changed, Grant Fuhr probably never would have won a Vezina. He earned it in 1987/88, despite what on paper might have seemed a mediocre season. His GA was 3.43, not much better than the league's goals-against average (LGA) of 3.7. In fact, no fewer than twelve regular NHL goaltenders posted better GAs than him that season, and eight teams recorded fewer total goals-against than his team, the Edmonton Oilers. As a raw number, Fuhr was on par with Rick Wamsley, who recorded the same GA as Fuhr while playing for St. Louis and Calgary that season.

But the media types who voted for Fuhr were responding to qualities that the simplistic GA could not convey. At a time when the practice of having two goaltenders share a team's netminding workload was well established, Oilers coach and general manager Glen Sather went with Fuhr for a record seventy-five of eighty regular-season games. The Oilers were a freewheeling offensive machine, recording the second-highest number of goals in the league that season through the efforts of players like Gretzky, Kurri and Messier,

and sometimes Fuhr was left to his own devices in keeping the score in Edmonton's favour. He recorded his lowest GA since his rookie season of 1981/82, and managed to amass his most shutouts to date, four. Once the regular season was over, Fuhr backstopped the Oilers all the way through the playoffs to his, and the Oilers', fourth Stanley Cup. In the process he also made it onto the first All Star team. No other goaltender in the eyes of the media had gotten the job done the way Fuhr had that season.

From 1926/27 to 1963/64, only the goaltender who had played the most games for a team with the lowest GA was awarded the Vezina. That changed in 1964/65, when Sawchuk insisted on sharing it with Bower. Had the pre-1964/65 system been followed in 1987/88, the Vezina would have been won by Patrick Roy instead of Fuhr. Had the system used from 1964/65 to 1980/81 been followed, Roy would have shared the Vezina with Brian Hayward, who played the bulk of the remaining Canadiens games. (Instead they won the Jennings.)

In recent years, GA has been seen as, at best, a thumbnail sketch of a goaltender's skill. More often today statisticians turn to a goaltender's save percentage. Rather than focusing on how many pucks get by a goaltender, the save percentage illuminates how many he manages to stop. GA has long been recognized as, in part, a team statistic. A team that stresses defence, and that allows the opposition few scoring opportunities, is going to have goaltenders whose GAs look very handsome indeed. If a game ends in a 3–3 tie, the goaltender who faced forty shots that night did at least as good a job as his counterpart who faced only twenty. Both had a 3.00 average on the night, but the former's save percentage was .925, while the latter's was .850. But not even goaltenders are happy with this statistical approach. Greats like Glenn Hall will insist that it's not the number of shots you face, but the quality. Twenty accurate ones are a lot tougher to deal with than forty routine ones, as North American goaltenders facing the great Soviet teams of the 1970s will attest. And if he gets too few shots in a game, a goaltender can lose his sharpness and be more vulnerable than one being shelled.

This book employs GA figures in its history of the game and its players because they are historically consistent and are still employed, despite the advent of the save-percentage figure. But it also strives to place the GA in perspective. It isn't appropriate or fair to compare GAs of goaltenders from different eras, as LGA in the NHL has fluctuated wildly over its eight-decade history. (See the chart "The Greats" on pages 14 and 15 for an historical overview of the changes in LGA and league-leading GAs in the National Hockey League. LGA trends for the original National Hockey Association appear on page 20, for the Pacific Coast Hockey Association and associated western leagues on page 23, and for the World Hockey Association on page 139.)

That is why, in the statistical presentations in this book, goaltender performances have been placed in their historical context. Individual GAs are plotted against a goaltending "sweet spot" of better than average performances, its upper range set by LGA, its lower range by the league-leading GA, the historic standard for Vezina awards. In this way the reader can gain a sense of how big an edge a team enjoyed over its opponents through the skills of its goaltender. And to give greater perspective, the average scoring output of the goaltender's team is also shown. Was he playing for a high-scoring team—one that favoured offence over defence, or was so powerful that few scoring chances got through to the goaltender? Or was he playing on a team with low scoring production—one that was either defensive-minded or just not very good? And how were all three of these trends changing over the career of the player?

Consider just two Vezina winners from the past and how different their circumstances were. Chuck Gardiner won a Vezina with the Chicago Blackhawks in 1931/32. Jacques Plante won one with the Montreal Canadiens in 1958/59. Gardiner won his with a GA of 1.92; at the time, LGA was 2.2. This means Gardiner gave the Blackhawks a netminding advantage of less than three-tenths of a goal per game over the league average—one of the lowest in the history of Vezina winners, and an indication of netminding parity at the time. But Chicago didn't do much with the advantage Gardiner gave them. The Blackhawks only averaged 1.79 goals per game in 1931/32, leaving themselves with a scoring deficit. Not surprisingly, the Blackhawks had a losing record that season.

Jacques Plante won the Vezina in 1958/59 with a GA of 2.16, not as good as Gardiner's 1.92 of 1931/32. But did that make Gardiner's effort the superior one? When Plante won the Vezina, LGA was 2.90—he was more than seven-tenths of a goal better (on paper) than whoever was at the other end of the rink on a given night. In producing its fourth successive Stanley Cup–winning season, the team pumped out a commanding 3.69 goals per game, producing a net scoring advantage of +1.53. The Blackhawks of 1931/32, on the other hand, had a scoring deficit of -0.13.

But as Plante's career illustrates, with goaltending statistics, location, as in real estate, is everything. Traded to the lowly Rangers in 1963, his GA leapt nearly a full goal. After playing for two seasons for a team that scored fewer goals than he allowed, Plante quit.

Plante and Gardiner were two skilled goaltenders separated by more than a quarter-century who turned in Vezina performances within very different contexts. In Montreal, Plante didn't have to toil behind a team that didn't do much scoring. Gardiner never had to face something called a slapshot, the rules in his era forbade

NUMBERS TELL THE STORY

A quick study of the career statistics of the Chicago Blackhawks' Chuck Gardiner provides a guided tour of the chart format used throughout this book.

In five of seven NHL seasons, Gardiner posted a GA (red line) within the league's goals-against "sweet spot" (blue background). The upper range of the sweet spot is defined by the league goals-against average (LGA), the lower range by the league-leading GA that season.

From 1926/27 to 1963/64, the Vezina was awarded to the goaltender who played the majority of games on the team with the lowest GA. This means that an individual's Vezina-winning GA could be lower than the team GA that brought him the trophy. In 1950/51, for example, Toronto's GA was 1.97, while the GA of its Vezina-winning goaltender, Al Rollins, was 1.77. Where the Vezina has been awarded to a single goaltender, his personal GA has been used to determine the league-leading GA. Where the GA has been shared by two goaltenders, their team GA has been used.

Gardiner's team, the Blackhawks, was often weak in scoring (goals-per-game production, in maroon). Even so, Gardiner produced Vezina-winning seasons in 1931/32 and 1933/34 (yellow dot). Below the graph, Gardiner's games played, shutout record, his team's playoff record and his All Star team appearances are listed ("1" for first team, "2" for second team). The NHL convened an All Star team for the first time in 1930/31.

Playoff formats have varied greatly in the NHL. Prior to the 1926/27 season, when the Stanley Cup was not the exclusive property of the NHL, playoff records are only shown for Cup finals. Otherwise, playoff records for the team on which a goaltender played that season are coded as follows: Blank—missed playoffs; QF—appeared in quarterfinal; PR—appeared in preliminary round; CC—appeared in conference championship; SF—appeared in semifinal; DSF—appeared in division semifinal; DF—appeared in division final; F—appeared in Stanley Cup final; W—won Stanley Cup.

CHICAGO

	27/28	28/29	29/30	30/31	31/32	32/33	33/34
GAMES	40	44	44	44	48	48	48
SHUTOUTS	3	5	3	12	4	5	10
STANLEY CUP				QF	F	QF	W
ALL-STAR TEAM				1	1	2	1

screening the goaltender, and with no icing rule his defence could quickly nullify an offensive press by dumping the puck in the other end. On the other hand, Gardiner was not allowed to hold the puck to get a faceoff when the heat was turned up. And until Plante, there was no such thing as a true face mask.

And context, ultimately, is what this book is about: not simply statistics, or the greatness conferred by them, but the very different circumstances in which goaltenders have played in hockey history. ○

c.1875–1924/25

IN *the* BEGINNING

NO PADS, NO SPECIAL GLOVES OR STICKS, NO HOLDING THE PUCK, AND NO FALLING DOWN: GOALTENDING IN HOCKEY'S INFANCY WAS "DIFFICULT" AND "THANKLESS"

THE MONTREAL CANADIENS PRACTISE AT AN OUTDOOR RINK IN VERDUN, QUEBEC, IN A STILL TAKEN FROM A FILM MADE IN JANUARY 1924. THE GOALTENDER AT THE FAR END OF THE RINK IS GEORGES VEZINA; THIS IS THE ONLY KNOWN IMAGE OF VEZINA IN A GAME SITUATION. THE IDENTITY OF THE GOALTENDER IN THE FOREGROUND IS NOT KNOWN. HE IS WEARING CRICKET-STYLE LEG PADS WITH HEAVY FELT BACKING, WHICH ARE ABOUT TO BE MADE OBSOLETE BY EMIL "POP" KENESKY'S LEATHER PADS.

ockey is not a timeless game. Its origins are obscure and endlessly debated, and its most fundamental rules were revised ceaselessly, even decades into its existence as a popular professional sport. Baseball as played in the 1920s was much the same as it is today, but a hockey fan transported back into a rinkside seat before the Depression would find the game decidedly odd. Even into the Second World War, there was much to hockey that would cause the time-travelling fan to scratch his head. Since the beginning, though, there have been undisputable constants: hockey is a team sport, it is played on ice by people wearing skates, it involves a projectile and sticks, and there are goals at either end of the rink. And there has always been a player standing in front of the goal, defending it at all costs.

Various North American centres, principally Montreal, Kingston and Halifax, lay claim to the game's invention. What is indisputable is that in 1886, the regulations employed in eastern Canada were codified as the fourteen-point "Montreal Rules," set down by delegates from Montreal, Ottawa, Quebec City, Toronto and Kingston at the Montreal Winter Carnival. It was in many aspects a winterized form of lacrosse. Like lacrosse, it was an "onside" game, with no forward passing. It used seven players a side in a similar configuration—the defensive "point" and "cover point" positions were straight out of lacrosse. And so were the goals: two posts six feet apart and six feet high, topped with flags. The goal height would soon be reduced to four feet, where it has remained. The regulations regarding goaltending were strict, and would survive, word for word, right through the First World War: "The goalkeeper must not during play, lie, kneel, or sit upon the ice, but must maintain a standing position." He was allowed no equipment other than a stick, and his stick was no different from that of any other player.

Hockey was also popular in the northeastern U.S.,

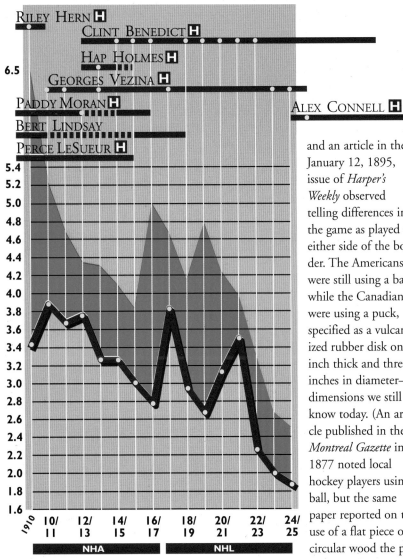

RILEY HERN **H**

CLINT BENEDICT **H**

HAP HOLMES **H**

6.5

GEORGES VEZINA **H**

PADDY MORAN **H**   ALEX CONNELL **H**

BERT LINDSAY

PERCE LeSUEUR **H**

5.4
5.2
5.0
4.8
4.6
4.4
4.2
4.0
3.8
3.6
3.4
3.2
3.0
2.8
2.6
2.4
2.2
2.0
1.8
1.6

1910 | 10/11 | 12/13 | 14/15 | 16/17 | 18/19 | 20/21 | 22/23 | 24/25

NHA   NHL

and an article in the January 12, 1895, issue of *Harper's Weekly* observed telling differences in the game as played on either side of the border. The Americans were still using a ball, while the Canadians were using a puck, specified as a vulcanized rubber disk one inch thick and three inches in diameter—dimensions we still know today. (An article published in the *Montreal Gazette* in 1877 noted local hockey players using a ball, but the same paper reported on the use of a flat piece of circular wood the previous year.) The *Harper's* writer noted that offside rules in Canada were strictly observed, "which obviates any necessity of the three-foot goal line." This suggests the Americans were using a privileged zone in which defending players could receive forward passes from their goaltender. Such a three-foot zone showed up in the Ontario Hockey Association rules in 1905 and was moved steadily outward to thirty feet. Allowing the goaltender alone to make forward passes, though permitted in the Pacific Coast Hockey Association, didn't come to the National Hockey League until 1921/22.

The *Harper's* article also makes clear that the Americans were the first to use a goal with a crossbar, since it noted that the Canadian goals are "four, not three feet high, and have no bar—an obvious advantage for the goal-keeper." Although nets may have been used by OHA teams earlier than the *Harper's* article, the device is known to have been introduced in Montreal in the winter of 1899 by the *Montreal Herald's* sporting editor, Bill Hewitt, father of broadcaster Foster Hewitt. He got the idea from a friend travelling in Australia, who probably saw them being used in field hockey. The Canadian Amateur Hockey League, with teams in Ottawa, Montreal and Quebec City, adopted a net in late 1899, when Frank Stocking and Arthur Scott of the Quebec Hockey Club presented a small model for approval by the CAHL at its annual meeting in Montreal on December 9. Stocking was the goaltender for the Quebec team from 1893 to 1901, and the net was needed to cut down on disputed goals. On December 30, Stocking and Scott's simple net was used in an exhibition game. It consisted of two wooden posts six feet apart and four feet high, with no connecting crossbar. There was no "lid" to catch rising shots that might pass between the posts but sail above the net. The net was approved for league use, and in short order the wooden uprights were replaced with uncapped steel ones. These hollow posts, it is said, were used as spittoons by the tobacco-chewing goaltenders of the era, their less accurate lobs staining the ice around them.

Despite the prohibition on special equipment in the 1886 rules, those players seconded to guard the goal were not going to put up with the resultant physical abuse for very long. The practice of wearing special leg pads appears to have arisen early, in Winnipeg, far from the rule sticklers back east. An 1891 photograph of a hockey team believed to be at the Winnipeg Military School shows a sensible goaltender wearing cricket pads. In the east, the earliest known use of cricket pads by goaltenders is 1895, when Fred Chittick of the CAHL Ottawa team wore them. They were popularized in 1896, when George "Whitey" Merritt of the Winnipeg Victorias became the first goaltender to wear them in a Stanley Cup game. On February 14, 1896, he used them to shut out the Montreal Victorias, 2–0. They created a sensation, and were soon being worn by goaltenders everywhere.

Frank Stocking would recall that, in addition to these shin pads, goaltending equipment in these years consisted of a fur cap stuffed down the front of one's

A BREED APART   20

THE FIRST KNOWN USE OF LEG PADS BY A GOALTENDER IS DOCUMENTED IN THIS 1891 PHOTO, THOUGHT TO HAVE BEEN TAKEN AT THE WINNIPEG MILITARY SCHOOL. THE WHITE CRICKET-STYLE PADS CAN BE SEEN CLEARLY.

pants, a pair of ordinary leather gloves and a stick similar to that of a defenceman. Goaltenders and defencemen used a stick with a wider than normal blade, achieved by attaching a strip of wood to the top of a regular blade with nails or wire. The sticks were otherwise of one piece, and very tough. Two-piece sticks, with a separate blade slotted and glued into the shaft, didn't appear until 1928 when hardwood became scarce.

The playing stick used by "skaters" in the late nineteenth century was fundamentally recognizable: the blade could be no wider than three inches (a maximum the game still employs) and no longer than thirteen inches. Before the First World War, goaltenders began using a "built-up" stick, which carried the three-inch width of the blade a foot or more up the front of the shaft. In 1911, Spalding was selling an "autograph" model endorsed by Riley Hern, goaltender of the Stanley Cup–winning Montreal Wanderers of 1907, 1908 and 1910.

The dimensions for the rinks of the modern North American game—200 feet by 85 feet—were established by the ice surface at Montreal's Victoria Skating Rink, home ice to the Montreal Amateur Athletic Association, which had been playing hockey there since the 1870s. (Tom Patton, the Montreal AAA goaltender, is thought to have brought hockey to Toronto in 1887; the Ontario Hockey

Association was formed in 1890.) But not every neighbourhood had a sheet of ice this size. The Ontario Hockey Association Rules of 1896 gave no suggested rink dimensions, but the Amateur Hockey Association of Canada in 1896 and the Amateur Hockey League of New York were specific: 112 feet by 58 feet. In its infancy, hockey was often played on curling rinks, a sport gaining popularity at the same time as hockey. Using the 112 by 58 prescription, a hockey rink could be created by limiting play to four or five curling sheets. The Amateur Hockey Association of Canada called for the goal line to be placed "at least five feet" from the end of the ice surface; rules of American amateurs called for at least ten feet, and not more than fifteen, a prescription more attuned than the Canadian one to the ten-foot gap the future National Hockey League would adopt.

In the seven-man game played before the First World War (which lasted until the 1922/23 season in the Pacific Coast league), the rulemakers were unanimous on the role of the goaltender. The regulations of the Amateur Hockey League of New York, the Amateur Hockey Association of Canada and the Ontario Hockey Association were virtually identical. As the OHA directed in 1896, "The goalkeeper must not during play, lie, sit, or kneel upon the ice; he may, when in goal, stop the puck with his hands, but shall not throw or hold it. He may wear pads, but must not wear a garment such as would give him undue assistance in keeping goal." These specifications held for another quarter-century—the 1920 amateur rules repeated the wording verbatim, although for some reason the NHL's forerunner, the National Hockey Association, formed in 1909, omitted the word "lie" from its rulebook, as evidenced by the surviving 1916/17 edition.

The regulations created a stand-up game with only minimal protection for the goaltender, who had to guard the same goal area—twenty-four square feet—as his modern counterpart. By 1916, the National Hockey Association allowed goaltenders a maximum stick width of 3.5 inches, thereby permitting the essential "paddle" shaft and large blade we know today. Regulations still limit the goaltender's stick width to 3.5 inches.

The goaltender's gloves underwent glacial changes. Because he was so limited in how he could handle the puck, there was little call for specialization beyond extra protection. The turn-of-the-century rules allowed any player to stop the puck with the skate "or any part of *Continued on page 25*

AT 200 FEET BY 85 FEET, THE "IDEAL" SIZE OF PROFESSIONAL HOCKEY RINKS WOULD DWARF THE EARLY AMATEUR GAME'S PRESCRIBED RINK (SHOWN IN LIGHT BLUE), 112 FEET BY 58 FEET. IN THIS LAYOUT FROM 1918/19, THE NHL'S SECOND SEASON OF OPERATION, GOAL LINES ARE SET TEN FEET FROM THE END OF THE RINK, WHICH WOULD REMAIN STANDARD FOR THE GAME UNTIL 1990/91, WHEN ANOTHER FOOT WAS ADDED. IN 1918/19, THE NHL BORROWED BLUELINES FROM THE PCHA, CREATING A CENTRE-ICE NEUTRAL ZONE IN WHICH FORWARD PASSING WAS PERMITTED. IN THEIR ORIGINAL POSITION (DOTTED BLUE LINES), THEY WERE SET TWENTY FEET TO EITHER SIDE OF CENTRE ICE. THE PCHA POSITIONED THEM SIXTY-SEVEN FEET FROM THE END OF THE RINK TO CREATE THREE EQUAL PLAYING ZONES (SOLID BLUE LINES).

Continued on page 25

IN THE BEGINNING

Go West, Young Men

SOME OF THE GAME'S GREATEST GOALTENDERS WERE STARS NOT OF THE NHL, BUT OF THE PCHA

It wasn't until the mid-1920s that the NHL emerged as the dominant brand of the professional game. The league did not become the sole proprietor of the Stanley Cup until 1927; for more than a decade, beginning in 1915, the trophy demanded an end-of-season match between the champion club of two leagues: the NHL (its predecessor, the NHA) in the east, and the Pacific Coast Hockey Association in the west, with the short-lived Western Canada Hockey League also becoming involved in Stanley Cup play in the early 1920s. During those years, some of the very best goaltenders in the game were associated with professional hockey in western Canada, sometimes exclusively.

Three of them, Hap Holmes, Hugh Lehman and George Hainsworth, have been inducted into the Hockey Hall of Fame.

The Pacific Coast league was the brainchild of Frank and Lester Patrick, both born in the east, both of whom played defence. In 1909, the brothers were working for their father's lumber business in British Columbia when they surrendered to a hail of contract offers from the fledgling National Hockey Association and signed on with the Renfrew Creamery Kings. The payroll of the

HUGH LEHMAN WAS A PERENNIAL ALL STAR, PLAYING IN EVERY ONE OF THE PCHA'S FIFTEEN SEASONS.

team was so outlandishly high—twenty-six-year-old Lester got $3,000, twenty-four-year-old Frank $2,000, for the twelve-game season, making them better paid on a per-game basis than the best American baseball play-

ers—that the team immediately became known as the Millionaires.

These shocking sums were being spent by Renfrew backer Amby O'Brien in a quixotic pursuit of the Stanley Cup. Like many sports entrepreneurs who would follow him, O'Brien discovered that money wouldn't necessarily buy him success—Renfrew finished third in the NHA for two seasons running, then folded.

By then, the Patrick brothers were back in B.C., joining forces with their father to launch a professional league of their own. Selling the lumber business, they built Canada's first artificial-ice arenas, in Vancouver and Victoria, added a third franchise venue, New Westminster, and in 1911 were up and running as the PCHA.

They had learned an important lesson from their experience with Renfrew: top hockey talent like themselves put fans in the seats, and damn the expense. The Patricks, star players themselves, launched a bidding war with their former employers in the NHA, luring away some major talents. Among them from the Renfrew lineup were Cyclone Taylor and goaltender Bert Lindsay, father of future NHL scoring star Ted Lindsay.

Lindsay and Lester Patrick had worked together as hired guns with the Edmonton Eskimos of 1908, who lost a Stanley Cup match to the Montreal Maroons. Bert Lindsay played four seasons with the Victoria Aristocrats, where Lester Patrick was team manager and captain while playing the defensive "point" position of the old seven-man game.

Lindsay was thirty-one when he finished up with the PCHA in 1915. In his second season he posted the league's lowest GA and was named to its All Star team, but he never did get to play in a Stanley Cup final against the easterners while with the Pacific Coast league. Cup competition wasn't yet open to PCHA teams when Lindsay and the Aristocrats went east to meet the Quebec Bulldogs, who had just won the cup, in 1913. The western team proved its worth by beating the Bulldogs 2–1 in a best-of-three exhibition series. The following season the Aristocrats were back east for a supposedly official cup series against the Toronto Blueshirts, Amby O'Brien's follow-up to the Renfrew team. But Lindsay didn't make the trip, and the Aristocrats lost a bitterly fought series, which, in any case, turned out to be unofficial because the Millionaires hadn't taken care of their paperwork in filing their challenge.

The NHA and the PCHA, however, had come to an agreement with the trustees of Lord Stanley's cup to have its possession decided every year by a series between the champions of the two leagues, with the location of the series alternating between coasts and individual games alternating between the rules of the two leagues. (Among other differences, the PCHA stuck to the old seven-man game.) In 1915, the cup match came west. Frank Patrick's

Vancouver Millionaires were ready for the Ottawa Senators with Cyclone Taylor still in the lineup and a sharp easterner, Hugh Lehman, between the posts.

Lehman was from Bert Lindsay's old stamping ground of Pembroke, Ontario. The record books list his year of birth as 1895, but this would have made him a ten-year-old when he began playing on professional and semi-professional teams in Sault Ste. Marie, Kitchener and Pembroke in 1905. A more likely year of birth is 1885. Lehman headed west for the debut of the PCHA. "Old Eagle Eyes" played twenty-three years of hockey, twenty-one of them professionally, and was on the ice for every single PCHA season. For the first three seasons he played for the New Westminster Royals; in his first season he posted the best GA; in his third, he was named to the All Star team. For 1914/15 he switched to Frank Patrick's Vancouver Millionaires.

Patrick himself played infrequently that year but was on the ice when Lehman and the Millionaires, in the first cup final on the coast, demolished the visiting Senators with scores of 6–2, 8–3 and 12–3. The Senators' young netminder Clint Benedict, a future star of the NHL, was humiliated by the drubbing. The quality of play in the PCHA could not be doubted.

Lehman played in five more Stanley Cups with Vancouver, four in a row from 1921 to 1924, but never won another. He was still one of the dominant goaltenders, vying for the league's top-goaltender honours with another eastern import, Harry "Hap" Holmes.

Born in Aurora, Ontario, Holmes joined the Toronto Blueshirts in 1912/13, and was with the team when they defeated Lester Patrick's Aristocrats in the 1914 Stanley Cup. When the Patricks decided to set up a new PCHA team in Seattle called the Metropolitans for 1915/16, they raided the Blueshirts payroll, hiring away Holmes, among others.

Holmes and the Metropolitans made it to the cup final the next season, meeting the Montreal Canadiens at home in Seattle. Seattle won the best-of-five decisively in four games, with Holmes outduelling Georges Vezina. The next season, 1917/18, Holmes won another Stanley Cup—this time as the goaltender of the Toronto Arenas in a one-season return to his old league, which had just been reincarnated as the NHL.

Holmes made it into his third straight Stanley Cup final in 1918/19, this time as a Metropolitan again, and again playing at home against Montreal. His netminding opponent was—again—Vezina, and the two men were a ready-made contrast for sportswriters. Holmes, who was never seen to crack a smile, was called "nerveless"; Vezina was "high strung"—a curious description of a man who was known as the Chicoutimi Cucumber for his trademark coolness. If he was uncharacteristically rattled in this series, he had good reason: in the first game, playing

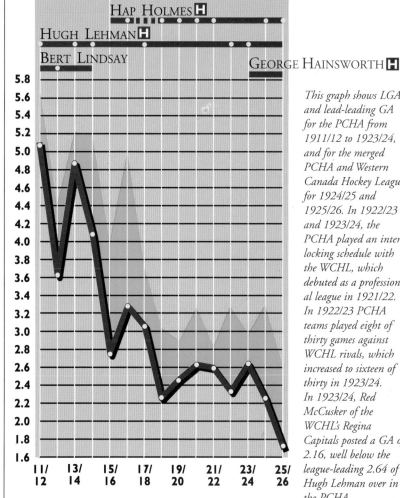

This graph shows LGA and lead-leading GA for the PCHA from 1911/12 to 1923/24, and for the merged PCHA and Western Canada Hockey League for 1924/25 and 1925/26. In 1922/23 and 1923/24, the PCHA played an inter-locking schedule with the WCHL, which debuted as a profession-al league in 1921/22. In 1922/23 PCHA teams played eight of thirty games against WCHL rivals, which increased to sixteen of thirty in 1923/24. In 1923/24, Red McCusker of the WCHL's Regina Capitals posted a GA of 2.16, well below the league-leading 2.64 of Hugh Lehman over in the PCHA.

under PCHA rules, Vezina was shelled 7–0. Seattle was leading the series 2–1 when an epic battle of defensive hockey erupted in game four. Played under six-man eastern rules, the two teams, with Holmes and Vezina the focus of attention, hammered away at each other like two ironclads, unable to make a dent. After eighty minutes of hockey, the two exhausted teams were still scoreless, and the match was declared a

HAP HOLMES OUTDUELLED SUCH NHA/NHL STARS AS CLINT BENEDICT AND GEORGES VEZINA IN STANLEY CUP MATCHES. HE ENDED HIS CAREER WITH THE NHL'S NEW DETROIT FRANCHISE.

draw. Montreal tied the series at two wins apiece, but then North America's influenza epidemic struck the team rosters; Canadiens defenceman Joe Hall went to hospital and died there. The series was cancelled, and for the first and only time in Stanley Cup history, there was a year without a winner.

Holmes played in three more Stanley Cup finals, winning once, as a Victoria Cougar (as the Maroons were renamed in 1921) in 1925 over the Canadiens, a match that produced another showdown between Holmes and Vezina, who was playing his last season before tuberculosis claimed him. By then the PCHA was struggling. A new rival arose in 1921 in the form of the Western Canada Hockey League, with teams in Edmonton, Calgary, Regina and Saskatoon. In 1922/23, the PCHA followed the example of the NHL and WCHL by dropping the rover and playing the six-man game so that it could play an interlocking schedule with the WCHL. In 1924/25, the two western leagues merged under the WCHL name. In its final season, 1925/26, it was known as the Western Hockey League.

Hap Holmes played on regardless of league transmogrifications. In a press description of a heroic Holmes effort against the Saskatoon Sheiks in 1925, he is a thirty-six-year-old warrior in "white pads, battered skates [and a] dinky skull cap" and covered, suggests the writer, with "horseshoes, four-leaf clovers and rabbit's feet."

In the last gasp of the PCHA/WCHL/WHL, Holmes and the Victoria Cougars lost the Stanley Cup in four games to the Montreal Maroons. Every win for Montreal was a shutout by Clint Benedict, with whom Holmes had tangled in the cup final of 1920, a series that had also gone Benedict's way as he played net for Ottawa. Benedict was the only goaltender to post a better lifetime GA than Holmes's (at 2.90) during Holmes's PCHA reign. Holmes had the best GA in the western league in seven of ten seasons. Yet he was regularly consigned to honourable mention at awards time, being named a second-team All Star seven times and a first-team All Star only once. Lehman earned ten first-team All Star placings. And as professional hockey in western Canada entered its final years, it provided the debut for a latecomer to the professional goaltending ranks:

George Hainsworth (see page 42).

When the WHL folded after the 1925/26 season, player contracts were sold to the NHL, which used them mainly to fill the rosters of its expansion clubs in New York, Detroit and Chicago. Hugh Lehman's contract was bought by Chicago, and he played forty-four games for them in their opening season. They finished third in the five-team American division, but also allowed more goals than any other team in the league. Lehman played four more games the following season, and was 1–2–1 when he replaced Barney Stanley (who had played with the Stanley Cup–winning Vancouver Millionaires of 1915) as coach at mid-season. In his first game behind the bench, Chicago lost 10–0 to Montreal. The Blackhawks won only seven games the entire season, and Lehman never coached another NHL game.

Hap Holmes played two seasons for Detroit. Despite being on an expansion team, Holmes posted reasonable GAs of 2.33 and 1.80, and in his second season recorded an impressive eleven shutouts in forty-four games. Holmes was thirty-nine at the end of the 1927/28 season, when his ambitions turned to ownership. He set up a franchise for the new International League in Cleveland, called the Falcons, but as the Depression set in Holmes could not hang on and Al Sutphin took over the ownership. When the American League was formed in 1936 from the remnants of the International League, Sutphin was in charge and the team became the Barons, but Holmes was at least still on the payroll. He died in 1940 while on vacation in Florida; the Barons ran a tribute to Holmes in its program for years. In 1947, Sutphin put up a trophy in Holmes's name to honour the American League's top goaltender, which is still being given out today.

Norman "Heck" Fowler, who was born in Saskatoon, spent eight seasons in the western professional game and made two All Star teams, but he was quick to light, attracting two fighting suspensions in 1921/22. He also liked to watch things light, and legend has it that his reputation as a fire nut cost him his job. In 1923/24, Fowler and the rest of Lester Patrick's Victoria Cougars were coming out of their Regina hotel to play a game when a fire truck went by. Fowler jumped on the back to see the blaze and the game had to be delayed until he was retrieved. An exasperated Patrick sold his contract to the Bruins, with whom he played seven games in 1924/25 before appearing in another eight back in the western league for Edmonton.

As for Bert Lindsay, he returned east after the 1914/15 season and played for the Montreal Wanderers and the Toronto Arenas of the newly formed NHL in 1917/18 and 1918/19. At the end of the Second World War, Lindsay tried to sell the NHL on a goal net with flexible safety posts. The league declined. ○

Continued from page 21

the body," but the OHA rules restricted stopping the puck with the hand to the goaltender alone. (This was known as "knocking on.") As with their first specialized sticks, goaltenders tended to use whatever the defence-men used. Gloves with extra padding in the thumb and back of the hand were available by 1915. The trapper-style catching glove and stick-side blocker were a long, long way in the future, and so, of course, was the mask.

In a game without slapshots and without players dressed like gladiators, the goaltender's role in hindsight might seem genteel, played as the game so often was by the refined, casual-looking Ivy Leaguers and gentlemen athletes who populated team photographs at the turn of the century. But accounts of the day leave no doubt that, even in the game's infancy, the goaltender's role was demanding. "[A] clever goal-tend intercepts many a try-for-goal, though at the cost of as many bruises where his body has met the flying puck," assured the 1898 *Ice Hockey and Ice Polo Guide*.[1] "He very rarely leaves his station between the goal-posts, and then only after signalling the point to fall back into his position, the goal-tend having left same in order to return a long 'lift' [a rink-long clearing shot in the days

before the icing rule] which has dropped back of and near the posts, the opposing forwards, of course, being at some distance down the rink.

"Through the agility of a clever goal-tend the score of a match is often kept down to a small number of goals, as he kills many tries which would score but for his good work. The rules forbid him to lie, sit or kneel upon the ice, and compel him to maintain a standing position. When a scrimmage occurs near his goal, his is the most difficult, and usually the most thankless, work of any man on the team. Though he may frequently gain a momentary possession of the puck, he seldom has room or time to pass it far down the rink or even directly to one of his own side. His play then is to shoot it off to one side of the rink, either to the right or left of the goal, thus preventing another try-for-goal until the puck is worked back again into a favorable position..."

Then, as today, goaltending was physically and mentally trying, and no team could hope for any success without a good "goal-tend" between its posts. The style of play of the early game—not falling down, not wandering from the net—would persist for decades as the model of the proper way to play the position, even after the rules that ordered him to stay on his feet were elimi-

S. MATSUMIYA, GOALTENDER FOR VANCOUVER'S ASAHI ATHLETIC CLUB TEAM OF 1919/20, WEARS STANDARD CRICKET-STYLE LEG PADS AND NOVEL THREE-DIGIT GLOVES.

---

[1] Ice polo, as played by the New England Skating Association at the turn of the century, employed a sheet of ice 150 feet long, with five players aside, sticks four feet long, and essentially followed the rules of polo, without the horses. The game was also popular in the Canadian Maritimes, but hockey overtook the sport in both locales.

nated. Ironically, in this most emphatic stay-at-home era of the profession, in 1905 and 1906 goals were actually scored by a goaltender named Brophy in CAHL games, one of them against Paddy Moran of the Quebec Bulldogs. And the fact that Riley Hern had played forward as well as goal suggests that these prototypic goaltenders were not as fixed in their assignments as the record might suggest. On balance, though, it was not a position given to roaming. It was not uncommon for goaltenders to play in a pair of boots rather than skates. Georges Vezina, who joined the Canadiens in 1910 at age twenty-three, didn't even learn to skate until he was eighteen.

There has never been an easy time to be a goaltender. The absence of a slapshot would have been of little comfort to the goaltenders who faced, with the most minimal protection, wicked, rising wrist shots and, worst of all, backhands fired (usually with little accuracy) from close in that were powerful and often inadvertently at head level. And a goaltender

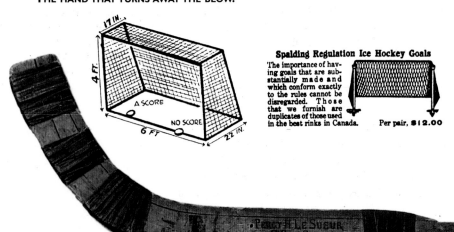

A MEMBER OF THE 1909 AND 1911 STANLEY CUP TEAMS, PERCE LESUEUR (SHOWN HERE ON AN IMPERIAL TOBACCO TRADING CARD OF 1910/11) WAS A NOTEWORTHY INVENTOR AS WELL AS A GREAT GOALTENDER.

IN 1912, HE DEVISED THE FIRST GOAL NET THAT COULD TRAP RISING SHOTS (SHOWN BELOW LEFT, AS PICTURED IN THE 1929 CAHA RULEBOOK). BEFORE THEN, NETS WERE OPEN AT THE TOP, AS IN THE CASE OF THE MODEL ADVERTISED BY SPALDING IN 1908 (BELOW RIGHT). HE ALSO CREATED A SPECIAL GAUNTLET GLOVE FOR GOALTENDERS, WHICH PROVIDED MORE PROTECTION TO THE FOREARMS. AFTER THE FIRST WORLD WAR, HE TURNED TO REFEREEING, AND COACHED THE NHL'S HAMILTON TIGERS IN THE 1920s. AS A HOCKEY COLUMNIST FOR THE HAMILTON SPECTATOR HE INTRODUCED THE "SHOTS ON GOAL" STATISTIC TO BOX SCORES IN 1923.

HIS STICK (BOTTOM), AN EARLY "BUILT-UP" MODEL, WAS USED FROM 1905 TO 1910. HE INSCRIBED IT WITH ALL HIS MAJOR WINS, AS WELL AS THE LATIN PHRASE FOR "THE HAND THAT TURNS AWAY THE BLOW."

could not get himself or his team out of trouble by grabbing or falling on the puck and securing a faceoff. As the 1909 American Amateur Hockey League Rules prescribed, "The player in the goal position may catch the puck, but if he does he must at once drop the puck to the ice at his own feet." The requirement that the goaltender immediately drop any puck he caught would be part of the game well into the 1930s. And a goaltender in the NHA who dropped to the ice was penalized with a fine.

The National Hockey Association, with teams in Quebec, Montreal and Ottawa, came up with an historic innovation for its 1911/12 season: a six-skater lineup. William Northey, secretary of the Montreal Arena Co., was credited with suggesting it, undoubtedly inspired by the money that would be saved on players, as the NHA was engaged in a salary war with the Pacific Coast Hockey Association (see "Go West, Young Men," page 22). The NHA dropped the rover from the forward ranks, and the defensive unit remained at three. In the seven-man game, the defence corps lined up lacrosse-style from the goal forward—the goaltender first, then the point (slightly off centre), then the cover-point. In the new, six-man game, and with the arrival of the blueline, which the easterners also adopted (from the PCHA in 1918/19), the defending players assumed the present configuration, with a goaltender and two defencemen, arranged left and right.

The NHA added another game innovation in its 1912/13 season: the modern goal net. Perce LeSueur, or Peerless Percy, a goaltender with the Ottawa Senators, was assigned by his league to design a standard net that would reduce controversies over whether or not the puck actually passed between the posts. LeSueur's was the first to use the crossbar and a webbed top to trap rising shots. LeSueur's rectangular net, maintaining the standard six foot by four foot opening, was seventeen inches deep at the top and twenty-two inches at the bottom. The net was used by the NHA and its successor, the NHL, until 1927, and it would remain a standard net in the CAHA rulebook right to the Second World War. In 1913/14, the NHA painted a goal line on the ice between the posts for the first time. The rink-wide goal line would not appear until the dawn of the Second World War, as the game had no icing rule.

The NHA was transformed into the NHL when team owners in Montreal, Ottawa and Quebec could no longer get along with their Toronto franchisee, Eddie Livingstone. (Toronto had joined the league as the Blueshirts in 1912/13.) They left

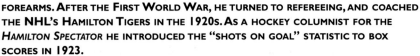

Spalding Regulation Ice Hockey Goals
The importance of having goals that are substantially made and which conform exactly to the rules cannot be disregarded. Those that we furnish are duplicates of those used in the best rinks in Canada.

Per pair, $12.00

Livingstone alone in the NHA, which promptly ceased to exist, and started afresh as the NHL in 1917/18 with their existing teams and a new Toronto squad, the Arenas. It was a hectic debut, with the Quebec Bulldogs deciding to sit out the season and the Montreal Wanderers withdrawing from competition after six games when Montreal Arena, home ice to both the Canadiens and the Wanderers, burned down. Only three teams—the Canadiens, the Ottawa Senators and the Toronto Arenas—completed a twenty-two-game schedule.

The league had decided to carry on under the NHA regulations, with one significant change: goaltenders were now allowed to fall to the ice to stop a shot. The amateur game did not take readily to this revolution. The 1920 amateur rules still insisted on the ban on lying, kneeling or sitting.

It was clear to the organizers of the professional game that the goaltenders were in need of a playing edge. Although the 1898 *Ice Hockey and Ice Polo Guide* had praised the ability of the "goal-tend" to keep scoring low, the game as played by the pros was a high-scoring one. In the NHA, LGA had declined steadily, from 6.46 in 1910 to 3.83 in 1915/16. But in 1916/17, it shot up more than a goal, to 4.99. Out west in the PCHA, there was a similar jump, and LGA was almost identical to the NHA's. Even with permission to flop to the ice, goaltenders in the infant NHL had GAs that were higher than at any other point in league history. LGA in 1917/18 was 4.65; the best GA in the league was 3.82, posted by Georges Vezina of the Canadiens.

For more than a decade, the league struggled to bring more balance to the offensive and defensive games, shifting it steadily away from the traditional onside game to one in which forward passing became increasingly tolerated, but with quick strikes reined in through the use of distinct playing zones. For its second season, 1918/19, the NHL introduced bluelines. Positioned twenty feet on either side of centre ice, these created a neutral zone in which forward passing (and kicking the puck) was allowed, as in the larger neutral zone of the PCHA, which consumed one-third of the ice surface. Forward passing was still banned in the defensive zones, but for the 1921/22 season goaltenders alone were allowed to pass the puck forward to their own blueline, a derivation of the OHA and PCHA rules.

The changes in passing rules, and the new ability of the goaltender to launch counterattacks with forward breakout passes, had immediate impact on goals-against figures. LGA tumbled to 3.25 in 1922/23, and kept on falling. In 1923/24, it was down to 2.66, and Clint Benedict of the Ottawa Senators registered the lowest GA to date, 2.25.

About this time, the goaltenders received a significant new weapon that helped push down their individual GAs and overall LGA: substantial leg pads. Emil "Pop" Kenesky of Hamilton, Ontario, is generally credited with their invention. Tradition has it he was watching a local Catholic league match and noticed how pucks were glancing off the curved surface of the goaltender's cricket-style pads and into the net. Kenesky modified an existing pad, increasing the padding and in the process widening it to twelve inches. The new pads caught on in the local league and in 1924 attracted the interest of Percy Thompson, coach of the Hamilton Tigers, who asked Kenesky to repair the pads of Jake Forbes. An eight-game losing streak ended the first time Forbes wore them, and Kenesky was off and running in a new career as he fielded orders from top goaltenders everywhere.

Kenesky may not have been the first man to make the big leather pads. Alex Connell of the Ottawa Senators was the first goaltender to have a set of Kenesky pads made from scratch, but Tiny Thompson, who became a star goaltender with the Bruins, was playing Senior hockey in Minnesota when he had his first pair made in 1924. Thompson never said where he got his (which he wore for his entire career), but it's doubtful he went all the way to Hamilton for them, and photos of Connell's and Thompson's pads reveal distinctive constructions. Still, if Kenesky didn't invent them outright, he perfected them, and remained the pad-maker of choice for goaltending's elite right through the 1970s.

From the goaltender's perspective, the league's rule-makers had a Midas touch—whatever changes they made to the game, their jobs became easier, if the downward spiral of LGA is any indication. Overwhelmingly, the next two decades would be devoted to finding a balance between offence and defence in the league's rules. In the process, the goaltender's duties would undergo their own evolution, rapidly closing in on a role the game today would recognize. ○

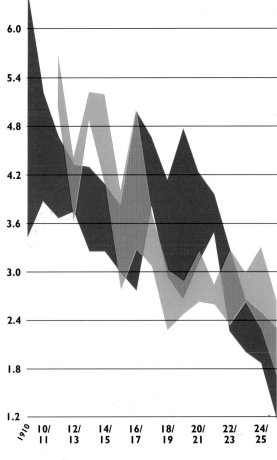

PLOTTED AGAINST EACH OTHER ARE THE GOALTENDING "SWEET SPOTS" OF THE NHA/NHL (IN RED) AND OF THE PCHA (IN BLUE). FOR ITS LAST TWO SEASONS, THE PCHA MERGED WITH THE WESTERN CANADA HOCKEY LEAGUE. THE UPPER RANGE OF EACH SWEET SPOT IS THE LEAGUE GOALS-AGAINST AVERAGE (LGA); THE LOWER RANGE IS THE BEST INDIVIDUAL GA IN THE LEAGUE THAT SEASON. IN ITS FIRST YEARS, THE PCHA PLAYED A MUCH HIGHER SCORING GAME, BUT FROM 1918/19 TO 1921/22, THE PCHA'S RANGE DROPPED SIGNIFICANTLY BELOW THAT OF THE NHL. THE RANGE IN THE WESTERN LEAGUE REMAINED RELATIVELY STABLE FOR THE REST OF ITS HISTORY, WHILE NHL GA PLUNGED WITH THE REFORMS IN OFFSIDE AND PASSING RULES. BUT THERE WAS LITTLE TO CHOOSE BETWEEN THE BEST GOALTENDERS OF THE TWO LEAGUES.

BLEU, BLANC *et* ROUGE

GEORGES VEZINA, THE MAN WHOSE NAME LIVES ON AS THE TROPHY EMBLEMATIC OF GOALTENDING EXCELLENCE IN THE

IMPERIAL TOBACCO ISSUED THIS TRADING CARD OF TWENTY-FOUR-YEAR-OLD VEZINA IN 1911/12 FOLLOWING HIS ROOKIE SEASON WITH THE CANADIENS. HE SPENT HIS ENTIRE FIFTEEN-SEASON CAREER IN MONTREAL, AND HAD TO BE HELPED OFF THE ICE IN HIS FINAL GAME IN 1925, WITH TUBERCULOSIS KILLING HIM.

National Hockey League, was a simple, decent man whose life was steeped in tragedy. Of the twenty-four children his wife bore, only two reached adulthood. Georges Vezina himself was only thirty-nine when he died, struck down by tuberculosis. The last Montreal Canadiens crowd to see him play saw him collapse on the ice and be assisted from it, coughing up arterial blood. He never got to play another game, and it broke his heart.

He was born in January 1887 in the town of Chicoutimi, in Quebec's Saguenay region. Hockey was so new as a sport it has been said that as a boy he played on the town's very first team. The game is thought to have been brought to town by McGill graduates who were working for the company Price Bros., which built the local rink as a result. He played goal in his boots on the ice, a not uncommon strategy in the game's early days, and didn't actually learn to skate until he was eighteen. He sharpened his skills by having friends throw rubber balls at him. His parents were the local bakers, and eventually his father Jacques bought the rink from Price Bros., an initiative that must have been a factor in honing young Georges' abilities.

Dates vary on precisely when Vezina was "discovered." It seems to have been the winter of 1910. The first hint that Vezina was an exceptional talent came with a visit by a touring Grand'Mère Senior club, which played the Chicoutimi team in preparation for an Allan Cup appearance. Vezina shut them out. Then came a visit in February 1910 by the Montreal Canadiens of the National Hockey Association, a team and a league in their first season of play.

Vezina's discovery came at an auspicious time in professional hockey. It had been a bewildering winter of manoeuvring in the eastern professional loops. On November 25, 1909, the Eastern Canadian Hockey Association had turned into the Canadian Hockey Association, comprising the Ottawa Senators, the Montreal Shamrocks, the Quebec Nationals and All-Montreal. Conspicuously absent was the Montreal Wanderers franchise, which had just been bought by P.J. Doran, owner of the Jubilee rink. His intention to hold his home games at this compact, 2,700-seat facility had caused him to be locked out of the reconstituted ECHA by the other owners.

It was a fatal error. At a secret meeting on December 2, six rooms away from where the CHA owners were holding their annual meeting in Montreal's Windsor Hotel, the National Hockey Association was created, composed of teams from the eastern Ontario town of Renfrew, the northern Ontario mining towns of Cobalt and Haileybury (on the west shore of Lake Temiskaming, headwaters of the Ottawa River) and the Wanderers. Tom Hare, who had the Cobalt team, was granted a franchise for a new Montreal team, to be called Les Canadiens, on the condition that it be transferred to sportsmen in the French Canadian community as soon as possible, and the team was granted exclusive right to sign French Canadian players in Montreal.

After playing a few games of their respective schedules, there was evidently too much hockey going on. Ottawa and the Shamrocks switched to the NHA, and the CHA died. A new season with all seven surviving teams began on January 15, 1910.

If Les Canadiens called on Chicoutimi that February, it was a quick dash in and out of town. The team had NHA games on February 2, 7, 12, 15, 24 and 26. Whenever they did come to town, Les Canadiens met with the same reception as the Grand'Mère Seniors. The Montreal professionals were shut out by the hinterlands crew that had Vezina between the posts.

Shutouts then were only slightly more common than a no-hitter in baseball. Riley Hern of the Wanderers would record the only one of the NHA's inaugural season on February 25, against Renfrew. Vezina himself wouldn't get one in the NHA until his third season. Vezina's back-to-back shutouts against powerful teams understandably impressed the Canadiens' netminder, Joseph Cattarinich, and tradition has it that for the next season, 1910/11, Cattarinich persuaded the Canadiens' new owner, George Kennedy, to sign Vezina, even though it would cost Cattarinich his position on the team. Cattarinich supposedly also urged Kennedy to sign Georges' brother Pierre, a forward, but Pierre chose to remain in Chicoutimi.

The signing of Vezina may well have eliminated Cattarinich's position, but he was something of a gentleman athlete who had only played three of twelve Canadiens games in 1910. The main Canadiens netminder, Teddy Groulx, had a GA of 8.56 in a league in which LGA was 6.46 and Riley Hern was the top goaltender at 3.42.

There is another problem with this oft-told tale of Vezina's recruitment. Kennedy (aka Kendall), a Montreal wrestler and sporting club operator, wasn't the owner of the Canadiens the following season, when Vezina did indeed take over the Canadiens goaltending job from Cattarinich and Groulx. Tom Hare was still the owner of the Canadiens at the league's annual meeting in November 1911, after Vezina had already played a full season. Cattarinich later became a partner in the ownership of the Canadiens, and the story of his selfless advocacy of Vezina sounds like an anecdote with which an owner would love to regale acquaintances.

If his birthdate of January 1887 is correct, Vezina was twenty-three when he joined the Canadiens, it's been said for $800. His maarriage has been dated to 1910, and it has also been written that his wife bore two sets of triplets in the first two years of marriage. Vezina was a quiet man who didn't speak much English, neither smoked nor drank, and ran a tannery business back in Chicoutimi.

The NHA was transformed after its truncated inaugural season; for 1910/11, when Vezina arrived, there were five teams: the Ottawa Senators, the Canadiens, the Renfrew Millionaires, the Montreal Wanderers and the Quebec Bulldogs. There was a formidable lineup of goaltending talent—Perce LeSueur in Ottawa (who would record the season's lone shutout), Paddy Moran in Quebec, Bert Lindsay in Renfrew and Riley Hern with the Wanderers. In his first season as a Canadien, Vezina's GA led the league. The next season, 1911/12, the NHA was down to four teams as the Renfrew Millionaires folded and the Patrick brothers, former Renfrew stars, formed the Pacific Coast Hockey Association and made off with a horde of high-priced talent, including Renfrew's Bert Lindsay. Again, Vezina's GA was the league's best, even though the Canadiens finished at the bottom of the standings.

The NHA found new strength in 1912/13 as two Toronto franchises, the Blueshirts (backed by Amby O'Brien) and the Tecumsehs, joined the circuit. It was Vezina's first ordinary season. The Canadiens were still struggling, and on GA Vezina finished in the middle of the pack, although he picked up his first NHA shutout, a 6–0 defeat of Ottawa. There were two new netminding stars: Clint Benedict, who began sharing the Senators net with Perce LeSueur, and Hap Holmes of the Blueshirts.

Vezina's first significant success came in 1915/16, when the Canadiens suddenly found greatness with offence provided by Newsy Lalonde and Didier Pitre; Vezina's GA was bettered only by Clint Benedict. The Canadiens won the league championship and met the Portland Rosebuds of the Pacific Coast league at Mount Royal Arena for the Stanley Cup. It was the first cup appearance for both the Canadiens and an American hockey club. Vezina was instrumental in the hard-fought Montreal victory, and the day after winning the cup, the

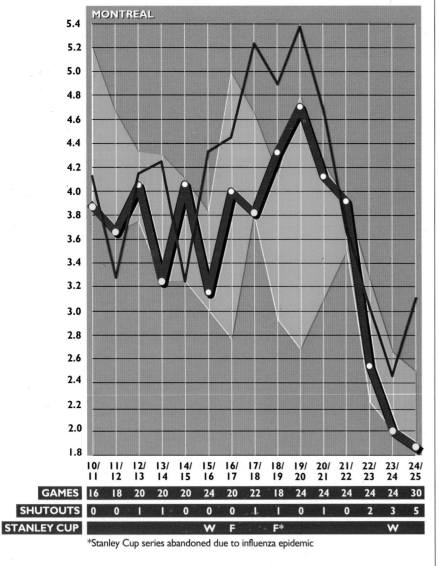

MONTREAL	10/11	11/12	12/13	13/14	14/15	15/16	16/17	17/18	18/19	19/20	20/21	21/22	22/23	23/24	24/25
GAMES	16	18	20	20	20	24	20	22	18	24	24	24	24	24	30
SHUTOUTS	0	0	1	1	0	0	0	1	1	0	1	0	2	3	5
STANLEY CUP					W	F		F*						W	

*Stanley Cup series abandoned due to influenza epidemic

Canadiens headed to Vezina's home town to play an exhibition match. Vezina was probably in a hurry to get home. The night of the winning game, one of Vezina's two sons who would survive to adulthood, Marcil, was born. By way of celebration, Georges gave him "Stanley" as his middle name.

The Canadiens won the NHA's 1916/17 championship, and so headed west for a Stanley Cup match against the PCHA's Seattle Metropolitans. Montreal won the first game 8–4, but only because Vezina had made a heroic stand against the Seattle offence. It could not last. Montreal then went down three straight, 6–1, 4–1 and 9–1. Two years later, the NHA was the NHL and Vezina and the Canadiens went west for a rematch with Seattle. It was during this series match-up between Vezina and Seattle's Hap Holmes that Vezina was described as "high strung", probably the only time in Vezina's career that the man known as the Chicoutimi Cucumber was referred to as anything short of unflappable. Vezina may have been rattled by a 7–0 opening-game loss, but Montreal was not through. The scoreless draw Holmes and Vezina battled to in game four, a hallmark of Stanley Cup lore, was overshadowed by the influenza epidemic that raged through Seattle, claiming the life of Montreal defenceman Joe Hall and compelling the trophy's trustees to abandon the series.

In all, Vezina played fifteen seasons for the Canadiens. If the team was on the ice, so was he: Vezina appeared in 328 consecutive league games and 39 playoff contests. Successes for the team after the abandoned 1919 series, though, were hard to come by as Ottawa dominated the four-team loop. In 1921, Leo Letourneau, Leo Dandurand and Joseph Cattarinich—the goaltender who had supposedly first spotted Vezina's talent—bought the team from the estate of George Kennedy for $11,000. They promptly gave Vezina his best financial return in hockey, a $7,200 salary.

In 1923/24, Vezina led the league on GA, ending a five-season dominance by Clint Benedict, and would repeat the feat the following season. Montreal won the 1923/24 NHL championship over Ottawa and Benedict, then met and defeated the Vancouver Maroons (as the Millionaires were renamed in 1922) of the PCHA and the Calgary Tigers of the Western Canada Hockey League in a two-tier Stanley Cup series at home. It proved to be Vezina's last.

Long after his playing and coaching career was over, Frank Boucher, who starred with the Vancouver Maroons in the 1920s, looked back on the goaltender who had faced him down in 1924. "The first thing that pops into my mind is that he always wore a toque, a small, knitted hat with no brim in Montreal colours—bleu, blanc et rouge. I also remember him as the coolest man I ever saw, absolutely imperturbable... He stood upright in the net and scarcely ever left his feet; he simply played all his shots in a standing position. Vezina was a pale, narrow-featured fellow, almost frail-looking, yet remarkably good

with his stick. He'd pick off more shots with it than he did with his glove."

Vezina was indeed pale and frail-looking. He was also seriously ill. In Montreal's home opener of the 1925/26 season on November 25, Vezina's Canadiens played a scoreless first period against the Pittsburgh Pirates. When Vezina arrived in the dressing room between periods, he had arterial blood in his mouth, and lost consciousness. Incredibly, Vezina returned to the ice for the second period. He had never not finished a game. During that period, he collapsed on the ice, and had to be carried off. He had a temperature of 102 and was dizzy and complaining of chest pains; it was thought he had a severe cold that was threatening pneumonia. But Vezina had been looking so poorly before the start of the season that the Canadiens owners had already taken the step of securing a backup, Alphonse Lacroix. It was soon apparent that Vezina was suffering from far more than pneumonia. He had tuberculosis, and had been suffering from it for some time.

At the end of the season, in late March, Vezina made his first visit back to the Canadiens since his collapse in the season-opener four months earlier. He turned up at game time and sat down in his corner of the dressing room. Dandurand would recall how he "glanced at [Vezina] as he sat there, and saw tears rolling down his cheeks. He was looking at his old pads and skates that [trainer] Eddie Dufour had arranged in Georges' corner, thinking he would don them that night." But Vezina was going nowhere near the ice. He had lost a shocking amount of weight, and TB had thoroughly ravaged his lungs. Vezina asked one favour of Dandurand—he wanted to have the sweater he wore in the last Stanley Cup. With that, Georges Vezina left. A few days later, he was dead. The Canadiens ownership promptly established the Vezina Trophy to honour goaltending excellence. When the Hockey Hall of Fame was founded in 1945, Georges Vezina was one of the first twelve players promptly inducted. ◯

IN MARCH 1926, A GRAVELY ILL VEZINA SAT IN HIS CORNER OF THE CANADIENS DRESSING ROOM WITH TEARS IN HIS EYES, LOOKING AT THIS PAIR OF SKATES, KNOWING HE WOULD NEVER WEAR THEM AGAIN. A FEW DAYS LATER, HE WAS DEAD.

AFTER TWELVE OUTSTANDING
SEASONS AS AN OTTAWA
SENATOR, IN 1924 BENEDICT
WAS SOLD TO THE MONTREAL
MAROONS, WITH WHOM HE
WON A FOURTH STANLEY CUP.

PRAYING BENNIE

IN 1964, CLINT BENEDICT WAS SEVENTY-TWO YEARS OLD, CONFINED TO A HOSPITAL BED WHILE RECOVERING FROM A FRACTURED HIP, WONDERING WHERE HE

had gone wrong. Unquestionably the greatest goaltending star of the game's early years, induction into the Hockey Hall of Fame had somehow eluded him. Hugh Lehman, whose Pacific Coast league career paralleled Benedict's in the NHA and NHL, was inducted in 1958. Perce LeSueur, Benedict's predecessor in the Ottawa Senators goal, made it into the Hall in 1961. Johnny Bower Hutton, goaltender for the Ottawa Silver Seven cup champions of 1903 and 1904, was elected in 1962, a year after George Hainsworth, who had starred alongside Benedict in the NHL in the 1920s. And Chuck Gardiner, whose career with the Blackhawks overlapped Benedict's, had been inducted way back in 1945, alongside Georges Vezina.

Reminiscing for a *Montreal Star* reporter, Benedict confessed to his disappointment. "I've been told I should be in there and maybe I should, but I seem to have 'crossed' someone somewhere along the way. Politics? Yes, I guess that's what you'd have to call it. Politics."

But the *Star* profile was read in the right circles,

and the following year, Benedict joined Lehman, LeSueur, Hainsworth, Vezina and Gardiner in the Hall. What "politics" had kept Benedict out so long? His career statistics were without parallel. He played seventeen seasons of professional hockey (a performance exceeded only by Lehman's twenty-one seasons in the era), won four Stanley Cups and almost singlehandedly forced the rulemakers to allow goaltenders to leave their feet. For nine seasons in the NHA/NHL, from 1914/15 until 1922/23, his GA was bested only once. Statistically, Benedict outshone even the great Georges Vezina, who was defending the Montreal Canadiens net while Benedict played for the Senators. He had also been the first goaltender to wear a face mask in a game.

It may have been Benedict's misfortune to record his greatest statistical seasons before there was a Vezina Trophy. It may also have been his misfortune to have played for two teams, the Ottawa Senators and the Montreal Maroons, that folded in the 1930s, taking his own performances with them into obscurity as the legacies of the Original Six franchises took priority in the 1950s and 1960s. Or it may simply have been his good fortune to have lived so long. Having avoided the tragic deaths that struck down the likes of Gardiner, Vezina and Hainsworth, Benedict had not provided the kind of reminder that can

CLINT BENEDICT'S SKATES

put the accomplishments of a long-forgotten career back in the public eye: an obituary. Yet George Hainsworth was not elected to the Hall until eleven years after his death. Though disheartened that it took him so long to gain the recognition of his sport, Benedict could take considerable solace in the fact that it did come within his lifetime.

Benedict's career was synonymous with the early history of organized hockey. Born in 1892, at age six he began playing goal for his school team. Cricket-style pads had just caught on with goaltenders, and he wore this style for his entire career, even for the half-dozen seasons he played after the thick stuffed leather pads perfected by Pop Kenesky took his profession by storm. At the tender age of fifteen, he began playing Senior hockey in Ottawa. At seventeen he appeared in his first professional game.

Like Perce LeSueur, Hap Holmes and Alex Connell, Benedict was an accomplished lacrosse player, playing semi-pro in the summers for the first five seasons he was with the Ottawa Senators. Perce LeSueur was the main Ottawa goaltender, and Benedict played in only eleven games in his first two seasons with the Senators, which he joined in 1912 at age twenty.

Benedict's early performances were impressive. His GA in four games in 1912/13 was only 2.75, well below the league-leading 3.75 set by Paddy Moran among the league regulars. And he managed to record a shutout, one of only four in the league that season.

The NHA was experiencing a changing of the guard among its goaltenders. The league had been dominated by such established stars as LeSueur, Moran and Riley Hern. Moran played sixteen professional seasons, all but one of them with the Quebec Bulldogs, and won the Stanley Cup in 1912 and 1913. His GA was rather mediocre even for the time—5.4 over 201 games—but it was an age when GA was not taken seriously as a measure of greatness. Riley Hern, who had played both forward and goaltending positions before settling on the net, was one of the professional hockey pioneers who were lured to Houghton, Michigan, in the state's northern copper country, to play for the famed Portage Lake team in 1903. He signed with the Montreal Wanderers in 1906, and won the Stanley Cup with them in 1907, 1908 and 1910. The next season, he gave up playing to concentrate on his business interests, staying in touch with the game as a referee and goal judge. LeSueur played one season for the Ontario Shamrocks after Benedict took over the Ottawa net before going into the army. And then there was Renfrew's Bert Lindsay, who jumped from the NHA to the Patrick brothers' new PCHA in 1911 for its inaugural season, but would return to play for the Montreal Wanderers and the Toronto Arenas in the NHL's first two seasons.

When Benedict took complete charge of the Senators goal in 1914, two wars were under way—the one in Europe and the one in hockey, as the NHA battled with the PCHA for the best players and bragging rights to the best team. Benedict became a Senators starter just as the trustees of the Stanley Cup agreed that the trophy should be contested annually between

A BREED APART | **34**

the two leagues. Benedict and the Senators headed to Victoria in 1915 to play the first Stanley Cup series on the west coast, in the Patricks' marvellous artificial-ice arena against the Vancouver Millionaires of Frank Patrick.

Patrick had an awesome lineup of talent, spearheaded by former Senators star Cyclone Taylor. His goaltender, Hugh Lehman, was an experienced professional out of Pembroke, Ontario, when Benedict came up against him in Victoria, and the best-of-five series was a humiliation for the Senators and the twenty-three-year-old Benedict. Every game turned out worse than the last as they went down 6–2, 8–3 and 12–3. Benedict's GA for the series was 8.67; Lehman's, 2.67. "We were beaten so badly that we took the $147 share from the series and went to the World's Fair in San Francisco until the heat went off," he recalled in 1966. The loss was so traumatic that Benedict would practically erase it from his résumé. "I seldom talk about the team. Usually I cite the main reasons why we lost—and their names were Frank Nighbor, Frank Patrick and Cyclone Taylor, to mention a couple. That was quite a team Vancouver had in those days." Nighbor was later a teammate of Benedict's in Ottawa.

It would be five years before Benedict got another shot at the Stanley Cup. By then the NHA had been reconstituted as the NHL, in the fall of 1917. That first season, the new league made a significant change in the rules it carried forward from the NHA, becoming the first league to permit goaltenders to drop to the ice. Benedict's play has long been credited as the motivating factor. He had devised an elaborate series of ruses to allow him to get to his knees—ruses that other goaltenders began copying. One routine allegedly saw him dropping to his knees to give thanks to God—a play that gave rise among outraged Toronto fans to the nickname "Praying Bennie."

Benedict proved a genius of deception, losing his balance in such a way that he got away with not only falling to the ice, but also smothering the puck in the process. Well after goaltenders were allowed to drop to the ice, they had to get rid of the puck immediately, should they catch it or land on it. Not Benedict. He was the master at getting whistles. "If you did it a little bit sneaky and made it look accidental, you could fall on the puck without being penalized," he recalled in 1964. Again, he was widely mimicked. "We all watched each other's tricks and that's one of mine which was copied and eventually became part of the game." In 1966, he would explain the need to force stoppages in play any way possible: "You had to do something. Quite a few of the players could put a curving drop on the shot, and the equipment wasn't exactly the greatest in those days."

His stick, which was shaped from a single piece of wood, "weighed a ton." Benedict wore the standard five-fingered gloves—"My fingers were as badly hurt as my face or legs." When interviewed in 1964, his knuckles were noted to be "wobbly and mishappen."

The game was brutal for him. He was known to perform injured, once practically without the use of one of his legs. "Getting hurt was nothing. I've been hit so hard [by the puck] that it bounced off my head and into the seats. They stitched me up and put me back in." And Benedict was intimately acquainted with the game's brawling nature. He once got in a tussle with the notorious Cully Wilson. The right-winger had been suspended by the Pacific Coast league after breaking Mickey MacKay's jaw with a vicious cross check, and came east to play for Toronto, Hamilton and Chicago in the 1920s. "Wilson and I threw a couple punches and both of us got penalties," Benedict recalled. "As we skated to the penalty box he seemed to have had enough, so when he invited me politely to enter first, I did. That was where I made my mistake. He hit me with a beautiful right hand shot in the jaw. You couldn't trust anybody in those days."

In the NHL's second season, 1918/19, Benedict began a five-season string of league-leading GAs, all of them as a Senator. He was the second goaltender in NHL history, after Vezina, to record a shutout. Vezina got his, a 9–0 performance against Toronto, on February 18, 1918. A week later, Benedict blanked Vezina and the Canadiens, 8–0. In 1919/20, he was sensational, leading the league with a 2.67 GA and recording five shutouts in twenty-four games—no other goaltender managed a single shutout. Benedict turned in this performance when LGA was 4.79, the highest in the NHL's history; his performance edge of more than two goals per game over the average goaltender has never been matched. Ottawa won the NHL league title, and the Seattle Metropolitans came east to contest the Stanley Cup. Hap Holmes was the Seattle goaltender, and the series went all five games before Benedict and the Senators prevailed, with the only shutout of the series going to Benedict.

These were years in which the Senators dominated professional hockey, winning three Stanley Cups in four seasons. In 1921, Benedict went west with Ottawa to play the Vancouver Millionaires. There would be no humiliation for Benedict on this trip to the coast. He again faced Hugh Lehman in the opposite net, and Lehman mesmerized the Senators with his forward passing, but Benedict and the Senators defended the cup in the second straight series to require all five games.

In 1923, the Senators were back in the west again, this time for a trying two-tier playoff series. The rise of the Western Canada Hockey League meant that the Senators were required first to meet and beat the PCHA champions before advancing to the Stanley Cup final against the WCHL champions. The PCHA had at last shifted to the six-man game, which meant the Stanley Cup series no longer had to alternate between seven-man and six-man hockey each game. The series against Frank Patrick's Vancouver Maroons (the name the team adopted in 1922) was one of the most punishing ever. In the first game, Benedict was cut and knocked unconscious by an accidental high stick, but returned to win the game 1–0. In game two, a shot by Mickey MacKay struck Benedict in the mouth, splitting his lip and loosening his teeth. He picked himself up off the ice and continued to play, and lost, 4–1. The Senators almost to a man were nursing injuries, but they won the Vancouver series and then beat the Edmonton Eskimos of the western league in two straight games. Frank Patrick called this squad of Senators the greatest team he had ever seen.

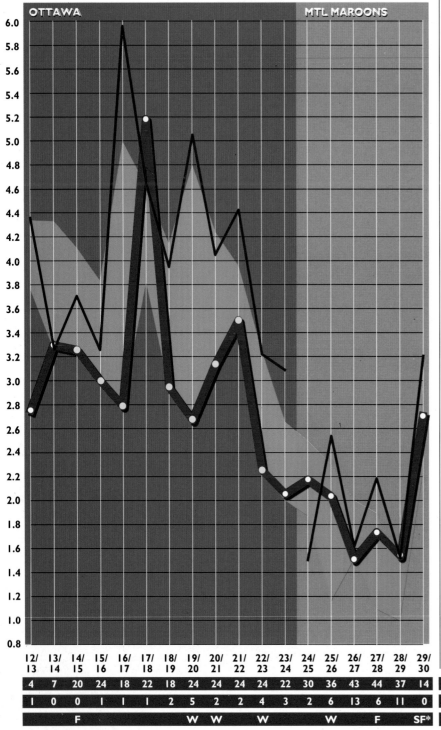

	12/13	13/14	14/15	15/16	16/17	17/18	18/19	19/20	20/21	21/22	22/23	23/24	24/25	25/26	26/27	27/28	28/29	29/30	
	4	7	20	24	18	22	18	24	24	24	24	22	30	36	43	44	37	14	**GAMES**
	1	0	0	1	1	1	2	5	2	2	4	3	2	6	13	6	11	0	**SHUTOUTS**
	F				W	W		W		W			W			F		SF*	**STANLEY CUP**

While Benedict's GA in 1912/13 was a league-leading 2.75, he played only four games. The season's top GA is attributed to Paddy Moran, at 3.75.
*Benedict did not participate in playoffs.

During these glory years of the Senators franchise, Benedict towered above the rest of the goaltending talent on strength of numbers. But by 1923/24, goaltending parity was more in evidence. Benedict's 2.05 GA that season, trailing Vezina's 2.00, was not far ahead of the LGA of 2.66.

In 1924/25, the NHL expanded, adding a franchise in Boston and welcoming the Montreal Maroons. To help strengthen the Maroons, Ottawa sold the team two players: Benedict, and his old teammate Harry "Punch" Broadbent. Ottawa replaced Benedict with rookie Alex Connell.

Benedict was an immediate star in Montreal. In his first season, he won the Mappin Trophy as the team's MVP. Connell dominated the regular season in goal, recording a GA of 1.17 and fifteen shutouts in thirty-six games. But Benedict, who had six shutouts and a 2.03 GA, took charge in the playoffs. Benedict's Maroons won the league title by defeating Connell's Senators, with Benedict recording a shutout in the final game. Buttressed by the arrival of Benedict, the Maroons made the Stanley Cup final in only their second season. It was the last match-up with a representative of a western league, since the Western Hockey League (as the merged PCHA and WCHL was known in the final season) promptly folded. Against the Victoria Cougars (as the Aristocrats were known beginning in 1922), Benedict was virtually impermeable. In the series' four games, Benedict recorded three shutouts and a GA of 0.75.

It was Benedict's last Stanley Cup win, though he was still at the peak of his game. In 1926/27, he notched thirteen shutouts in forty-three games; in 1928/29, eleven shutouts in thirty-seven games. In 1926/27, the league awarded the first Vezina Trophy in honour of the Canadiens' late, great goaltender. Benedict missed winning it by the slightest of margins. The trophy was awarded to the goaltender on the team allowing the fewest total goals. The Canadiens had allowed sixty-seven goals, the Maroons sixty-eight. Thus the trophy went to Vezina's successor, George Hainsworth, newly arrived from the collapsed western league. Their individual records were virtually identical. Benedict had missed one game—Flat Walsh played his first game in seven seasons of serving as the Maroons' backup—and in forty-three games allowed sixty-five goals, with thirteen shutouts, for a GA of 1.51. Hainsworth allowed sixty-seven goals in forty-four games, with fourteen shutouts, for a GA of 1.52. It was a time of great parity among the top goaltenders. Lorne Chabot's GA in New York that season was 1.56; Alex Connell's in Ottawa, 1.57.

Benedict had another three NHL seasons before him, but he would never again come as close to leading the league in GA as he did that first Vezina Trophy season. Still brilliant, Benedict nonetheless was now in his mid-thirties and still wearing the old-fashioned cricket-style pads as a new generation of netminding stars, sporting great leather pads, arose—notably Chabot in New York, Connell in Ottawa and Gardiner in Chicago. Benedict made it to one more Stanley Cup final, in 1928 against the New York Rangers, which the Maroons lost. It was the series in which Lester Patrick came from behind the Rangers bench to replace the injured Lorne Chabot in game two, and won an unlikely goaltending duel against Benedict when the Rangers scored in overtime. Benedict still set a league record by recording four shutouts in nine playoff games against Ottawa, the Canadiens and the Rangers that season. ("I just used to keep yelling, 'Don't let them shoot!' ")

Silverware was hard to come by for Benedict. The Vezina Trophy eluded him. There was no award for playoff performance; the Conn Smythe Trophy wouldn't be dedicated until 1964. And though the award for most valuable player, the Hart Trophy, had made its debut in 1923/24, it too passed him by. His teammate Nels Stewart won it twice in those years, in 1925/26 and 1929/30. When the journalists who voted on it did decide to give it to a goaltender in 1928/29, it was to Roy Worters of the New York Americans.

Without warning, Benedict's career was derailed on January 7, 1930 in a game against the Canadiens. As the great Howie Morenz closed in, defenceman Jim Ward cut in front of Benedict, trying to break up the play. Using Ward as a screen, Morenz fired the puck high from twenty-five feet out. "I saw it at the last, split second and lunged," Benedict would recall. "Wham, I'm out like a light and wake up in the hospital."

The shot had smashed into Benedict's cheekbone and nose. Two seasons later, a reporter would write that the puck had "crushed in the side of Benny's face like an eggshell."

"I wasn't right for a month," Benedict remembered. "I was in bed for a month and eventually it was that injury that forced me out of hockey because my vision was affected."

Whether to protect his fragile face or his now-precarious confidence, Benedict set out to create the game's first face mask. There are two stories on its origins. One says he had a Boston firm make him one out of leather, built around a football face mask in use at the time. Another has it that the Maroons trainer modified a black leather face mask boxers wore in sparring by riveting a thick black bar across the front to protect Benedict's nose and cheekbone. The confusion is heightened by the fact that a Benedict mask in the collection of the Hockey Hall of Fame doesn't look like the mask Benedict wore in a photo (see page 123). Whatever it was, it didn't work. "The nosepiece protruded too far and obscured my vision on low shots." After losing 2–1 to Chicago wearing it, "I threw the darn thing away. I blamed it for the loss and that was that." He then tried a wire cage–style protector, like a baseball catcher's mask, "but the wires dis-

tracted me. That's when I gave up."

To make matters worse, later that season another Morenz shot struck him in the throat, again putting him out of commission. He never held the mishaps against Morenz; Benedict said they were friends before the incidents, and continued to be afterwards. But his career in the NHL was over. "You know, if we had been able to perfect the mask, I could have been a twenty-year man," he would suggest. "I broke in when I was seventeen and played seventeen seasons. I'm pretty sure that's a record for a goaltender." (In total seasons, at least, Hugh Lehman outlasted him.)

The next season, the Maroons sent Benedict down to their farm club, the Windsor Bulldogs of the International League. Benedict allowed ninety goals in forty games for a GA of 2.25, with one shutout. The Bulldogs won the league championship, which proved to be Benedict's swan song. He was thirty-nine years old, and bitter that his career had come to such an end in such a place. He headed to Saint John, New Brunswick, to coach the Beavers of the old Big Four loop.

Then, in 1934, he made a drastic change. The Empire Pool and Sports Arena opened at Wembley, England, that year. With seating for 10,000, it became a focal point for the revved-up British ice hockey league. For four years, Benedict managed and coached the Wembley Lions.

When the war arrived, Benedict returned to Canada. He managed a Sherbrooke team, but took a job with the city of Ottawa and suffered increasingly poor health. His sterling NHL career was almost, but not quite, forgotten. He died in an Ottawa hospital in 1976, ten years after he finally became a Hall of Famer. ○

BENEDICT WAS BITTER THAT HIS CAREER SHOULD COME TO AN END WITH THE WINDSOR BULLDOGS, A MONTREAL MAROONS FARM TEAM. HE WORE THIS SWEATER IN HIS FINAL SEASON.

CHAPTER 2

1925/26–1938/39

DEFINING *the* ROLE

AS THE NHL SOLVED ITS CRISIS IN GOAL-SCORING, IT ALSO MADE GREAT STRIDES TOWARD CREATING THE MODERN GOALTENDER

I n a league in which average goals against (LGA) was tumbling season after season, the ceaseless activity in the pages of the NHL rulebook from the mid-1920s through the Second World War speaks of a struggle to find some balance in the offensive and defensive aspects of the game. Inevitably, goaltenders were a focal point of this struggle. Over about fifteen seasons, the position and the game around it underwent enormous changes and moved within striking distance of their modern forms.

After an uncertain start, the National Hockey League had found relative stability in the early twenties as a four-team loop; the Quebec Bulldogs franchise had resumed play in 1919/20, and moved to Hamilton the next season. The game gained an unprecedented mass audience when Foster Hewitt made hockey's first radio broadcast in March 1923. In 1924/25, the NHL began to expand as professional sports across North America blossomed. The Montreal Maroons and the first American franchise, the Boston Bruins, appeared. In 1925/26, two longstanding hockey hotbeds received franchises: the Hamilton Tigers were sold for $75,000 and resumed play as the New York Americans at Madison Square Garden, and Pittsburgh's amateur Yellow Jackets joined the NHL and became the Pirates. Franchises were also awarded to Chicago and Detroit in 1926.

It was a period of consolidation as professional hockey in western Canada collapsed after the 1925/26 season, unable to keep up with the bidding war for play-ers it had launched against the National Hockey Association, the NHL's forerunner, in 1911. The Stanley Cup was now wholly the domain of the NHL. But as players and managers (including the Patrick brothers, founders of the Pacific Coast league, which had launched the professional game out west) moved over to the NHL, they helped instigate one important revision for the 1926/27 season. A larger neutral zone was created by positioning the bluelines sixty feet from the goal lines,

THE GOALTENDER FOR THE NEW YORK AMERICANS "TAKES A SWIM IN A FROZEN POND" IN THIS GOALMOUTH SCRAMBLE AGAINST THE TORONTO MAPLE LEAFS IN 1933. THE IDENTITY OF THE GOALTENDER IS NOT KNOWN, BUT IT IS NOT STARTER ROY WORTERS, WHO DIDN'T WEAR A CAP.

rather than twenty feet to either side of centre ice. This created a neutral zone sixty feet wide on a full-size rink—twenty feet wider than in the NHL the previous season, and seven feet narrower than in the western game. And for the 1926/27 season, the Toronto St. Patricks franchise became the Maple Leafs as Conn Smythe (who had assembled the New York Rangers lineup, only to be cashiered as general manager in favour of Lester Patrick) engineered a takeover.

But even as the league expanded, the game was in danger. LGA was continuing its steady slide—4.65 in 1917/18, it was down to 2.0 in 1926/27—as the NHL descended into a dull defensive gridlock.

As the dominant league, the NHL would no longer follow hockey practices set by the amateur organizations. Borrowing some of its revisions from the western professional game, it began to create its own version of basic elements: the rink on which it played, the roles the players should fill. As a professional game charged with providing entertainment, it was less hidebound than the amateur game when it came to fiddling with the basic rules. Already, in the NHL's inaugural 1917/18 season, it had allowed goaltenders to drop to the ice, well before the amateurs were willing to do the same.

The NHL first mentioned rink dimensions in its rulebook for the 1927/28 season. The "ideal" rink size was set at 200 feet by 85 feet, although these dimensions didn't necessarily have to be adhered to, as the cramped arenas in Chicago and Boston attested. The ten-foot goal line was spelled out, and the LeSueur net of 1912 was replaced by the double-bulge Art Ross net, whose shape was meant to trap the puck when shot from virtually any angle.

In 1924/25, LGA had sunk, again,

to 2.5, aided in part by the appearance around 1924 of the quasi-modern goaltender's leg pad. Pioneered by Pop Kenesky of Hamilton, Ontario, these custom leather pads, stuffed with felt and horsehair, would change very little in essential shape over the next five decades.

The Kenesky-style pads were huge—some measured fourteen inches across and seemed to reach clear to the goaltender's waist. For 1925/26, the league introduced a twelve-inch limit on their width. And in an effort to break up defence-obsessed strategies, the league introduced two new rules: it forbade more than two skaters from remaining behind their own blueline once the puck had left the defence zone, and faceoffs were called whenever a player was judged to be killing time by skating aimlessly with ("ragging") the puck, unless his team was shorthanded. LGA continued to fall regardless, to 2.31. The following season, 1926/27, the change in the measurement of the blueline position served to reduce the defence zone's size and put more of the play in the neutral zone, where forward passing was permitted. But still LGA fell, to 2.0.

For 1927/28, the goaltender's maximum leg pad width was cut to ten inches to give shooters more open net; the pad measurement would remain at ten inches for sixty years. And if a player delayed the game, usually to rescue his team from an offensive press, by shooting the puck out of the rink, he was now assessed a minor penalty. That season, LGA drooped to 1.9 and Alex Connell of the Ottawa Senators set the league record of six straight shutouts—in all, 446 minutes and 9 seconds of continuous scoreless hockey.

I t was a time when superb goaltenders turned in superlative performances. Connell, known as the "Ottawa Fireman" because he was secretary of the capital's fire department, was a great lacrosse and baseball player as well; in baseball he played catcher, a position a number of professional goaltenders would be attracted to. It is said that Connell started playing goal in the army in Kingston during the First World War, but he only turned sixteen on February 8, 1918, near the war's end. At any rate, he didn't turn professional until 1924, at age twenty-two, signing with the Senators when the great Clint Benedict was sold to the Montreal Maroons. In his second season—the last in the league before there was a Vezina Trophy—Connell led the NHL with a GA of 1.17, more than a full goal better than the LGA of 2.31, and assembled fifteen shutouts in a thirty-six-game season. The next season, 1926/27, when he and the Senators won the Stanley Cup, he recorded thirteen shutouts in forty-four games, and the following season, still at forty-four games, he notched fifteen more.

Connell played on through 1932/33, every season with Ottawa except 1931/32, which he played in Detroit as the Senators temporarily suspended operations with the Depression biting hard. When the Senators were revived for 1932/33, he returned to play for them for fifteen games, but the team died for good at the end of the season. Connell played one game for the New York

Americans the following season and retired, but in 1934/35, the Montreal Maroons coaxed him back. As a result, Connell suffered the indignity of becoming the first goaltender in NHL history to be scored on by a penalty shot, a novelty borrowed from the defunct western league that season. He made amends in the playoffs, completely shutting out Chicago in the quarterfinal and eliminating the Rangers in the semifinal, then outperforming George Hainsworth of the Maple Leafs by allowing only four goals as the Maroons won the Stanley Cup in three straight games.

Connell sat out the next season, and the Maroons replaced him with Lorne Chabot, a Vezina winner who had become somewhat notorious in 1932 when he and a number of name-brand stars around the league held out for higher pay after the league introduced a salary cap of $7,500—at the time the average Canadian production worker was making $844. (Chabot gained a different sort of notoriety when Lester Patrick, in Chabot's New York days, tried to create a fan attraction for the city's Jewish community by renaming his goaltender Chabotsky.) In 1931, the diminutive New York Americans netminder Roy Worters, having just won the Vezina, had demanded a princely salary of $8,500 in U.S. funds, which were worth twice as much as Canadian dollars, and had gotten it. But in 1932, Chabot and the other holders didn't get their way, and it proved to be Chabot's last of five seasons in Toronto.

The Maroons didn't advance past the semifinal with Chabot in 1935/36, and in 1936/37, Connell was back in the NHL, again in a Maroons sweater. The Maroons were stopped short of a Stanley Cup appearance in the semifinal, and it proved to be, at last, Connell's final tour of duty. He never did win the Vezina, but his performances were outstanding. In twenty-one career playoff games, he recorded four shutouts and allowed only twenty-six goals—a GA of 1.19. His career GA of 1.91 surpassed even that of Benedict, who played all but one of his seasons before the league's LGA leap in 1929/30.

By the time Connell played his last NHL game, LGA had doubled, and it had done so in a single spasm of change. At wit's end in the late 1920s as LGA had continued its tumble, the league tried to inject more offence by liberalizing the forward passing rules in a manner that initially proved disastrous. In 1928/29, forward passing was permitted by a team in its defensive zone and in the neutral zone, but not in the attacking zone (the other team's defensive zone). The rules would, however, allow an attacking player to receive a forward pass in the attacking zone provided he was on the neutral-zone side of the blueline when the pass was released. But a team was still not allowed to make a forward pass across its own blueline. As can often happen, a rule designed to create more offence only served to create a game that stressed more defence, as strategists protected against the plays the new rule permitted. The league's

LGA tumbled from 1.9 to 1.45. George Hainsworth won his third straight Vezina that season with an astonishing GA of 0.98, a league record that still stands and will certainly never be broken.

For 1929/30, the league scrapped the new passing rules and began afresh. In a measure also adopted by the amateur game, forward passing would be allowed in all three zones, but never across a blueline. At mid-season, it was decided to elaborate on the matter of attacking players and the blueline: a loophole was closed by declaring that no attacking player could cross the blueline ahead of the play. The league was very close to the nub of the modern offside rule. The modern rule—no offensive player could cross the the blueline ahead of the puck— came the following season.

The minimum defensive bodies rule of 1924/25 was tightened. A minor penalty would now be assessed for the first two times in a game a team was caught with more than two skaters behind their blueline keeping their goaltender company once the play had moved up ice; on the third time, it became a major penalty. The rules regarding the goaltender and the puck were made explicit. He was permitted to stop a shot "any way he chooses except by throwing his stick, but must not hold the puck and must not pass it forward with his hands but may pass it laterally or backward with his hands."

Continued on page 44

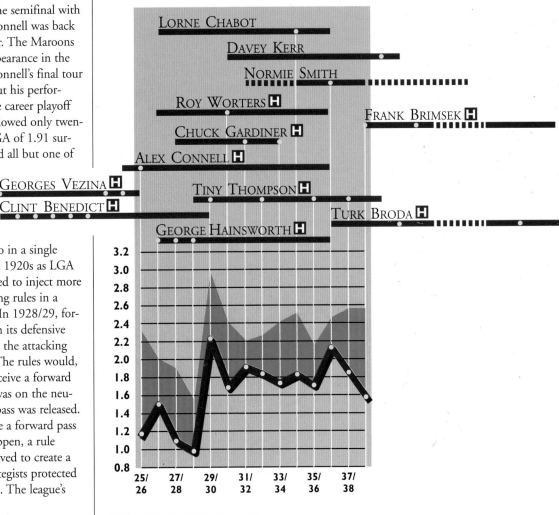

GEORGE HAINSWORTH

"ALL I CAN DO IS STOP PUCKS," HE ONCE APOLOGIZED. THE CANADIENS' FANS READILY FORGAVE HIM FOR HIS LACK OF CHARISMA

"I'm sorry I can't put on a show like some of the other goaltenders," George Hainsworth apologized after a game. "I can't look excited because I'm not. I can't shout at other players because that's not my style. I can't dive on easy shots and make them look hard. I guess all I can do is stop pucks."

Hainsworth had stopped every puck that night, and his performance delivered the Montreal Canadiens the 1930/31 Stanley Cup. At the other end of the rink, in the Chicago Blackhawks net, had been Chuck Gardiner, who, to quote Montreal journalist Elmer Ferguson, "bounced and dived around, shouted an endless flow of encouragement or advice to his teammates, occasionally exchanged jovial repartees with nearby customers, and often shouted jibes at opposing players as they bore in on him." Gardiner was one of the game's effervescent new stars, and Hainsworth was a colourless, though genial, old-reliable. He was a small man, only five-foot-five, but his quickness covered a lot of net. "Hainsworth plays goal in a debonair, nonchalant fashion that at times looks to verge on actual carelessness, but isn't," one account stated around the time of the 1930/31 cup victory. "And this isn't done for effect. He makes the tough shots look easy." Another called him "almost mechanical in his perfection." At that time, Hainsworth figured he'd stopped 19,000 pucks and recorded 160 shutouts since he had started playing goal in his home town of Kitchener, Ontario.

Born in Toronto in 1895, Hainsworth had moved with his family to Kitchener (then known as Berlin) when he was a young boy. Keen on baseball and hockey, he began playing hockey in the City League at age fifteen. Two years later, this natural talent was in the net for the city's Junior team; working his way up to the Senior level locally, he won the Allan Cup, the national Senior title, in 1918.

He took his time moving over to the professional game. He was twenty-eight when he headed west in 1923 to play (for $2,500) for the Saskatoon Crescents of the Western Canada Hockey League, where the former Canadiens star Newsy Lalonde was the player-manager. He spent three seasons out west. In his second season, when the PCHA teams came under the WCHL umbrella (and the Crescents became the Sheiks), he had the league's second-best GA; in his final season, with the circuit now known as the Western Hockey League, he was the All Star goaltender and, again, second-best on GA.

The western league folded after the 1925/26 season, and his rights were fought over by the NHL's Toronto St. Patricks and the Canadiens, a tussle the Canadiens won. Georges Vezina had died in the spring of 1926, and the team was desperate for a quality starter. Alphonse Lacroix, whom the Canadiens ownership had secured at the start of the 1925/26 season to back up the ailing Vezina, was not up to the job, nor was Herbert Rheaume, who played thirty-one games that season for Montreal.

Hainsworth came into the NHL as the league was sliding toward its lowest LGA in history; by moving from the defunct WHL to the NHL, his average dropped from 2.12 to 1.52, and his shutouts rose from four to fourteen. In 1928/29, he amassed twenty-two shutouts in forty-four games and a GA of 0.98 as LGA hit its historic rock bottom of 1.45. What made the performance, and particularly the shutouts, even more remarkable, is that the Canadiens only won twenty-two games all season. He earned his

	WCHL/ WHL SASK.			MONTREAL								TORONTO			
Season	23/ 24	24/ 25	25/ 26	26/ 27	27/ 28	28/ 29	29/ 30	30/ 31	31/ 32	32/ 33	33/ 34	34/ 35	35/ 36	36/ 37	
GAMES	30	28	30	44	44	44	42	44	48	48	48	48	48	7	
SHUTOUTS	4	2	4	14	13	22	4	8	6	8	3	8	8	0	
STANLEY CUP				SF	SF	SF	W	W	SF	QF	SF	F	F	QF	
ALL STAR TEAM		★													

Hainsworth played for the Montreal Canadiens at the end of 1936/37 season. He did not appear in Toronto's quarterfinal games. Montreal was eliminated in the semifinal.

third straight Vezina—he was the only goaltender to have won a Vezina, as the trophy had only been dedicated in 1926, Hainsworth's NHL rookie season.

In 1950, Hainsworth revealed that the trophies were stored in the attic of his Kitchener home. When Hainsworth won them, they brought no accompanying cash award—just a replica of the original Vezina Trophy, which Canadiens' co-owner Leo Dandurand had told him cost sixty dollars each. "I suggested he give me the sixty dollars and put a little shield on the original trophy for each of the two additional ones. Leo didn't like the idea."

The Canadiens won the Stanley Cup in 1929/30 and 1930/31, but as the Depression set in, the franchise fell on hard times. The Canadiens made Hainsworth their captain for the 1932/33 season, the first time a goaltender had been so honoured in the NHL. Montreal won only eighteen of forty-eight games, and Hainsworth was traded to Toronto for Lorne Chabot. Hainsworth was a respected veteran now, but no longer at the peak of his profession. He was never named to an NHL All Star team—not even in the first season of the prize, when he and the Canadiens won their last cup together. (The flamboyant Chuck Gardiner made the first team that season, and Boston's Tiny Thompson was named to the second team.) And he would not win another Vezina.

It may have been that the game had changed too much for Hainsworth when the offside reforms of 1929 ushered in a new era in offence. But it may have been simply that his best years were behind him. After all, he had been twenty-eight when he first turned professional with Saskatoon, at which time he was already a seasoned amateur and Allan Cup winner, and was thirty-one as a rookie in Montreal. His last season was 1936/37, when he alternated with newcomer Turk Broda for the first half-dozen games. Hainsworth retired and left the Leaf net entirely to Broda, but the Canadiens coaxed him back later in the season; in all, he played only seven games in 1936/37.

He returned to Kitchener, becoming active in local politics and amateur sports. On Thanksgiving Day, 1950, he was killed in an auto accident. He was elected to the Hockey Hall of Fame in 1961. ○

GEORGE HAINSWORTH APPEARS IN A RATHER RATTY MONTREAL CANADIENS UNIFORM IN MARCH 1930, A FEW MONTHS FROM HIS THIRTY-FIFTH BIRTHDAY.

Continued from page 41

FORMED IN 1931, THE
PRESTON RIVULETTES
RULED WOMEN'S
HOCKEY IN CANADA
FOR A DECADE. THE
TEAM WON TEN
STRAIGHT ONTARIO
TITLES, ALMOST
EVERY NATIONAL
CHAMPIONSHIP, AND
LOST ONLY TWO
GAMES IN THEIR
HISTORY. GAS
RATIONING AT THE
START OF THE SECOND
WORLD WAR FORCED
THE BARNSTORMERS
TO DISBAND. THE
GOALTENDER IN THEIR
INAUGURAL SEASON
(SHOWN HERE AFTER
WINNING THEIR FIRST
PROVINCIAL TITLE)
WAS NELLIE
RANSCOMBE.

For all this legal work, the league was richly reward-ed. Goal scoring doubled—LGA rose to 2.95—and Hainsworth's Vezina-winning 0.98 GA shot up to 2.57. Although LGA would sink several points over the next few seasons as players and coaches adjusted to the new rules (and yet more new rules), the NHL was finally out of the woods. With offence safely restored to the game, the role of the goaltenders, rather than the scorers, came under fresh scrutiny.

The 1929/30 season was a watershed in goaltend-ing. Twice as many pucks were now getting past even the best goaltenders, and the ranks of the best underwent a critical revision. Clint Benedict, at thirty-nine, played his last NHL season, his face smashed by a Howie Morenz shot. A new generation was emerging—Connell in Ottawa, Chuck Gardiner in Chicago, Roy Worters (at first with the Pittsburgh Pirates, then with the New York Americans), Davey Kerr with the Rangers and George Hainsworth (who had come over from the western league) with the Canadiens and later the Maple Leafs.

The new decade saw the rulemakers stew about how much control these goaltenders could have over the puck, and how much protection they deserved from the opposition. The goaltender's unique role in the game had always been obvious, but in the 1930s his separateness began to be encoded. He acquired special privileges, as well as special limitations.

Holding or smothering the puck had long been one of the game's taboos. The puck was to stay in motion; it was the job of the "skaters" to put the puck in the net, the job of the goaltenders to keep it out of the net, and there was to be no funny stuff. The routine stoppages in

play the game knows today, when the goaltender catches the puck or sits on it, or when a defenceman throws himself on it, were strongly discouraged then. It cannot be overstated how fundamental the passing and offside rules were to defining the goaltender's lot. The fact that his teammates could only move the puck out of their own defensive zone by stickhandling it out, or passing it laterally to a fellow player, meant that it was easy for a team to get bottled up in its own end. (Mind you, they were still allowed to lob it down the rink, as there was no icing rule.) And opportunities for the goaltender to shut down an offensive press by forcing a stoppage in play were next to nil. Just to be sure everyone understood the taboo, in 1931/32 the league elaborated the ban on the goaltender's holding the puck to include the words "arms" as well as "hands." No one was going to get a whistle by tucking the puck into his elbow.

The following season, 1932/33, NHL goaltenders received an important concession. They were the only players on the ice allowed to fall on the puck within ten feet of the net (a privilege never adopted by the ama-teurs). According to the rules, they were still required to get rid of the puck once they'd landed on it, but they were understandably loath to do so.

The rules encouraged the goaltender to compile a broad spectrum of ruses to get a whistle, and get himself and his team out of a tight spot. Clint Benedict had made an art of this in the 1920s, and the goaltenders who followed him elaborated on his routines. "You tried a bit of everything," says Chuck Rayner, who played Junior hockey in the 1930s before making his first NHL appearance in 1939/40. "I used to grab the puck and shove it in my pants. Referees were looking and looking and looking, and could never find out where the hell it went. That was the favourite move with everybody. Either that, or shove it down your glove—any way to stop the play. The referees would come over, and they would warn you a couple times. And you'd say, 'Oh, I didn't do that. It went in itself.' But they weren't bad, really, unless it was done really deliberately. They knew what the setup was.

"At that time I used to shoot the puck over the boards a lot, too. If it was on edge, I'd flip it right over, and they'd call the play." Although the rulebook did call for a penalty for any player deliberately sending the puck out of the rink, Rayner says he would only receive a warning from the referee. And while the ten-foot rule called for the goaltender to get rid of the puck once he'd fallen on it, and the amateur game forbade him from deliberately falling on it at all, "A lot of times you fell on it in such a way that you'd tuck it underneath you. Once the puck was out of sight, the referee had to blow the whistle."

While the NHL's ten-foot zone was not marked on the ice, the new rule was the first step in defining a spe-cific territory for the goaltender. The rules underlined the separateness of the goaltender by assessing a major penal-ty for cross-checking or charging a goaltender who was

Continued on page 46

A BREED APART | 44

HOME ICE

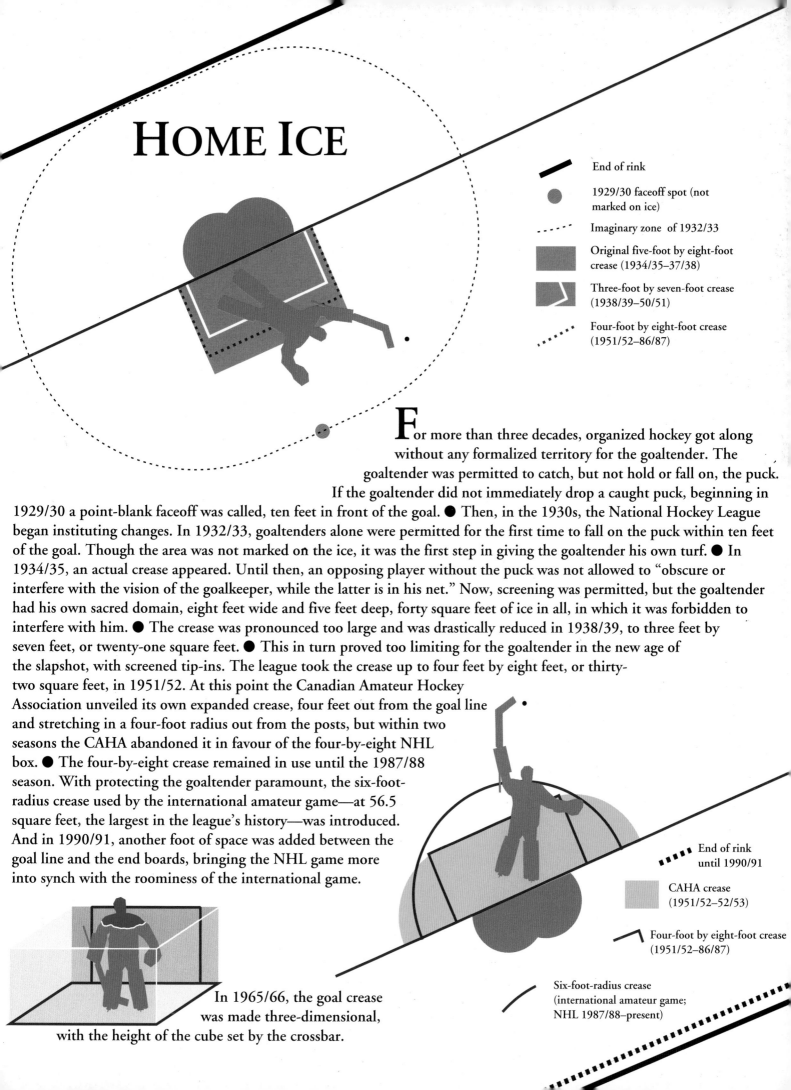

Legend:

- End of rink
- 1929/30 faceoff spot (not marked on ice)
- Imaginary zone of 1932/33
- Original five-foot by eight-foot crease (1934/35–37/38)
- Three-foot by seven-foot crease (1938/39–50/51)
- Four-foot by eight-foot crease (1951/52–86/87)

F or more than three decades, organized hockey got along without any formalized territory for the goaltender. The goaltender was permitted to catch, but not hold or fall on, the puck. If the goaltender did not immediately drop a caught puck, beginning in 1929/30 a point-blank faceoff was called, ten feet in front of the goal. ● Then, in the 1930s, the National Hockey League began instituting changes. In 1932/33, goaltenders alone were permitted for the first time to fall on the puck within ten feet of the goal. Though the area was not marked on the ice, it was the first step in giving the goaltender his own turf. ● In 1934/35, an actual crease appeared. Until then, an opposing player without the puck was not allowed to "obscure or interfere with the vision of the goalkeeper, while the latter is in his net." Now, screening was permitted, but the goaltender had his own sacred domain, eight feet wide and five feet deep, forty square feet of ice in all, in which it was forbidden to interfere with him. ● The crease was pronounced too large and was drastically reduced in 1938/39, to three feet by seven feet, or twenty-one square feet. ● This in turn proved too limiting for the goaltender in the new age of the slapshot, with screened tip-ins. The league took the crease up to four feet by eight feet, or thirty-two square feet, in 1951/52. At this point the Canadian Amateur Hockey Association unveiled its own expanded crease, four feet out from the goal line and stretching in a four-foot radius out from the posts, but within two seasons the CAHA abandoned it in favour of the four-by-eight NHL box. ● The four-by-eight crease remained in use until the 1987/88 season. With protecting the goaltender paramount, the six-foot-radius crease used by the international amateur game—at 56.5 square feet, the largest in the league's history—was introduced. And in 1990/91, another foot of space was added between the goal line and the end boards, bringing the NHL game more into synch with the roominess of the international game.

- End of rink until 1990/91
- CAHA crease (1951/52–52/53)
- Four-foot by eight-foot crease (1951/52–86/87)
- Six-foot-radius crease (international amateur game; NHL 1987/88–present)

In 1965/66, the goal crease was made three-dimensional, with the height of the cube set by the crossbar.

Continued from page 44

busy "defending his goal, with his body." Furthermore, since 1932/33 an opposing player without the puck could not "obscure or interfere with the vision of the goalkeeper while the latter is in his net." This no-screening rule, which was part of both professional and amateur play, gave some protection against interference and allowed the goaltender a clear view of incoming pucks. But it also begged the question: what constituted "in his net"?

In 1934/35, both the NHL and the Canadian Amateur Hockey Association chose to define the goaltender's territory by painting it right on the ice. The rule-makers were feeling generous, and for this first crease laid down a rectangle with a red border 1.5 inches wide, five feet deep and eight feet wide, thus extending one foot to either side of the goalpost and encompassing forty square feet of ice. The existing rule forbidding an opposing player without the puck from obscuring or interfering with the vision of the goaltender was confined to within the dimensions of the crease. The absolute ban on screening the goaltender's view was thus lost, although he was still allowed to drop on the puck within ten feet of the net, and he was now allowed three seconds in which to get rid of the puck after nabbing it. (The three-second rule didn't come to the amateur game until 1939.) To look at it another way, the referee was now giving the goaltender three seconds in which to cough up the puck. Beginning in 1936/37, he could face a penalty shot for not doing so.

The amateur rules did provide a loophole for getting a stoppage in play that goalkeepers could exploit and that wasn't spelled out in the NHL rulebook. Beginning in 1934/35, with the debut of the crease, the CAHA specified that in the event of "a pileup inside the crease," if the referee lost sight of the puck, he was to bring play to a halt and order a faceoff ten feet out, at the side of the rink. The amateur game also insulated the goaltender from attacks from behind the goal. In 1934/35,

the CAHA declared a pass-out from the corner or the back of the net by an attacker to be legal, but a second pass-out could not be made on the same play.

The crease was an innovation that Chuck Gardiner never saw. The young goaltending marvel played his entire seven-season NHL career in Chicago: after turning pro with the Winnipeg Maroons, he had come to the Blackhawks in 1927/28, to refine his craft under the guidance of former PCHA goaltending star Hugh Lehman, who arrived in Chicago following the death of the western league at first to play and then to coach. The Blackhawks were awful, and in Gardiner's second season, during which Lehman coached, the team won only seven games, producing only 0.75 goals per game while allowing 2.85 goals against—at the time, LGA was 1.45. But when the league introduced its major offside reforms in 1929/30, the Blackhawks clicked; although their scoring was still below average, Gardiner gave them a GA edge of nearly half a goal over the league's typical netminder. That season, one of the Blackhawks' coaches was Bill Tobin, another former western league goaltender, who would serve as the team's general manager from 1942/43 to 1953/54. In 1930/31, with another western league alumnus, Dick Irvin, behind the bench, the Blackhawks made it to the Stanley Cup final and were leading the series at one point, but could not hold back the Canadiens, who had George Hainsworth—yet another former western league goaltender—in net. Gardiner just missed winning the Vezina when Roy Worters allowed four fewer goals.

Over the next three seasons, Gardiner won the Vezina twice. Without question 1933/34 was his greatest season. In a rare turn for a goaltender, he served as team captain. Most important, he won the Vezina, and Chicago the Stanley Cup. Gardiner was instrumental in the victory, which had provided him with a second chance against Hainsworth,

FRANK BRIMSEK IS IN THE NET FOR BOSTON IN HIS ROOKIE SEASON IN A GAME AGAINST THE NEW YORK AMERICANS AT MADISON SQUARE GARDEN, DECEMBER 29, 1938. COWBOY ANDERSON OF THE AMERICANS IS ATTEMPTING TO LASSO THE PUCK WHILE APPLYING A GLOVE TO THE FACE OF THE BRUINS' JACK PORTLAND. IT WAS NOT A TYPICAL GAME FOR BOSTON OR BRIMSEK AS THEY LOST, 4-2. THE BRUINS WENT ON TO WIN THE STANLEY CUP AND BRIMSEK THE VEZINA.

now playing for Toronto. Gardiner recorded a double-overtime shutout in the deciding fourth game; before the final game, Chicago defenceman Roy Jenkins promised Gardiner he'd push him around Chicago's "loop" district in a wheelbarrow if he could shut out the Leafs. Jenkins ended up doing just that.

Eight weeks later, Gardiner, only twenty-nine years old, was dead. On June 13, he collapsed in the street in Winnipeg and died on the operating table, of either a brain hemorrhage or a brain tumour. The following autumn, the professional and amateur leagues painted the creases on the ice, and the Blackhawks played the season without a captain.

Other changes followed the introduction of the crease. In 1937/38, the NHL granted the goaltender the sole right to hold the puck against the boards; players in general, provided they were being checked by an opponent, earned this right the following season. But after several seasons of progress, the goaltender's domain began suffering setbacks. In 1936/37, the league began awarding penalty shots whenever a goaltender threw the puck forward, in addition to awarding one for not clearing the puck in three seconds.

In 1937/38, the crease was drastically reduced by professionals and amateurs alike, to three feet by seven feet, nearly halving its total area. The league also introduced the "icing" rule that season, thereby depriving defencemen of the one strategy they had enjoyed since the dawn of the game for taking the pressure off their goaltender—sending the puck to the other end of the rink. In 1939/40, the NHL goaltender lost his ten-foot zone for falling on the puck. He could now only do so within his (shrunken) crease. He still had to get rid of the puck three seconds after catching it, and only by throwing it laterally or backwards. (The amateur game was still strict about how the goaltender got rid of a puck. He could only throw it behind him, not forward or even laterally.) And the NHL rules were now explicit about forbidding him from getting a stoppage in play by dropping the puck into his pads (nothing about dropping it down his pants or inside his gloves) or throwing or batting it into the spectators. As a consolation, in 1940/41 opposing players were allowed to enter his crease only if the puck was in it. Already, in 1934/35, the amateurs had been explicit about an attacking player being forbidden to stand in or on the lines of the goal crease to take a pass; doing so constituted interference.

From 1933/34, when the three-second rule went into effect, until 1939/40, when the game began to change as a consequence of war, LGA in the NHL stabilized around 2.5. The goaltender was now very close to his present-day role. His leg pads were recognizably modern. His stick was also reasonably modern, although his gloves were still primitive. The trapper-style catching glove was a world war away, but there was some movement toward a blocker on the stick side. Extra padding appeared on the back of the glove—a felt sheath over both gloves was being used by some—and during this period Roy Worters has been credited with advancing the use of the back of the stick hand as a puck deflector. There was still no mask, although in his final season, 1929/30, Clint Benedict had briefly worn one to protect a broken cheek and nose.

The most important innovation of those years had assuredly been the crease. Chuck Gardiner had been known for roaming from the net to play the puck, as had Hugh Lehman out west. The crease, arriving soon after Gardiner's death, formalized the area in which the goaltender was "safe." It gave him a defined territory, but it also served to cage him, and in the process to formalize a notion that goaltending was a "stay at home" job. For a time in the 1930s, the goaltender had enjoyed his imaginary zone of privileged activity stretching ten feet from the net in all directions. Now, goaltenders who wandered from their position—their position now being the crease—were deemed not to be playing the game the way it was meant to be played. This view was reinforced by the arrival of a new star, Frank Brimsek, who joined the Boston Bruins lineup in 1938 and quickly came to define goaltending excellence.

In 1938/39, his rookie season, Brimsek recorded the lowest Vezina-winning GA since the offside reforms of 1929/30, a paltry 1.58. An American, Brimsek had played goal for the same Eveleth, Minnesota, high school team as Chicago netminder Mike Karakas, who won the Calder in 1935/36. (Eveleth also produced Tom Karakas, who played for the University of Minnesota and tier two American professional teams. There was also Sam LoPresti, who was two years younger than Brimsek and played goal for Chicago in 1940/41 and 1941/42. Sam's son Pete played goal for Minnesota and then Edmonton from 1974/75 to 1980/81.) The Bruins handed Brimsek a daunting assignment when he was selected to replace Tiny Thompson, whom Boston sold to Detroit. The Bruins fans adored Thompson, and were not prepared to greet Brimsek warmly. And in his first appearance as Thompson's successor, a home game against the indifferent Canadiens, Boston lost 2–0. Brimsek came back and recorded three straight shutouts, and six in his first eight games. At the end of the season, Brimsek had ten and was known as Mr. Zero, and the Bruins were the Stanley Cup champions. He was named to the first All Star team, and over the course of his nine-season career he made the first team twice and the second team six times.

Brimsek knew this newfangled device called the crease, and he stuck to it. Other goaltenders watched him, admired him and above all imitated him. Brimsek became a model for how goaltending was played—and would be played, long after he had retired. O

"THE SHRIMP"

HE WAS CALLED "SHRIMP" FOR OBVIOUS REASONS: ROY WORTERS WAS ONLY FIVE-FOOT-TWO, AND WEIGHED AT THE MOST 130 POUNDS. WHEN HE GOT INTO HIS CROUCH, THE BACK OF HIS HEAD

could touch the crossbar. By the standards of size alone he was an enigmatic figure in sport, but there was much more to the enigma of Worters than superficialities like his height and weight. Other goaltenders were on the small side—Jake Forbes and Georges Vezina were about five-foot-five—but few netminders could boast of a career with such an intriguing combination of accomplishment and controversy. His career was bookended by extraordinary incidents, and the years in between distinguished by perseverance and no small amount of pain.

His career was almost over before it began. As a member of the Timmins team, he was caught up in a scandal in the Northern Ontario Hockey Association's Senior playoffs of 1921. The twenty-year-old Worters was from Toronto; he had grown up playing in Jesse Ketchum Park alongside childhood friends Charlie and Lionel Conacher, and in 1920 Worters won the Canadian Junior title with the Toronto Canoe Club team. Worters ended up playing Senior hockey in Timmins as a typical ringer of the era, put on the payroll of the Dome and McIntyre mine operation, which sponsored the club, and brought into town to play so-called amateur hockey as the burghers of Timmins chased after an Allan Cup title.

In its one-game playoff meeting with Iroquois Falls,

Timmins won, but the game was ordered replayed when one of Worters' teammates turned out not to have a proper league registration card. A lot of money was riding on the rematch in both communities, and to make sure its team's chances of repeating the victory remained high, persons unknown in Timmins bought off two of the Iroquois Falls players for $25 each. Timmins won the game, 6–4, but then word of the payoff leaked. The two Iroquois Falls players were suspended, and so was Worters, the only player on the winning side to be punished. The reason: he knew about the fix, and goaltenders should never be in on fixes, no matter which side of the fix they're on. Worters was subsequently reinstated, although the taint of scandal hung over him in informed circles.

The stain on his reputation was unfortunate, but his association with Damon Runyon types was typical of his career. No one ever accused him of deliberately getting out of the way of pucks, however. He played the game with a tenacious dedication that was almost self-destructive. His face was laced by more than two hundred stitches, and he became famous for refusing to take time off. When his buddy Charlie Conacher hit him in the throat with a shot during an NHL game, Worters clung to the crossbar for support and refused to leave the

WORTERS LEADS THE LINEUP OF THE 1933/34 NEW YORK AMERICANS.

WORTERS WORE THIS NEW YORK AMERICANS JERSEY AFTER HIS CONTRACT WAS PURCHASED FROM THE STRUGGLING PITTSBURGH PIRATES. HE BECAME THE FIRST GOALTENDER TO WIN THE HART TROPHY, BUT NEVER MADE IT TO A STANLEY CUP FINAL.

ice. He finished the game and only then went to hospital; he couldn't eat solid food for two weeks. A hand fracture kept him out of the line-up for two games. He played in a cast, with his stick and glove taped to his arm. His only extended spell out of the game came when Ching Johnson fell on him and hurt his knee, causing him to miss six weeks of play.

Worters had taken his game south in 1924 with Lionel Conacher to play for the Pittsburgh Yellow Jackets, a nominally amateur outfit. When the Yellow Jackets joined the NHL in 1925 (and became the Pirates), Worters hit the big leagues, but he was still fre-quenting the shady margin of organized sport, in which he had been tainted in Timmins. The Pirates were run by a former world lightweight boxing champion named Benny Leonard. "Being a fighter," Conn Smythe said in his memoirs, "he thought all sports were crooked." Leonard would talk to Smythe about "my turn" to win. He once cut off a ten-minute overtime in a home game against Smythe's Leafs at thirty seconds, to preserve a tie. "Well, timekeepers sometimes could be influenced in those days," Smythe explained.

Worters played for them for three years, and the Pirates had reasonable seasons—Worters left them just as they started to become truly awful. In his first season,

Worters was part of a record-setting goaltending nightmare. In a game between his Pirates and the New York Americans, 141 shots were fired, 73 of them on Worters. Amazingly, the final score was only 3–1 for the Americans.

In 1928/29, Worters followed Conacher to the charismatic Americans, a tough-luck outfit owned by the notorious bootlegger Bill Dwyer. When the Pirates hit hard times and moved to Philadelphia in 1930, play-ing as the Quakers for one season before folding, Dwyer stepped in at mid-season and essentially took over the team. By then Dwyer had acquired Worters by offering Leonard an estimated $20,000 plus the Americans' reserve goaltender.

At his very first Americans practice, Worters was cut behind the left ear by a Babe Dye shot. Later that season, playing the Leafs in Toronto, left-winger Danny Cox caught him square in the mouth. The puck knocked out two teeth, broke off two more, and cut him for two stitches on the outside and three on the inside of his upper lip.

Worters' attitude to injuries was nothing if not philosophical. "People have the wrong idea about injuries you get in hockey," he once said. "A fellow gets hit in the mouth or on the forehead or over the eye, and it bleeds a lot, and everybody says: 'Ooh! Looka the blood! And he's staying there, too. What a game guy he is!' Why shouldn't he stay in there? It doesn't hurt to bleed, and the chances are the injury looks much worse than it is. A cut around the head—unless it's right in the eye, so that the sight is blurred—shouldn't bother anybody. The injuries that stop you are on the arms or legs, so that you can't move around. Then if you don't get out you're crazy, because you're only handicapping your team."

In Pittsburgh the word "wizardry" was applied to his work; they called him "the Phantom" in New York because of the magic of his performances. The Americans had a good season in 1928/29, finishing second to Montreal in the inappropriately named Canadian division, but were eliminated by the Rangers in the playoffs. Still, Worters' performance was so impressive that season that he became the first goaltender to earn the Hart Trophy, awarded to the player judged most valuable to his team. In securing a shutout against the Bruins, for example, Worters had turned away seventy-two shots.

He spent part of the following season with the Canadiens, then returned to the Americans for the rest of his career. In 1930/31, Worters won the Vezina with a GA of 1.68, nearly six-tenths of a goal below the GA Tiny Thompson posted in winning the Vezina the previous season. With that achievement on his résumé, Worters went to Dwyer and demanded a three-year contract for $8,500 a year, and he wanted it in U.S. funds. The salary was an extraordinary sum, and the U.S. funds made it even more extraordinary, as the Canadian dollar, badly devalued in the Depression, was converting at rates upwards of forty-eight per cent. Dwyer gave Worters what he asked; it was said that Dwyer was always amused by the performances his pint-sized goaltender turned in.

With that contract, Worters committed himself to a career backstopping a sad-sack franchise, as the Americans slipped into the league cellar during the Depression years. In most seasons, Worters' GA was worse than the LGA, but he was viewed as the classic Great Goaltender on a Bad Team. He was named to the second All Star team, behind Chicago's Chuck Gardiner, in 1931/32 and 1933/34. His childhood friend Charlie Conacher called him the best goaltender he ever shot a puck at. His teammate and roommate Red Dutton would recall Worters "using the backs of his hands to

divert pucks to the corners, so you very seldom scored on a rebound on Roy. His hands took terrible punishment and I marvel at the little guy and the way he had splints put on his fingers before a game."

The Americans returned to the playoffs after a six-season absence in 1935/36, to be eliminated by Toronto in the semifinal. It was something of a swan song for both Worters and Dwyer: Worters would never have another playoff game, and the Depression had left Dwyer so impoverished that the league had to take over the team. Dutton stopped playing to become coach and general manager, and from 1943 to 1945 served as the league's interim president.

In 1936/37, with two games left in the season, Dutton made an appalling discovery: that Worters "had a hernia and that it was a bad one, and that he had played five previous games with this hernia and had told no one about it. He pleaded with me to allow him to play as there were only two games to go. He wanted to finish his season as he said it was going to be his last."

He did play the games, and the season was his last. Worters retired with happy consequences. He went into the hotel business, buying a spot with a tavern in Toronto's Italian neighbourhood. A good second baseman with some of the leading amateur teams around Toronto when he was a kid (he had even played football, despite his size), Worters became a devotee of the professional Maple Leafs ball club, and liked to talk baseball strategy with whoever was the team manager. He sold his hotel in 1949 and prepared himself for early retirement, but went back into the business in the 1950s when he teamed up with Charlie Conacher to build the Skyline Hotel near Malton Airport, and then the Conroy (an amalgam of their names) on Dufferin Street. Conacher would quip that he hadn't seen his business partner in two years—Worters was too busy playing the stock market. Worters had just retired for the third time in 1957 when throat cancer claimed him. He was elected to the Hockey Hall of Fame in 1969. ○

	25/26	26/27	27/28	28/29	29/30	30/31	31/32	32/33	33/34	34/35	35/36	36/37
GAMES	35	44	44	38	37	44	40	47	36	48	48	23
SHUTOUTS	7	4	10	13	2	8	5	5	4	3	3	2
STANLEY CUP	SF		QF	QF								SF
ALL STAR TEAM							2		2			

Worters spent part of the 1929/30 season with the Montreal Canadiens.

"THE SHRIMP"

TINY THOMPSON BATTLED HIS NERVES AND TH

TINY, PERFECT

EAGUE TO WIN AN UNPRECEDENTED FOUR VEZINAS

Boston Garden

OFFICIAL PROGRAM 35¢

"TINY" THOMPSON 1927-28 — 1925-26 ALL TIME BRUINS ALL STARS SERIES

Sport News

BOSTON BRUINS HOCKEY

Cecil "Tiny" Thompson was not tiny. Roy "Shrimp" Worters, who was the greatest goaltender in the game, as far as

THOMPSON WAS FETED IN THIS OFFICIAL BOSTON GARDEN PROGRAM, SHORTLY BEFORE THE BRUINS SOLD HIM TO DETROIT. THE ILLUSTRATION IS BASED ON THE PHOTOGRAPH ON THE PRECEDING PAGE, TAKEN AFTER THE BRUINS WON THE 1928/29 STANLEY CUP WITH THE ROOKIE NETMINDER.

Thompson was concerned—now there was a goaltender who lived up to his billing. But Thompson, who stood five-foot-ten, managed to do what neither Worters nor any other goaltender before them had done: he won four Vezinas. It wasn't until Bill Durnan came along that his performance was surpassed.

Thompson was like Durnan—like a lot of goaltenders—in that the game was a battle of nerves for him. He would begin the season around 170 pounds, and when it was over (forty-four games later at the beginning of his career, forty-eight at the end) he had shed ten of them. Some of them went to sweat, but it was said that some of them went to anxiety. At the end of the day, goaltending to Thompson could be classified as a business of relative failure: the less you failed, the better you were. And when you failed, somebody wrote it down as a statistic. Watching the 1970 Stanley Cup, he noted, "The pressure in cases like these has to be on the goalie—if he misses, the error is in the book, a goal against. When the shooter blows one, it is forgotten."

The 1970 final was of particular interest to him. Chicago was playing Boston, and as Chicago's chief scout, Thompson had a professional involvement. But the series also pitted brother against brother—Tony Esposito in goal for Chicago, Phil Esposito at centre for Boston. There was a lot of back and forth in career lines in that series. Phil had played for Chicago for four seasons before being dealt to Boston; Tiny Thompson had spent most of his career in Boston, before becoming a Chicago scout at the beginning of the Second World War. Then there was Tiny's older brother, Paul, who'd spent eight of his thirteen NHL seasons in Chicago. That was where the 1970 series became personal for Thompson, because he, too, had played against his brother when the cup was at stake. In his very first season in the league, Tiny had faced down Paul in the final, when Paul was playing left wing for the Rangers. Tiny had come out ahead in that encounter. In 1970, it would be the sniping brother's turn.

Paul Thompson was never a sniper the way Phil Esposito would be, but for six straight seasons as a Blackhawk in the 1930s he led the team in scoring. And in 1935/36, the brothers made it onto the All Star team

together—Tiny on the first team, Paul on the second. The only other brothers to have been picked together were Lionel and Charlie Conacher, in 1933/34. But it would happen again with those Espositos—in 1969/70, 1971/72, 1972/73 and 1973/74.

The Thompsons came out of Alberta, and though Paul's NHL career started sooner, in 1926/27, Tiny was the older brother, by eighteen months. They were precocious kids. Tiny was playing Junior hockey with the Calgary Monarchs in 1919/20, when he was only fourteen, and over three seasons played for three different Alberta Junior clubs, the last of them in Bellevue, a southern mining town. In 1922, at seventeen, he began a two-season stint with the Bellevue Bulldogs, a Senior club.

In 1924, Tiny was playing Senior hockey for the Duluth Hornets of the Minnesota Central League. Amateur hockey was only nominally amateur: he was almost certainly getting paid to play. Thus, when he was traded to another Senior club, the Minneapolis Millers, in 1925, it was probably a moot point that he became a professional in 1926, playing for the above-board professional Millers team in the American Hockey Association.

In 1924, Tiny got his first set of leather leg pads. In later years he never said who made them. He got them just as Pop Kenesky of Hamilton, Ontario, was starting to make them for the elite ranks, and while it's possible he ordered a set from Kenesky, it's more probable he had them made right in Duluth. He would remember them as enormous, fourteen inches wide, and it was said that to close the gap between his legs Thompson would have to overlap the pads. As the maximum pad width was cut to twelve, and then ten inches, Thompson took the pads to a harnessmaker to have them recut. Remarkably, these were the only pads he wore in his entire career.

In 1928, the Boston Bruins came calling. It was a young franchise beginning its fifth season; after a horrible debut in which the team won only six games, the Bruins had steadily improved. They'd finished first in the league's American division in 1927/28, but had been eliminated in the semifinal. The Bruins bought the contracts of two Minneapolis players: Thompson, and Ralph "Cooney" Weiland, a small, agile centre who turned twenty-four that autumn. Tiny Thompson was twenty-three. When they got to camp, Weiland was teamed up with Dit Clapper and Dutch Gainor, and the Bruins had the Dynamite line. Hal Winkler, an old pro from the western league, was the Bruins starting goaltender. He'd played for Edmonton and Calgary from 1922 to 1926, and when the western league folded he landed with the Rangers, who then dealt him to Boston. He was about to start his third NHL season, and he was thirty-six years old. The Bruins' new coach, Cy Denneny, decided to start Thompson in the opener against the Pittsburgh Pirates, and after that never bothered to switch back to Winkler, who didn't play another NHL game.

It was an oddball year in the league. The ongoing efforts to increase offence backfired spectacularly with the zone passing reforms, which still didn't allow players to pass the puck across any blueline. LGA sank to its historic low of 1.45, and in Montreal George Hainsworth posted his record GA of 0.98. In New York, Roy Worters of the Americans picked up thirteen shutouts in thirty-eight games, posted a GA of 1.21 and won the Hart Trophy, becoming the first goaltender to be named the league's most valuable player. Thompson certainly did all right. He recorded twelve shutouts and a GA of 1.18, and played superbly when it mattered most. In the best-of-three playoff semifinal and final, Thompson logged three shutouts in five games. In the semifinal, he outduelled Hainsworth, and in the final, John Roach played well, but not well enough, for the Rangers as Boston won the cup in two straight games. Thompson's playoff GA was 0.60.

I t was a brilliant start to what would be a brilliant career, but for Boston there would not be another Stanley Cup for more than a decade, even though a superb Bruins team emerged from the blueline offside reform of 1929/30 that ushered in a new era of offence. That season, the Bruins won thirty-eight of forty-four games, Cooney Weiland won the scoring title and Thompson won the Vezina, but the team could not win the Stanley Cup as Hainsworth's Canadiens swept them two straight. Thompson would later say that he had great respect for the veteran Hainsworth (he turned thirty-five after that cup series), even though he didn't see him in his prime. If Thompson didn't think the 1930 Stanley Cup was Hainsworth at his best, then he must have thought that Hainsworth had once

been a superhuman goaltender.

"He worries a lot," one contemporary writer said of Thompson. He worried so much in 1931/32 that he was unable to play four games. The Bruins started a fellow Albertan, Percy Jackson, in his stead, and Jackson performed respectably in his first NHL games, recording a 2.07 average. Tiny became "frantic" at the idea he was washed up. His wife was so distraught that she left Boston, staying home in Calgary during all succeeding seasons. But Thompson did come back, and the following season, 1932/33, won his second Vezina.

In April 1933, Thompson played what he would describe as both his hardest and his best game. It was game five in the semifinal series with the Maple Leafs, which the Leafs led two games to one. Lorne Chabot was in goal for Toronto, and through all of regulation time he and Thompson kept the game scoreless. The game went into overtime, and appeared destined to stay there. At about one o'clock in the morning, there was even talk of deciding the game with a coin toss. They kept on playing, and a Maple Leaf substitute player named Ken Doraty took to the ice. Doraty was never more than a fringe player, but he showed a flair for playoff hockey, registering seven goals and two assists in the fifteen post-season games in which he appeared. Doraty came into the game with fresh legs, skated around Boston's exhausted defensive great Eddie Shore, and after 104 minutes and 46 seconds of overtime, put the puck past Thompson. An estimated 200 shots had been stopped by both goaltenders in what became known as the Doraty Derby. Three seasons later, Chabot, now with the Maroons, staged another shutout marathon, this time with Normie Smith of Detroit, in the opening game of the Stanley Cup. When Mud Bruneteau finally scored on Chabot, 176 minutes and 30 seconds of overtime had been played. It remains the longest game on record, the Thompson–Chabot duel the second longest.

The only truly poor season Thompson and the Bruins had was 1933/34, when Thompson, for the one time in his Boston career, allowed more goals than the team scored; it was also the second and last time that his GA was above LGA while in Boston, the first time having been in his nerve-wracked 1931/32 season. When the Senators had returned to competition after a one-year Depression hiatus in 1932/33, they hired Cy Denneny, who had coached the Bruins to their 1928/29 Stanley Cup. Denneny bought the Bruins' captain, Cooney Weiland, and his linemate, Dutch Gainor. At first Boston shrugged off the loss, winning their division that season. But the team went into the cellar in 1933/34, winning only eighteen of forty-eight games.

The next season the Bruins were right back on top of their division.

It was the season that the NHL introduced the penalty shot, an innovation of the defunct western league. Alex Connell of the Montreal Maroons was the first goaltender to be beaten by one, and when Thompson's career was over he would be proud of the fact that no one had beaten him on a penalty shot, ever.

Despite the ups and downs of the Bruins, Thompson was consistently on top of the goaltending game. After making the second All Star team in 1930/31 (the first season in which the league had an All Star team), he returned to the second team in 1934/35 and made the first team in 1935/36 and 1937/38. Thompson won his third Vezina in 1935/36, and became the first goaltender to register an assist when he fed a pass to defenceman Babe Siebert and Siebert scored. Thompson's fourth Vezina came in 1937/38, the season the Bruins unveiled the "Kraut" line of Milt Schmidt, Woody Dumart and Bobby Bauer. Boston was a great team through these latter years, finishing first or second in their division, but the Bruins could not convert their sterling regular seasons into a Stanley Cup.

Like Davey Kerr of the Rangers, Thompson subscribed to the theory that using your eyes too much was bad for them, so he didn't do much reading. "The only thing a goaltender has," he would explain, "is his eyes." At the beginning of the 1938/39 season, Thompson, citing an eye ailment, sat out two games. In his stead Boston played a twenty-three-year-old prospect from its American league affiliate, the Providence Reds. The previous season, Frank Brimsek had recorded a GA of 1.79 in Providence, an AHL record that still stands. When Thompson was ready to play again Brimsek was sent back to Providence, but Bruins GM Art Ross saw the future with 20/20 clarity. Tiny was the reigning Vezina-winner and first-team All Star, but he was also thirty-three. On November 28, Ross cut a deal with Detroit's Jack Adams, selling Thompson for $15,000, a good Depression-era price for a top goaltender. After playing nine games of the new season with Providence, Brimsek became a Bruin.

Thompson had long been a fan favourite in Boston, but Brimsek quickly made the customers forgive Ross, and forget Thompson, by recording six shutouts in his first eight games. That spring, the Bruins with Brimsek finally won the Stanley Cup that had been eluding them all through the 1930s. Detroit finished fifth of seven teams, scoring twenty-one fewer goals than Thompson allowed, and were eliminated in the semifinal.

In 1938/39, Paul Thompson played his last NHL game and took over as coach of the Blackhawks. Tiny played one more season before hanging up his own skates and joining his brother in Chicago, where he became the team's chief scout. In 1944, Tiny appeared in a game for the RCAF Mustangs. When the game was over, he threw away the pads he'd had for twenty years.

Tiny Thompson was elected to the Hockey Hall of Fame in 1959. He died in Calgary in 1981. ○

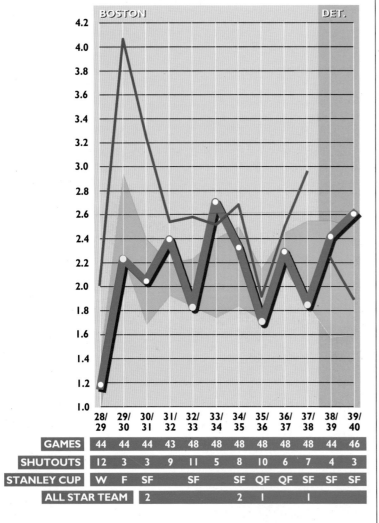

	28/29	29/30	30/31	31/32	32/33	33/34	34/35	35/36	36/37	37/38	38/39	39/40
GAMES	44	44	44	43	48	48	48	48	48	48	44	46
SHUTOUTS	12	3	3	9	11	5	8	10	6	7	4	3
STANLEY CUP	W	F	SF		SF		SF	QF	QF	SF	SF	SF
ALL STAR TEAM			2				2	1		1		

TOOLS *of the* TRADE

Equipment from the interwar years

Above: skates worn by Roy Worters, who starred with the Pittsburgh Pirates and the New York Americans, 1925/26 to 1936/37.

Above right: gloves worn by Lorne Chabot, who played from 1926/27 to 1936/37 with the New York Rangers, Toronto, the Montreal Canadiens, the Montreal Maroons, Chicago and the New York Americans. The gauntlets, made of fibreboard about one-eighth of an inch thick, originally may have been covered with leather. It's also possible these gloves were worn inside a pair of defenceman's gloves. The gloves are thickly padded and of soft leather.

Right: leather leg pad worn by John Ross Roach, who played for Toronto, the New York Rangers and Detroit from 1921/22 to 1934/35.

Below: stick used by Georges Vezina at the end of his career with the Montreal Canadiens (1910 to 1925/26). The original tape is missing, revealing the stick's construction: a regular stick with wood strips added to increase its width on the blade and shaft to 3.5 inches.

CHAPTER 3

"*Hey,* ABBOTT!"

WHEN GOALTENDERS WENT DOWN, THE STRANGEST REPLACEMENTS WOULD STEP IN. THESE WERE MOMENTS OF UNPREDICTABLE HEROISM

An oddity of professional goaltending for decades was that, while it may have been the most specialized, the most dangerous and perhaps the most demanding position on the ice, if not in all team sports, it also was, at times, played by men who were less than prepared for the task at hand. In addition to the sometimes doubtful talents pressed into service during wartime, there were the hapless individuals who came to play for a game or less simply because nobody else was available. No one ever hears of an untried amateur being directed to the mound to pitch in the opening game of a World Series, or pushed onto the playing field to quarterback a Super Bowl team. Yet it seemed that hockey was a rodeo at which at any moment some poor soul could be hauled out of the stands and thrust onto the back of a furious bull.

The reason was parsimony. Owners of professional teams did their utmost to keep costs down, and one of the easiest ways was by maintaining a minimum player lineup. In the professional game's earliest days, teams sometimes used more than one goaltender, as the Ottawa Senators did just before the First World War in employing both Clint Benedict and Perce LeSueur. But cutting costs soon put an end to that. During the 1920s, NHL teams routinely hit the road with only ten men; in 1928/29, league rules called upon teams to dress at least eight but no more than twelve players, exclusive of goaltenders. And when it came to goaltenders, the professionals thought one was just fine. The 1929 Canadian Amateur Hockey Association rulebook, in contrast, stated that each team was allowed ten players for a match, two of whom must be goaltenders.

It wasn't until the 1965/66 NHL season that league rules made it mandatory for teams to have two fully suited, ready-to-play goaltenders at every game. In 1950/51, the league called upon the home team to have an emergency goaltender in attendance, in full equipment, at every game, to be used by either team in the event of illness or injury. This was often a young amateur from the home team's farm system, installed (not quite dressed to play) in the press box. The Detroit Red Wings would offer up assistant trainer Lefty Wilson, who would turn in dogged, creditable performances against his own team,

THE MOST FAMOUS GOALTENDING SUBSTITUTION IN HOCKEY HISTORY WAS MADE BY LESTER PATRICK, WHO AT AGE FORTY-FIVE CAME OUT FROM BEHIND THE NEW YORK RANGERS BENCH IN THE 1927/28 STANLEY CUP TO REPLACE AN INJURED LORNE CHABOT—AND WIN THE GAME.

much to their disgust. But before 1950/51, injured goaltenders had to be replaced by whatever warm body was available, and only with the approval of the opposing team.

There were many occasions on which an injured goaltender wasn't replaced at all; he played on, knowing there was no one adequate to fill his skates. In the third game of the 1929/30 Stanley Cup final, Detroit goaltender Wilf Cude was accidentally struck in the face by the stick of Blackhawks right-winger Rosie Couture when he dropped to block a shot near the end of the second period. The blow knocked him unconscious, but he returned from the dressing room ten minutes after being carted off the ice. His face was bloody and his right eye was nearly closed up, but he finished the game and preserved the Red Wings' 5–2 lead.

The policy of substitutions produced some of the game's most absurd, and most dramatic, moments. The first person listed in the alphabetical directory of NHL goaltenders is George Abbott, who played one game for Boston in 1943/44. Boston was in Toronto for a road game and, in the revolving-door goaltending mess in which the Bruins found themselves after Frank Brimsek entered the Coast Guard, they had no starter when Brimsek understudy Bert Gardiner came down with the flu. The Maple Leafs helpfully came up with Abbott, who happened to be an ordained minister and who suited up in the Bruins dressing room in an advanced state of terror. Bruins captain Dit Clapper, moving to ease the nerves of the reverend (who was busy putting his skates on the wrong feet), declared, "Don't worry, Abbott. We'll get the bastards. Those sons of bitches won't beat us." The Bruins lost, 7–3. Hence, Abbott's lifetime NHL GA of 7.00.

The playoffs saw some remarkable substitutions. In 1938, Chicago's Mike Karakas broke a toe in the final game of the semifinal and was lost for the first few games of the final against the Maple Leafs. Chicago coach Bill Stewart and general manager Bill Tobin wanted to replace him with the Rangers' sensational Davey Kerr, but the Leafs were having none of that. On game day the Leafs' assistant GM, Frank Selke, told the Blackhawks that Alfie Moore would be a suitable choice. A Toronto resident, Moore had played eighteen games for the New York Americans in 1936/37, and in the past season had been in goal for the Pittsburgh Hornets, the Leafs' American League farm club.

According to Blackhawks tradition, Chicago left-winger John Gottselig was dispatched to fetch Moore. He headed for Moore's house, where he found Moore's wife, but not Moore. She told him to check a local bar. Moore wasn't there, either, but at that bar Gottselig was directed to yet another bar, where Moore was ensconced, quaffing beer. Whether or not Moore was soused is a matter of debate. When he saw Gottselig walk in, he reputedly asked him if he had a spare ticket for the big game. Gottselig, of course, had the perfect viewing spot for Moore: the Blackhawks net.

Foster Hewitt would recall that a "messenger" was sent out to find Moore, while Stewart and Tobin continued to argue back at the Gardens with Leaf GM Conn Smythe and Selke for the right to use Kerr. It's been said that the Blackhawks were put in this goaltending bind because there was no time to bring in their practice goaltender, Paul Goodman, who was under contract with Chicago but playing in Wichita, Kansas. But it seems that the Blackhawks were trying to pull a fast one, and had intended all along to use Kerr in the final. After all, Karakas's injury had come in the preceding series, not the night before, and in the last Stanley Cup, when starter Normie Smith was injured in the first game, the Red Wings showed up for the second game with a minor-league backup, Earl Robertson, as his replacement. (As with so

THE INJURY OF CHICAGO GOALTENDER MIKE KARAKAS (BELOW) SHORTLY BEFORE THE 1938 STANLEY CUP TOOK MINOR-LEAGUER ALFIE MOORE (RIGHT) OFF A TORONTO BARSTOOL AND DEPOSITED HIM IN THE BLACKHAWKS NET FOR THE OPENING GAME AT MAPLE LEAF GARDENS.

many untested goaltenders, Robertson proved equal to his assignment: the Red Wings won, 4–2, and went on to win the cup.)

The Blackhawks were very much the underdogs, having finished the regular season in third place in the four-team American division, with only fourteen wins in forty-eight games, while the Leafs had finished atop the Canadian division with ten more wins. Chicago had produced the least number of goals, 97, while Toronto had produced the most, 151, and Chicago had allowed 139 goals compared to Toronto's 127. Without Karakas, the Blackhawks would need brilliant goaltending to keep the Toronto offence down to a dull roar and allow their own lukewarm firepower to make a game of it. Kerr seemed to be more of a ringer than an emergency fill-in.

With less than an hour to go before the opening faceoff, the management of the two teams were still bickering over who would appear in the Chicago net. Right by the press box, Stewart accused Selke of stiffing him with a half-drunk substitute and of lying about Moore's quality. Conn Smythe boiled over. A veteran of the First World War, Smythe had personally dispatched a German soldier with his service revolver, and was not a man to inflame. By way of defending the honour of his old friend Selke, Smythe lunged at Stewart. It took several men to pull them apart.

According to Hewitt, the Blackhawks were openly cool to Moore when he, and not Kerr, entered their dressing room to suit up. Contentedly seated on a bar stool hours earlier, he had been transformed into an unwelcome palooka in the most important match in hockey. As far as the Blackhawks were concerned, clever Conn Smythe had managed to roll a hand grenade right into their lineup. Thus, when Moore took to the ice, he stood alone against everyone in Maple Leaf Gardens— against his own teammates, against the hometown fans, against the opposing Leafs and against the Leaf brass, who had made him a minor leaguer in favour of Turk Broda.

The first Leaf shot beat Moore, but then he buckled down, or sobered up, and shut down the Leafs. The Blackhawks rose to the occasion of his unexpected performance and put three unanswered goals behind Broda. A delighted Tobin asked Moore how much the win was worth. Moore asked for $150. Tobin gave him $300.

For the next game, Smythe declared Moore ineligible to play, and league president Frank Calder ordered Chicago to use Goodman. He had never played an NHL game, and the Leafs swamped the Blackhawks, 5–1. Chicago brought back Karakas and fitted his skate with a steel guard to protect his broken toe. Chicago won the cup by sweeping the next three games. When the victory was celebrated back in Chicago, the team brought in Moore and presented him with an engraved gold watch.

Moore's performance in the 1938 Stanley Cup tends to be cast as a lone moment of glory for an embittered minor pro, but he proved to be a very good goaltender in the American League. The season that followed his

Stanley Cup heroics, Moore made the second All Star team with the Hershey Bears. He made brief returns to the NHL: two games with the Americans in 1938/39, and one game with Detroit in 1939/40. Perhaps, as some were wont to suggest, he was one of those very good goaltenders who got stuck toiling for subpar teams. As for poor Goodman, he played quite well for Chicago in fifty-two games over the next two seasons, logging six shutouts and recording a GA of 2.17. Karakas ended up playing in the American League with Providence, making the first All Star team in 1940/41 and the second team in 1942/43 before returning in 1943/44 to the Blackhawks for three more seasons. He joined his fellow Minnesotan Frank Brimsek in the U.S. Hockey Hall of Fame.

No goaltending substitution is more famous than that of forty-five-year-old Lester Patrick, who came from behind the bench to play goal for his New York Rangers in the 1928 Stanley Cup. The Rangers were playing the Montreal Maroons in the best-of-five series and were already down a game when their star netminder, Lorne Chabot, was knocked unconscious by a Nels Stewart backhand early in the second period of the second game. The game was in Montreal—the entire series was in Montreal, because the Barnum & Bailey Circus was occupying Madison Square Garden—and Patrick, the Rangers coach, attempted to bring the Ottawa Senators' great goaltender, Alex Connell, down from the stands to plug the gap. Maroons general manager Eddie Gerard refused to agree to the Connell substitution. Patrick had ten minutes to come up with a replacement. His centre, Frank Boucher, nominated Patrick himself.

When Boucher was starring in the old Pacific Coast league with Frank Patrick's Vancouver Maroons, he had played against Lester Patrick. He may have been forty-five during this Stanley Cup final, but two seasons earlier, Lester had played twenty-three games, virtually a full season, on defence for his Victoria Cougars. And when the short-tempered Cougars goaltender Heck Fowler received two fighting suspensions in 1921/22, Patrick had taken his place in the net. At Boucher's urging, Patrick donned Chabot's equipment. Patrick was six-foot-one and lanky, with a shock of white hair. Facing the Rangers at the other end of the rink was Clint Benedict, perhaps the greatest goaltender of the era.

Patrick made for a stunning, unthinkable sight, and his players protected him ferociously, forcing the Maroons whenever possible to shoot from far out or from bad angles. A rinkside cheering section of league managers—Conn Smythe from Toronto, Leo Dandurand of the Canadiens, and Jack Adams of Detroit—shouted encouragement to Patrick and instructions to both Patrick and his players. The game remained scoreless through to the end of the period, and thirty seconds into the third, Rangers captain Bill Cook gave his team the lead. But with only minutes to play, Stewart, who had already KO'ed Chabot, beat Patrick with a rebound and tied

the game. After seven minutes of overtime, Boucher ended Patrick's forty-six-minute nightmare by scoring on Benedict and tying the series. For the rest of the series, New York brought in Joe Miller, who had played twenty-eight games for the New York Americans that season, and the Rangers won the cup.

Patrick, needless to say, never played goal again. He lives on in the record book with a sparkling 1.30 GA as a result of that single, harrowing game. Miller moved on to the dreadful Pittsburgh Pirates (and its last-season incarnation, the Philadelphia Quakers) for three seasons. The series loss was Benedict's last Stanley Cup appearance. Two seasons later, the facial injuries he suffered when hit by a Howie Morenz blast forced him out of the NHL. And after being struck by Nels Stewart's backhand, Chabot never again played for New York. The next season, Patrick dealt the goaltender whose injury had forced him to tend net to the Maple Leafs. ○

CHAPTER 4

1939/40–1944/45

A *damned* <u>war</u> COMES ALONG

WHEN THE WORLD WENT TO WAR, GOALTENDING WENT WITH IT. AND WHEN THE STARS RETURNED, THEY RETURNED TO A GAME THAT WAS ALMOST UNRECOGNIZABLE

T he Second World War played havoc with professional hockey, as it did with so many aspects of North American life. For six seasons, the NHL struggled to ice a quality product—even to ice a product at all. Goaltending suffered greatly, and the game suffered because of it.

LGA in the NHL had run around a steady 2.5 from 1933/34 to 1938/39, but as soon as hostilities erupted, it soared: to 2.7 in 1940/41, 3.1 in 1941/42, 3.6 in 1942/43 and a peak of 4.08 in 1943/44. But why LGA climbed so rapidly cannot be answered simplistically. True, the bulk of the game's great goaltending stars did join the military, but they didn't do so until well into the war. When the Bruins set two records that still stand for shots on goal—most in a single game (eighty-three) and most in one period (thirty-three)—on March 4, 1941, against Chicago, they still only won the game 3–2. Paradoxically, it wasn't until Frank Brimsek, Turk Broda, Johnny Mowers, Sugar Jim Henry and Chuck Rayner were all out of the league, in 1943/44, that LGA began its decline to normal levels. There was more at work than diluted rosters: the game was undergoing important changes, not only in who was playing it but in how it was played.

At the beginning of the war, the NHL was packed with extraordinary goaltending talent, led by Brimsek in Boston. He won two Vezinas and two Stanley Cups in the years leading into war, and made eight straight All Star appearances in the seasons he wasn't in the military. Three other goaltenders won the Vezina between 1939/40 and 1942/43: Walter "Turk" Broda in Toronto, who had come into the league in 1936/37, the veteran Davey Kerr of the Rangers and Johnny Mowers, who was twenty-four when he took over the Red Wings' goal from Normie Smith in 1940/41.

Kerr was one of the greatest goaltenders of the

TURK BRODA (FAR RIGHT), STAR GOAL-TENDER OF THE TORONTO MAPLE LEAFS, WEARS A DIFFERENT KIND OF UNIFORM CIRCA 1943. BRODA SPENT THE WAR PLAYING SOFTBALL AND HOCKEY OVERSEAS ON CANADIAN ARMY TEAMS. HIS CONTROVERSIAL ENLISTMENT IGNITED A NATIONAL DEBATE OVER THE PREFERENTIAL TREATMENT GIVEN PROFESSIONAL ATHLETES BY THE MILITARY.

A BREED APART

1930s, but honours came to him late in his career. (Even today, he is absent from the Hockey Hall of Fame.) His performance in 1939/40, which earned him a Vezina with a GA of 1.60, helped bring the Rangers the Stanley Cup, and allowed him to edge out Brimsek for the first-team All Star berth. It was his signature season, and nearly his last. He did not get along with Rangers GM Lester Patrick: the two men were constantly at odds at contract time. Kerr retired after the 1940/41 season, at the peak of his game, and went into the hotel business.

Kerr's former teammate and coach, Frank Boucher, later described him as "a solidly built fellow with good, strong legs and arms. He was very agile and could do the splits with one skate firmly anchored against one goalpost and the other skate stretching right across the goalmouth to the other post. In this fashion

DAVEY KERR HAD PIERCING LIGHT BLUE EYES WHICH HE CONSCIENTIOUSLY PROTECTED BY WEARING SUNGLASSES WHEN READING AND AVOIDING MOVIE THEATRES ON GAME DAYS. AFTER A BRILLIANT SEASON IN 1939/40, IN WHICH HE WON THE VEZINA AND THE RANGERS THE STANLEY CUP, KERR QUIT AT THE END OF THE 1940/41 SEASON, TIRED OF HAGGLING OVER HIS SALARY.

he made his saves with those big fat leather pads of his…. In a commanding way, Davey was able to shout at his defencemen, giving them guidance without offending them, and getting them to do the job he wanted done in front of him, talking continually when the puck was in our end. I don't ever remember hearing Dave accuse a defence player of a mistake when a goal was scored against him. He always assumed the blame."

He'd begun his NHL career with the Montreal Maroons in 1930, having won the Allan Cup with the Montreal Athletic Association's Winged Wheelers in 1929. He joined the Rangers in 1934 after several seasons of bouncing in and out of the minor leagues. "When I joined the Rangers," Kerr would reflect in 1957, "I replaced Andy Aitkenhead. They tell me he got so he'd lock himself in his room after a game and play the game over and over. By the time the next game rolled around, he'd played forty-eight games in that room."

"There's pressure on a goalkeeper," Kerr noted. "The last few years I was with the Rangers, I used to take a wine cocktail before my dinner to relax me." He considered himself fortunate that in eleven seasons around the NHL, he'd only been cut for one stitch, in the back of the head.

Kerr was a more acrobatic goaltender than Brimsek, but like Brimsek was known as an "angle goalie." The introduction of the crease in 1934/35 gave goaltenders a frame of reference on the ice, and with it they developed a closely studied art of exactly where to position themselves to deny the shooter as much net as possible. "He had it all figured out," his teammate Murray "Muzz" Patrick (son of Lester and brother of Lynn) would recall. In practice, Kerr would tell Patrick: "Just keep your man outside a certain spot. No, not there. Back up a couple of feet, Muzz. Now six inches to the left. That's it. Keep him outside of there and if he scores, it's my fault." He defended his crease tenaciously, using his stick to whack the ankle of anyone who came too close.

It was Kerr's theory that the goaltender's greatest assets were his reflexes and his eyes, and he went to great lengths to protect his eyesight. He wore sunglasses when there was snow, even when he was reading, and never went to the movies on a game day, to "save" his eyes. This was a widely held philosophy among athletes. Baseball's great hitter Rogers Hornsby similarly steered clear of movie theatres in the 1920s. In the mid-fifties, when Muzz Patrick was coaching the Rangers, he suggested to his young netminder, Gump Worsley, that he try wearing sunglasses too. "What do I look like, a Hollywood character?" shot back the Gumper.

When Kerr left the league, there was still a solid lineup of goaltenders. The war still seemed like a remote conflict in the United States, where five of the NHL's seven teams were located. The nation wasn't caught up in the hostilities the way Canada was, with

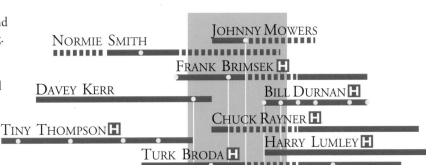

NORMIE SMITH

JOHNNY MOWERS

FRANK BRIMSEK H

DAVEY KERR

BILL DURNAN H

CHUCK RAYNER H

TINY THOMPSON H

HARRY LUMLEY H

TURK BRODA H

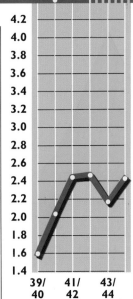

its ties to Great Britain, and the NHL was still thriving.

That changed on December 7, 1941, when the Japanese bombed Pearl Harbor. That night, Boston played the Rangers in New York. After the game, the Bruins milled dejectedly about the Hotel Lincoln. The Bruins had lost 5–4, but it was clear to them that more than a game had been lost. The Japanese attack meant the end not just of an illusory peace at home, but also possibly of their careers, as the nation angrily prepared to strike back. "You just get established in a business like hockey," Brimsek grumbled that night, "and you have to give it all up. The — Japs bomb Pearl Harbor and a damned war comes along."

The league finished the season, with Broda and the Leafs defeating Mowers and the Red Wings for the Stanley Cup, but there was serious doubt as to whether there would be another one. In September 1942, the NHL was preparing to suspend operations. Players were either enlisting or answering draft notices, and general sentiment was that it was both cowardly and frivolous for young men to be making money playing games while their brothers and neighbours were off risking their lives for democracy.

Like other professional sports, the league was in a terrible position. It had to choose a course that was supportive of the war effort, but team owners were frankly appalled at the possibility that their players—their investments—would march off to be killed, and have the game killed with them.

National authorities felt that the entertainment industry, of which professional sports was a part, should carry on for the sake of public morale. Rangers coach Frank Boucher helped engineer a timely, if controversial, compromise that would allow players to meet their military obligations without getting shot at. Boucher got together with Cecil Duncan of the Canadian Amateur Hockey Association and a friend in the Canadian civil service to form an all-star army team in Ottawa, the Commandos, composed entirely of professional players who would be invited to enlist for the exclusive purpose of playing hockey.[1] Boucher arranged the enlistments of Rangers Neil Colville, Mac Colville, Alex Shibicky, and goaltender Jim Henry. The civil service friend brought aboard Ken Reardon of the Canadiens and Bingo Kampman of the Leafs. Boucher himself went into the army as a commissioned officer as a result.

Though the all-star team was shortlived, its basic strategy was employed throughout the armed forces. The Royal Canadian Air Force assembled the Flyers, which included the intact Boston "Kraut" line of Woody Dumart, Milt Schmidt and Bobbie Bauer. (Dumart and Schmidt then went to England with the Canadian Bomber Group as player-coaches.) Traditional military sports teams turned into clubs packed with professionals. At the Cornwall base, the army signed on as officers Punch Imlach and Tommy Ivan, both of whom would be giants in NHL coaching and management after the war. The Maple Leafs entering military service congregated in the Toronto Scottish Regiment. After two weeks of basic training, they became hockey players with the Toronto Army Daggers and then attended sixteen night drills, according to Foster Hewitt. Billy "The Kid" Taylor starred with HMCS *York* in Toronto Military District competition. Four Leafs—Joe Klukay, Jackie Hamilton, Gaye Stewart and Bob Goldham— played for the HMCS *Cornwallis* team in the Halifax defence league between 1943 and 1945.

Whether serving on active duty or entertaining on skates, players began to leave the NHL in droves beginning in 1942/43, the first season to follow Pearl Harbor. In all, about eighty players had entered the service in some fashion by then. With a game limit of fourteen players per team, and six teams, that meant a turnover in virtually the entire NHL roster. The enlistment/draft stampede cleaned house of nearly every quality netminder. Having already lost Davey Kerr to retirement, the Rangers saw Jim Henry enter the Canadian military. After the collapse of the New York Americans, Chuck Rayner joined the navy and played hockey in Victoria and Halifax before shipping out on a

Continued on page 68

---

1. There was actually nothing new about the "sports regiment" phenomenon. During the First World War, the Northern Fusiliers, or 228th Battalion, was a Canadian army team composed entirely of hockey players. They played in the National Hockey Association during the 1916/17 season until controversy–mainly they were too good for the rest of the league–sent them overseas. Other players during that war were granted deferments, provided they did not play any hockey.

TURK BRODA

WHEN THE STANLEY CUP—AND PLAYOFF PAY—WAS ON THE LINE, THE TURKEY WAS TOPS

As a story during the 1948/49 season so gracelessly put it, "In the nets, he looks like a harmless, jolly tub of lard, but the Leafs goalie dives for a puck like an angry cat." Walter "Turk" Broda may have had breadth, but he also had depth—in skill and in heart. When he died in 1972, he still held the record for most playoff shutouts (thirteen) and most playoff games by a goaltender (101). He had won the Vezina twice, and would have won a third time in 1950/51 if the Vezina rules followed from 1964/65 until 1981/82 had been employed, and both goaltenders on the team with the lowest number of goals allowed were awarded it. Instead, Al Rollins alone won it for the Leafs, even though Broda had played thirty-one of seventy games.

He was called "Turk" not because he was Turkish—he was actually of Polish extraction—but because in his childhood in Brandon, Manitoba, his freckles made the other kids think of a turkey egg, or because his neck turned red when he angered. But an angry Turk was a difficult thing to imagine. He was one of the most affable characters the game ever produced. Leaf captain Ted Kennedy remembers him as a rarity in that you could actually kid him about a bad goal as you fished the puck out of the net.

He played goal because as a kid he was judged too small to play defence. After playing his Junior hockey in Brandon and Winnipeg, he turned professional with the Detroit Olympics of the International League. During his Olympics days he was the property of the Red Wings, but fate intervened in the person of Conn Smythe, who came out for an IHL game in 1935/36 to scout another Detroit-system goaltender, Earl Dickerson, playing for Windsor, as a possible successor to the aging George Hainsworth. It turned out not to be Dickerson's night, as Windsor lost 8–0 to Broda and the Olympics. When Detroit's Jack Adams pressed Smythe to cut a deal for Dickerson, Smythe declared that he wanted that Broda fellow. Broda's GA that season for the Olympics was 2.00; in the playoffs, 1.33. Adams thought highly of the twenty-two-year-old prospect. Even before Broda reached the NHL, Adams avowed that Broda "hasn't a nerve in his body. He could tend goal in a tornado and never blink an eye." Smythe got him, for an estimated $8,000. For the first six games, Broda and Hainsworth alternated games for the Leafs, then Hainsworth was gone.

Broda's performances were solid but unremarkable under coach Dick Irvin. When Smythe replaced Irvin with Hap Day in 1940/41, Broda's game moved up a big notch. Day wasn't convinced the big man's hands were fast enough, and began a practice regimen of taking away Broda's stick and having a line of players fire a volley of pucks at him. It

BRODA AND BILL DURNAN WERE GOOD FRIENDS; BRODA WAS THE ONLY GOALTENDER TO DENY DURNAN A VEZINA

was a routine followed for fifteen minutes for every practice during the rest of his career under Day. He was also skated as hard as any other player to help fight a never-ending battle with his waistline.

In 1940/41, Broda made the first All Star team and won the Vezina against the likes of Davey Kerr, Johnny Mowers and Frank Brimsek. The next season, Broda was in the net when the Leafs dug themselves out of a 3–0 series deficit to win the Stanley Cup.

His entry into military service as a goaltender in uniform in 1943 set off a national debate over how hockey players and other athletes were getting preferential treatment in the call to arms. After missing two and a half seasons of NHL action, he returned to the league in early 1946 to reclaim his rightful place among the netminding elite. In his absence, Bill Durnan had appeared as the game's dominant goaltender. The two men became friends, and Broda was the only one to deny Durnan a Vezina in the postwar years when he won in 1947/48.

At the start of the 1949/50 season, Broda was the focus of a famous bit of calculated Smythe intimidation when Smythe benched his star netminder until he had worked off seven pounds. Much publicity was generated for the team as Broda sweated off the weight and made it back into the starting lineup.

Broda was instrumental in the four Leaf Stanley Cup victories that followed the Second World War. He was known as the man you wanted in the net when there was a championship and bonus pay on the line. "Going for the money," Smythe would say of him, "Turkey was tops." While his career GA was a solid 2.53, in playoff hockey he drove it down to 1.98.

After winning a final Stanley Cup in 1950/51, Broda played one more game before retiring. He coached a variety of amateur and second-tier professional clubs over the ensuing years, including the Toronto Marlboros when they won two Memorial Cups in the mid-1950s. To the young men in his charge, Turk seemed to be more of a team mascot than a strategist and disciplinarian. Billy Harris, who played for Broda as a Marlie before becoming a Maple Leaf, has written: "He blamed himself for our terrible play, our poor conditioning and our lousy power play...we fell in love with the guy and were willing to go through concrete walls for him." That he was never offered the Leaf coaching job was a disappointment to him, but Smythe was never convinced that Broda was responsible enough to handle it. He had a one-season spell as coach of the Quebec Aces in the American League in 1969/70, in which the team won twenty-seven of seventy-two games and had the third worst GA in the league. At the end of his life in 1972, he was spending plenty of time around Woodbine racetrack. He'd been working as a PR man for Leaside Construction Co., whose principal, Marc Cavotti, invested in race horses and even owned one named Turk Broda.

During the September 1972 series between Canada and the Soviets, Broda was seen poised in front of a television at Woodbine, popping in and out of a crouch. "I was playing goal for Ken Dryden," he explained.

He died of a heart attack within a month of the Canada–Soviet series, and two weeks before the death of Durnan, at age fifty-eight. ○

TURK BRODA'S MAPLE LEAFS JERSEY

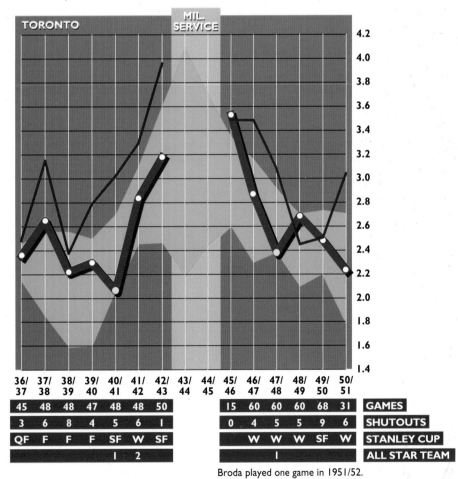

	36/37	37/38	38/39	39/40	40/41	41/42	42/43	43/44	44/45	45/46	46/47	47/48	48/49	49/50	50/51	
	45	48	48	47	48	48	50			15	60	60	60	68	31	GAMES
	3	6	8	4	5	6	1			0	4	5	5	9	6	SHUTOUTS
	QF	F	F	F	SF	W	SF				W	W	W	SF	W	STANLEY CUP
						1	2					1				ALL STAR TEAM

Broda played one game in 1951/52.

Continued from page 65

frigate. In 1943/44, the league was also without Johnny Mowers, Turk Broda and Frank Brimsek. Brimsek went into the Coast Guard, and played goal for the Coast Guard Clippers in the Eastern U.S. amateur league before joining a supply ship in the South Pacific. Mowers entered the RCAF, Broda the Canadian army.

It was Broda's entry into the military that touched off a national controversy. Broda's draft notice required him to report for enlistment no later than midnight, October 18, 1943. It was assumed that he would enlist in Toronto and mind net for the Daggers, but on the evening of the 18th, Broda was on a train to Montreal, in the company of a staff sergeant from Montreal's military district. At 11:18 p.m., the RCMP boarded the train, took Broda into custody on the grounds that he was about to breach his draft notice by not enlisting before midnight, and hauled him back to Toronto to have him enlist there.

PAUL BIBEAULT WAS A BUSY JOURNEYMAN DURING THE WAR. HE PLAYED FOR THE CANADIENS UNTIL DURNAN CAME ALONG, WENT INTO THE ARMY, PLAYED FOR THE LEAFS AND BOSTON TO FILL IN FOR THE ABSENT BRODA AND BRIMSEK, AND FINALLY LANDED IN CHICAGO AFTER HOSTILITIES HAD CEASED.

The Montreal *Gazette* accused Toronto Military District of engineering a "kidnapping" of Broda so that he could play for the Daggers. It was soon alleged that Broda had been offered $2,400 above and beyond his base military pay if he enlisted in Montreal and played his military hockey there. Toronto Army had reputedly only been able to offer him army pay plus a subsistence allowance.

Many Canadians were already upset with the special treatment hockey stars received as the nation went to war. Players were routinely paid salaries by their professional clubs while drawing military pay, and those who did make it to active duty often took a long time to see any action, as commissioned officers more interested in assembling hockey powerhouses than military fighting machines squirreled away their star enlistments. "It is an obvious fact that many prominent hockey players who enlisted one or two years ago are still in Canada and appear on the rosters of armed service teams," a *Calgary Herald* editorial fumed on October 20. And there were surely some players who were happy playing military hockey rather than being shot at.

Broda would spend more than two years in the Canadian army playing hockey and softball. He went to England and played there for army teams, and as the Allied forces marched across Europe after the D-Day invasion, the YMCA moved in behind them, refurbishing rinks so that hockey could be played by servicemen. Broda was a roving ringer within the military. He recorded eight straight shutouts with the 32nd Self-Propelled Artillery while in England, and as a softball catcher played on a championship team. In Holland he had nine shutouts in ten games with the 4th Division team. He played his way into Czechoslovakia, stopping pucks fired by the locals.

Broda was apparently frustrated by military life. Conn Smythe, majordomo of the Leafs, had formed his own battery and saw action in France, in which he was wounded. Assisting Frank Selke in assembling the Hall of Fame nomination for Broda in 1967, he wrote Selke that Broda "applied to come to my Battery so he could go to France, and through the usual army skullduggery his O/C kept him at the Base in England and would not release him to us."

His stint as a military goaltender so tried him that he announced he was quitting the game for good in January 1946. While waiting to be shipped home in Amsterdam, he had been hit in the face by a puck fired from three feet away in a practice with the Canadian forces all-star team. The shot cost him six teeth. "Can you imagine getting it from some joker after catching the best from the best of them?" he exclaimed.

There's no question that the diluted talent, not just in goaltending but in all positions, was the major factor in the LGA runup of the war years. The NHL would not see another increase like it until the expansion years, when there wasn't enough talent to go around to effectively fill the rosters of the ballooning league. But with so many star goaltenders still in the league in those years, the rise may have been a case of one or two weak teams inflating the overall LGA, since Vezina-winning GAs didn't experience the same inflation. At the beginning of the war, the NHL was a seven-team loop, with the New York Americans grimly hanging on and the Montreal Canadiens in poor shape; already the Depression had claimed the Montreal Maroons, in 1938. Both the Canadiens and the Americans were routinely shelled by the opposition at the beginning of the war. In 1941/42, the Americans' last season (in which they relocated to Brooklyn), they allowed 175 goals, compared to 118 in Boston, where Brimsek was starring. That same season, Montreal allowed 173.

But beginning in 1942/43, the shrinking pool of quality players definitely played a major role in the LGA runup. Franchises with limited depth could not easily replace stars the way a leading team like the Toronto Maple Leafs did. Boston went from being a perennial Stanley Cup favourite to a cellar-dweller in one dreadful season. In 1942/43, Boston finished second overall with twenty-four wins. In 1943/44, the Bruins won only nineteen games and finished fifth, missing the playoffs.

The Rangers, Stanley Cup champions in 1940/41, were even more badly decimated. In 1941/42, the Rangers finished at the top of the standings with twenty-nine wins. In 1942/43, they won eleven games and finished last. With Sugar Jim Henry in the net in 1941/42, the Rangers allowed 143 goals. With Henry in the military in 1942/43, the Rangers allowed 253 goals, sixty-two more than Montreal, the next worst offender, and more than twice as many as Detroit, the season's champion and Stanley Cup winner. The Red Wings still had Johnny Mowers, the Vezina winner that season.

In 1942/43, the Rangers went through three goaltenders trying to come up with a replacement for Rayner and Henry. One was Steve Buzinski, a twenty-five-year-old plucked out of the Intermediate ranks in Swift Current, Saskatchewan, by an optimistic Lester Patrick. He had never played in an NHL game. Coach Frank Boucher would not forget his first glimpse of Buzinski at practice: "a scrawny guy all dressed up in a Ranger uniform and goaltender's pads, a little short fellow who was, so help me, the most bow-legged goaltender I ever saw in my life." Buzinski turned out to be a genius in practice, but he was out of his league in a regular game. "He was a lovely little fellow, earnest and sincere, and we all liked him tremendously, but that simply didn't stop pucks," Boucher would reflect. Buzinski lasted nine games, with a GA of 5.89.

Another goaltender New York turned to was Bill Beveridge. At thirty-three, he had been out of the NHL for four seasons, having concluded an eight-season stretch (the last three with the doomed Montreal Maroons) in 1937/38. Beveridge played seventeen games with a GA of 5.24. "I always felt particularly sorry for Beveridge," recalled Boucher, "who was a real good goaltender but had always played with bad clubs." After one brutal loss with New York, Beveridge reminded Boucher

of how Boucher and the Rangers had run up the score on him back when he was toiling for the Maroons. Beveridge had always wanted to see the same thing happen to the Rangers, and now, he realized, he had.

The bulk of the season, twenty-three games, was shouldered by Jimmy Franks, a twenty-eight-year-old with only slightly more NHL experience than Buzinski. He had played in one game, back in 1937/38, with Detroit. Franks recorded a GA of 4.48 and was good enough to collect another nineteen games with Detroit and Boston the following season.

Things didn't get any better in New York as the war raged on. With almost its entire starting lineup in the military, the Rangers were winless for the first fifteen games of the 1943/44 season, a league record. The team was in such bad shape that Boucher came out of retirement at age forty-two to play centre for fifteen games. For the last two seasons of the war, NHL neophyte Ken "Tubby" McAuley got the goaltending job. Boucher felt that McAuley "should have been awarded the Croix de Guerre if not the Victoria Cross," for taking the punishment the porous New York defence subjected him to. Of the ninety-six games he played for New York, he won only seventeen and recorded one shutout.

The bewildering turnover in goaltenders was not restricted to the Rangers roster. It was a marked change from the prewar years, when teams could depend on the same solid goaltender for season after season. Like the Rangers, the Detroit Red Wings ran through at least five different goaltenders during the war after they lost the services of Mowers.

Journeymen like Paul Bibeault and Bert Gardiner moved from team to team as clubs strove to ice a presentable lineup. Bibeault was twenty-one when he played his first four games with Montreal in 1940/41; the club's regular starter in the 1930s, Wilf Cude, was at the end of his career. A popular performer with the hometown francophone fans, Bibeault played the better part of two seasons with the Canadiens, until Montreal signed up Bill Durnan; he landed in Toronto, where a replacement was needed for Broda. After playing twenty-nine games of the 1943/44 season in Toronto (during which time he was part of the Canadian army reserve), he was sent by the Leafs as a kind of lend-lease goaltender to Boston, struggling to fill the skates of the absent Brimsek. In December 1945, he came back to Montreal to sub for an injured Durnan; the return of Brimsek early in 1946 then eliminated his job in Boston. He moved to Chicago for the 1946/47 season, his last in the NHL. Meanwhile, Bert Gardiner was doing his own tour of duty with a revolving door of NHL teams. Gardiner was twenty-seven when he came to the Canadiens in 1940/41 to share the netminding job with Bibeault. He had already played in the NHL back in 1935/36, when he appeared for a single game as a New York Ranger. In the intervening years, he had been a star with the Philadelphia Ramblers of the new American League, making its first All Star team in

AMONG THE **NHL** PLAYERS WHO ENLISTED IN THE CANADIAN ARMY AND PLAYED ON ITS ALL-STAR TEAM WAS GOALTENDER SUGAR JIM HENRY, A NEW YORK RANGER WHO AFTER THE WAR PLAYED FOR THE RANGERS, THE BLACKHAWKS AND THE BRUINS. HE APPEARS HERE IN THE LINEUP OF THE 1942/43 ARMY TEAM. CELEBRITY MILITARY PLAYERS HELPED BOOST MORALE OF THE MILITARY RANK AND FILE BY ACTING AS ENTERTAINERS, BUT THE PHENOMENON RAISED SOME HACKLES ON THE HOME FRONT.

1938/39 and the second team in 1939/40. With Bibeault emerging as the main Canadiens netminder, Gardiner was shipped to Chicago for 1942/43. Chicago then sent Gardiner to Boston as a Brimsek fill-in for 1943/44, where he played his final NHL games before being replaced by Bibeault—who, of course, was then replaced by the returning Brimsek.

In some cases the vacancies created by wartime allowed genuine new goaltending stars to be discovered. In 1943/44, the Red Wings seized upon a future Hall of Famer, a seventeen-year-old from Owen Sound, Ontario, named Harry Lumley, acquiring him from the Rangers, who were patiently awaiting the return of Rayner and Henry. On January 23, 1944, Detroit mowed down the hapless Ken McAuley and the Rangers 15–0, a blowout that set the league record for most consecutive goals in a game by one team. And in Montreal the revolving door of goaltending was brought to a halt when the Canadiens convinced Durnan to move up from their Senior affiliate, the Montreal Royals. Durnan played seven seasons and won the Vezina six times.

The Maple Leafs, with their great depth of talent, soldiered on. The military had cost them not only Turk Broda, but his understudy, Baz Bastien, who played for Cornwall Army. After trying out Bibeault for a season, the Leafs hit upon twenty-six-year-old Frank McCool.

By 1944/45, the league was stabilizing, even though the war was still on. Players who had signed on for tours of duty in reserve regiments were now receiving discharges and trickling back into the league. And while there may still have been weak outfits in places like New York, the league in 1944/45 had some exceptionally strong teams. New young scoring stars, like Ted Lindsay in Detroit and Maurice Richard in Montreal, were appearing. The Montreal Canadiens, who hadn't won the Stanley Cup since 1930/31, began to emerge as a league power-house, as did Detroit. Thus, McCool came to play against clubs with far from inferior talent. He had a terrific rookie season, winning the Calder and backstopping the Leafs into the Stanley Cup final against Detroit, who had their own wartime rookie, the eighteen-year-old Lumley. It was an awesome defensive engagement, with only nine goals scored in seven games. Toronto won the cup on the strength of McCool's performance, as he logged three shutouts to Lumley's two. But the brooding McCool was driven off the ice and into the dressing room in the deciding game, plagued by nerves. As McCool gulped down ulcer medication, Toronto coach Hap Day quietly told him, "There's no one else." McCool calmly replied, "I can finish," and did. McCool never shook the feeling that the fans saw him only as a temporary substitute for their beloved warrior Broda. When Broda returned to the Leafs in the latter half of the 1945/46 season, McCool quit the Leafs and the NHL.

As the war drew to a close, LGA had begun another precipitous descent, a predictable result of the league's return to full strength. But there had been other culprits besides diluted talent and punching-bag teams in the LGA runup of the early war years. New rules were chipping away at the goaltender's territory and rights. In 1938/39, the crease had been drastically reduced, from five feet by eight feet to three feet by seven feet, and the icing rule was introduced, which meant defending players could no longer fire the puck down the ice to take the heat off their goaltender. In 1939/40, the goaltender lost his right to fall on the puck within ten feet of the net—he could now only fall on it in his much-reduced crease. Interference with the goaltender was now deemed to occur only within the crease. Once outside it, he was treated like any other player. In 1932/33, the league had instituted a major penalty for "cross checking or charging a goalie while defending his goal, with his body." In 1940/41, this penalty was limited to infractions occurring within the twenty-one square feet of the crease. As the war years progressed, the goaltender was being hemmed in by the rules.

It was also a time when the penalty shot came into broad use. When introduced to the NHL in 1934/35, the shot had to be taken from inside a ten-foot circle located thirty-eight feet from the goal. Beginning in 1938/39, the shooter was allowed to skate right in on the goaltender. In 1941/42, the use of penalty shots was 'elaborated, with new classifications of major and minor. The major category was reserved for the spoiled break-away, for which a shooter was allowed to skate in to point-blank range. The minor penalty shot was awarded for goaltenders holding the puck beyond the three-second count, or throwing the puck forward. For this, the shooter had to tee off from a line located twenty-eight feet from the goal (initially thirty feet from the goal in the amateur game).

Davey Kerr of the Rangers rehearsed an unorthodox penalty shot style in practice. He would lay his stick across the ice in front of him, place a skate against either post, and prepare to stop any shot with his hands alone. The stick was meant to prevent a shot along the ice from getting between his legs. As much as he practiced it, his coach, Frank Boucher, could not recall him ever actually using it in a game, which suggests that the penalty shot was, then as now, rarely awarded.

(It should be noted that if a goaltender incurred a major penalty, such as fighting, that did not result in a penalty shot, the goaltender himself had to serve it. Another player on the team could take his place in net, but it was only in 1939/40 that this player could use the goaltender's stick and gloves, although no other piece of his equipment.)

On balance, the league's increasing enthusiasm for penalty shots probably had minimal effect on LGA in the early war years. A more likely factor was a chink discovered in the defensive armour of the game. It was clear to observers like Ted Kennedy, the future Maple Leafs captain, during the 1941/42 Stanley Cup final. Kennedy, a hot young amateur from Port Colborne, Ontario, watched one of the early games in the series from up in the cheap seats in Maple Leaf Gardens. From his lofty perch, he couldn't help noticing that all the skate marks were inside Toronto's blueline. The Red Wings had perfected a dump-and-chase offence that handcuffed the Leafs. The defensive style of the day had been to meet the incoming attackers outside one's own blueline. Detroit in particular learned that a more successful strategy than trying to stickhandle around these defencemen was simply to shoot the puck right past them and go after it. During the Stanley Cup, Detroit would fire the puck into a corner and then flood the Toronto zone with all five skaters in what was known as a "ganging attack." When a Toronto player touched the puck, he was hammered. The offside rules forbade a defending team from making a forward pass across its blueline, and the introduction of the icing rule in 1937/38 had removed the option of sending the puck the length of the ice, so the puck had to be stickhandled out, a task the bottled-in Leafs found well-nigh impossible. The Red Wings ran up a 3–0 series lead before Hap Day shuffled the Leaf lineup and marshalled a remarkable turnabout in playoff fortunes as the Leafs stormed back to win four straight games.

Day's strategic triumph didn't remove the essential problem of the ganging attack. The NHL was now playing a game in which the defending team could become trapped in its own end, unable to break out, and the goaltender had to go to extraordinary lengths to get a whistle that would allow his team to regroup.

Frank Boucher is credited with coming up with the solution: the two-line offside. Though he was coaching one of the worst teams in the league, Boucher consistently produced inspired strategies for the game. He had played in the old Pacific Coast league for Frank Patrick's Vancouver Maroons, and was now employed by Lester. He seemed to tap into that vein of hockey genius for which the Patricks were renowned. Already during the war years Boucher had contributed two important innovations: pulling the goaltender on the fly (rather than waiting for a stop in play) in favour of an extra attacker, and the box configuration for penalty killing. The first time Boucher tried pulling Kerr while play was under way, the bewildered referee called a penalty for too many men on the ice when he saw six Rangers sweaters swirling around the rink.

Boucher would recall that he came up with the two-line offside in concert with the CAHA's Cecil Duncan, with whom Boucher was working to harmonize the professional and amateur rulebooks. Bruins general manager Art Ross helped Boucher push for the change in the game, which was adopted for the 1943/44 season by both the NHL and the CAHA. A centre line was added to the ice (where it did not already exist for decorative purposes) and it was prescribed that a team could now pass the puck across its own blueline, provided the puck did not also cross the centre-ice red line.

At first, the controversial new measure created even more scoring. For wartime goaltenders already labouring through the weaknesses in their team's or their own skills, the two-line offside was a horrid development. Defencemen didn't adjust immediately to the quick changes in the flow of the game, and the result was a quantum leap in the number of breakaways. LGA made a half-goal jump, to 4.08, in one season; a league record was set that season when Montreal and Toronto combined for six goals in three minutes, fifteen seconds on January 4, 1944. The second-fastest five goals came the following season, when Montreal and Detroit put them away in one minute, thirty-nine seconds on November 15, 1944. And on January 21, 1945, Boston set the record for the fastest four goals by one team, notching them up in one minute, twenty seconds as they stung poor Tubby McAuley for a total of fourteen goals in defeating the Rangers by an eleven-goal margin. That same season, of course, Maurice Richard terrorized goaltenders far and wide as he set his record of fifty goals in fifty games.

But coaches and players adjusted to the blitzkrieg

A DAMNED WAR COMES ALONG

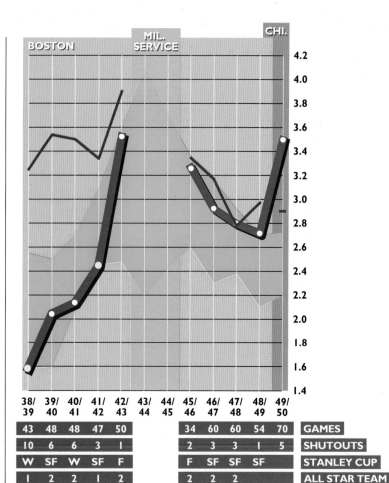

attacks of the two-line offside, and while some of the best goaltenders in the league may have been in the service, LGA tumbled nonetheless. With the offside innovation, NHL hockey entered its modern era, becoming a much faster game—a "head-manning" game, with breakout passes that created rushes faster than one player could skate, yet less scoring overall.

Ironically, Frank Boucher became one of the innovation's greatest detractors, and in subsequent seasons tried to get the league to move the bluelines closer to centre ice, or to choose between keeping the bluelines or the centre line—to no avail. Hockey, to Boucher's disdain, changed dramatically with the new offside rule. The 1943/44 season proved to be a watershed in the game's history, on one side of which fell decades of rule tinkering and expansion and contraction in the size of the league, and on the other a new stability in the number of teams and the game they played. In 1942/43, the league had solidified as a six-team loop with the collapse of the Americans franchise; this Original Six configuration would be maintained for a quarter-century.

The goaltenders who had gone away to war by the end of the 1942/43 season returned to a game that was almost unrecognizable. But they had gone away greats, and when they returned to a transformed game, they resumed their rightful place at its pinnacle. Only newcomers Bill Durnan and Harry Lumley could not be dislodged by the old stars. Turk Broda, still a relatively young man at thirty-one, returned to play with the Leafs and helped them win three straight Stanley Cups, and then another, and along the way earned his second Vezina. Chuck Rayner returned to a debilitated New York Rangers, losing more games than he won but gaining the enduring respect of the game's practitioners. Sugar Jim Henry shared the New York netminding duties with Rayner before being traded to Chicago. Only Johnny Mowers found his job taken. He returned to the game from the RCAF, hampered by back trouble, with Harry Lumley firmly in place as the Detroit netminder. After playing a few games in 1946/47, Mowers retired, and coached Indianapolis in the American League the following season. He then gave up on hockey for good and went into the insurance business.

Frank Brimsek, a year younger than Broda, resumed his career in Boston, playing thirty-four games in the 1945/46 season. Brimsek was now part of a Bruins team that could not quite recover its prewar glory. When he had left the league, the Montreal Canadiens were a laughingstock. When he returned, they were a juggernaut. Maurice "The Rocket" Richard had played only sixteen games for Montreal in 1942/43, Brimsek's last season before entering the Coast Guard. When Brimsek returned in 1945/46, Richard was a star, having scored his fifty-in-fifty the previous season.

In that first postwar season, the Bruins showed promise of becoming the Bruins of old, finishing second overall and making it to the Stanley Cup final. But this was a new era of firewagon offence, and strong

goaltending was not enough. Not a single Bruin made the top-ten scoring list in 1945/46. In the final, they were overwhelmed by Durnan and Richard and the rest of the Canadiens, going down in five games.

Brimsek's GA in his first season back, at 3.26, was only slightly better than the 3.35 of the league as a whole. For the next three seasons, his GA was as good as, or slightly better than, the LGA. That he was still a great player, however, was never doubted. He made the second All Star team in each of his first three seasons back.

In 1949/50, Brimsek was replaced as the Bruins starter by Jack Gelineau, a Toronto native who came out of the McGill University Redmen ranks to be named the league's rookie of the year. Boston dealt Brimsek to the Blackhawks, just as Tiny Thompson had once been dealt by Boston to Detroit to make way for the young Brimsek. The trade at least put him closer to his Minnesota roots. The Blackhawks finished at the bottom of the standings, winning twenty-two of seventy games; Brimsek played every one of them, recording a 3.49 average; LGA was 2.73, and Bill Durnan won the Vezina with a GA of 2.20.

Brimsek then retired. The very next season, Bernie "Boom Boom" Geoffrion made his NHL debut with the Canadiens, and introduced to the league the first fully developed slapshot. The two-line offside had changed the rhythm of the game, and the lot of the goaltender. The slapshot revolutionized the game and changed virtually every position in it. No player had more changes to adjust to than the goaltender. ○

	38/39	39/40	40/41	41/42	42/43	43/44	44/45	45/46	46/47	47/48	48/49	49/50	
	43	48	48	47	50			34	60	60	54	70	GAMES
	10	6	6	3	1			2	3	3	1	5	SHUTOUTS
	W	SF	W	SF	F			F	SF	SF	SF		STANLEY CUP
	1	2	2	1	2			2	2				ALL STAR TEAM

BONNIE PRINCE CHARLIE

ON A TEAM
THAT LOST
MORE
OFTEN
THAN
IT WON,
CHUCK
RAYNER
WAS A SPARK OF
NETMINDING GENIUS

H

E NEVER WON A VEZINA. IN 424 REGULAR-SEASON GAMES SPREAD OVER TEN SEASONS, HE WON 138, TIED 77 AND LOST 209. HE SAW PLAYOFF ACTION IN ONLY

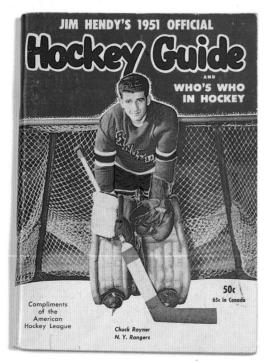

JIM HENDY'S 1951 OFFICIAL
Hockey Guide
AND
WHO'S WHO
IN HOCKEY

50¢
65¢ in Canada

Compliments
of the
American
Hockey League

Chuck Rayner
N. Y. Rangers

two seasons, and never won a Stanley Cup, though he came achingly close in his only cup final. Few fans of the game know his name today the way they do Plante, Vezina, Sawchuk, Dryden and Hall. Yet Claude Earl Rayner—aka Chuck, aka Charlie, aka Bonnie Prince Charlie—was recognized in his own day as one of goaltending's great talents. Glenn Hall, whom many consider to have been the greatest between the posts, ranks Rayner second, behind Sawchuk, in his assessment of historic talent. In an era dominated in the public imagination by Turk Broda, Bill Durnan and Frank Brimsek, Chuck Rayner was a star, if not in the record books then certainly among his peers. And as a mentor, he provided a critical bridge between the game as it had been played by Tiny Thompson in the 1930s and the game as it would be played by Hall (and all those who came to admire and imitate Hall) in the 1950s, '60s and '70s.

Rayner was one of those players whose misfortune or destiny it was to spend their careers in the service of struggling teams. For virtually his entire career, his own performances and those of his team straddled the wrong sides of the league goals-against average. In eight of ten seasons, his GA was higher than LGA; in only two of ten seasons was his team's scoring higher than LGA.

Rayner was born in Sutherland, Saskatchewan, now a neighbourhood of Saskatoon, in 1920; the province, with its pond-dotted prairies, was a font of NHL players, and among them many fine goaltenders, including Glenn Hall, Johnny Bower, Emile Francis, Bert Gardiner and Al Rollins. His teams were the teams of New York, teams that exhibited idiosyncratic genius yet could not find success in the standings. When Rayner broke into the NHL for a twelve-game stint in 1940/41, the Rangers were the defending Stanley Cup champions. But Rayner was across town, toiling for the sad-sack New York Americans, who finished deep in the basement of

the standings with only eight wins in forty-eight starts. Playing goal for the Americans meant facing a fusillade of shots; it was, says Rayner, like "a visit to the Goodyear rubber factory." In his first horrific exposure to the NHL, his GA was nearly a full goal higher than the league average. The next season, the Americans moved to Brooklyn, where in their last-gasp incarnation they again finished at the bottom of the league, this time with sixteen wins in forty-eight starts. Playing thirty-six games, Rayner posted a GA a half-goal higher than LGA.

The Brooklyn Americans lasted only this one season, and when the team vanished from the league, so did Rayner. He left professional hockey for three seasons during the war, serving with the Canadian navy and playing some hockey for navy teams in Victoria and Halifax before shipping out on a frigate on the North Atlantic run. When he returned in 1945/46, his rights were held by the Rangers, with whom he spent the final eight seasons of his career. The war had turned the powerhouse Rangers of 1939/40 into the doormat of the league after its entire starting lineup entered the armed forces. When the hostilities were over, so was any hope of building a Rangers dynasty. Stars like Bryan Hextall and Neil Colville had been lost for three seasons, and when they returned, their best days were behind them. The Rangers didn't even make the playoffs in the first two seasons following the war. Yet Rayner's skills were so obvious that he was chosen as the league's second-team All Star in three straight seasons, from 1948/49 to 1950/51, breaking up the All Star monopoly held by Bill Durnan of Montreal, Frank Brimsek of Boston and Turk Broda of Toronto.

Rayner's game had been forged under the intense heat of Eddie Shore, the much-admired, much-feared and much-loathed Boston Bruins defenceman who in 1939 had acquired the Springfield Indians franchise, a New York Americans farm team in the new American League, a tier-two professional loop formed in 1936. Eddie Shore became known as a merciless taskmaster, and it was Rayner's strange good fortune to come to play for Shore's Indians when he turned professional. Rayner didn't like Shore—few players who toiled for him ever did—but he could not help but admire his hockey sense.

"He was the greatest goaltending coach I ever had," says Rayner. "Before that, there wasn't such a thing as a goaltending coach. Nobody told you anything. You went out and did your best, got hell for the goals you didn't stop, and no praise for the ones you did."

Rayner says Shore's ideas on goaltending were greatly influenced by the example of his old Bruins teammate Tiny Thompson. Long before anyone had ever heard about power skating, Shore was fanatical about hockey's most essential skill, and the ever-expanding Shore mythology would include stories of Shore making his players take dancing lessons to improve their footwork. In practice, he skated Rayner as hard as any other player. "I had to skate with everybody. If they had stops and starts, I had to go with them. I went around and around that rink until I'd just about drop. He figured skating gave you balance. The more I think of it, the more I think he was so right." Balance was particularly important to Shore's goaltending theories, because he hated to see a goaltender drop to the ice. One story has it that in practice Shore once put a noose around a goaltender's neck and tied it to the crossbar, so that if he dropped to his knees he'd hang himself.

Though a proponent of the stay-on-your-feet game, Shore wasn't enthusiastic about the era's other goaltending tenet: sticking to the crease. In practice, he would sometimes put an iron cage in front of the net to prevent a goaltender from backing up too much, ensuring that he played his angles properly.

None of the legendary Shore props and gimmicks—the dancing lessons, the noose, the iron cage—were in evidence when Rayner played for him. Instead, there was hard work, which included Rayner's developing the strength in his stick hand, to make him efficient at clearing loose pucks. "He used to dump a pail of pucks and I had to keep shooting them against the boards until my wrists got so sore I couldn't move them."

True to the mystique surrounding him, Shore also had some interesting theories about blood circulation and nerve signals that led him to make Rayner play with a board-straight back and bent knees, holding his stick several inches above the top of the paddle. Rayner saw good sense in Shore's theories, and the distinctive playing style stayed with him when he came to the NHL.

After the war, when he came to the Rangers, Rayner's career fell under the tutelage of another hockey original: New York coach and general manager Frank Boucher. As the game returned to full strength and took on a greatly expanded schedule, Boucher became concerned with the wear and tear it inflicted on the men in the nets. He became the first coach or general manager to employ a two-goaltender roster in the NHL, despite the extra salary. Boucher paired Rayner with "Sugar Jim" Henry, who had played one season with the Rangers in 1941/42 (while Rayner was across town with the Americans) before joining the Canadian army and playing on the all-star services team Boucher had helped conceive. Unable to choose between Rayner and Henry, he alternated them for the first twenty games of the

1945/46 season. For the first three or four games, Boucher tried switching Rayner and Henry with every third line change, but this coming and going of netminders during the game was too much for Conn Smythe, and because of the Toronto GM's objections it was abandoned. Rayner played the bulk of 1945/46, but for three seasons Boucher persisted in employing two major-league goaltenders. Rayner also played most of the 1946/47 season, and Henry started the majority of games in 1947/48. It was a good arrangement for Rayner and Henry, as it meant they both had contracts that would pay them NHL salaries; otherwise, one of them would have been playing exclusively for the Rangers' American League affiliate in New Haven.

The system worked because Rayner and Henry were good friends. They had played against each other in Junior hockey—Rayner for the Kenora Thistles (after starring with the Saskatoon Wesleys), Henry for the Brandon Wheat Kings. Rayner had made it to the Memorial Cup final with the Thistles against the Oshawa Generals, a series Oshawa won. Rayner and Henry also came to New York at the same time—Rayner to play for the Americans, Henry for the Rangers. They even went into business together, establishing a fishing camp called Hockey Haven on northwestern Ontario's Lake of the Woods, near the Manitoba border. (Henry was from Winnipeg, for which Lake of the Woods serves as a recreational getaway, and Kenora, where Rayner had played Junior hockey, was the nearest big Ontario town to the lake.) For a while they ran a hockey camp out of the lodge, and in 1948 a kid from Humboldt, Saskatchewan,

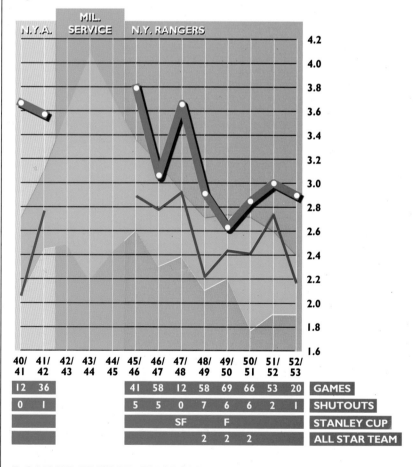

	40/41	41/42	42/43	43/44	44/45	45/46	46/47	47/48	48/49	49/50	50/51	51/52	52/53
GAMES	12	36				41	58	12	58	69	66	53	20
SHUTOUTS	0	1				5	5	0	7	6	6	2	1
STANLEY CUP							SF		F				
ALL STAR TEAM									2	2	2		

named Glenn Hall, who was playing Junior hockey in Windsor, came up to the camp.

After three seasons of employing two goaltenders, the Rangers decided they could no longer afford the luxury and dealt Henry to the Blackhawks in exchange for Emile Francis. He stayed there one season before moving on to the Bruins, where he took over from Jack Gelineau, the sparkling young replacement for Frank Brimsek who ultimately chose the insurance business over the stress of netminding. Rayner took charge of the Rangers goal, despite the fact that 1947/48, the last of his tag-team seasons with Henry, was statistically one of Rayner's worst seasons. Playing only twelve games, his GA was 3.65, LGA was 2.92 and Turk Broda won the Vezina with a GA of 2.38. But with a team as anaemic in offence as the Rangers, stats were never much to go on when assessing a goaltender's skills. The team did make its first playoff appearance in six seasons, though bowing out in the semifinal.

In 1948/49, the Rangers finished last and missed the playoffs, but Rayner made his first of three consecutive second-team All Star appearances, even though his GA exceeded the LGA. Rayner could not be confused with any other goaltender in the league. Boucher called him "brilliantly aggressive." Although Boucher had pioneered the strategy of pulling the goaltender on the fly for an extra attacker, in the case of a delayed penalty he was inclined to leave Rayner on the ice and let him play as a sixth skater. He regularly ventured as far as his blueline in playing the puck. Emile Francis, who went on to become the Rangers' coach and general manager, remembers a game in which he was playing goal for Chicago when Rayner skated right into the Blackhawks' end.

Rayner's glory year was 1949/50. The Rangers finished fourth, winning only twenty-eight of seventy games and failing to put a single player on the top-ten scorers' list. But Rayner kept the team in the fight, and in the playoffs the Rangers came alive. In the best-of-seven semifinal against Montreal, New York raced to a 3–0 series lead. It proved to be the undoing of Montreal star Bill Durnan, who was an off-ice friend of Rayner. ("We all got along real well," Rayner says of the small circle of goaltenders at the time. "We got together, had a beer and discussed the shooters.") The celebrated Montreal goaltender quit the game, unable to face New York again. Gerry McNeil stepped in for him, and New York won the series in five games, reaching the Stanley Cup final for the first time since 1940.

Their opponents were Detroit, who had overwhelmed the league with thirty-seven wins and locked up the top of the scorers' list with their Production Line of Sid Abel, Gordie Howe and Ted Lindsay. Because the circus was booked into Madison Square Garden, the Rangers had to use Toronto as home ice. Detroit took a 2–0 series lead, but Rayner then came to the fore; after three straight wins, two of them in overtime, the unlikely Rangers were a win away from taking the cup. But Detroit, smarting at the thought of losing a third straight

Stanley Cup final, regrouped and tied the series, forcing a deciding game. The climactic game was tied 3–3 at the end of regulation time, and the two teams were scoreless through the first overtime period. Eight minutes into the second overtime period, Detroit's George Gee won a faceoff in the Rangers' end and fed the puck back to Pete Babando, who blindly fired it past Rayner. The dream season was over. While there was no Conn Smythe Trophy at the time for playoff performance, Rayner's role in the team's remarkable season could not be ignored. He became only the second goaltender, after Roy Worters, to win the Hart Trophy as the player judged most valuable to his team.

For the next three seasons, the Rangers returned to their wartime ways. They failed to make the playoff round every season. Rayner's third, and final, All Star selection came in 1950/51. In his last season, 1952/53, he played twenty games. Rookie Gump Worsley played the other fifty and won the Calder. Chuck Rayner was thirty-three, and his NHL career was over.

In the spring of 1972, the New York Rangers made their first return to the Stanley Cup final since Rayner's heroic stand of 1950. New York lost again, this time to the Bruins. The experience must have turned a few heads back in the direction of Rayner's signature season. In the twenty-two seasons that followed it, only two other goaltenders—Al Rollins in 1953/54, Jacques Plante in 1961/62—had won the Hart. In 1973, Bonnie Prince Charlie was inducted into the Hockey Hall of Fame. ❍

ABOVE: RAYNER IS BACK IN BUSINESS, SUITING UP FOR THE RANGERS' HOME OPENER ON NOVEMBER 7, 1945, AFTER SPENDING THREE YEARS IN THE CANADIAN NAVY. OPPOSITE: THE PRINCE OF STICKWORK AWAITS AN INCOMING PUCK.

MIRROR MAN

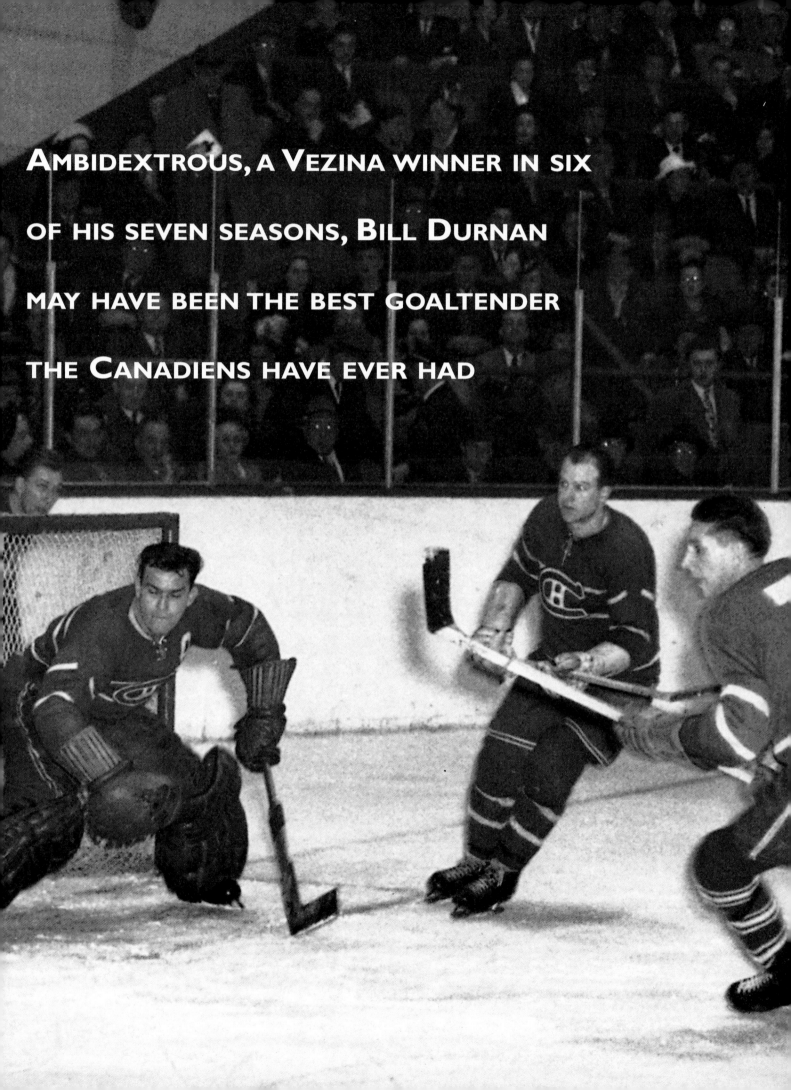

AMBIDEXTROUS, A VEZINA WINNER IN SIX
OF HIS SEVEN SEASONS, BILL DURNAN
MAY HAVE BEEN THE BEST GOALTENDER
THE CANADIENS HAVE EVER HAD

THE SEASON THE TWO-LINE OFFSIDE ARRIVED IN THE **NHL** WAS THE SEASON **BILL** DURNAN ARRIVED. DURNAN WAS TWENTY-EIGHT, AND THE **NHL** WAS BEGINNING ITS TWENTY-SEVENTH

DURNAN'S GREATEST WEAPON WAS HIS AMBIDEXTERITY. HE WORE IDENTICAL GLOVES WITH WHICH HE COULD BOTH CATCH AND BLOCK, ALLOWING HIM TO SWITCH HIS STICK FROM ONE HAND TO THE OTHER TO SUIT THE SHOOTER.

season. It was the fall of 1943. The new passing rule changed the sport entirely, and for the next seven seasons Bill Durnan was the dominant goaltender of what would turn out to be the modern game. He left before the game could destroy him, having won six Vezinas in seven seasons, and he left behind an enduring impression of his pre-eminence.

Durnan was born in Toronto in January 1915; his genealogy included two keepers of the lighthouse at Gibraltar Point on the Toronto Islands. His mother died when he was five, and he was raised by his father. In recalling his modest upbringing on Ossington Avenue, he would note, "We lived a half a block from the firehall, and across the street from the city dump."

He excelled as both a goaltender and a softball pitcher, and it seemed at times that throwing a ball would serve him better than stopping a puck. But he learned one of his most valued goaltending skills early.

Playing net at Dovercourt school and for the Westmoreland church team, he was taught by his coach, Steve Faulkner, to hold his goal stick in either hand. "I was big, awkward, and not too fast," Durnan would recall. "Steve told me I would have to be able to play from both the right and the left sides with my stick to make up for the lack of speed." Drilled by Faulkner, Durnan became completely ambidextrous, able to catch the puck with equal skill in either hand.

It's been said that as a Westmoreland Bantam, he shut out the opposition for an entire season. His skills attracted the attention of hockey recruiters in Sudbury. In the 1930s, northern Ontario teams, flush with money from mining profits in company towns, went to great lengths to attract star players from around the country for the Junior and Senior amateur clubs in pursuit of the Memorial and Allan cups. Durnan was not yet sixteen when he joined the Sudbury Cub Wolves for the 1930/31 season. Returning home, he played Junior hockey in North Toronto, which Durnan described as being at the bottom of the Toronto Maple Leaf farm system. Nonetheless, Frank Selke secured Durnan's rights for the Leafs.

A promising career was quickly put on hold when Durnan, horsing around with friends at Wasaga Beach in the summer of 1933, badly wrenched his knee. The Leafs lost interest in him, and Durnan lost interest in hockey. After playing with the Toronto All Stars in 1933/34, Durnan came out for only three games the following season before quitting.

He continued to play softball, and was one of the country's top pitchers. In 1936, the north came calling again, this time mainly because of his pitching arm. Bill Brydge, a former New York American, was putting together a powerhouse Senior hockey team for Kirkland Lake, the Lakeshore Blue Devils, and he picked up four players in Toronto. Brydge also decided to take along Durnan as a spare goaltender, but mainly to pitch for the local ball club. With the Blue Devils, Durnan returned to form as a goaltender, and played with them for four seasons, each summer returning to Toronto to play ball in the mercantile league.

In 1939, Durnan won the City of Toronto title, and his pitching for the Ford team got him a job in the stock room in the spring of 1940. That same spring, Durnan and the Blue Devils won the Allan Cup. Durnan's performance convinced Montreal Canadiens director Len Peto to sign him, bring him to Montreal to play for the club's Senior farm team, the Royals, and give him a desk job at Peto's steel company.

Durnan is sometimes portrayed as an amateur pining for his big break in the NHL, but in fact Big Bill was making too much money playing so-called amateur hockey and softball, with a guaranteed off-ice job and none of the pressures of the major league. With the talent drain brought on by the Second World War, the Canadiens themselves were pining for a first-class netminder, but Durnan wasn't budging off the Royals roster. Toe Blake, who had been a good friend of Durnan's since Durnan's spell with the Cub Wolves, became the captain of the Canadiens in 1940, but still Durnan held off. In 1943, he was finally persuaded to play for the Canadiens, perhaps in part by Peto threatening to yank his steel company desk job out from under him if he didn't. Even then, the story goes, Durnan had still not signed a contract only minutes before he was supposed to start his first Canadiens game. At the last moment, Durnan assented to a salary offer of $4,133 from general manager Tommy Gorman, dashed down the corridor to the dressing room to put on his equipment, and with scarcely time for a warmup went out and played the Bruins in a 2–2 tie.

His arrival in Montreal was politically charged. A favourite son of the francophone fans, Paul Bibeault, was losing his starting job as a result, but Durnan's performances quickly won over most Canadiens supporters. The Forum crowds didn't see Durnan lose that sea-

son, because in 1943/44 Montreal never lost a home game, and lost only five on the road. With offence provided by the likes of Rocket Richard, who was playing his first full season, Montreal won the season's championship and swept Chicago in the Stanley Cup. Durnan was runner-up in Calder voting to Toronto's Gus Bodnar, who finished tenth in scoring, but he took the Vezina by allowing only 109 goals, an astonishing 68 goals ahead of Detroit, which had the second-best defensive record. The last-place Rangers allowed almost three times as many goals as Durnan did.

His sophomore effort delivered a jarring bump. On January 30, 1945, he was stung 9–0 by New York, which dropped him behind Detroit's Harry Lumley in the Vezina race. Durnan took the Vezina seriously, and took the shellacking by the lowly Rangers as a wake-up call. "He changed completely," his coach, Dick Irvin, would recall. "In practice he used to just go through the motions guarding the nets. He'd wave an arm or kick a skate, but he wouldn't exert himself. But after that 9–0 game he went to work...even in practice drills. He drove himself to get in shape. He was the first player to hit the sack at night. He watched his diet. He became as sharp and as alert as any player I've ever seen, and I've seen a lot of great ones." Durnan's turnaround in the last half of the season produced one of the greatest performances in goaltending history. He won his second Vezina by allowing 121 goals in 50 games and building a 40-goal margin over Detroit.

No one else in the net looked quite like Durnan. He was a big man who occasionally had to battle with his waistline. But his most striking characteristic was that he wore a catching glove on each hand. Davey Kerr in New York before him had been ambidextrous, but never so flamboyantly. Durnan would switch the stick from hand to hand, depending on the shooter and which side of the net he was playing.

Detroit's Normie Smith, who had won the Vezina in 1936/37 and filled in for rookie Harry Lumley for one game in 1944/45, offered his own praise of Durnan that season. "Normally, a goalie's good side is where he catches the puck. Because he can catch with either hand, Durnan is almost equally good on either side of the net. Watch him, and you will find that when a puck carrier comes in on right wing, Durnan will switch his stick to the left side of the net. Then he can catch the puck with his right hand on the big side of the net. And vice versa. Unlike other players, he doesn't use the posts much in shifting about. Instead, he glides back and forth."

As great as his performances were, in his first two seasons Durnan, like Frank McCool in Toronto, played under a cloud of opinion that ascribed his success to the fact that all

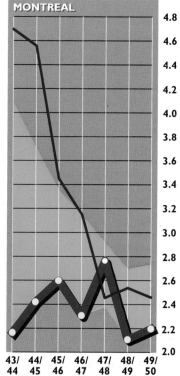

	43/ 44	44/ 45	45/ 46	46/ 47	47/ 48	48/ 49	49/ 50
GAMES	50	50	40	60	59	60	64
SHUTOUTS	2	1	4	4	5	10	8
STANLEY CUP	W	SF	W	F		SF	SF
ALL STAR TEAM	I	I	I	I		I	I

the real talent was away at war. He had arrived in the NHL just as virtually all of the quality netminders were entering the military. He also had to endure a simmering resentment among the Canadiens fans that he had displaced Bibeault, a situation complicated by the fact that Bibeault married the daughter of Canadiens GM Frank Selke. In December 1945, Woody Dumart hit Durnan in the back of the hand while he was switching his stick from one hand to the other. The shot cracked the bones, and Bibeault, to the delight of his supporters, was brought in from Boston for ten games. But when Bibeault went 4–6, the fans were ready to welcome Durnan back.

Unquestionably the disarray in the goaltending ranks contributed to Durnan's huge Vezina margin in his first season. Fourteen goaltenders played on the six teams as the league tried to keep the game afloat in 1943/44; some, like Ben Grant and Jim Franks, played for two different teams that season. And in his second NHL season, Durnan was a polished thirty; his closest competitor in the Vezina race, Harry Lumley, was only eighteen.

As to his being strictly a wartime talent, he proved his critics overwhelmingly wrong. When the league returned to strength in the 1945/46 season, Durnan kept on winning. When he won his third straight Vezina that season, the Bruins, who regained Brimsek in mid-season, turned in the next best effort, twenty-two goals back. Today, Brimsek says Durnan was the greatest goaltender he ever saw, the greatest goaltender Montreal has ever had. He set a league record by winning four straight Vezinas, paused for a season while Turk Broda earned one, then won two more in a row. If there was a disappointing aspect to Durnan's career, it was that his stellar regular-season performances produced only two Stanley Cup victories, in 1943/44 and 1945/46. But Durnan could not be blamed: his career NHL GA was 2.36 in the regular season, and dipped to 2.08 in the playoffs. While the Maple Leafs went on a tear, winning four Stanley Cups between 1944/45 and 1948/49, Durnan still dominated his profession. He won the 1946/47 Vezina with thirty-four goals to spare, the 1948/49 Vezina by a nineteen goal margin.

Near the end of the 1948/49 season, he set a modern shutout record, going 309 minutes, 21 seconds without being scored on. The week after the streak ended, following a game against the Leafs, sportswriter Baz O'Meara heaped praise on the thirty-three-year-old marvel. "Bill has something that no other goalies seem to possess. In addition to baseball hands, a sweeping stick, fine timing, he is the best fielder or icer in the nets. He is a regular third defenceman. Not the way that Hughie Lehman used to be when he raced out of his net, sometimes almost to the blueline, but as a forward feeder. For Bill made almost as many well calculated passes as Elmer Lach had [against Toronto] and that is saying a lot. He batted the puck away like a Vezina, he made passes behind his net, once he caught a forward scouting out to the blueline and fed him a pass which sent him on his way. He uses his stick to the best advantage of any goalie in hockey today. It was wise old Clint Benedict...who remarked [in 1948] that he found modern goalies relied too much on skate saves. 'The stick is your best friend and shots on the ice should be handled as much as possible with the old weapon. That gives you a chance to sweep the puck away, control it if you have to, or make a pass.'"

Durnan found an obvious friend in Turk Broda, who was the only goaltender to win a Vezina while Durnan was in the league.

Durnan was a great softball pitcher and Broda was a none too shabby catcher, although he never played at Durnan's level. They both loved the horses, and both were affable types who didn't seem to have a mean bone in their body. Both also were cursed by eating habits that were a half-step ahead of their metabolisms.

When Broda won the Vezina in 1947/48, Durnan endured a rare poor season, as did the team as a whole. The Canadiens missed the playoffs, and Durnan's goals-against record was well off the Vezina pace, twenty-six goals back and fourth in the six-team league. The cat-calls arose for another return of Bibeault. Halfway through the season, though, an ankle fracture forced Toe Blake's retirement, and he passed the captain's "C" to Durnan, who wore it for the rest of the campaign before turning it over to Butch Bouchard. He was only the third NHL goaltender to serve as a team captain, after Chicago's Chuck Gardiner and Montreal's George Hainsworth, and remains the last to date. Durnan recovered from his indifferent 1947/48 season, and put together another Vezina-winning performance in 1948/49. The fans lobbied for the Hart for him, but it went to Detroit's Sid Abel.

He had played six seasons, and he was ready to quit. The game was becoming hair-raising for all goaltenders, with its aggressive screening and ever-longer seasons. When Durnan joined the Canadiens in 1943/44, the NHL played a fifty-game season. It moved to sixty games in 1946/47, and in 1949/50 would increase to seventy. Durnan has been credited with arguing for a regular two-goaltender lineup, which the Rangers tried with Henry and Rayner, but at the same time he was not eager to share his job. Years later, he said when he was playing he felt that the best place for a backup goaltender was five hundred miles away. "I liked to play *all* the games. A reserve goalie was someone who was after my job. I wasn't going to give him a chance."

But it was a job he had trouble taking seriously as a long-term prospect. He was still playing mercantile league ball in the summer, always with an eye to an opportunity off the ice. When one arrived, he promised, he'd be gone. When he first signed with the Canadiens, "I remember saying to Tommy [Gorman], 'I figure hockey is a one-year career.' I still think of it that way. I figure I may be fired next week, or I may decide to quit the week after. In that way, I gear myself for shock. If it doesn't come, so much the better. I carry on the best I can."

At the beginning of the 1949/50 season, facing ten more games than the previous season, Durnan was ready to quit. Dick Irvin and Frank Selke talked him out of it. He played well enough to earn his sixth Vezina, but the game was consuming him. "It got so bad that I couldn't sleep on the night before a game. I couldn't even keep my meals down. I felt that nothing was worth that kind of agony."

The beginning of the end came on March 2, 1950, when his head was cut badly in a road game against the Blackhawks. When he got off the train in Montreal, he was met by another old Sudbury cohort, Murph Chamberlain, who had played his last NHL game the previous season with Montreal. According to Red Fisher, Chamberlain was told by Durnan, "That's it. I don't want any more of this. I've had enough."

He finished the season and earned his Vezina, fourteen goals ahead of Lumley, but came apart in the playoffs. In the semifinal, the second-place Canadiens were paired with the fourth-place Rangers. The teams were well matched in offence, Montreal having scored 172 goals that season, the Rangers 170. But the Rangers had been weak defensively, allowing thirty-nine more goals than Montreal. In the playoffs, New York came together, tightening up a defence that gave the required support to the sparkling Chuck Rayner. The Rangers raced to a surprising 3–0 series lead. Durnan couldn't play what threatened to be the game that would eliminate them. He went to Irvin and told him to use his long-standing backup, Gerry McNeil, instead. For the first time in his life, Durnan was ready to make way for his understudy.

McNeil had long idolized Durnan, and was not raring to shove him aside. "It was tough the night I replaced him," McNeil remembers. "I didn't want to take his place. Dick Irvin said, 'You're playing,' and I said, 'I'm not playing unless *Bill* tells me to play.' So Bill told me. At first I'd thought he was getting kicked out. But it was him that didn't want to go out."

The Canadiens won that night with McNeil, but the Rangers took the series in five games. At thirty-five, Durnan did not attempt a comeback.

Out of hockey, Durnan invested in an Ottawa hotel, which went bankrupt. He'd held a sales job with Labatt's in the off-season while with Montreal, and ended up back in the sales business with an assortment of breweries—O'Keefe's, then Dow, then Carling. He also tried his hand at coaching, at first in Noranda, then with the Ottawa Senators of the Quebec Senior league, finally the famed Kitchener-Waterloo Dutchmen Senior team. The Dutchmen stint ended badly. The team had been selected to represent Canada at the 1960 Olympics, but they performed poorly in 1959/60 regular-season play. In December 1959, Durnan resigned as coach, and the Dutchmen won Olympic silver at Lake Placid, behind the Americans.

Durnan ended up working in the promotions department of Canadian Breweries, attending sports banquets and charity promotions. When he could, he'd join his old adversary Turk Broda at the track.

Durnan was elected to the Hall of Fame in 1964; Brimsek, who also made 1949/50 his last season, made it in 1966; Durnan's pal Broda, who hung in through 1950/51, with a single game in 1951/52, followed in 1967. Rayner, the goaltender who helped drive Durnan from the game, waited for his election until 1973.

On October 17, 1972, Turk Broda died. On October 31, so did Bill Durnan, of kidney failure, at age fifty-seven. ◯

CHAPTER 5

1945/46–1966/67

WELCOME *to the* SHOOTING GALLERY

A SEVENTY-GAME SEASON, A FASTER, MORE BRUTAL STYLE AND THE ARRIVAL OF THE SLAPSHOT ALL CONSPIRED TO TEST THE ENDURANCE OF THE POSTWAR GOALTENDER

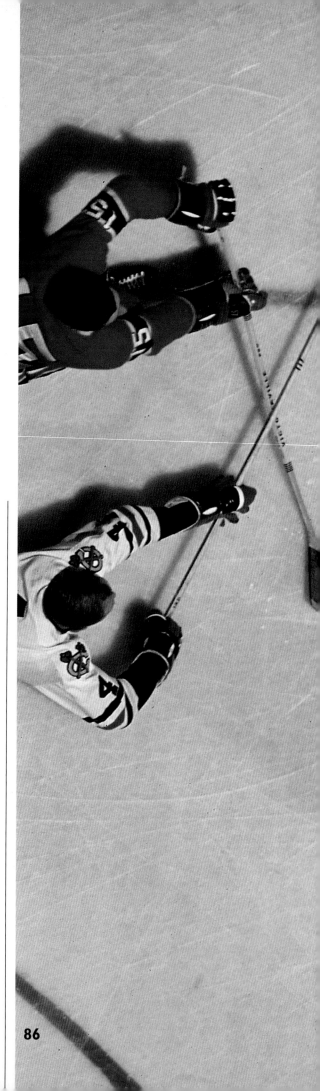

Hockey underwent a rapid, and traumatic, revolution in the immediate postwar seasons. The two-line offside reform of 1943/44 had broken the game wide open, allowing faster attacks and more breakaways. Perhaps it was the speed that encouraged it, but the game also became much more brutal. In 1942/43, the league's top-ten scorers were incurring only three-tenths of a minute per game in infractions, or one minor penalty every six games. By the mid-fifties, the league's offensive stars—pugnacious players like Detroit's Ted Lindsay and Montreal's Rocket Richard— were accumulating on average minor penalties every other game. Even goaltenders were getting in on the act. Returning to the Leaf lineup after the war, Turk Broda found himself challenging Lindsay in an attempt to break up a fight near the Leaf goal. Before the Lindsay–Broda set-to could progress beyond a Lindsay punch to Broda's face, Broda was tackled by Detroit netminder Harry Lumley.

THE MONTREAL CANADIENS PRESS FOR A GOAL AGAINST THE CHICAGO BLACKHAWKS' DENIS DEJORDY, WHO WON THE VEZINA TROPHY WITH GLENN HALL IN 1966/67.

This new game also featured ferocious jousting that spilled over into the goaltender's domain as attacking players drove for the net and took up station on the edge of the tiny three-foot-by-seven-foot crease. As defencemen started scuffling with attacking players, they inevitably fell into the crease itself, sometimes bowling the goaltender over, and if it was judged that the defenceman had done the pushing, it wasn't the attacker's fault that he was in the crease, on top of the helpless goaltender. As Johnny Bower recalls, this was Montreal forward John Ferguson's modus operandi—if a defenceman shoved him, his chosen trajectory was right at the goaltender.

In the first few seasons after the war, New York Rangers coach and general manager Frank Boucher looked

A BREED APART

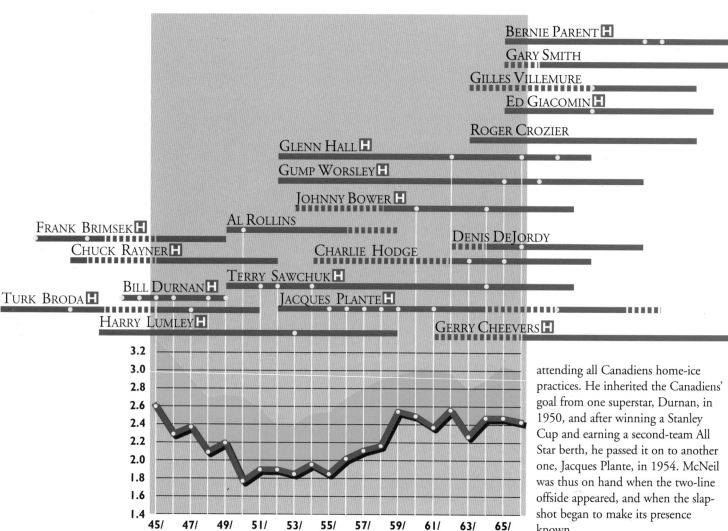

BERNIE PARENT H

GARY SMITH

GILLES VILLEMURE

ED GIACOMIN H

ROGER CROZIER

GLENN HALL H

GUMP WORSLEY H

JOHNNY BOWER H

FRANK BRIMSEK H

AL ROLLINS

DENIS DEJORDY

CHUCK RAYNER H

CHARLIE HODGE

TERRY SAWCHUK H

BILL DURNAN H

TURK BRODA H

JACQUES PLANTE H

HARRY LUMLEY H

GERRY CHEEVERS H

| 3.2 |
| 3.0 |
| 2.8 |
| 2.6 |
| 2.4 |
| 2.2 |
| 2.0 |
| 1.8 |
| 1.6 |
| 1.4 |

45/46 47/48 49/50 51/52 53/54 55/56 57/58 59/60 61/62 63/64 65/66

at the game he had re-engineered with the two-line off-side and suspected it had all turned out worse for the men in the nets. "Goaltenders were being subjected to a much more difficult assignment than they'd ever known before," he would reflect. "Power plays, deflected shots, and pileups in front of them that blocked their vision were presenting them with tensions and obstacles and injuries almost unknown five years earlier." After a game in Montreal in January 1949 in which his goaltender, Chuck Rayner, had been subjected to wave after wave of bleu, blanc et rouge piling up in his crease, an exasperated Boucher told the press he wanted to see the crease depth extended from three to four feet. It wasn't until 1951/52 that Boucher got his way. A foot was added to both crease dimensions, increasing the rectangle to four feet by eight feet. By then, the imperative to give the goaltender more turf had been made more emphatic by the arrival of a terrible new offensive weapon in the NHL: the slapshot.

Gerry McNeil was a goaltending bridge between the war years and the glory days of the Original Six. His first training camp as a Canadien had come as a seventeen-year-old in 1943, and for the next seven seasons he was Durnan's understudy, playing for the Montreal Royals of the Quebec Senior league and

attending all Canadiens home-ice practices. He inherited the Canadiens' goal from one superstar, Durnan, in 1950, and after winning a Stanley Cup and earning a second-team All Star berth, he passed it on to another one, Jacques Plante, in 1954. McNeil was thus on hand when the two-line offside appeared, and when the slapshot began to make its presence known.

Credit for inventing the slapshot has long been given to Bernie "Boom Boom" Geoffrion, who played his first games as a Canadien in 1950/51. He was almost certainly the first to use it consistently and well in the postwar NHL, but there was nothing new about the shot itself. It had been around in one form or another since the 1930s. The reason it wasn't used much before Geoffrion, says Frank Brimsek, is that it was so inaccurate. "Bun Cook had the best I'd ever seen," says Brimsek, who retired at the end of the 1949/50 season, before Geoffrion arrived in the league. Cook played in the NHL from 1926/27 to 1936/37, every season but the last as a New York Ranger; Cook then coached Brimsek in Providence in the American League. "He was the only guy with a slapshot who knew where it was going," maintains Brimsek. "He knew *exactly* where it was going." The shot Brimsek feared was not the slapshot, but the drop shot of Rangers star Bryan Hextall. Brimsek swears Hextall's shot could drop four feet on the way to the net. If you set up to take it on the chest, you had to make sure you kept your pads together as it could wind up shooting between your ankles.

McNeil saw plenty of the slapshot as it took firmer hold after the war. Unlike other goaltenders who faced Geoffrion's blast every fifth game, McNeil confronted it day in, day out, in practice. But he was never that impressed with the slapshot as an offensive weapon. McNeil frankly saw the shot as little more than showboating, a crowd pleaser. "A chap would wind up at the blueline, and if you played the angles, you didn't care where the hell it went. It was going to hit you, or hit the glass. But the people loved it because it hit the glass with a bang. I didn't think much of it for scoring."

Besides, the slapshot made for sloppy hockey. It wasn't a finesse tool, like the clever passing and needle-threading wrist shots that made the goaltender of McNeil's era stick close to the net and play his angles carefully. The slapshot seemed to be fired with no particular part of the net in mind, or propelled wildly into a screen of bodies in the slot in the hope that it would bounce somehow past the goaltender—off a stick, a leg, anything. (While attacking players had always taken up station on the goaltender's doorstep, the physical "slot" didn't arrive until 1942, when the introduction of faceoff circles created a discernible territory defined by the crease on one end and the inner arcs of the two circles to either side.)

Glenn Hall, who played his first NHL games in 1952/53, saw the slapshot's effectiveness not in its accuracy (of which it had very little) but in its ability to intimidate the goaltender. It was fast, it could hurt, it increased the shooter's range and so could arrive through a screen of bodies, and, most unnervingly, it could be tipped and rise unnoticed into the goaltender's face.

Even when the slapshot was a well-established part of the game, its potency in the hands of an NHL star could be a terrifying revelation to a young goaltender entering the professional ranks. "You've no idea how hard National Leaguers can shoot that puck until you've been hit a few times. It comes as a great shock," Gerry Cheevers recalled in 1971. "My first professional camp was with Toronto in 1961. The first time Frank Mahovlich hit my shoulder

(Bower says Mahovlich's slapshot was particularly dangerous because it was a rising one.)

When Glenn Hall reaches for words with which to pay tribute to Dave Dryden, who served as his backup in Chicago in the 1960s, his choice is telling: "He could hold the crouch." Goaltending was a profession of technique, true, but it was also, and perhaps ultimately, one of nerves. In Hall's succinct compliment, holding the crouch implies doing what every nerve fibre in your body was screaming at you not to do when someone like Bobby Hull wound up. Your instinct was to flinch, to come out of your stance and draw yourself taller, to raise your catching glove out of its low position to protect your face, which had no mask to preserve it. The impulse was stronger when the shot was screened. You had no idea where it was going to come from unless you got down in your crouch, covered the net, did your job and actively looked for the approaching shot. Your job was to get in the puck's way, and it didn't matter that the puck, in this new era of the slapshot, could do devastating harm, even when you did see it coming.

The slapshot did not purge the game of the traditional wrist shot—far from it. In the hands of skilled players, the wrist shot was still an effective tool, assuredly the most effective scoring tool. "The Rocket had the most accurate shot," says Bower. "He had a wrist shot he could put anywhere, and it was never the same place." But with the arrival of the slapshot, the goaltender had no choice but to move out from the crease, to take the net away from a distant shooter coming in on the

Continued on page 91

with a shot, I staggered back and my shoulders banged into the crossbar. It was as much from the surprise as the force of the shot. I just hadn't expected a puck could feel like that. It was as though somebody had wound up ten feet in front of me and thrown a rock as big as an orange."

A Really Big Deal

Al Rollins and Harry Lumley were the focal points of one of the game's blockbuster trades

They were born a month apart in 1926, though miles apart—Harry Lumley in Owen Sound, Ontario, Al Rollins in Vanguard, Saskatchewan. It would take twenty-six years for their lives to complete their unusual collision course, when two talented goaltenders who fell under the sway of Maple Leafs magnate Conn Smythe figured in one of the game's biggest trades.

Harry Lumley had broken into the NHL as a seventeen-year-old Junior player with the Barrie Colts, when Detroit acquired his rights from New York and put him on the ice in a three-game tryout in 1943/44 before assigning him to the Indianapolis Capitols of the American League. These were the war years, when goaltending talent was hard to come by, and Lumley turned out to be a stellar replacement for Johnny Mowers, who was in the Canadian air force. Lumley played another twenty-one games in Indianapolis in 1944/45 before moving up to the Red Wings for good. He held the Maple Leafs to nine goals and shut them out twice in

the seven-game defensive gridlock that was the 1944/1945 Stanley Cup. The Leafs won that series, but Lumley won Conn Smythe's admiration. In 1947/48, Lumley was back again facing Toronto, this time on the receiving end of a four-game Stanley Cup sweep by the Leafs.

After the Red Wings and Lumley finally won the Stanley Cup in their third consecutive attempt in 1949/50, Detroit seized upon another new netminding star, Terry Sawchuk, and dealt Lumley to Chicago. The Blackhawks were a defensive sieve; in Lumley's first season with them, they allowed twice as many goals as the regular-season champions, Lumley's old Red Wings.

Meanwhile, Al Rollins was making his way into the NHL. His unlikely break came when Baz Bastien, the heir apparent to Turk Broda, lost an eye to an errant shot at the first day of the Leaf training camp in September 1949. Broda played another full season in the Leaf net, relieved for two games by Rollins, who was called up from Kansas City in the U.S. League, a minor pro loop a notch below the American League. In 1950/51, Rollins played forty of seventy games (Broda took the rest), recorded a paltry 1.77 goals-against average and won the Vezina as the Leafs won the Stanley Cup. The next season he played every single game for the Leafs, posted a very respectable 2.22 goals-against average and finished second to Terry Sawchuk in the Vezina race. But it wasn't enough. The Leafs thought they could do better.

The Toronto fans and media had never forgotten Lumley's performances in the 1944/45, 1947/48 and 1948/49 Stanley Cups. Even with the struggling Blackhawks, Lumley continued to impress. "When he was with Chicago, he played awfully, awfully well," says Ted Kennedy, the Leaf captain at the time. "Chicago was strong offensively, but not defensively. Any time Chicago beat us, it was because of Lumley. The Toronto press were lobbying the Leafs to get him."

As it happened, Blackhawks GM Bill Tobin had long hankered after some of the talent in the Leafs superlative defensive corps. Back when Bastien was injured, Tobin, up at the Blackhawks training camp in North Bay, was willing to give up a goaltender if Toronto were willing to send him in return a proven defenceman, either Jimmy Thomson or Gus Mortson. Smythe turned him down—at the time, Tobin didn't have a goaltender of Lumley's calibre to deal. But just before training camp in 1952, the Leafs and the Blackhawks were ready to do business. Lumley came to Toronto. In return, Toronto sent Chicago an astonishing package: their Vezina-winner, Rollins, their star centre, Cal Gardner, a minor-league prospect, Ray Hannigan, and the defensive standout Tobin had long coveted, Gus Mortson, who became the Blackhawks captain.

Although neither team built a Stanley Cup winner out of the trade, Rollins and Lumley continued to star. Lumley stayed in Toronto for four seasons, winning the

After winning a Stanley Cup and a Vezina in Toronto, Al Rollins (below) was traded to Chicago, where he won the Hart Trophy. The trade brought Harry Lumley (opposite) to the Leafs, with whom he won a Vezina.

Vezina in 1953/54 with a GA of 1.86 and making the first All Star team in 1953/54 and 1954/55. The Leafs then signed a promising goaltending rookie, Ed Chadwick, who became the runner-up in Calder voting in 1957; Lumley dropped out of the NHL and reappeared in Boston in 1957/58. He spent three seasons with the Bruins, who lost the Stanley Cup final to Montreal in 1957/58, before retiring in 1959/60. Rollins endured five trying seasons in Chicago with a GA routinely over 3.00. Although he was never named to an All Star team, in 1953/54 Rollins became only the third goaltender to win the league's coveted Hart Trophy, having already been a runner-up to Gordie Howe in Hart voting in 1952/53. In 1957, Glenn Hall arrived in Chicago from Detroit, replacing Rollins as an NHL starter. He was playing in Winnipeg when he resurfaced for nine games with the Rangers in 1959/60. Rollins then went into coaching and management in minor pro hockey in the western U.S., and also coached in the WHA.

Harry Lumley was elected to the Hockey Hall of Fame in 1980. Despite having won the Hart, a Stanley Cup and a Vezina, Al Rollins has still not been elected to the Hall. ○

Continued from page 89

wing or standing back at the blueline. He had to find some compromise between moving out far enough to cut down the angle, but not so far that the speeding puck, reaching him quicker than if he had stayed back in the crease, cut down his available reaction time. A puck clocked at 100 miles an hour is travelling 147 feet a second. That means it moves from the shooter back at the point to the goal line sixty feet away in 0.41 seconds. If the goaltender moves out ten feet, the puck reaches him in 0.34 seconds. And once out of the crease, he was vulnerable to being caught out of position by a feigned shot that became a cross-ice pass, by a long rebound or by a shot that missed the net entirely and ricocheted off the boards or the glass to an open man.

He was leaving the crease not only to take away the net from the distant shooter, but to play the puck, feeding breakout passes, moving behind the net, as Plante showed, to intercept dump-in shots wrapping around the back boards. Now that the goaltender was in the territory of the skaters, he had to skate like never before, to cover as much ice as possible. But those goaltenders who did wander, who knew they had to wander to play the puck as a third defenceman, often had to overcome the prejudices of management. "Staying in the net has always been a team philosophy instead of an individual philosophy," says Glenn Hall. "I was told: Don't stop a puck that's going to miss the net. You might deflect it in. Well, if you're that bad, you shouldn't be playing. The goalkeeper's idea of how the position should be played often varied quite a bit with management's idea." Gump Worsley has observed: "Coaches tell you never to kick at the puck with your skates because you might kick it backwards into the net. What do they know?"

The advent of the slapshot was a watershed in the goaltender's profession. It added a recklessness and degree of violence hitherto unseen. It set off an arms race between the attacking player and the goaltender that escalates still. The slapshot came to dominate the game, the sticks grew curves, the shots became ever harder and (in the hands of some practitioners) more accurate. The tactics of offence and defence adjusted markedly to accommodate it. And goaltenders made their own changes—in equipment, in playing style.

For the most part, goaltending was still a standup job. This was partly a matter of survival. With no mask, and slapshots, sticks and skates flying, you wanted to keep your head above the fray. "If we went down," says Johnny Bower, "we got up real quick." The rare netminders who did drop to the ice as a matter of course, like Gump Worsley or Jack Gelineau, were known as "flip-flops." When they were on the ice, they were said to be taking a swim in a frozen pond.

Stylistic variations did emerge. Terry Sawchuk would sink into a "gorilla crouch," doubled over so that his face seemed scarcely to clear his knees, hands at the ready. Glenn Hall introduced the butterfly style: knock-kneed, feet wide apart to cover the corners of the goal, hands and stick at the ready to cover the new scoring spot, the "five hole" between his legs. The changes came as the goaltenders responded to the realities of the new offensive game, and as they brought to bear new weapons of their own.

The equipment with which goaltenders had first greeted the new game wasn't up to the job. "You're wearing up to forty pounds of padding as you stand there in front of a cage that is four feet high and six feet wide, and you're expected to be as agile as a ballet dancer," Worsley has noted.

The goaltenders took it upon themselves, often with considerable frustration, to get the manufacturers to make equipment that actually worked. "The only difference between a monkey and a goalkeeper is a goalkeeper has one arm turned forwards," says Hall, referring to the arm that holds the stick. "That's where I wanted the padding, and I couldn't get it across to the people that I was no longer a monkey. I was totally out of the tree and I wanted one arm turned."

Gloves experienced a rapid evolution, initiated by the goaltenders themselves as they strove to come up with an equaliser for the new offensive style (see pages 96–97). But there was still much work to be done. Johnny Bower wore a three-finger catching glove made by Pop Kenesky that "weighed ten pounds. If I couldn't catch the puck, I knocked it down with it."

The pads pioneered by Pop Kenesky underwent very few changes. Harry Lumley introduced the use of a "scoop," a crease or pocket at the shins which made pucks drop to the ice rather than rebounding. Turk Broda had the padding extend along either side of the skate to improve blocking around the blades. But that, fundamentally, was it. They were still made of horsehide, felt and rubberised canvas, with kapok for stuffing in the front and deer hair on the sides.

The canvas might have been rubberised, but that didn't mean the pads stayed dry. They were notorious for gaining weight as a game progressed, soaking up so much water that they felt like two sacks of wet cement on the legs. "I can close my eyes and think of how heavy they were in the third period," says Hall. "*Heavy*," McNeil recalls. "It was unbelievable. The felt got wet and stayed wet for a long time, and just about doubled the weight of the pads. I would love to start over and try the new equipment." Brimsek notes that sweat would also weigh down the equipment and the wool jerseys, although he personally wasn't bothered that much by the weight. For Bower, the weight was noticeable, and he would try to prevent the pads from soaking up water by treating them with dubbin (waterproof grease) and wrapping his legs in dubbin-treated tape. Wet ice was even more treacherous to the goaltender in that he had difficulty controlling his slide when he went down. Rinks with soft ice, like Madison Square Garden and Boston Garden, were the toughest for netminders to play in because of the sloppy conditions.

Although players like Tiny Thompson had owned their own equipment back in the 1920s and 1930s, by the war years equipment generally was the property of the team. A good set of Kenesky pads, conscientiously waterproofed and regularly repaired, could last four seasons, and teams hated coughing up for a new set. "You had such difficulty getting new pads," says Hall. "They never wanted to trade a goalkeeper with new pads. They wanted to trade him with old pads. So you would say to the trainer: Is there a trade coming? How come I can't get new pads?"

No one wore them into a game fresh out of Kenesky's shop. Brimsek says he liked to wear a pair for at least two weeks in practice. Glenn Hall and Johnny Bower practised with a new pair for three to four months before they were ready to take them into a game. "You might get a new pair prior to playoffs, but they weren't good," says Hall. "You didn't have them broken in. Now you can take them right off the rack, put them on and have no problem. After having a new pair in the playoffs, you'd go to training camp, and you'd have a pretty good pair, but you'd get them soaking wet and they would deteriorate like you wouldn't believe."

The goaltenders were, as always, a fraternity. Some, like Brimsek, never felt anything less than a full member of their team; others, like McNeil, were conscious of the separateness of their role. "That was one of the things told to me by management when I first came up," says McNeil. "You're by yourself. Don't take sides with defencemen. Just stay out of it. You couldn't sit down with someone playing the same position and talk something over. There was no one else around." But as a group, their ties cut across team barriers. They were virtually self-taught. Some coach or manager always had a particular theory about how the position should or should not be played, but for the most part they developed their skills on their own, which gave them distinctive styles, probably more distinctive than at any future point in the game. Brimsek blames today's similarity on the media. Back then, "you learned it yourself. Today they watch television and they copy that. In my day there was no television, and that was good. You learned to play a style that was best for you."

They learned by watching the goaltender at the other end of the rink. "If you didn't watch the opposing goalkeeper, you weren't paying attention," says Hall. It was by studying Jack Gelineau in his brief Boston career, says Hall, that he really appreciated the blocking possibilities of the stick-side glove. When Johnny Bower was playing for the Cleveland Barons in the American League, the team's general manager, Jim Hendy, sent him to Detroit to watch the young Terry Sawchuk play. Bower took notes on Sawchuk's style, and reviewed them with Hendy back in Cleveland. "I had a three-quarters crouch then," says Bower. The field trip to watch Sawchuk led him to adopt a more compressed crouch. And when Bower came up to the New York Rangers for the 1953/54 season, the man he was replacing, Chuck Rayner, told him his stick work was poor. Rayner gave him some tips on the poke check, and Bower became

one of the best at it, knocking away the puck as well as taking out the feet of the player without incurring a penalty. Rayner also passed along one of his ruses for beating the three-second rule for goaltenders getting rid of a caught puck: buy time by juggling it in your glove in such a way that you don't appear to have gained control of it. Emile Francis was a young hopeful in the Rangers net when Frank Brimsek, playing for the Bruins, took time after a game to dispense some advice. Like a lot of hockey players of the era, Francis was keen on baseball in the off-season, playing shortstop. Brimsek told Francis he was playing goal too aggressively, coming out too quickly, just like a shortstop going after a grounder, then having to back up. Brimsek advised him to hold back before committing himself as a shooter approached. And Francis made a huge contribution to goaltenders everywhere when he introduced the baseball-style catching glove (see page 96).

For many goaltenders, the changes the game underwent from the middle of the Second World War forward were too much to bear. It was bad enough that offence had become so aggressive, that the slapshot had arrived and that they wore no mask. What made it literally unbearable for some was the length of the season.

In the professional game's early years, two dozen games would constitute a season. The NHL season had jumped from twenty-four to forty-four games between 1923/24 and 1926/27, but even with that increase, goaltenders managed to have long careers right through the 1930s. Until midway through the Second World War, the league played a forty-eight-game schedule. In 1942/43, with the reduction of the league from seven to six teams after the New York Americans folded, the schedule underwent a nominal increase, to fifty games.

Continued on page 98

UNMASKED: WHEN GERRY CHEEVERS ARRIVED IN THE NHL IN THE MID-1960S, HE PLAYED BAREFACED, BUT NOT FOR VERY LONG. HIS MASK, COVERED IN STITCHES, BECAME A PERSONAL TRADEMARK AND A SYMBOL OF THE MOST DANGEROUS JOB IN TEAM SPORTS.

| *WELCOME TO THE SHOOTING GALLERY*

JOHNNY BOWER

AFTER THIRTEEN YEARS AS A MINOR-LEAGUE PHENOMENON, THE MAN WHO WOULD WIN FOUR STANLEY CUPS AND TWO VEZINAS FINALLY GOT OFF THE BUS IN TORONTO

He spent, in his own words, "thirteen years riding the bus." Indeed, John William Bower had an entire career in the American Hockey League, from 1945/46 to 1957/58, before he at last found stardom in the NHL with the Toronto Maple Leafs. He'd been one of the brightest lights of the AHL for, it seemed, forever. It had also seemed that the six-team NHL loop, with only one goaltender per team, was never going to find room for him.

He got his first chance to show he belonged in the big league in 1953/54 when called up by the Rangers; by then he had toiled for eight seasons with the Cleveland Barons of the AHL. He had a solid season in New York, playing all seventy games and recording five shutouts and a 2.60 GA for a team that won only twenty-nine games. The Rangers mystified him by shipping him back to Cleveland and reverting to Gump Worsley, who had been the Calder winner with New York in 1952/53 but had been sent back to the minors after recording a GA of 3.06 with two shutouts in fifty games. Bower was retrieved by New York for seven games over the next three seasons, but nothing came of it. He

appeared in danger of having his career unfold like that of his AHL contemporary Gil Mayer, who in six seasons was named a league All Star five times and its outstanding goaltender four times, but could not break into the NHL. Bower settled back into the routine of the bus, sure he was going to make it someday.

He finally got there in the fall of 1958, when Punch Imlach, newly hired as the coach and general manager of the struggling Toronto Maple Leafs, drafted him. Bower was the top goaltender in the AHL at the time. In 1957/58, he won the league's most valuable player award for the third straight season. It was also the third straight season he had been the league's first-team All Star goaltender, an honour he held five times. The season also brought him his second straight—and third career—top-goaltender award. And he had just turned in an outstanding performance for Cleveland in the playoffs against Imlach's Springfield Indians. About to turn thirty-four, Johnny Bower was finally getting a real shot at the NHL.

He didn't squander the opportunity, although he was at first reluctant to take it, having become so established in Cleveland. With the rejuvenated Leafs he played for eleven more seasons, won the Vezina twice and the Stanley Cup four times.

The long and tortuous road to glory for Bower had begun in the northern Saskatchewan town of Prince Albert, where he was born in 1924 (despite persistent rumours that he is a lot older than the record books say, Bower insists on that birthdate). There wasn't a lot of money around when he was growing up in the Depression. The favourite source of cheap hockey pucks for Bower and his chums was the horses that came into town on weekends. When the horse droppings froze solid, they made perfect pucks. "You didn't want to get hit in the mouth with one," he remembers.

Bower went into the army during the Second World War, and while overseas looked into playing goal for a military team, but the teams were so loaded with professional talent like the Leafs' Turk Broda that he wasn't judged good enough. Bower had entered the Canadian army in 1940 as an underage sixteen-year-old. When he came out of the service in 1944, he was twenty, and still eligible to play a year of Junior hockey. But he didn't have a birth certificate to prove it, and while Bower did play another Junior season, it served as the source of the rumour mill about his true age—some people weren't prepared to believe that he could have spent four years in the military and still be eligible for Junior play. In 1945, he joined Cleveland of the AHL.

As a Maple Leaf, Bower was instrumental in the Stanley Cup victories of the 1960s, yet his résumé is surprisingly thin on official accolades. He was named to only one NHL All Star team. He only won his second Vezina because fellow Toronto netminder Terry Sawchuk insisted on

	IN AHL	N.Y. RANGERS		TORONTO										
	53/54	54/55	55/56	56/57	57/58	58/59	59/60	60/61	61/62	62/63	63/64	64/65	65/66	66/67	67/68	68/69
GAMES	70	5		2		39	66	58	59	42	51	34	35	24	43	20
SHUTOUTS	5	0		0		3	5	2	2	1	5	3	3	2	4	2
STANLEY CUP				SF		F	F	SF	W	W	W	SF	SF	W		QF
ALL STAR TEAM								1								

Bower played one game for Toronto in 1969/70.

GAMES
SHUTOUTS
STANLEY CUP
ALL STAR TEAM

A BREED APART   94

sharing the trophy and prize money with him. The trophy's rules at the time specified that the prize go to the goaltender who had played the most games on the team with the lowest GA, and Sawchuk had played thirty-six games to Bower's thirty-four. The league relented, and from then on the Vezina was shared by the regular goaltenders on the team with the lowest GA. The performance of Bower and Sawchuk also encouraged the league to make it mandatory for teams to have two dressed-to-play goaltenders on hand for every game, beginning in 1965/66.

Yet by rights there should have been more awards for Bower. In three other seasons he posted a personal GA better than the team GAs that won other players the coveted Vezina, but Bower had nothing to show for it. Bower was an affable old pro, a standup goaltender whose reflexes defied his age, whose importance to the success of the Leafs failed to register with the media types who overlooked him in All Star voting.

By 1968/69, time was catching up with him. At forty-four, his play still sparkled, but his eyesight was weakening, and to preserve it he reluctantly decided to

don a mask. He never really got used to the device—like other goaltenders, he found it restricted his vision, and he tended to lose sight of the puck when it was down around his feet. When a long shot beat him, Bower protested to an angry Imlach that he had been screened. Imlach played him the game film: "There wasn't anybody within twenty feet of me."

The decision to hang up the pads was simplified by the firing of Punch Imlach at the end of the 1968/69 season after the Leafs were blown out of the quarterfinal in four straight games (and a combined score of 17–0) by the Bruins. Within minutes of the Imlach sacking, Bower publicly announced his retirement. He was one of a handful of players in a team otherwise united in their loathing of Imlach who had always respected the boss without ever kowtowing to him.

He played one game in 1969/70, then moved into scouting with the Leafs, and later served as a goaltending coach. In 1976, he was elected to the Hockey Hall of Fame. He still runs a goaltending school, and on November 8, 1994, Johnny Bower says he really did celebrate his seventieth birthday. ○

JOHNNY BOWER HAD A FULL CAREER WITH THE CLEVELAND BARONS IN THE AMERICAN LEAGUE BEFORE MOVING UP TO THE NHL WITH THE TORONTO MAPLE LEAFS.

Hands
of Time

Considering how many goaltenders were enthusiastic baseball players, it took a remarkably long time for the fraternity to add a proper catching glove to its tool kit. Catching gloves right into the Second World War were little more than heavy-duty defenceman's gloves. Players like Frank Brimsek can recall wearing a kid leather glove inside their regular glove to take some of the sting out of nabbing a puck virtually barehanded. By the end of the war, gloves with rudimentary cages were appearing, but it took the initiative of a teenage goaltender who also happened to be a hardball shortstop to make the great leap forward.

Emile Francis, who went on to become coach and general manager of the New York Rangers, was playing Junior hockey for the Moose Jaw Canucks at the start of the Second World War. He took a Roger McGuinn model three-finger first baseman's glove made by Rawlings to a shoemaker and had him sew on a regular hockey glove gauntlet. He used the glove without incident in Junior hockey, and it caused no fuss when he was called up by the Chicago Blackhawks in 1946/47 and played his first NHL game, against Boston. The second game, a Thursday-night match in Detroit, was another matter. The Red Wings coach and general manager, Jack Adams, spied the glove on Francis during the pregame warmup, and summoned referee King Clancy to the Detroit bench. "Adams is pointing at me. I'm looking at my pads, looking around, trying to figure out what's wrong. Finally King Clancy skates over and says, 'Let me see that glove you've got there.' I took it off and showed it to him. He says, 'You can't used that. It's illegal. It's too big.' I said, 'Who says so?' He says, 'Jack Adams.' I told him, 'I tell you what, King. If I can't use this glove, you've got no game tonight.' Those days a team only had one goalkeeper." Clancy agreed to allow him to wear it, but on the condition that Francis showed the glove to league president Clarence Campbell that Saturday at the NHL head office in Montreal, when the Blackhawks would be in town playing the Canadiens. Campbell gave Francis's glove his blessing, and goaltending

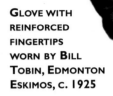

GLOVE WITH REINFORCED FINGERTIPS WORN BY BILL TOBIN, EDMONTON ESKIMOS, C. 1925

LIKE MANY GOALTENDERS, TURK BRODA OF THE MAPLE LEAFS WAS KEEN ON BASEBALL, PLAYING SOFTBALL AS A CATCHER IN THE OFF-SEASON

THREE-FINGER KENESKY MODEL

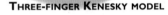

TRAPPER WORN BY MANNY LEGACÉ, GOALTENDER FOR CANADA'S 1993 WORLD JUNIOR CHAMPIONS

TRAPPER WITH EARLY "CHEATER" EXTENSION ON THUMB, WORN BY PELLE LINDBERGH, PHILADELPHIA FLYERS, 1985/86

acquired an entirely new dimension of play.

"I should have patented it," Francis laments. He didn't, and his three-finger prototype became a production standard.

In time, the catching glove came to resemble less a first baseman's glove than a catcher's mitt. The trapper-style glove had more padding and, most important, more area overall. There was (and is) nothing in the NHL rulebook about precise dimensions of the catching glove, only a proviso—added at the time of Francis's innovation—that the cage could be no larger than the span between thumb and forefinger. Through this loophole Mike Palmateer, who tended net for Toronto and Washington from 1976/77 to 1983/84, was able to introduce the "cheater," an extension of the outside edge of the thumb that increased the glove's overall area. Combined with the slablike pad along the wrist, the cheater has made the modern catching glove as much a blocker as a device with which to snag the puck.

The stick-side glove underwent a parallel evolution. Before the Second World War, goaltenders either wore heavy-duty defenceman's gloves, or added protection to the glove with a felt sheath. Extra padding began to appear—Frank Brimsek used a wrap with bamboo ribbing. Mitts began to appear that had heavy padding built into them, and, gradually, a slablike rectangular blocker became standard by the end of the Original Six era. The Cooper "waffle board" became a virtual standard. Today's blockers have lost the waffle look and are more flexible, with the top portion angled outward to help direct rebounds. ○

PADDED STICK-HAND MITT
WORN BY GERRY COLEMAN, A
MONTREAL JUNIOR CANADIEN
GOALTENDER IN THE 1940S

COOPER "WAFFLE-
BOARD" BLOCKER
WORN BY ED
GIACOMIN, 1977/78

EMILE FRANCIS, WHO INVENTED THE
BASEBALL-STYLE CATCHING GLOVE
WHILE PLAYING JUNIOR HOCKEY IN
THE 1940S, HAS PADDING APPLIED TO
THE BACK OF HIS STICK GLOVE AS A
CHICAGO BLACKHAWK,
C. 1947

BLOCKER
WORN BY
MANNY LEGACÉ,
GOALTENDER FOR
CANADA'S 1993
JUNIOR WORLD
CHAMPIONS

Continued from page 93

In 1946/47, with the league stabilised in its Original Six configuration, the schedule was expanded to sixty games. Then Leaf GM Conn Smythe called for an increase to seventy games, and he wanted roster sizes increased from seventeen to eighteen skaters so he could carry six dressed-to-play defencemen, rather than the normal five. Smythe got his way on the number of games, but not on the number of players. The teams would have to get by with seventeen skaters, exclusive of goaltenders. And when it came to goaltenders, owners still generally thought one per team was just fine.

The league began to churn through goaltending talent at an alarming rate. The first casualty was Bill Durnan, whose career ended in the middle of the 1950 playoffs when he could not bring himself to return to the ice. Gerry McNeil, who replaced him, could endure the game for only four seasons.

With the careers of veterans ending during and after the war years, and because, during the war years, teams were running through goaltenders like so much Kleenex, genuine goaltending talent, particularly new blood, was never more valued. Bill Durnan was runner-up for the top rookie award, the Calder, in 1943/44, and Frank McCool won it in 1944/45. From 1949/50 to 1956/57, the Calder was practically a goaltending trophy. In 1949/50, Jack Gelineau won it; in 1950/51, Terry Sawchuk won it and Al Rollins was runner-up. Gump Worsley won it in 1952/53. Glenn Hall took it in 1955/56, and Ed Chadwick was runner-up in 1956/57. Goaltenders also figured in the Hart, which went to the player judged most valuable to his team. In 1949/50, Chuck Rayner became the first goaltender to win the Hart since Roy Worters in 1928/29; Al Rollins took the honour in 1953/54, and in 1961/62, Jacques Plante would become the last one to win it to date.

The talent that wasn't replaced quickly, that managed to stick with the job and make a full career of it, often paid a price. Terry Sawchuk aged rapidly under the stress of the postwar game and was considered washed up after five seasons. Harry Lumley became a different person when a game was imminent. "When he came into the dressing room at 6:30 or 7:00 prior to the game," Leaf captain Ted Kennedy recalls, "he went into a complete shell. No one spoke to him. He was psyching himself up for the game, I guess, but you never kidded with him. That was Lum. But after the game, he was completely relaxed, the life of the party." Gump Worsley impressed everyone with his seemingly happy-go-lucky nature, but was driven into temporary retirement in November 1968 by a nervous breakdown. Jack Gelineau inherited the Bruins goal from the beloved Brimsek, but he didn't last even as long as McNeil, playing only two full NHL seasons before deciding that his future lay in the insurance business.

By the mid-1950s, the goaltending profession fell into its old pattern of established practitioners enjoying long careers. Despite Frank Boucher's concerns about the unprecedented pressures on the goaltender, the game weeded through a formidable talent pool and came up with a handful of players who could perform with consistent skill and who were determined, for better or for worse, to stick with the job. It had always been a profession whose members seemed to get better with age, once they had overcome the initial terrors of the big-league game. Experience improved them, much as it did defencemen. (In 1971, Gerry Cheevers recounted how Bernie Geoffrion, who had become a scout, hailed Cheevers and his netminding partner, Eddie Johnston, as they left a St. Louis hotel. "You're in great shape, Eddie," Geoffrion said. "You're only thirty now. You've hardly started.") There were a lot of tricks of the trade to master, and defencemen and goaltenders didn't have the pressures of high-speed play that put a premium on fresh young legs. Forwards might get better with age too, but there was a point at which experience could not compensate for tiring bodies and a weaker shot. With goaltenders, as long as they could maintain their reflexes, their eyesight and their nerves, their careers could stretch into the double digits in seasons. Jacques Plante, Gump Worsley, Johnny Bower, Terry Sawchuk, Glenn Hall and Charlie Hodge all had long careers in the Original Six that extended into the NHL's expansion era.

That the top goaltenders managed to hang in so long is a tribute to their fortitude, for when the curved stick showed up, the goaltender's lot became even more hellish, if that were possible. Although Andy Bathgate of the Rangers experimented with the novelty in the late 1950s, the true development took place in Chicago, beginning in 1961. Stan Mikita and Bobby Hull experimented with different ways to bend the blade and arrived at a compromise in shape that would allow them still to stickhandle and give and receive passes while gaining the shooting benefits of the blade. The curve of the blade turned the slapshot into an entirely new and terrible creature. To borrow from baseball, what had been a fastball became an even faster fastball that behaved like a knuckleball. But Ed Giacomin, who was a baseball catcher in the off-season, makes an important distinction between the goaltender facing a curved-stick slapshot and a catcher facing a knuckleball. The catcher signals the pitcher, and knows exactly what is coming his way.

In the Bryan Hextall days, players created their drop shots with straight blades by "cutting" the puck—striking on an angle to induce spin. The curved blade added much more spin to the puck, and on the way to the net it danced and dipped and behaved in entirely unpredictable ways. The shooter didn't know where it was going any more than the goaltender did. It was the ultimate siege weapon, and it elevated the shooter's art of intimidating the goaltender to its apex. Sticks reached such monstrous curves that in 1968/69 the curve limit was set at 1.5 inches, but even that proved excessive. In 1969/70, the curve was limited to an inch, and in 1970/71 it was reduced again to half an inch. Gerry Cheevers would remark on how frightening Bobby Hull's

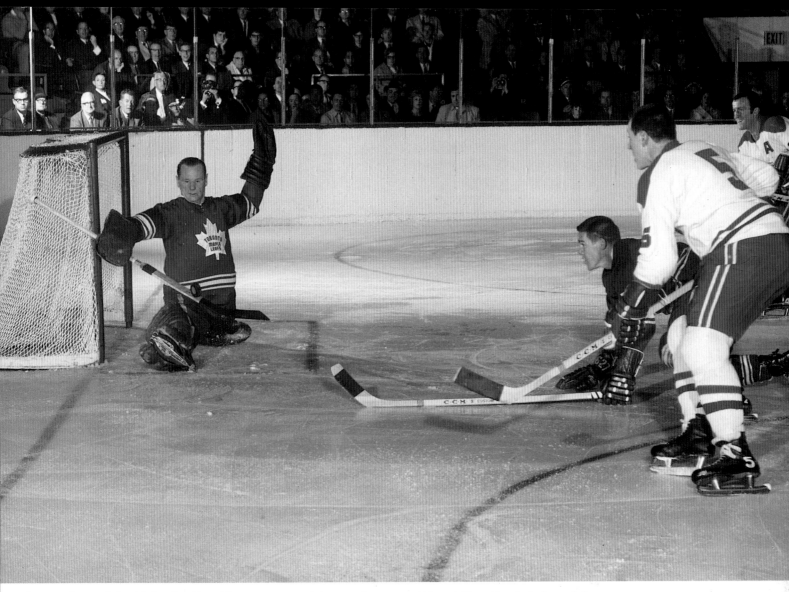

shot was, but said that his brother Dennis's was even worse: the younger Hull, he was convinced, had absolutely no idea where his slapshot was going. Goaltenders were working in a shooting gallery, and the shooters were wielding bazookas with wonky sights. Every now and then, a player managed to rifle a shot past the goaltender from centre ice.

 The new ability of shooters to make the puck drop or dance with a slapshot propelled by a curved stick was not something management was necessarily quick to grasp. Johnny Bower was once beaten by a Geoffrion blast from just inside the Leaf blueline. Bower was sure the shot was going to go over the crossbar, but when he stuck out his glove to catch it, it shot between his legs. "That puck dropped three feet. I looked over to the bench, and Punch pulled his hat down over his face. All I could see was his nose. I thought, 'Oh boy, I'm in trouble.' " When he tried to explain to Imlach that the puck had dropped, Imlach wasn't having any part of it. "Pucks don't drop!" he told Bower.

The debut of the mask in 1959 gave netminders like Jacques Plante, who introduced it, the will to continue playing in this era of terrible new offensive weapons. The innovation didn't exactly sweep the league. A mask was considered all right for practices,

but not for games. Although Terry Sawchuk donned the device during the Original Six era, veterans like Johnny Bower and Glenn Hall only wore one at the very end of their careers, in the expansion era. It took hold most firmly among the young prospects still making their way toward the professional ranks. Even then, some of them had to be convinced the hard way of the mask's appropriateness in the evolving world of slapshots and curved sticks. Gerry Cheevers would become famous in Boston for his face mask adorned with stitches, which became a visceral public image of the carnage the mask prevented. But when Cheevers came up to the professional game in 1961, like the majority of goaltenders he was still playing barefaced. In his first exhibition game with the Leafs, Leo Boivin of Boston hit him above the eye with a shot that dazed him and required stitches. He had never been cut in his amateur days. Cheevers carried on barefaced, but was finally convinced of the need for the mask while playing for the Leafs' American League farm team, the Rochester Americans. In a January 1965 game, Cheevers was nailed by a shot from Red Berenson of the Springfield Indians. It wasn't a slapshot but a backhand; it knocked out three upper and three lower teeth and cut him for thirty-five stitches. "It was a mess," he would write. "I was spitting blood and teeth as they led me to

Continued on page 102

JOHNNY BOWER SHUTS THE DOOR ON THE MONTREAL CANADIENS. HE WAS A CLASSIC STANDUP GOALTENDER. "IF WE WENT DOWN," HE SAYS, "WE GOT UP REAL QUICK."

GUMP WORSLEY

BEST REMEMBERED AS A STANLEY CUP STANDOUT WITH THE CANADIENS, HE FIRST HAD TO SERVE ELEVEN SEASONS IN THE "JAILHOUSE" OF NEW YORK

Lorne "Gump" Worsley had an evocative way of describing his job: when he was in the crease, he was "in the barrel." He made the ride over the NHL's Niagara Falls 932 times, and despite a few crash landings and some scary leaks, after twenty-one seasons he was able to walk away with his body and mind intact.

Worsley was the hard-living product of a dirt-poor Depression childhood. He dabbled in juvenile delinquency in Montreal's working-class north end neighbourhood of Point St. Charles, and quit school to go to work at fourteen. He picked up the nickname "Gump" as a kid, his flat-top brushcut reminding a friend of the cartoon character Andy Gump.

He didn't start playing goal until his final year of Juvenile eligibility, when a coach told him he was too small to play any other position. Despite being a native Montrealer, he was no fan of the Canadiens. His parents were from Scotland, and his dad had followed the old Maroons, the city's anglo team. Although he saw Bill Durnan play at the Forum, his netminding idols were Frank Brimsek of the Bruins and Davey Kerr, the old Rangers star.

The family was so poor—Worsley's father was out of work for five years during the 1930s—that he had to borrow goalie equipment from the Montreal Boys Association when he tried out for the Quebec Junior A's Verdun Cyclones. When he made the team, he was the only English-speaking kid in the lineup, and the experience taught him French in a hurry.

Verdun was a newly minted farm team of the New York Rangers, which made it Worsley's destiny to play for the star-crossed Rangers teams of the 1950s, which were nothing like the ones Kerr had starred on. At five-seven, Worsley was shaped like the barrel in which he imagined himself riding. He covered the net in an acrobatic style, standing out in an era in which the standup style was de rigueur.

Despite being cast against type, he made steady progress in the Rangers system, but in 1953 he suffered the first of several professional indignities. In 1952, Worsley had been brought up from the Saskatoon Quakers of the minor pro Pacific Coast league to replace the veteran Chuck Rayner. While his GA in his debut season was a mediocre 3.06, this was New York he was toiling for, and he earned the league's Calder Trophy. Worsley was astonished when Rangers GM Frank Boucher decided to send him to the Vancouver Canucks of the Western Hockey League instead of playing him in New York the very next season. Boucher had decided to try instead a new signing from the American League, Johnny Bower. Boucher's latest find had an even better season on paper than Worsley's, with a GA of 2.60. But then it was Bower's turn to be baffled as he was shipped back to the American League and Worsley was retrieved from Vancouver for 1954/55.

This time Worsley was able to stick with the starting job, but it wasn't necessarily a change for the better. The team as a whole struggled under the erratic leadership of coach Phil Watson, and the strain of losing season after season got to Worsley. After 1958, Worsley has recalled, "The next three years were pure misery for me—the darkest of my career. I was doing a lot of drinking then, using the bottle to chase all those bad games and bad goals."

Publicly, Worsley came across as an impish, happy-go-lucky sort; privately, the game weighed on him as heavily as it did any goaltender. "I suffered fits of depression after many losses. I found it hard to sleep. I'd toss and turn in bed, get up and have a smoke, pace the floor, and then climb back into bed. Instead of counting sheep, I'd

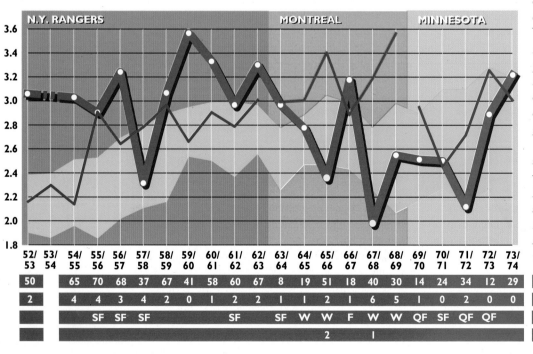

find myself seeing the pucks that beat me or almost tore my head off."

Worsley suffered facial cuts requiring more than 200 stitches during his career, but when Jacques Plante introduced the mask to the league in 1959, Worsley was one of the fraternity's diehard critics of the new device. When anyone asked him why he didn't wear a mask, his standard reply was: "My face is a mask."

His life and career were delivered a badly needed reprieve on June 4, 1963, a date Worsley would refer to as "the day I got out of the Rangers jailhouse." Worsley was part of a seven-player deal between the Rangers and the Canadiens that saw a stunned Jacques Plante go to New York and an ecstatic Worsley return to his home town.

The trade, initially at least, didn't work out well for either goaltender. Plante boasted about winning yet another Vezina, but found out how hard it is to keep a GA below 3.00 when playing for the Rangers. After a season and a half, New York sent him to Baltimore of the American League, thereby provoking his retirement. As for Worsley, a hamstring injury at the start of the 1963/64 season sent him to the Quebec Aces of the American League for what was supposed to be a recuperative stint. It turned into a season and a half in the minors as Plante's former backup, Charlie Hodge, took the starting job and won a Vezina.

Worsley finally got a taste of hockey glory in the 1964/65 Stanley Cup. After playing only nineteen games for the Canadiens that season, he was expected to carry Montreal through the playoffs. A torn thigh muscle put him out of action for three games of the final against Chicago. Coach Toe Blake then dumbfounded the recuperating Worsley by tapping him, rather than Hodge, for a ride in the barrel in game seven. Worsley shut out the Blackhawks 4–0 and learned, at last, what it was to be a champion.

He repeated the experience in 1965/66 and in 1967/68, winning the Vezina in both seasons—the first time with Hodge, the second time with Rogie Vachon. He also made the All Star team in both seasons. But Worsley also had the dubious privilege of being the winning goaltender in two Stanley Cups in which the losing goaltender won the Conn Smythe. Detroit's Roger Crozier won it in 1965/66, Glenn Hall of St. Louis in 1967/68. Worsley was annoyed on both occasions. In the 1965/66 playoffs, Worsley would recall, "I'd played all ten playoff games and had allowed only twenty goals. Roger had given up twenty-six in twelve games and

wound up on the losing team." In the 1967/68 playoffs, Worsley couldn't help but note that his GA was 1.88, while Hall's was 2.43.

The November following the Stanley Cup victory over St. Louis, Worsley suffered a nervous breakdown. Expansion in 1967 now meant lots of time in airplanes, of which Worsley was petrified, and the cumulative seasons of stress were provoking hallucinations. It all caught up with him on a flight from Montreal to Los Angeles. When the Canadiens' flight stopped over in Chicago, Worsley got off, announced his retirement, got on a train and returned to Montreal. For the next month, he visited a psychiatrist every day to conquer his anxieties and control his fear of flying. When Montreal tried to demote him to its new Montreal Voyageurs American League farm team the next season, Worsley quit.

He was then drafted by the Minnesota North Stars, and made a four-season comeback, teamed with the lanky Cesare Maniago in a pairing known as "Mutt and Jeff." In his final season, 1973/74, Worsley gave in to the arguments of his wife and donned a mask. The final goal scored on him, number 2,624, was from the stick of Philadelphia enforcer Dave Schultz. Worsley noted that Schultz was born in 1949, the year he had played his first professional game. He was forty-four when he climbed out of the barrel for the last time. His election to the Hockey Hall of Fame came in 1980. Today, the Gumper lives in Montreal. ❍

WORSLEY KEEPS HIS EYE ON THE JOB DURING HIS YEARS IN THE NEW YORK RANGERS "JAILHOUSE."

Continued from page 99

the infirmary. I can still see a couple of those teeth landing in my glove." Cheevers embarked on two seasons of experimenting to come up with a mask he could live with.

Contriving a suitable mask was partly a matter of overcoming the visibility limitations that had foiled Clint Benedict back in 1930. Like many experienced goaltenders donning a mask for the first time, Cheevers found it restricted his vision when he looked down at his feet. He finally found one he liked through Bruins alumnus Woody Dumart, who had a sporting goods store in Boston. A former plumber named Ernie Higgins had come into the store one day to show Dumart a mask he'd made for his son. Dumart put Higgins in touch with Cheevers; for $125 Cheevers had a mask he liked and Higgins had a newfound career supplying other NHL goaltenders, like Eddie Johnston, Les Binkley, Al Smith and Doug Favell. Cheevers' experience was typi-

cal. For years masks were custom made by garage-based entrepreneurs or even goaltenders themselves, rather than mass-produced.

But the advent of the mask also required a change in the goaltenders' mentality. In 1964, Clint Benedict rejected the idea that machismo had held off the perfection of the mask. "We took such a beating anyway that nobody would have thought it sissified," he said. "No, it was a case of not developing one that was practical." But Cheevers saw hockey culture as definitely playing a role in the mask's slow acceptance. By the fall of 1967, when he first wore a model he could live with at the Bruins' training camp, "most of the stigma attached to mask-wearing had disappeared. And there was a stigma—or, at least, there had been." As Ed Giacomin recalls, wearing a mask could get you labelled "chicken." When someone asked Plante if wearing a mask made him a coward, he shot back: Does jumping out of an airplane without a parachute make you brave?

A BURNT-OUT CASE: TERRY SAWCHUK'S CAREER WAS ALL TOO TYPICAL IN THE GOAL-TENDING TRADE IN THE EARLY 1950S. AFTER FIVE SUPERB SEASONS, HE WAS CONSIDERED WASHED UP.

League managers and owners were slow to recognize that employing more than one steady goaltender would be a sensible solution to the game's rising number of burnouts. And goaltenders in general helped the old system persist by demanding to play every game possible—partly out of pride, partly out of not wanting to have to compete for their job with an equal on the roster. For nearly two decades after the war, teams were content to stick with a single starter, and if he could no longer cut it, there was always some other young hopeful willing to give it a go. Frank Boucher had tried to buck that trend in New York, using both Chuck Rayner and Sugar Jim Henry after the war, but in the end the accountants deemed it too expensive and Henry was traded to Chicago. The stability in goaltending ranks that took hold in the mid-1950s seemed to obviate, for a time, any need to provide relief. And the arrival of the mask, which gave some of the position's great stars the nerve to stay at the job, cut down further on turnover.

It wasn't until the early 1960s that the NHL again began to see tag-team goaltending lineups in the manner of Rayner and Henry. In Toronto, Don Simmons, who had been acquired from Boston, came to share a significant part of the netminding workload with Johnny Bower, playing twenty-eight games in 1962/63 and twenty-one in 1963/64, and making valued contributions to the Stanley Cup wins in both seasons.

The most famous, and most influential, tag-team approach arose in Toronto in 1964, when Maple Leafs GM and coach Punch Imlach acquired Terry Sawchuk from Detroit to share the net with Bower. The NHL wanted teams to have two dressed-to-play goaltenders on hand for the 1964/65 playoffs, but they could still use only one during the season. Imlach was a genius at getting extra miles out of veteran players. Bower had been playing professionally since 1945, Sawchuk since 1947, and Imlach figured they could both produce excellent performances if only the NHL played a thirty-five-game season. To achieve the same end, Imlach split the goaltending assignment between them, and Toronto had the lowest GA in the league that year.

Imlach didn't have a schedule for who was playing when. He based his decision on who would start the game on how the goaltenders performed in the pregame warmup. "I needed about thirty to forty shots to get warmed up," says Bower. "With Terry, about ten seemed to be enough. He was ready." Notes Dave Keon, who began his fifth season with the Leafs when Sawchuk came aboard, "With Terry, the fewer shots in warmup the better. John wanted as close to game conditions as possible." It worked out that in 1964/65 Sawchuk played thirty-six games, Bower thirty-four.

When the league tried to give Sawchuk the 1964/65 Vezina, since he had played two more games for Toronto than Bower, he refused it. It had been Bower's shutout performance in the final game of the season that allowed the Leafs to permit two fewer goals-against than Detroit rookie Roger Crozier, who played every game for the Red Wings. Sawchuk wanted

Bower's name on the trophy, too, and the prize money split between them. (Bower also had the lower GA of the pair, 2.38 to Sawchuk's 2.56.) The league acquiesced, and not only changed the rules of the Vezina, but recognized the wisdom in Imlach's strategy, regardless of the age of the players, and made it mandatory the following season for teams to dress two goaltenders for each regular-season game.

The two-dressed-to-play rule helped ease in a new generation of netminders just as the league prepared itself for expansion. Gerry Cheevers, Ed Giacomin and Bernie Parent, among others, made their first appearances in the waning years of the Original Six, so that when the league doubled in size in 1967, and kept on growing, they had the experience of the league at its most intensely competitive. During the 1960s, the difference between Vezina-winning GAs and the LGA was routinely three-tenths of a goal or less, and stayed that way until 1969/70, when the diluted talent of the expansion years began driving a statistical wedge between the very best goaltending and LGA.

In 1964/65, a new prize was added to the league's silverware collection: the Conn Smythe Trophy, awarded to the most valuable player in the Stanley Cup playoffs in the opinion of the league board of governors. Remarkably, in only its second season, the Smythe was awarded to Roger Crozier, whose Red Wings had lost the series 4–2 to Montreal. Two seasons later, in 1967/68, the board of governors again awarded the trophy to a member of the losing team, and again, the recipient was a goaltender, Glenn Hall of the new expansion club, the St. Louis Blues. Goaltenders have long figured prominently in the trophy's history. Of the thirty recipients to date, ten have been in the net.

For many observers, the glory years of the Original Six era also came to represent the glory of the goaltending trade. The netminders faced the fully developed slapshot, propelled by an alarmingly curved stick. Few wore a face mask, and the equipment, despite having evolved considerably, was still cumbersome; leg pads were two inches narrower then and the catching glove didn't cover nearly the area of open net it does today. The four-by-eight crease was much smaller than the six-foot-radius semicircle introduced to the NHL in 1987/88, and the safety of the goaltender did not have the priority it enjoys in today's game. The three goaltenders most commonly cited as the greatest ever—Glenn Hall, Jacques Plante and Terry Sawchuk—were synonymous with the era. But if goaltending's glory years are behind it, Hall, now the goaltending coach of the Calgary Flames, is not one to say so. "The position," he says, "has never been played better." ○

THE MASSIVELY CURVED STICK OF THE 1960S (THIS ONE WIELDED BY CURVE INNOVATOR STAN MIKITA) MADE THE GOALTENDER'S JOB EVEN MORE HELLISH, IF THAT WERE POSSIBLE. THIS SCYTHE TURNED THE SLAPSHOT INTO A FASTBALL THAT BEHAVED LIKE A KNUCKLEBALL.

| *WELCOME TO THE SHOOTING GALLERY*

KING OF PAIN

TERRY SAWCHUK EXEMPLIFIED THE DARKER ELEMENTS THAT MAKE FOR GREAT GOALTENDING

WHEN GOALTENDERS ARE ASKED TO NAME THE GREATEST PLAYER AT THEIR POSITION, EVER, THEIR OPINIONS ARE INEVITABLY SHAPED BY THE PARTICULAR ERAS IN WHICH THEY PLAYED. TERRY

Sawchuk is one exception who manages to rise above all eras. On January 28, 1952, Frank Boucher, who had played against the likes of Georges Vezina and gone on to coach and manage in the era of Frank Brimsek, Bill Durnan and Chuck Rayner, dispensed with all equivocation. "Terry Sawchuk is the greatest goalie in the history of league hockey," he pronounced.

On paper, Sawchuk's career was not distinguished with quite the same superlatives as his fellow Original Sixers Jacques Plante and Glenn Hall. In his first five full NHL seasons, during which Boucher made his pronouncement, he was sensational, earning an All Star berth in every one of them. He was the first goaltender since Brimsek both to win the Calder and to land on the first All Star team in his rookie season. He also won three Vezinas in five seasons, being edged out by a single goal in the other two. But the last fifteen seasons of his career were a constant struggle to reaffirm his greatness. In the end, he died tragically, broken by life and by the game, a sobering example of the burden an overwhelming talent can place on a player's shoulders, and also of the darker elements that can make for great goaltending.

Born in 1929 in Winnipeg, Sawchuk was raised in the north end neighbourhood of Morse Place, excelling on both the rink and the ball diamond. He was such a good baseball player that he would attract tryout offers from the St. Louis Cardinals and the Pittsburgh Pirates. One of his opponents in minor league hockey in Winnipeg was Don Rope, who went on to play hockey for Canada in two Olympics. "When Terry's team was well ahead in the second period," says Rope, "he'd take his goal pads off, leave on his goal skates and play defence. That amazed me, that he could play with those skates on."

His talent was apparent so early that

he scarcely had a chance to have an amateur career. Professional hockey was desperate for new recruits at the end of the Second World War, and Sawchuk was swept up in one of the successive waves of Canadian teenagers who turned professional at the time. Detroit already had its eye on him when he was twelve. At fifteen he was playing Junior hockey for the Winnipeg Rangers. His professional rights were secured by Detroit, and he was transferred to Galt in the Junior A OHA. Detroit then moved him to the Windsor Junior Spitfires, but the season had just begun when the Red Wings signed the seventeen-year-old to a professional contract and shipped him to Omaha of the U.S. League, a midwestern loop, in 1947.

After winning rookie of the year honours in the U.S. League, he moved up a notch to the Indianapolis Capitals of the American League, where he won his second straight rookie of the year award in 1948/49. "Sawchuk displayed remarkable fortitude during the late stages of the season, playing his position although suffering painful injuries, which only forced him to miss one game," noted the league's 1949/50 statistical "red book" of his rookie-season performance. In Omaha, he had nearly had his career ended by a three-stitch cut to his eye. There would be no shortage of injuries over the remainder of his career. A bad fracture in his right arm, suffered as a kid playing football, necessitated three operations and caused the arm to heal two inches shorter than the left one, and his elbow would be a ceaseless source of bone chips—about sixty in all (some twenty of which Sawchuk collected in a jar and displayed on his mantel).

Sawchuk would experience a punctured lung in a car accident in 1954, torn tendons in his hand, an emergency appendectomy, ruptured spinal discs and a wide assortment of facial cuts. In 1966, *Life* magazine published a photo of Sawchuk with his face a mass of scars, most of them convincingly added by a makeup artist to illustrate what Sawchuk would look like if he hadn't followed Jacques Plante's lead and started to wear a mask. But Sawchuk's scars ran much deeper than those an artist could apply. He was plagued by injuries, but also defined by them. Privately, some goaltenders feel that pain was not simply a consequence of the job for Sawchuk, but actually *was* the job. He felt it, and in some terrible symbiosis, embraced it in a way that no goaltender had since Roy Worters. The essential darkness of his career was foreshadowed by the death from heart failure of his seventeen-year-old brother Mike when Terry was just ten. Sawchuk inherited his goaltending equipment, and so set forth on his career in a dead man's armour.

He was called up for seven games by Detroit in 1949/50, when Harry Lumley sprained his ankle. The Red Wings won the Stanley Cup on their third successive attempt that spring with Lumley, but Sawchuk was so startling a young talent that Detroit general manager Jack Adams dealt away Lumley to Chicago while he was still hot to make room for Sawchuk. A few months shy of his twenty-first birthday, Sawchuk had a starting job in the NHL.

In his third professional league, Sawchuk won yet another rookie of the year trophy, led the league with eleven shutouts, produced a GA of 1.99, one goal shy of the Vezina, and made the first All Star team. The next season, Sawchuk played a central role as Detroit capped its fourth straight regular-season title by sweeping Montreal in four games in the cup final. The Red Wings didn't lose one playoff game, and in his eight appearances, Sawchuk allowed only five goals. His 1.90 GA for the season brought him the Vezina and a return to the first All Star team.

In 1951/52, "Boom Boom" Geoffrion was rookie of the year as he brought the slapshot into the postwar game. Sawchuk's unorthodox style—the "gorilla crouch" that saw him compress his body so that his face was well down below the crossbar—allowed him to keep his eye on incoming pucks, but in the new era of the slapshot and aggressive screening of the goaltender, the technique took extraordinary nerve.

Detroit won yet another season title in 1952/53; Sawchuk, with his 1.90 GA, picked up another Vezina and still another first-team All Star appearance. But in only his third season, the game was taking its toll. A big man, he had ballooned to nearly 230 pounds in Omaha, and at training camp in 1951/52 weighed in at 220. He'd gotten down to 195 that season, and in 1952/53 he resolved to lose weight again. He shed it at an alarming rate, dropping below 170. Gaunt and temperamental, Sawchuk

made the second All Star team, missed the Vezina by one goal again and saw the team through to another Stanley Cup victory.

In 1954/55, Sawchuk made another second-team appearance, earned his third Vezina and helped Detroit win another Stanley Cup in a seven-game final against Montreal. But the greatest goaltender ever was coming apart. After surrendering eight goals to the Bruins in February 1955, the worst performance of his career, the Red Wings gave him a holiday to pull himself together. While Sawchuk was recuperating, Detroit brought in prospect Glenn Hall. Hall was so good that Detroit viewed Sawchuk as another Lumley: still a hot property who should be traded to make way for fresh talent. The Bruins, in the market for a goaltender, negotiated with Detroit for one, thinking the tight-lipped Adams was prepared to deal Hall. They were amazed when it turned out to be Sawchuk, who was part of a record nine-player swap between the two clubs.

It was a professional and personal catastrophe for Sawchuk. The Bruins were entering some lean seasons, winning only twenty-three of seventy games in 1954/55 and 1955/56. In 1955/56, Sawchuk's first season in Boston, the Bruins missed the playoffs and for the second straight season didn't put a single player in the top-ten scorers' list. Things actually went well for Sawchuk in 1955/56, as he played sixty-eight games and recorded a reasonable GA of 2.66, with nine shutouts, but it was his first full NHL season in which his GA wasn't below 2.00.

In his second Boston season, Sawchuk tired visibly. In December, he was diagnosed with mononucleosis and hospitalised for two weeks. When it came time to return to play, he couldn't find his form and withdrew into a shell, saying he was quitting the game. His own physician declared he was "on the verge of a complete nervous breakdown." Boston GM Milt Schmidt suspended him

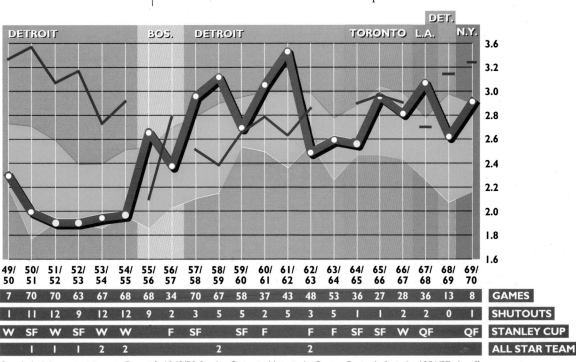

	49/50	50/51	51/52	52/53	53/54	54/55	55/56	56/57	57/58	58/59	59/60	60/61	61/62	62/63	63/64	64/65	65/66	66/67	67/68	68/69	69/70	
GAMES	7	70	70	63	67	68	68	34	70	67	58	37	43	48	53	36	27	28	36	13	8	
SHUTOUTS	I	II	12	9	12	12	9	2	3	5	5	2	5	3	5	I	I	2	2	0	I	
STANLEY CUP	W	SF	W	SF	W	W		F	SF		SF	F		F	F	SF	SF	W	QF		QF	
ALL STAR TEAM		I	I	I	2	2			2			2										

Sawchuk did not participate in Detroit's 1949/50 Stanley Cup win. He quit the Boston Bruins before the 1956/57 playoffs.

could be close to his wife and children again. He got his way. Detroit sold Hall to Chicago and brought Sawchuk home. In 1959, Sawchuk became an American citizen.

Sawchuk never completely recovered from his purgatory in Boston. He always seemed frailer than he had before mononucleosis had sidelined him; he was certainly leaner, and his accumulating injuries did not help. Nor would he ever again post the kind of save statistics that had distinguished his first five seasons in Detroit. As well, the Red Wings he returned to were not the Red Wings of the early 1950s. In his first season back, Detroit finished third overall and were swept by Montreal in the semifinal. The team finished last in 1958/59, missed the playoffs again in 1961/62 and finished fourth in the intervening seasons. Gone were the days when Sawchuk could record a season GA below 2.00. For two seasons in fact, it rose above 3.00.

But Sawchuk was not finished. He was still capable of a game-saving performance, and his decision to follow Jacques Plante's lead and begin wearing a mask in games (he'd been wearing one in practice for several seasons) in 1962/63 gave him renewed confidence. The Red Wings made it to the Stanley Cup finals in 1962/63 and 1963/64; his 1962/63 season was as good as any he had experienced in nearly a decade as he made the second All Star team.

In December 1963, Sawchuk followed up an early-season slump with a bout of back trouble. The Red Wings tried out a new goaltender, Roger Crozier,

indefinitely after he failed to show up for a practice, but showed sympathy by allowing that Sawchuk's mental health problems, if legitimate, would give him an out.

Sawchuk fled back to the Detroit suburb of Union Lake, where his American wife, Patricia, and children lived. He was so upset by his treatment in the Boston press that he threatened to file lawsuits. Patricia also filed for divorce. Sawchuk was able to patch up the marriage, and asked that he be traded back to Detroit so that he

for fifteen games, and while his GA was 3.40, compared to the 2.60 of Sawchuk, the twenty-two-year-old Crozier was the franchise's future. At the end of the season, Detroit elected to leave the thirty-five-year-old Sawchuk off its protected list. Punch Imlach snapped him up and made him a Maple Leaf.

Imlach already had one veteran goaltender, Johnny Bower, on the roster, and even though the league did not require teams to employ two goaltenders in the regular season, Imlach had found success using Don Simmons to relieve Bower for fifty-eight games over the previous three seasons. With the thirty-five-year-old Sawchuk and the forty-year-old Bower, Imlach now had two star veterans who could relieve each other. They ended up splitting the season almost exactly down the middle, and together they won the Vezina.

Sawchuk and Bower were very different goaltenders. Sawchuk was a bigger, rangier man. Bower was a practice goaltender—he worked hard when a game wasn't on the line, which is what Punch Imlach liked to see in any player. Sawchuk wanted nothing to do with the puck when the shooting didn't count. A dozen shots would constitute a pregame warmup for him. His mechanics were always fundamentally there. What mattered was whether or not Sawchuk, on that night against that team, was prepared to make the sacrifices one of his great performances demanded. Sawchuk had been hurt badly time and again, and seemed to understand that pain, or the willingness to experience pain, was an inextricable part of his game. He didn't need someone shooting at him to figure out if he could stop a game full of pucks. He just had to decide he was prepared to stop the ones ahead of him that night in any way possible. His donning of the mask, long before contemporaries like Bower, Worsley and Hall joined him in following Plante's lead, was his one significant concession to his own well-being.

In 1966/67, Sawchuk was at the heart of the Leafs' return to Stanley Cup glory. The team, overwhelmingly staffed by veterans, finished third overall, with nine fewer wins and sixty fewer total goals than the Blackhawks, who set a league scoring record. But in their semifinal series, the big guns of Chicago, with their menacing slapshots propelled by sticks curved like scythes, could not put enough pucks past Bower and Sawchuk, whose finest moment came in game five, with the series tied two-up. Bower played the first period, but Sawchuk took over in the second. Despite firing forty-nine shots at him over the final two periods, the Blackhawks could not score on him and lost 4–2.

"I'd never had any trouble scoring against Sawchuk, ever, while he was with Detroit," Bobby Hull recalled for writer D'Arcy Jenish. "We started the period on a power play and I drilled a shot that hit him in the shoulder, and he lay on the ice for about fifteen minutes. He got up and he was as loose as a goose. I had eleven shots on him and couldn't put a pea past him. I broke the handle of his stick twice. He was laying prone on the ice, and I fired one upstairs. He threw his leg up, and I stuck the puck right on the end of his skate. He just played fantastic." The win broke the back of the Blackhawks, and Toronto went on to meet Montreal in the final.

Sawchuk started the opening game and bore the brunt of a 6–0 loss. Imlach switched to Bower, who helped them take the series lead. When Bower strained a muscle warming up for game four, Sawchuk stepped in, and surrendered another six goals as Montreal tied the series. But Imlach stuck with Sawchuk, and gave him the assignment for game five in Montreal. It was the right

decision: Toronto won 4–1, and returned home to win the last Stanley Cup of the Original Six era with Sawchuk backstopping a 3–1 win. Sawchuk had just won his first Stanley Cup in twelve seasons. In voting for the Conn Smythe Trophy, awarded to the most valuable player of the playoffs, he was edged out by Dave Keon, but Leaf management awarded him its J.P. Bickell Trophy as the team's top player. In the dressing room after the victory, he announced that he didn't care if he never played another game. "I'm going to leave it in good style," he decided.

The Leafs had been able to win because Sawchuk, particularly against Chicago, had been willing to go out and inflict on himself whatever harm was necessary. His capacity for the physical abuse that came with the position seemed infinite, but it wasn't. He might not have cared to play another game after the 1966/67 Stanley Cup, but he tried to, and there was no glory in it.

His life rapidly unravelled. In the expansion draft he was picked up by Los Angeles, whose coach, Red Kelly, had been on the ice with Sawchuk the previous spring in the Leaf cup victory. In a game against the Blackhawks in the dreaded Chicago Stadium, a shot by Pit Martin hit him in the mask so hard that both of his eyes closed up with the swelling. His old team, Detroit, retrieved him for 1968/69, but he only saw action in thirteen games.

When the pain was no longer delivered by the game, it was as if Sawchuk had to inflict the pain upon himself. The Rangers signed him on for 1969/70, but by then Sawchuk was battling the bottle and was deeply despondent, separated from his wife, cut off from his seven children. At the end of the season, in which he played only eight games, he brought the roof down on himself. Sawchuk had been sharing a rented house on Long Island with teammate Ron Stewart, and they fell into an argument about money owed on the rent and Sawchuk's lack of enthusiasm for cleaning the place up before they vacated it. Sawchuk attacked Stewart, at first outside a neighbourhood bar, again on the lawn of the house. In the confused scuffle, Sawchuk injured himself falling on either Stewart's knee or a barbecue. He was rushed to hospital, where his gall bladder was removed, but a lacerated liver meant two more trips into the operating room. After a month in hospital, Sawchuk died. A formal investigation was held into Stewart's role, but Sawchuk had completely exonerated him while in hospital, blaming himself entirely.

He was forty years old and had played 63,496 minutes of regular-season and playoff hockey in the NHL and allowed 2,668 goals. He had played in eleven All Star games, second only to Glenn Hall's thirteen appearances. He had 103 shutouts, nine more than George Hainsworth. He had appeared in the most regular-season games of any goaltender—971, 65 more than Glenn Hall. And he had 435 wins. Jacques Plante would fall short of tying his mark by one win.

Sawchuk had the swiftest election to the Hockey Hall of Fame of any player. He was enshrined the year after his death. ○

"MR. GOALIE"

GLENN HALL: THE GOALTENDER WHO "DOES IT ALL"

PERHAPS NO GOALTENDER HAS HAD SO LASTING AN EFFECT ON HIS PROFESSION AS GLENN HALL. WHEN YOU WATCH ALMOST ANY STAR GOALTENDER TODAY, BE HE ED

HALL CAME OUT OF HUMBOLDT, SASKATCHEWAN, TO PLAY FOR THE WINDSOR SPITFIRES, THE RED WINGS' JUNIOR AFFILIATE ACROSS THE DETROIT RIVER.

Belfour or Felix Potvin, you are watching someone whose technical skills descend in a straight line from Hall's revolutionary butterfly style. If their puck-handling, particularly with their stick, is noteworthy, there, too, they owe a debt to Hall. And if they show daring in their pere-grinations from the crease, and skill in their skating, Hall is in them there, too. Most important, if they approach their profession methodically, with the most careful preparation, they should know that Hall was there before them, as prepared as anyone for the job at hand.

Hall did not have an exclusive claim to goaltending's fundamentals, but he embodied all of them in a way that few practitioners ever have. His monicker "Mr. Goalie" was entirely deserved. Glenn Hall was everything a great goaltender was supposed to be.

His greatness was impressively consistent. He won the Calder and made the second All Star team when he played his first full NHL season in 1955/56; thirteen seasons later, in 1968/69, he won his third Vezina and made the first All Star team, his eleventh such appearance. And in his final season, 1970/71, he was still at the top of the class, capable, if he had been so inclined, to go right on playing and winning.

Born in Humboldt, Saskatchewan, in 1931, Hall came from a corner of Canada that produced a bumper crop of hockey players in general and goaltenders in particular. The province had produced Johnny Bower in 1924, Emile Francis and Al Rollins in 1926, and Chuck Rayner in 1920. It was Rayner who made a lasting impression upon him when Hall visited the goaltending camp Rayner and his business and netminding partner, Jim Henry, ran out of their fishing camp, Hockey Haven, on Lake of the Woods in northwestern Ontario

in the late 1940s. Today Hall ranks Rayner second to Terry Sawchuk in all-time goaltending talent. Hall was playing Junior hockey in Windsor, Ontario, at the time, and made the trip to Hockey Haven in the company of another young goalkeeper, Bill Tibbs. "The goalkeepers were more of a fraternity then," Hall says. "We drove up, and they were just really, really nice to us."

There was less emphasis in that encounter with · Rayner and Henry on particular tricks of the trade than on a general approach to the profession. Rayner was famous with the Rangers for his aggressive approach to the game, which was anchored in his skating and stick skills. These would become fundamental skills for Hall as well. "If you can't skate, you're not going to be a very good goalkeeper," he maintains. "If you can skate, you can adapt to the conditions thrown at you." And as the slapshot came to the fore, skating skill became an essential part of the goaltender's ability to adjust his style to the radically altered offensive strategies and the pressures they placed on him. Puck-handling with the stick also became critical. "I remember how strong Charlie Rayner was with the stick. I didn't really learn to use the stick until I was thirty years old, partly because I wasn't strong enough.

"When I'm talking to young players," Hall adds, "the first things I stress are skating and effort. In the old days, the expression was: Don't think, because you'll weaken the club. Do everything that's automatic. It's about preparation, getting the mind set properly. I don't particularly care for kids coming to the rink and saying, 'I hope I play well.' They should be saying, 'I *should* play well. I've practised well, I know the opposition, I'm in good shape, I've looked after myself, I've eaten properly.' It's no guarantee that you *will* play well, but at least you're prepared."

"Glenn took the job really seriously," says Dave Dryden, who was Hall's backup in Chicago in the 1960s before Dryden became a regular starter with the expansion Buffalo Sabres. "Some of the ways goaltenders took it seriously destroyed them. Glenn's way was to be well rested and prepared and to look after himself."

Hall began his professional career in 1951 with the American League's Indianapolis Capitals, a troubled outfit embarking on its final season. He then moved for three seasons to the Edmonton Flyers of the Western Hockey League, a very good tier-two loop that emerged after the Second World War. The team boasted an exceptionally talented lineup of future NHL stars, including Hall, Johnny Bucyk, Vic Stasiuk and Norm Ullman. He saw minimal action with the NHL team that owned his rights, the Red Wings, coming up for six games in 1952/53 and two games in 1954/55. In those years, Detroit had Sawchuk, who had also played Junior hockey briefly in Windsor. But Detroit was burning out Sawchuk, who had entered the NHL in 1949, and traded him to Boston in 1955 in a four-for-five swap that helped overhaul the lineup that had just won Detroit the Stanley Cup. Sawchuk was the cornerstone of the deal, having just won his third Vezina in four seasons. With Sawchuk out of the way, Hall came up to the big league.

He had a superb rookie season in 1955/56, winning the Calder and making the second All Star team as he played all seventy games for Detroit and recorded twelve shutouts and a GA of 2.11. Detroit made it to the cup final again, but the Canadiens, with the new Vezina winner, Jacques Plante, in net, took the series in five games. Montreal would win five straight cups, and Plante five straight Vezinas.

Hall took his place in the elite ranks of goaltending as the slapshot was completely overhauling traditional notions about offence, and with it defence. "The game changed," says Hall. "You were looking at more screens, and then I got into the butterfly kind of by accident."

The butterfly style, pioneered by Hall while in Detroit, did not immediately supplant more traditional goaltending techniques, but it took hold with the next generation of players, in particular Tony Esposito, and is the essential inspiration for the inverted-V style and outright butterfly of today's goaltenders. It was widely disparaged because it broke— or seemed to break—two sacred tenets of goaltending: you stayed on your feet, and your kept your legs together. But notwithstanding the rules on how goaltenders were supposed to play, the fact was that so-called standup goaltenders often found themselves on the ice, as any survey of game photos will reveal. And they often had their legs apart. With the butterfly, the lanky Hall, who was six feet tall and weighed about 160 pounds, had his feet widely spaced, but his knees close together with the pads backstopping the stick.

"People talk about the drop shot going between the legs," says Hall. "Well, any shot is capable of going between the legs. You had to play with your legs a little wider to pick up post shots. When you were playing with your legs wider apart, you were vulnerable to the 'five hole.' I found that with the legs open I

wasn't strong enough to stop the puck with the stick. If I did the butterfly, I could get the stick back to the pads." That, and his hands, took care of the five hole. And when he dropped to the ice, Hall kept his knees together and splayed his legs to either side, creating a leather wall ten inches high across the goal.

But it was still seen as falling to the ice, which grated on purists. "A lot of people call it going down, but it's not," he insists. "Your body is still erect." It's hard to argue with Hall. When traditional standup goaltenders went down, they tended to look completely helpless— lying on their stomachs, their sides, their backs, limbs flailing. Hall was still upright from the knees up, on the job, able to get back to his feet again quickly.

Hall lasted only two seasons in Detroit, despite being an All Star in both seasons. When an effort to form a league players' association was crushed in 1957, most vigorously by Jack Adams in Detroit, several organizers were banished to the Chicago Blackhawks, among them Ted Lindsay and Hall of the Red Wings in a six-player deal. In getting rid of Hall, Adams brought Sawchuk back from Boston. But Dryden suspected that the butterfly style, as much as any labour organizing, was behind Hall's trade. "I always thought that Glenn must have had some real run-ins in Detroit with the way he played. He had just started to use the butterfly style, and I had the feeling, from the way we talked, that Detroit management didn't think that was the way you played the game. But it's the enduring style. Glenn was right on so many blessed things. He was the best that I ever saw play. There's no question. He always seemed kind of tragic because he didn't get the recognition he should have had."

He came to play in one of hockey's truly unique environments: the cramped confines of Chicago

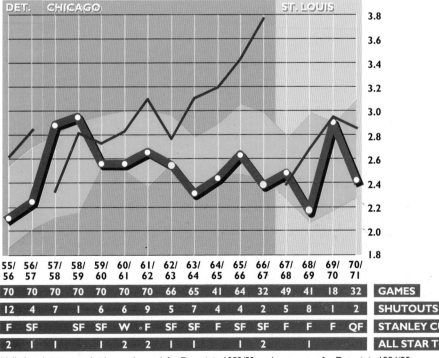

	55/56	56/57	57/58	58/59	59/60	60/61	61/62	62/63	63/64	64/65	65/66	66/67	67/68	68/69	69/70	70/71	
	70	70	70	70	70	70	70	66	65	41	64	32	49	41	18	32	GAMES
	12	4	7	1	6	6	9	5	7	4	4	2	5	8	1	2	SHUTOUTS
	F	SF		SF	SF	W	⋄F	SF	SF	F	SF	SF	F	F	F	QF	STANLEY CUP
	2	1	1		1	2	2	1	1		1	2		1			ALL STAR TEAM

Hall played six games (with one shutout) for Detroit in 1952/53, and two games for Detroit in 1954/55.

Stadium, its ice surface fifteen feet shorter than the standard rink and with peculiar corners that seemed to funnel the play right into the goaltender's face. The ice was also some of the worst in the league. "We had terrible ice in Chicago," Hall says. "They used to flood it with a hose, and any time you flooded with a hose it would chip out."

When Stan Mikita and Bobby Hull developed the curved stick in the early 1960s and created with it a terrifying slapshot, a Blackhawks game became the most feared stop on a visiting goaltender's road trip. They came down with what became known as the "Chicago flu," begging off sick out of the numbing dread of the shots that awaited them in that raucous shooting gallery. Cesare

HALL'S BUTTERFLY STANCE HAS PROVEN TO BE GOALTENDING'S ENDURING STYLE. HE DEVELOPED IT WHILE IN DETROIT, AND WON A STANLEY CUP, THREE VEZINAS AND A CONN SMYTHE WITH IT WHILE IN CHICAGO AND ST. LOUIS.

Maniago, who had a crouch as compressed as any goaltender, seemed to grow to his full height of six-three as Hull's missiles, clocked as fast as 118.3 miles an hour, compelled him to straighten up and get his head out of the way.

"One of the frustrations Glenn had was that he liked to work hard, practise hard," says Dryden. "But the way things were set up in Chicago when he was there, and the way the game was going with the curved stick and everything else, it simply wasn't *safe* for a goaltender to practise hard. He got into that fix of: Shoot, I want to practise hard, but I can't, so I don't feel good about that. He did things like standing over in the corner of the rink while guys were on line rushes, and then the guys would drill shots at him in the corner. He'd get so bloody upset, and they'd say, 'Come on, Glenn, work hard.' And he'd say, 'I want to work hard, but the drills are going to kill me.' And he was exactly right. Billy Reay, the coach, convinced him he didn't need to work in practice. Glenn would go out and skate hard and do some things, but then he would get off the ice fast. And I think that worked."

Hall became a netminding ironman, playing 502 consecutive league games from 1955/56 through 1961/62, and in his first seven seasons in Chicago he made the All Star team six times. It was in the 1960/61 playoffs that Hall and the Blackhawks reached sporting nirvana. The third-place Blackhawks met in the semifinal the first-place Canadiens, who had won five straight Stanley Cups and been in the final for eleven consecutive seasons. The Blackhawks hadn't made it to a Stanley Cup final in seventeen seasons, but in game five in Montreal, with the series tied 2–2, they took a tantalizing step closer when Hall shut out the Canadiens 3–0. When the two teams came back to Chicago for game six, 20,000 delirious Blackhawks fans were waiting. When the announcer introduced Hall as "Mr. Goalie," the roof of Chicago Stadium almost caved in. He lived up to his new handle, shutting out Montreal 3–0 for the second straight game and sending the Blackhawks into the final against Detroit. The Blackhawks took the cup, their first since 1937/38, in six games.

The 'Hawks could not bring home another cup, despite the continued presence of stars like Hall, Hull and Mikita, and lost to Toronto in their defending bid of 1961/62. In 1962/63, Hall won his first Vezina. But Hall never placed much importance on raw numbers as a measure of skill. "In those days you could lose 4–2 and still have a good game. Maybe even more so now, they look at the score to see if the goalkeeper played well. But this isn't anywhere close to assessing the situation. I did assess each goal, but I'd say, Could *we* have stopped it?" To Hall, and to many goaltenders, keeping the puck out of the net was a team responsibility, and Dave Dryden says

Hall had a remarkable ability to recall where everyone was on the ice on a particular goal.

After his invention of the butterfly, Hall is probably best known as the goaltender who threw up before every game, even between periods. It has helped create a picture of Hall as a cowering victim, a man terrified by his chosen profession. But Dryden, who roomed with Hall as well as backing him up, says this has been exaggerated. It didn't happen every game, and Hall never played like an intimidated man. Certainly if Hall had any reason to dread his performances, it was because he was so determined to get in the way of the puck. "I felt more comfortable after the game than before the game," Hall says. "After the game, I was whistling and happy. Before the game, I was hyper as hell. I couldn't wait for them to drop the puck. Let's *go*. And the better the team you played against, the more you were going to be like this."

"We roomed together and used to sleep like crazy after a game," Dryden recalls, "but sometimes after a game Billy Hay, who was a good friend of Glenn's, would come up to the room, too. They'd sit and talk and maybe have a beer. Then Glenn started bringing encyclopedias along with him. I'd say, 'What are you reading?' And he'd say, 'Tonight, I've got "A." ' And the next trip he'd bring 'B.' He got such delight out of it. He'd say, 'Do you realize such-and-such is the case? It's right here on page 36.' When I idolized him like I did, I didn't expect that from him. I had imagined this real hardened guy with no sense of humour. But he was just terrific."

In 1966/67, Hall combined with Denis DeJordy to win his second Vezina. By now Hall was routinely retiring at the end of every season, only to be lured back by larger contracts. In 1967/68, the new St. Louis Blues franchise picked him up in the expansion draft. The league was split into two six-team divisions, with the Original Six teams in one and the expansion clubs in the other. The champions of both divisions met in the Stanley Cup final, and the Blues weren't given much of a chance against the Canadiens in the 1967/68 cup. But Hall made a series of it. Although Montreal won in four straight, every game was decided by a single goal, and two ended in overtime. Hall became the second goal-

tender (after Roger Crozier in 1965/66) on the losing team to win the Conn Smythe.

The next season, the Blues brought on board the veteran Jacques Plante to tag-team with Hall. With a combined GA of 2.07, they became the first expansion-club goaltenders to win the Vezina, and Hall was named to the first All Star team. The Blues again met Montreal in the cup final, but this time the Canadiens made a more convincing four-game sweep. The Blues and Hall were back for a third cup appearance in 1969/70, this time to be swept in four by the Bruins.

Hall turned thirty-nine at the beginning of the 1970/71 season. As far as Gerry Cheevers was concerned, Hall was still the best of their breed. "Glenn Hall does it all," effused the man who had been in the net for Boston when the Bruins defeated Hall's Blues in the 1969/70 cup. Hall played thirty-two games and decided that this was, absolutely, his final tour of duty. He retired to his farm in Stony Plain, Alberta, and continued to be active in the game as a coach. In sixteen NHL seasons, he'd been an All Star eleven times. Four years after retiring, Mr. Goalie was in the Hall of Fame. ○

HALL WAS A GOALTENDING IRONMAN, LOGGING 502 CONSECUTIVE GAMES AS A BLACKHAWK.

MASKED MARVEL

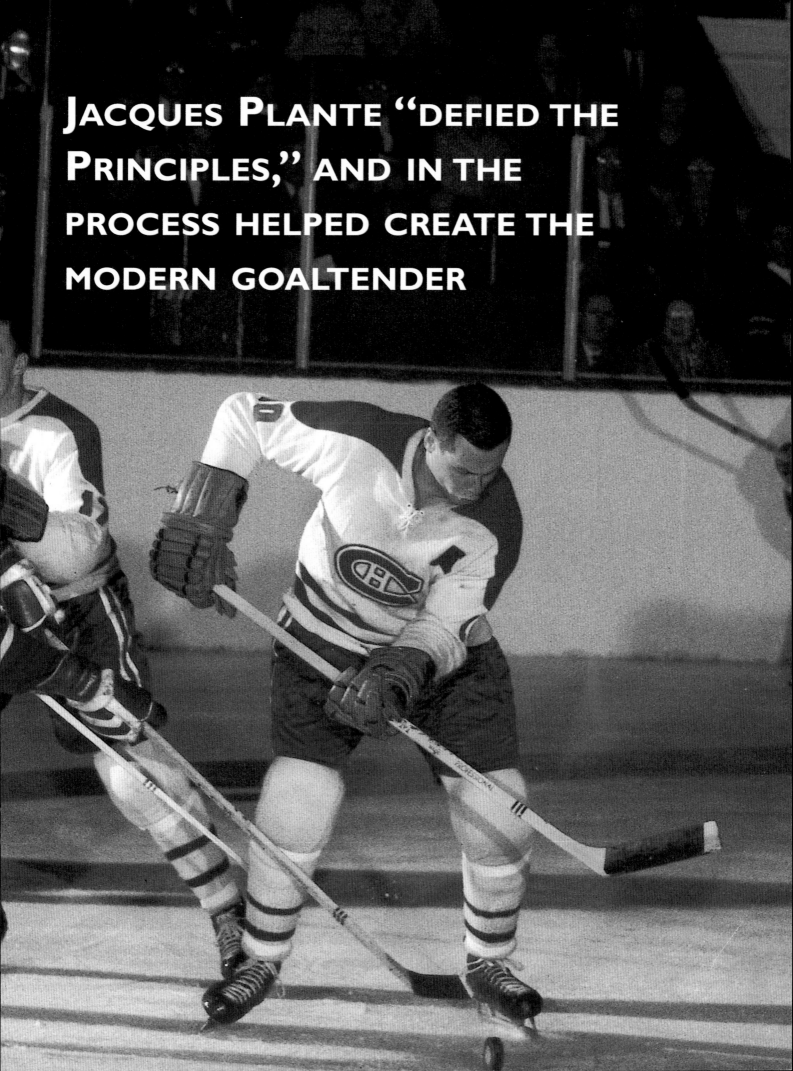

JACQUES PLANTE "DEFIED THE PRINCIPLES," AND IN THE PROCESS HELPED CREATE THE MODERN GOALTENDER

He MAY OR MAY NOT HAVE BEEN THE ALL-TIME GREAT AT HIS POSITION, BUT JACQUES PLANTE ENDURES AS A DOMINANT IMAGE OF THE *CHARACTER* OF

the goaltender: eccentric, daring and marked by violence. His "firsts" are not necessarily firsts at all. He is routinely praised as the first goaltender to have wandered from the goal, but Chuck Rayner was doing just that, and just as spectacularly, in New York a half-dozen seasons before Plante arrived in the league. Credited with being the first goaltender to wear a mask, he was beaten by twenty-nine seasons to the distinction by Clint Benedict of the old Montreal Maroons. But bragging rights notwithstanding, Jacques Plante's accomplishments were indisputable landmarks in the postwar game. And he gave them more cachet by winning, and winning. Ultimately, he became as famous within the goaltending fraternity for what he did wrong as for what he did right. During his career, he committed several cardinal sins against the most treasured tenets of the brotherhood, but in the process he helped reshape the goaltending art. Even when he was wrong, Jacques Plante was very often right.

Plante was born at Mont Carmel, Quebec, a small town near the south shore of the St. Lawrence about eighty miles northeast of Quebec City, on January 17, 1929. His birth came in the middle of the last season of record-low GAs in the NHL—George Hainsworth won the Vezina that year with a GA of 0.98. For much of Plante's youth, the NHL franchises of Montreal produced lame teams, the Canadiens limping through the Depression and scarcely surviving the financial strains that claimed the Maroons in 1938. For his part, Plante was growing up in a family of eleven children in Shawinigan Falls (a town just north of Trois-Rivières), helping make ends meet by taking home fifty cents a game with a factory team in 1944/45 at the age of fifteen and pitching in with the knitting piecework of his mother. When he continued to knit to relax as a professional hockey player, his eccentricity was firmly established.

After playing Junior hockey in Quebec City, he turned pro in 1951 with the ostensibly amateur Quebec Senior league, minding net for the Canadiens farm team, the Montreal Royals. The Canadiens had begun to emerge as a league powerhouse, thanks to the brilliance of Bill Durnan's netminding and the ferocious genius of

scorers like Rocket Richard. When Plante joined the Royals, the Canadiens had just lost the Stanley Cup final to the Maple Leafs in a series that ended in overtime in all five games. The Canadiens goaltender was Gerry McNeil, who had replaced an emotionally drained Bill Durnan in the middle of the 1949/50 semifinal.

Plante had his first taste of the NHL in 1952/53, appearing in three games on a call-up from the Buffalo Bisons of the American League. At twenty-four, he was clearly ready for the top-flight professional league, allowing only four goals in his three games for a GA of 1.33. The Canadiens starter was McNeil, who was named the second-team All Star, but in the playoffs history repeated itself. Just as Durnan had gone to coach Dick Irvin during the 1949/50 semifinal against New York, asking to be replaced by McNeil, in the 1952/53 playoffs McNeil asked Irvin to play the rookie Plante during the semifinal against Chicago. Montreal was trailing Chicago 3–2 in games, and Plante delivered them the series by allowing only one goal over the deciding two games.

In the final, Plante enjoyed a 4–2 victory over Boston in the opening game. He unleashed a dose of egotism that would become routine over the next two decades, and therein committed his first sin: talking down a fraternity brother. "They had twenty-seven breakaways on me in Buffalo this season before they scored on me," he boasted. "Gerry is a great goaltender but he's so small that he has to move twice as fast as me to cover the same area."

The Bruins cut Plante down to size in the next game, winning 4–1, and Irvin decided to go back to McNeil, who had regained his nerve. With both McNeil and Sugar Jim Henry of Boston playing on broken ankles deadened by freezing, a heroic duel unfolded, with McNeil prevailing in all three games to deliver Montreal the cup it had been chasing since last winning in 1945/46.

McNeil played on for one more full season, with Plante relieving him for seventeen games. In the playoffs, Irvin chose McNeil over Plante, and when McNeil lost the seventh game of the Stanley Cup to Detroit in Olympia Stadium in 1954, it seemed to be time for him to hang up the pads. Plante had recorded a GA of 1.59

that season, well below the 1.86 that won Toronto's Harry Lumley the Vezina, and in 1954/55 he took over the Canadiens' starting assignment. McNeil retired to run a gas station, coming back in 1956/57 to relieve Plante for nine games.

McNeil was brooding and self-critical, and would take the game home with him. Plante could be self-confident to the point of arrogance. "He was a guy who was always right," says McNeil. "A goal was never his fault—it was the defenceman's fault. It was a great way to go to sleep. I was the opposite. I would figure if I did it this way or that way, I could have stopped it."

Plante took over the Canadiens job just as Montreal embarked on a lengthy domination of the NHL. They won five straight Stanley Cups between 1955/56 and 1959/60, and Plante collected five straight Vezinas to go with them, then added a sixth in 1961/62. Along the way, Plante made six All Star appearances, three of them on the first team. The Canadiens' offensive power and Plante's netminding skill produced one of the most daunting scoring advantages in league history. Their most impressive seasons were 1957/58 and 1958/59, when Plante's Vezina-winning average was about 0.7 below LGA, and Montreal's goals production, combined with Plante's performances, gave them a net margin of about 1.5 between the number of goals per game the team typically scored and the number of goals Plante typically allowed. For a half-decade, the Canadiens offence and Plante delivered a one-two punch not seen since Clint Benedict and the Ottawa Senators terrorised the league in the 1920s.

Dave Keon, who played with Plante at the end of the netminder's career, cites Plante's ability to maintain his focus as one of his great assets. "When he was playing with those great teams in Montreal, he was getting twelve to fifteen shots a game. That's one every four minutes. With a penalty, he'd get three or four of those in two minutes, so he sometimes went even longer between shots. His concentration was great, to be able to go that long between shots."

Plante's wandering from the goal area was his next sin. To McNeil's astonishment, he got away with it. "He would go after everything. He defied the principles. If I went out of the net, they got after me. With him, it was okay."

As noted, Chuck Rayner was known for it well before Plante, but Plante was doing it in Montreal on a wildly popular winning club, which gave his antics more publicity. He also added a new dimension to wandering by going behind the net to intercept dump-in shots that were wrapping around the boards. He said he got into the habit of chasing pucks behind the net on a lousy amateur club he'd once played for. Plante's peregrinations flew in the face of the way Canadiens coach Toe Blake believed the position should be played. But as long as Plante wasn't allowing bad goals while he was doing it, he was going to get away with it.

Plante was one of those goaltenders who understood that the best way to deal with the slapshot's long-range scoring threat was to come well out of the crease. This not only cut down on the angle, taking away net from the shooter—it also helped prevent injuries to the goaltender. Most slapshots rose higher the farther they went. If the goaltender hung back around his crease, he would have to deal with them at head level. If he came out from his crease and cut down the distance between himself and the shooter, the same puck would meet him at chest level. The technique spelled the difference not only between a goal and a save, but between a glove save and a trip to the infirmary.

One of his most dramatic techniques was "fielding" the blooper slapshot, a kind of fad shot that caught on for a time. A player would let a high, lazy one go from back at centre ice, deliberately making it bounce in front of the goaltender. The traditional netminder who stuck to the crease and tried to play the puck as it bounced often was beaten by it. Plante resolved to charge the incoming shot and trap it against the ice as it made its first bounce. His long, sliding saves were heartstopping, but effective.

He committed the next sin on November 1, 1959, when he left the ice of Madison Square Garden eight minutes into the first period to take seven stitches in a nasty cut to his nose and cheek, the souvenir of an Andy Bathgate backhand. Teams did not carry backup goaltenders at this time, and Plante delivered an ultimatum in the first aid room: he would only return to the ice if he could wear a face mask.

Plante had had one made out of fibreglass that conformed to the contours of his face at the beginning of the season. By then, he had been cut for 200 stitches, and had had his nose broken four times, his cheekbones twice and his skull once. Coach Toe Blake, however, had refused to let him wear it. Now, with no one else to turn to, Blake consented to have Plante return to the ice wearing his contraption. It was the first time a goaltender had been seen in a mask in the NHL since Clint Benedict had tried one unsuccessfully in February 1930.

The Canadiens won the game 3–1, and Plante continued to wear the mask, extending a seven-game unbeaten streak to eighteen games. In the eleven games of the streak in which he wore the mask, Plante was scored on only thirteen times.

Blake would continue to allow him to wear it, so long as he kept playing well. The mask found a permanent place in Plante's game. McNeil still marvels at Plante's ability to defy authority. "If I'd worn one," he says, "they would have sent me home."

Within the culture of professional hockey, which even frowned on helmets for skaters, the mask was slow to gain acceptance. Terry Sawchuk was a rare convert; otherwise the leading goaltenders of the day refused to wear one. Partly it was the machismo of the sport; partly it was the fact that goaltenders who tried one didn't like the way it restricted their vision. But ten years after Plante put his on, almost every goaltender in the game was wearing one.

Montreal's domination began to recede in the 1960s, as Chicago and then Toronto began to win Stanley Cups. Plante continued to shine. In 1961/62, he won his sixth Vezina and became the first goaltender to win the Hart (and the last to date) since Rayner in 1949/50. But Montreal, which had led the league in the regular season for the fifth straight time, was derailed by Glenn Hall and the Blackhawks in the semifinal. In the final two games of the series, Plante allowed six goals, Hall none. That season, Plante had been named to the first All Star team, ahead of Hall. But when the Chicago Stadium announcer introduced Hall as "Mr. Goalie" at the start of game six, it was the first hint that Plante's days at the top of the profession were coming to an end. After winning five straight Stanley Cups, he would not win another.

Plante had another outstanding season in 1962/63. While Montreal finished third overall and won only twenty-eight games, with Plante playing the bulk of the season the Canadiens allowed only five more goals than Chicago's Hall, who won the Vezina. Johnny Bower, whose Leafs allowed two more goals than the Blackhawks, anchored a five-game rout of the Canadiens by the Leafs in the semifinal. Montreal decided the time had come for a change. Plante was traded to New York for Gump Worsley.

Thereupon Plante committed his next sin: he quit while he was behind. After playing nine full seasons with the legendary Canadiens, Plante was suddenly toiling for a losing club. In his absence, Charlie Hodge, who had relieved Plante off and on since 1954/55, played sixty-two of seventy games for the Canadiens, registered a 2.26 GA, and won the Vezina. Plante's GA leapt nearly a full goal, to 3.38, as New York won only twenty-two games and missed the playoffs. In 1964/65, the Rangers missed the playoffs again, with Plante's GA stuck at 3.37, while in Montreal Gump Worsley, after ten ugly seasons in New York, finally discovered what it was like to win a Stanley Cup.

When Plante, humiliated by his demotion to Baltimore of the American League, quit to take a sales job with Molson's, he provided his critics with the necessary fodder to talk down his achievements. Maybe his two seasons in New York had been the real litmus test for him. Maybe he had logged all those Vezinas in Montreal because he had such a great team in front of him. Plante may not have been able to stand losing, but he was thirty-six, after all, and a more charitable response would be that, after all his successes, and all his stitches and fractures, he was entitled to pack his bags.

His retirement lasted three seasons. With expansion in 1967, the league turned into a seller's market for veteran players. The general manager of the new St. Louis Blues was Lynn Patrick, who had brought in Glenn Hall from Chicago in his opening season and now wanted Plante to share the next season with him. Patrick offered him $35,000 to come out of retirement in 1968/69. Plante left the beer business to join Hall for two seasons. They made it to two Stanley Cup finals, and in their first season together shared the Vezina with a 2.07 GA— Plante contributed a personal GA of 1.96.

Now over forty, Plante was enjoying a second coming as a goaltending wizard. Though his wanderings tended to get him the most notice, Plante was also one of the most technically excellent netminders. He played his angles as well as anyone else in the league, and his manual on goaltending basics was a bible for young netminders. He never left a shooter with much net to aim for, and that skill was still with him, nearly twenty years after playing in his first Stanley Cup.

The Maple Leafs acquired him for 1970/71, and he ended up staying for three seasons. He became a favourite of Toronto fans, who had become used to having battle-hardened netminders like Bower and Sawchuk keep their team in the game. But in Toronto, Plante allegedly committed his next sin: the word in the fraternity was that he messed with a brother to keep his GA looking handsome.

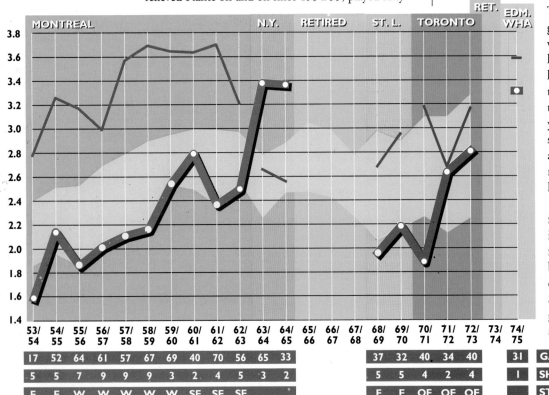

Plante played three games for Montreal in 1952/53. He played for Boston in the 1972/73 playoffs.

Goaltenders always say that numbers are no indication of quality, but at contract time GA is often the bottom line in negotiations with management. Plante knew how important GA could be to a goaltender's esteem (and to his market value) having won six Vezinas in seven seasons in Montreal. In Toronto, the fraternity openly suspected him of dickering with his playing schedule to his advantage, and at teammate Bruce Gamble's expense. "He picks the games where the Leafs have a good chance to win, playing at home against expansion teams," Gerry Cheevers said in 1971, adding that poor Gamble was left to deal with the tough road games.

"I don't know that he planned it that far ahead," Keon says, dismissing the idea that Plante might have sat down at the start of the season and crossed out the games he wouldn't play. But he does remember that when Bernie Parent was Plante's backup in Toronto, it was understood that Parent would play all the games in Chicago Stadium.

In his first tour of duty with Toronto, Plante played forty of eighty games, recorded four shutouts and allowed seventy-three goals for a GA of 1.88. The Vezina that season was won by Ed Giacomin and Gilles Villemure. Plante's performance landed him on the 1970/71 second All Star team. And while Cheevers might have thought Plante was finagling with his sched-

ule, he still had fulsome praise. "There's not a better mechanical goaltender in the game. You don't beat Plante with a fluky goal, you always beat him where you should beat a goaler—on the far side or wherever he gives you that inch of space."

Far from being an iconoclastic loner, Plante in Toronto was a committed team player, happy to help his teammates put pucks in the opposite net. "He talked to me about scoring," recalls Keon, "about how far the goaltender could go out, if he played his angles."

At the end of the 1972/73 season, Plante was acquired from the Leafs by Boston for the playoffs—the Bruins had lost Gerry Cheevers to the World Hockey Association before the season started. The Bruins bowed out in the quarterfinal, and Plante embarked on his second retirement. Two seasons later, he was back in uniform, this time with the Edmonton Oilers of the WHA.

He played thirty-one games in 1974/75, had a respectable (for the WHA) 3.31 average and came back for more the next autumn. At forty-five, he went through the entire training camp, a consummate professional. The season had just begun when he learned one of his children had committed suicide. This time Plante really quit the game. In 1978, he was elected to the Hockey Hall of Fame, and in 1986 the brotherhood lost Plante to cancer. ○

PLANTE TOOK WANDERING FROM THE CREASE TO A NEW LEVEL OF DARING. HIS EXCURSIONS BEHIND THE NET TO INTERCEPT DUMP-IN SHOTS AND FEED BREAKOUT PASSES ARE NOW AN ESTABLISHED PART OF THE GOALTENDER'S TOOL KIT.

CHAPTER 6

Face VALUE

WHO WERE THOSE MASKED MEN? A VISUAL SURVEY OF MORE THAN SIX DECADES OF GOALTENDERS STRIVING TO KEEP THEIR HEADS ABOVE THE FRAY

NO MASK HAS EVER EXPLOITED THE ABILITY OF THE DEVICE TO MAKE A STATEMENT BETTER THAN THIS FELINE NIGHTMARE MADE BY GREG HARRISON FOR GILLES GRATTON. THE LION MOTIF WAS INSPIRED BY GRATTON'S ASTROLOGICAL SIGN, LEO. GRATTON WORE IT AS A NEW YORK RANGER IN 1976/77.

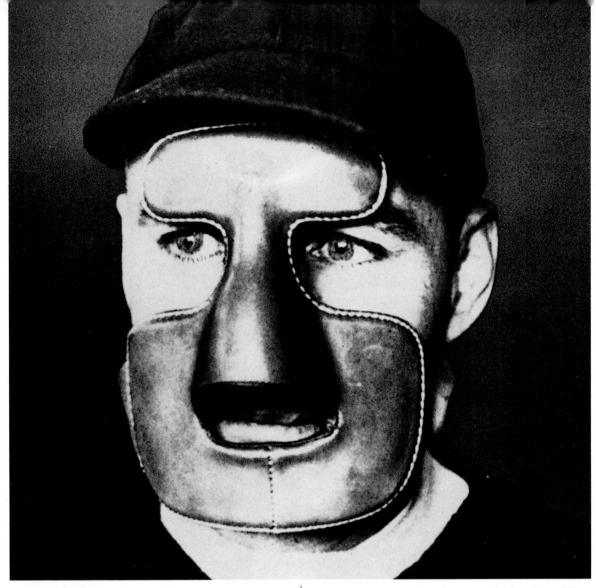

When a Howie Morenz shot smashed Clint Benedict's nose and cheekbone on January 7, 1930, the Montreal Maroons goaltender turned to a makeshift mask (based on either a football face guard or a guard worn by sparring boxers, according to conflicting stories) in hope of mounting a comeback. The mask, alas, did not work: Benedict had trouble seeing around the nosepiece, and after two games gave up on it.

Benedict's experiment did go down in the record books as the first goaltender's mask. Nearly thirty years would pass before a truly functional one next appeared in the NHL, on the face of Jacques Plante. In the interim, Benedict encountered a mask that actually worked, worn by an unheralded young Canadian.

When Benedict's playing career was over, he turned to coaching and managing, and in 1934 went to England to coach the Wembley Lions of the British ice hockey league. There, he found a young goaltender from Winnipeg named Roy Mosgrove. "Mosgrove had to use glasses all the time and would not risk playing without protection," Benedict would recall. And so, in Winnipeg and then in England, Mosgrove donned a wire-cage face protector worn by baseball catchers. It worked, and it would work thirty years later when a young Tony Esposito in Sault Ste. Marie, Ontario, could not play goal without his glasses, and borrowed the same piece of equipment from the sandlot.

It would take decades for the players and inspired tinkerers to see the wisdom of Roy Mosgrove, and to incorporate the wire cage into mask design. This chapter traces the route taken back to Roy—a route that takes in both a Wembley Lion and a Leo named Gilles.

PIONEER *spirit*

Jacques Plante had a knack for what Gerry McNeil, his predecessor in the Montreal Canadiens goal, calls "defying the principles." When he set out in the late 1950s to develop the first mask seen in the NHL since Clint Benedict's failed experiment of 1930, he also set himself at odds with management and the culture of the game. But by then the multiple Vezina winner had absorbed enough stitches and fractures to justify his defiance.

At the time, a clear plastic shield–style protector was being manufactured by Delbert Louch of St. Mary's, Ontario. "Relaxes goal keepers by eliminating fear and nervous tension, giving goal keeper more confidence," went the sales bumf. Samples were distributed through the professional ranks and used in practice; among the recipients were Gump Worsley, Terry Sawchuk and Plante. Initial complaints focused on the fact that it fogged up in a cold hockey rink; Louch countered that with an oil solution. But he couldn't do anything about Worsley's main complaint: he was distracted by lights reflecting on the inside of the shield. The Louch Protector never caught on.

For his first experimental mask, Plante eliminated this problem by shaping his Louch model to the contour of his face and cutting out a broad hole for the eyes. While he used the mask in practice, Plante never wore it in a game. It lacked adequate protection for the eyes and nose, and didn't extend far enough to shield the forehead.

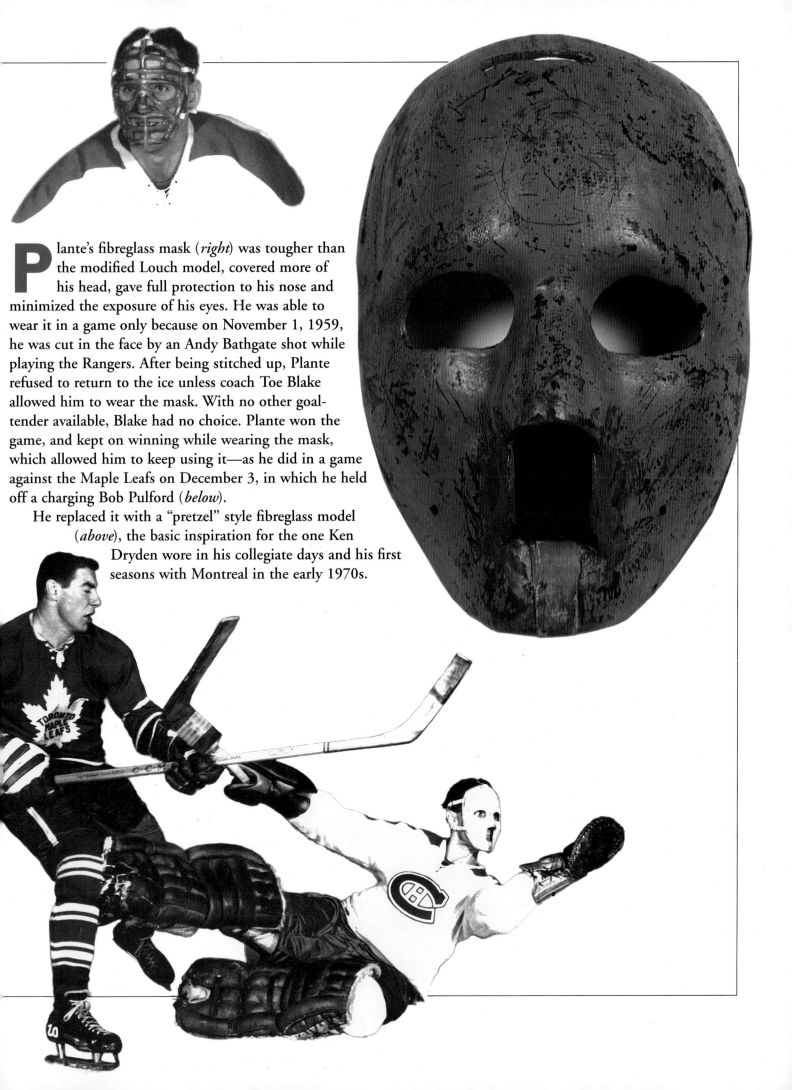

Plante's fibreglass mask (*right*) was tougher than the modified Louch model, covered more of his head, gave full protection to his nose and minimized the exposure of his eyes. He was able to wear it in a game only because on November 1, 1959, he was cut in the face by an Andy Bathgate shot while playing the Rangers. After being stitched up, Plante refused to return to the ice unless coach Toe Blake allowed him to wear the mask. With no other goaltender available, Blake had no choice. Plante won the game, and kept on winning while wearing the mask, which allowed him to keep using it—as he did in a game against the Maple Leafs on December 3, in which he held off a charging Bob Pulford (*below*).

He replaced it with a "pretzel" style fibreglass model (*above*), the basic inspiration for the one Ken Dryden wore in his collegiate days and his first seasons with Montreal in the early 1970s.

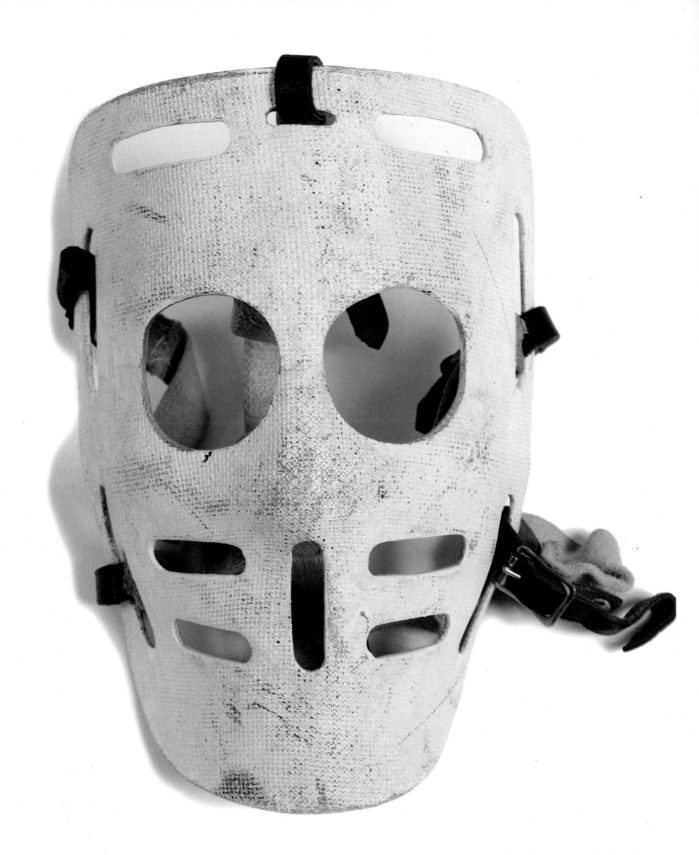

The most popular style of mask in the 1960s was the "Sawchuk" style, so called because of Terry Sawchuk, one of the first NHL goaltenders to follow Jacques Plante's example in donning a mask; Sawchuk began wearing his in regular games in 1962. This type was made by Detroit Red Wings assistant trainer Lefty Wilson, a sometime substitute goaltender in the days before two dressed-to-play netminders. Wilson produced them for goaltenders around the league, using five sheets of fibreglass, and charged $35. This one was worn by Roy Edwards, who followed Sawchuk as a Detroit Red Wings goaltender in 1967.

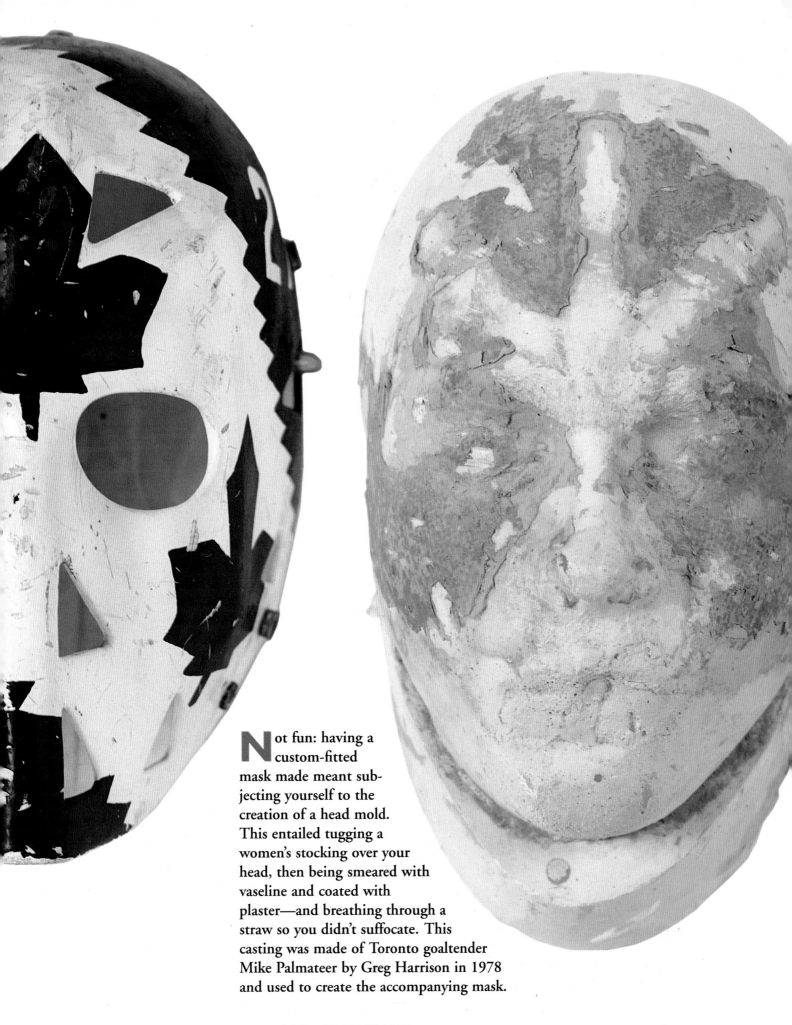

Not fun: having a custom-fitted mask made meant subjecting yourself to the creation of a head mold. This entailed tugging a women's stocking over your head, then being smeared with vaseline and coated with plaster—and breathing through a straw so you didn't suffocate. This casting was made of Toronto goaltender Mike Palmateer by Greg Harrison in 1978 and used to create the accompanying mask.

MAKING
a statement

Plain white fibreglass just wouldn't do. Gerry Cheevers got the trend going by having stitches painted on his mask; his buddy Doug Favell took the trend to the next level by spray-painting his mask orange for a Halloween game. The first _artistic_ mask—one with a full paint job and colour scheme— probably belonged to Glenn "Chico" Resch of the New York Islanders. In 1976 Resch had a new mask made by Ernie Higgins, who created Cheevers' and was the craftsman of choice in the early 1970s. The plain white mask intrigued Linda Spinella, a friend of the Islanders' trainer studying art in New York, and Resch let her loose on it. She painted not only the mask, but the rear headpiece that held it in place.

About this time, a young Torontonian named Greg Harrison came on the scene. A goaltender himself, he had played varsity hockey at the University of Toronto and at the Senior level in Barrie. He had made his first mask for himself at age fifteen using a fibreglass car repair kit. In the mid-seventies, combining his construction skill with artistic talent, he became the leading mask-maker for major-league goaltenders, with the graphic designs becoming increasingly ornate—none more so than the heraldry-inspired Cleveland Barons mask of Gilles Meloche.

WAYNE STEPHENSON
WASHINGTON CAPITALS—1980

GLENN "CHICO" RESCH
NEW YORK ISLANDERS—1976

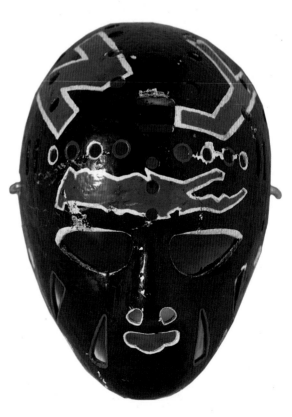

GILLES MELOCHE
CLEVELAND BARONS—1978

GARY SIMMONS
CALGARY/CLEVELAND/ LOS ANGELES—c. 1976

STEVE "BROADWAY" BAKER
NEW YORK RANGERS—1981

GARY EDWARDS
MINNESOTA—1979

Custom masks were the product of plumbers, dentists and other inspired artisans working in garage workshops. An exception was Dave Dryden, who as a professional goaltender made his own. Around 1972, the old Sawchuk style and others like it began to be replaced by masks that provided greater protection to the sides and top of the head. Dryden built a new mask around the one he'd worn as a Buffalo Sabre, and used it from 1974 to 1979 in the WHA. When he moved from the Chicago Cougars to the Edmonton Oilers in 1975, his friend Bob Pelkowski, a Chicago artist, overpainted the Cougars colour scheme with these Oilers oil drops.

A BREED APART   130

The neck was an area even the best masks left vulnerable. One solution arrived at was a hinged guard that swung forward so that the goaltender could tilt his head down without the bottom of the mask hitting his chest. Billy Smith wore this one with the New York Islanders in 1976/77.

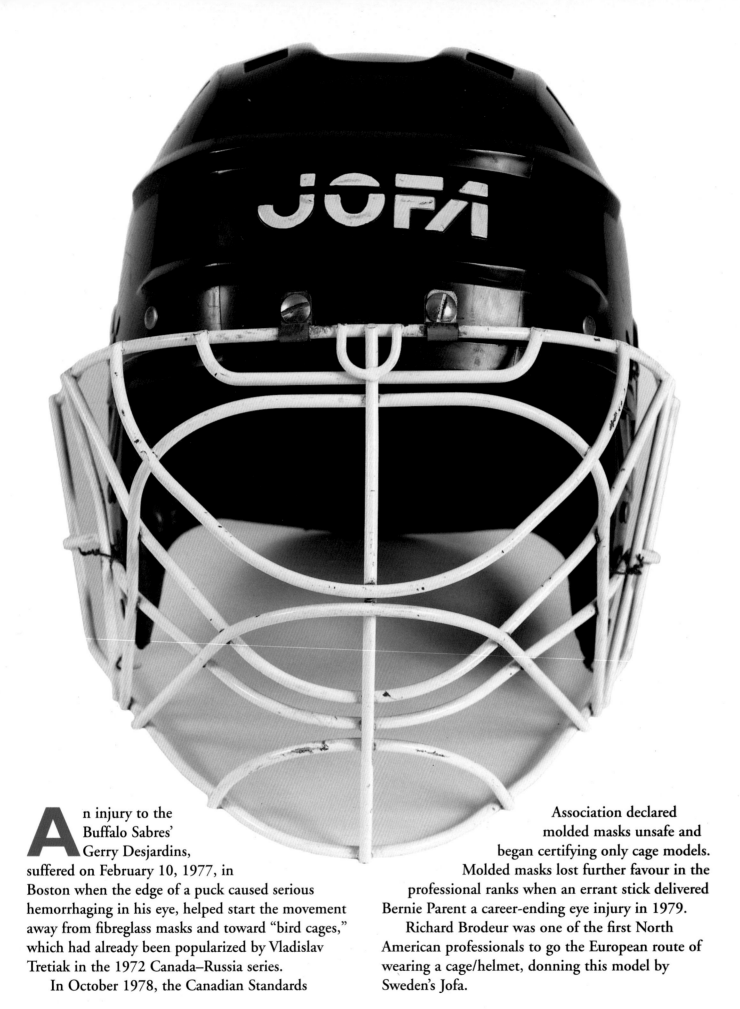

An injury to the Buffalo Sabres' Gerry Desjardins, suffered on February 10, 1977, in Boston when the edge of a puck caused serious hemorrhaging in his eye, helped start the movement away from fibreglass masks and toward "bird cages," which had already been popularized by Vladislav Tretiak in the 1972 Canada–Russia series.

In October 1978, the Canadian Standards Association declared molded masks unsafe and began certifying only cage models. Molded masks lost further favour in the professional ranks when an errant stick delivered Bernie Parent a career-ending eye injury in 1979.

Richard Brodeur was one of the first North American professionals to go the European route of wearing a cage/helmet, donning this model by Sweden's Jofa.

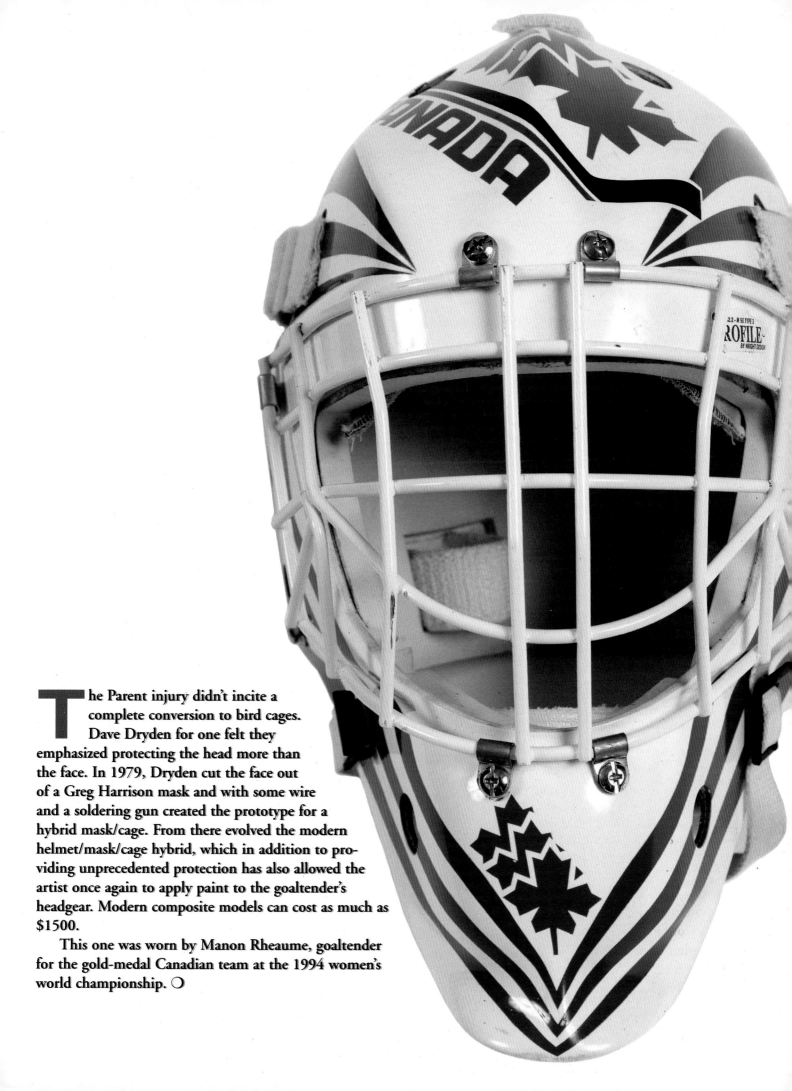

The Parent injury didn't incite a complete conversion to bird cages. Dave Dryden for one felt they emphasized protecting the head more than the face. In 1979, Dryden cut the face out of a Greg Harrison mask and with some wire and a soldering gun created the prototype for a hybrid mask/cage. From there evolved the modern helmet/mask/cage hybrid, which in addition to providing unprecedented protection has also allowed the artist once again to apply paint to the goaltender's headgear. Modern composite models can cost as much as $1500.

This one was worn by Manon Rheaume, goaltender for the gold-medal Canadian team at the 1994 women's world championship. ○

CHAPTER 7

1967/68–1980/81

The MORE *the* MERRIER

IN TEN YEARS, BIG-LEAGUE HOCKEY WENT FROM EMPLOYING SIX TO MORE THAN SIXTY FULL-TIME GOALTENDERS. BUT THERE WAS NO SECURITY IN NUMBERS

F or two decades following the Second World War, goaltending was a profession with limited employment opportunities. The National Hockey League emerged from the war as a six-team loop; a territorial agreement with the American Hockey League limited its expansion opportunities in the east, and team owners were not interested in taking their product west of Lake Michigan. The AHL, for its part, had shrunk from a high of eleven teams to six teams after the war. This meant that there were only a dozen "elite" professional clubs offering jobs to goaltenders, and each club had only one such job to offer.

When the NHL introduced its "two dressed to play" goaltender rule in 1965/66, goaltending employment in the premium league immediately doubled. It doubled again in 1967/68, when the league at last expanded, to twelve teams, with new franchises in Minnesota, Philadelphia, Oakland, Los Angeles, St. Louis and Pittsburgh. Two more franchises, in Buffalo and Vancouver, arrived in 1970/71.

In 1972/73, the job market for goaltending, and for players in general, exploded with the debut of the new twelve-team World Hockey Association. By mid-decade, the WHA had fourteen teams, the NHL eighteen, and each team needed at least two goaltenders. Where there had been only six starting goaltending jobs in the NHL in the early 1960s, by the mid-1970s there were sixty-four in the NHL and the WHA. (In the meantime, the AHL had been transformed into a development league for the NHL.)

While this exponential increase in professional teams meant that goaltenders of average professional skill could now have something approaching a career, expansion brought other consequences. In the 1960s, the six-team NHL had enjoyed the greatest parity of its history. Vezina-winning GAs, as we have seen, routinely bettered LGA by three-tenths of a goal or less. While you couldn't win without great goaltending, there was no excuse for a team not

DAVE DRYDEN OF THE BUFFALO SABRES COUNTERS A BREAKAWAY BY THE VANCOUVER CANUCKS WITH A POKE CHECK. BOTH TEAMS JOINED THE NHL IN 1970. DRYDEN BECAME PART OF ANOTHER GREAT EXPANSION IN PROFESSIONAL HOCKEY WHEN HE CROSSED OVER TO THE WORLD HOCKEY ASSOCIATION IN 1974.

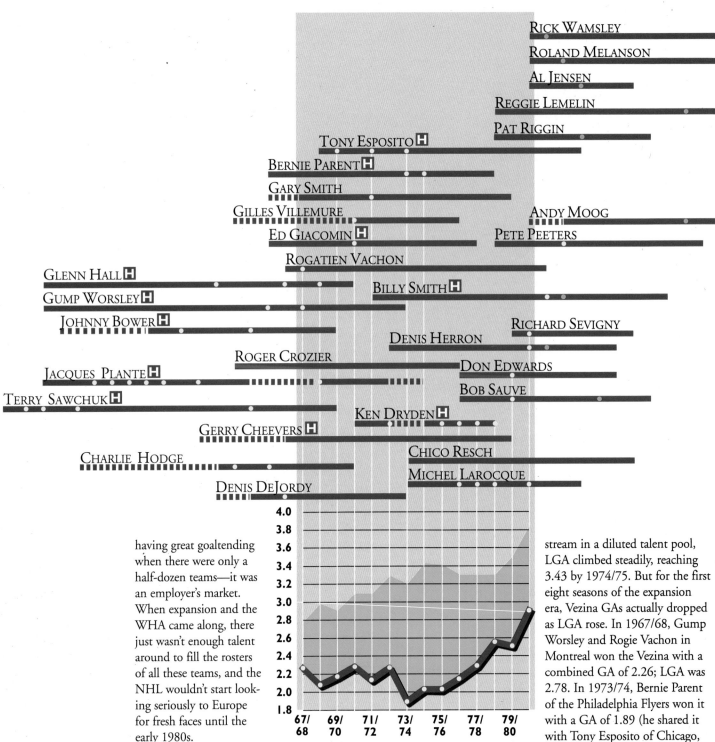

RICK WAMSLEY
ROLAND MELANSON
AL JENSEN
REGGIE LEMELIN
PAT RIGGIN
TONY ESPOSITO
BERNIE PARENT
GARY SMITH
GILLES VILLEMURE
ANDY MOOG
ED GIACOMIN
PETE PEETERS
ROGATIEN VACHON
GLENN HALL
GUMP WORSLEY
BILLY SMITH
JOHNNY BOWER
RICHARD SEVIGNY
DENIS HERRON
ROGER CROZIER
DON EDWARDS
JACQUES PLANTE
TERRY SAWCHUK
BOB SAUVE
KEN DRYDEN
GERRY CHEEVERS
CHARLIE HODGE
CHICO RESCH
MICHEL LAROCQUE
DENIS DeJORDY

4.0 3.8 3.6 3.4 3.2 3.0 2.8 2.6 2.4 2.2 2.0 1.8

67/68 69/70 71/72 73/74 75/76 77/78 79/80

having great goaltending when there were only a half-dozen teams—it was an employer's market. When expansion and the WHA came along, there just wasn't enough talent around to fill the rosters of all these teams, and the NHL wouldn't start looking seriously to Europe for fresh faces until the early 1980s.

The results, from the goaltending perspective, were threefold. Some teams tried to get by with a revolving door of mediocre netminders. Some very good netminders ended up playing for indifferent teams whose rosters were stocked with raw amateur recruits, journeymen of middling talent and over-the-hill vets, none of whom would have been on the ice back in the glory days of the Original Six. And those teams that were very good, and had very good goaltending, stood head and shoulders above the rest of the league. Some of the greatest spreads between Vezina-winning GAs and LGA were recorded in the 1970s.

As the decade progressed and more teams came on

stream in a diluted talent pool, LGA climbed steadily, reaching 3.43 by 1974/75. But for the first eight seasons of the expansion era, Vezina GAs actually dropped as LGA rose. In 1967/68, Gump Worsley and Rogie Vachon in Montreal won the Vezina with a combined GA of 2.26; LGA was 2.78. In 1973/74, Bernie Parent of the Philadelphia Flyers won it with a GA of 1.89 (he shared it with Tony Esposito of Chicago, whose GA was 2.04). Parent's GA was the lowest in Vezina history since Jacques Plante's 1.86 of 1955/56. When Plante won it, LGA was 2.53; when Parent won it, LGA was 3.2. A huge gap had arisen between the very best and middle-of-the-road in goals-against statistics.

The early expansion years were littered with blowout games and absurdly powerful individual clubs from the Original Six who beat up most mercilessly on the expansion teams. The Buffalo Sabres were only a few months into their first season when they

Continued on page 142

ROGATIEN VACHON'S PERFORMANCE IN THE 1976 CANADA CUP WAS ONE OF THE OUTSTANDING GOALTENDING EFFORTS OF THE DECADE. HE SURRENDERED ONLY SIX GOALS IN THE SIX-GAME ROUND-ROBIN.

ANOTHER
game *in* TOWN

WHEN WHA DOLLARS LURED AWAY PLAYERS FROM NHL PAYROLLS, GOALTENDERS WERE AT THE FRONT OF THE LINE

For seven seasons in the 1970s, the upstart World Hockey Association provided hockey fans in North America with an alternative to the NHL. The league has mainly been credited with setting off a massive escalation in player salaries, but the WHA deserves more credit than it normally gets for bringing European talent and their style of play to this side of the Atlantic. In addition to Swedish scoring stars like Anders Hedberg and Ulf Nilsson (imported by the Winnipeg Jets of the WHA, swiped away by the New York Rangers of the NHL), the WHA also introduced from Finland goaltender Rainer (Markus) Mattsson, who played with the Quebec Nordiques and the Winnipeg Jets for the last two seasons of the WHA. When the Jets joined Quebec, the Edmonton Oilers and the Hartford Whalers in moving into the NHL after the WHA folded in 1979, Mattsson made the transition as well, and played four seasons in the NHL in Winnipeg, Minnesota and Los Angeles. Mattsson was in his final NHL season, in Los Angeles in 1983/84, when he snapped Wayne Gretzky's record-setting point-scoring streak after fifty-one games.

The WHA got its start signing journeymen NHLers and just enough big stars to make the new league a serious contender for the public's affections. Bobby Hull's defection from the Chicago Blackhawks to the Winnipeg Jets was the most famous, but for its first season of operation the WHA also scored big by landing Boston goaltender Gerry Cheevers for its Cleveland Crusaders franchise. Cheevers had won the Stanley Cup the preceding spring; when he reported to Cleveland, he did not simply take the money and run. He stuck with Cleveland for two and a half seasons before the Barons' financial problems and a dispute with its management sent him back to the Bruins.

The WHA had less success with

GERRY CHEEVERS WAS ONE OF THE WHA'S FIRST STAR SIGNINGS, JOINING THE CLEVELAND CRUSADERS IN THE LEAGUE'S OPENING SEASON AFTER WINNING THE STANLEY CUP WITH BOSTON.

Bernie Parent, who only stayed one season with the Philadelphia Blazers before money matters made him switch to the Philadelphia Flyers of the NHL, with whom he promptly won two straight Stanley Cups, Vezinas and Conn Smythe trophies.

In all, forty-four goaltenders who played in the NHL also played in the WHA. Many of them, like Parent and Cheevers, tried out the new league for a season or two before returning to the old league. Gerry Desjardins had been around the NHL for six seasons when he crossed over to the Baltimore Blades, a one-season phenomenon, in 1974/75. When Baltimore folded, Desjardins returned to the NHL to play for Buffalo. After Desjardins arrived in Buffalo, Gary Bromley left, spending two seasons in the WHA, with Calgary in 1976/77 and Winnipeg in 1977/78, before returning to the NHL to play for Vancouver.

The WHA allowed some aging veterans and second-stringers from way back to enjoy something of a return to the limelight. At age forty-five, Jacques Plante came out of retirement to play thirty-one games for Edmonton in 1974/75. Two aging backup goaltenders, Marcel Paille and Robert Perrault, also secured some ice time. Paille, who had been a substitute goaltender for the Rangers from 1957/58 to 1964/65, was forty when he relieved Parent for fifteen games with the Blazers in 1972/73. Perrault had played thirty-one games with Montreal,

Detroit and Boston between 1955/56 and 1962/63; he was forty-one when he played one game for the L.A. Sharks in 1972/73. Jack McCartan, goaltender for the 1960 U.S. Olympic champions, resurfaced as a Minnesota Fighting Saint in 1972.

In its efforts to attract fans, the WHA resorted at times to gimmickry. A coloured puck was tried, and for a spell the league allowed a goal scored in the final two minutes of play to count as two goals. The WHA was overall a higher-scoring league than the NHL, and its best team GAs were generally as high as the NHL's LGA, partly because the WHA used overtime for regular-season games. Goaltenders were solid rather than spectacular, and a few made homes for themselves in the WHA. Les Binkley had played five seasons for the Pittsburgh Penguins when he switched to the new league in its inaugural season, playing a total of four seasons, mainly in relief, for Ottawa and then Toronto. Joe Daley, who had played in Pittsburgh, Buffalo and Detroit, switched to the Winnipeg Jets and was in the net for Winnipeg for every one of its WHA seasons. Dave Dryden left Buffalo to play with the Chicago Cougars (he had been Glenn Hall's backup with the Blackhawks in the 1960s) in 1974/75. He then spent four more seasons in the WHA with the Edmonton Oilers while his brother Ken was starring in the NHL with Montreal. Gary Kurt, who had played for the California Seals, switched to the WHA in its first season and stayed there for five seasons.

Don McLeod had played eighteen games as a backup in Detroit and Philadelphia when he joined the new league, and spent six full seasons with it. Wayne Rutledge had been a regular in the net for the L.A. Kings for three seasons when he joined the Houston Aeros, and was a stalwart goaltender there for six seasons. Ernie "Suitcase" Wakely had been around the NHL since 1962 when he joined the Jets for their first season, and played on five different teams in the WHA right through to its last season. Al Smith was a backup in Toronto from 1965/66 to 1968/69 before he landed a starting position in Pittsburgh and then Detroit from 1969/70 to 1971/72. He, too, jumped to the new league, playing for New England for three seasons. Then it was back to the NHL and Buffalo for a backup job for two seasons before returning to the starting job in New England. When New England joined the NHL (as Hartford) in 1979/80, Smith came along, and then played one more season in Colorado. Andy Brown had been a backup in Detroit and Pittsburgh from 1971/72 to 1973/74 when he joined the Indianapolis Racers (where Wayne Gretzky made his professional debut) for three seasons.

As the seasons passed, the WHA was able to get to goaltenders before they had played their first NHL game. Jean-Louis Levasseur, for example, was around the WHA for four seasons, but saw most of his ice time with Minnesota, New England and Edmonton in 1976/77 and 1977/78. After the league died, he appeared in one

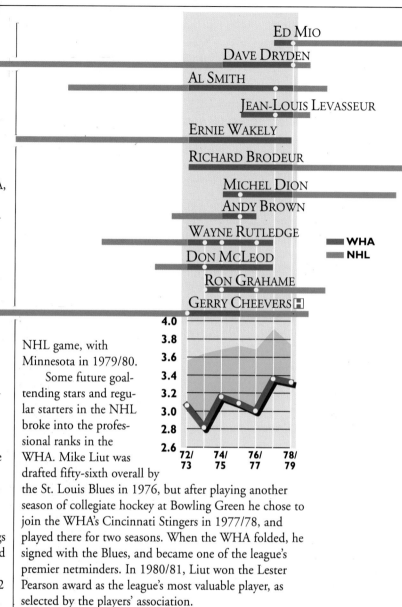

NHL game, with Minnesota in 1979/80.

Some future goaltending stars and regular starters in the NHL broke into the professional ranks in the WHA. Mike Liut was drafted fifty-sixth overall by the St. Louis Blues in 1976, but after playing another season of collegiate hockey at Bowling Green he chose to join the WHA's Cincinnati Stingers in 1977/78, and played there for two seasons. When the WHA folded, he signed with the Blues, and became one of the league's premier netminders. In 1980/81, Liut won the Lester Pearson award as the league's most valuable player, as selected by the players' association.

Pat Riggin played in Birmingham in the WHA's final season, then came over to the NHL for nine solid seasons, the best of them with the Washington Capitals in the mid-1980s. In 1983/84, Riggin and Al Jensen shared the Jennings.

Ed Mio played in Indianapolis and Edmonton for the last two WHA seasons. Moving over to the NHL, he spent seven seasons with Edmonton, the Rangers and Detroit. Ron Grahame was one of the best goaltenders the WHA ever had, and he spent four seasons with the champion Houston Aeros before coming over to the NHL for four seasons in Boston, Los Angeles and Quebec. Michel Dion played more than four seasons in Indianapolis and Cincinnati; when the WHA folded he was good enough to play six seasons in the NHL in Quebec, Winnipeg and Pittsburgh. Finally, Richard Brodeur carved out a solid career in both leagues. He starred with the Quebec Nordiques for the entire life of the WHA. Nine quality seasons in the NHL, most of them with Vancouver, followed. ○

ROGATIEN VACHON

POISED TO INHERIT THE CANADIENS GOAL FROM GUMP WORSLEY, "ROGIE" INSTEAD BECAME THE TOAST OF L.A.

Just before the start of the Stanley Cup final of 1966/67, Leaf coach and general manager Punch Imlach let fly with a classic put-down of a player. Sizing up the not very big and not very well known Montreal Canadiens goaltender, twenty-one-year-old Rogatien Vachon, Imlach quipped, "Do they think they can win from us with a Junior B goalie in the net?"

As it turned out, Montreal couldn't. An aging Leaf team won the cup in six games. But in the process, Rogie Vachon made it known that he was anything but Junior B quality. At five-foot-seven, one of the smallest men ever to play the position professionally, he was to be a giant in the game.

Imlach's jab was a half-truth. Vachon indeed had only progressed as far as Junior B as a teenager. One of eight kids born to a dairy farmer in Palmarolle, about fifty miles from Noranda-Rouyn in Quebec's northern mining country, he had come south to try out for the Junior A Canadiens, only to be sent east to the townships south of Quebec City to play for the Thetford Mines Junior B outfit.

But after this stint, he rose rapidly through the

hockey hierarchy. Turning pro, he was moved by Montreal to the Quebec Aces of the American League for ten games in 1966, then to Houston of the Central League for 1966/67. When Houston starter Gerry Desjardins injured his knee, Vachon got the chance to shine, putting in thirty-four impressive games. The Canadiens brought him up for nineteen games in 1966/67 to spell Gump Worsley, and from then on he was an NHL fixture.

Thwarted by Imlach's aging Leafs in 1966/67, he won his first Stanley Cup in 1967/68. That season, he and Worsley shared the Vezina with a combined 2.26 GA, the best performance the trophy had inspired since Jacques Plante in 1958/59. In the 1968/69 playoffs he took over from Worsley when the veteran dislocated his finger, and completely shut down the emerging Bruins, recording a playoff GA of 1.42 as Montreal won another cup. When a nervous breakdown ended Worsley's Montreal career the following autumn, Vachon inherited the Canadiens net. But when Boston won its first Stanley Cup since forever that spring, Vachon's Montreal career began to unravel.

He blew hot and cold the following season, 1970/71, and as the playoffs approached the Canadiens unveiled a secret weapon. Ken Dryden, nine inches taller than Vachon, beat back the big Bruins shooters in Montreal's famous quarterfinal victory, then won the Conn Smythe as Montreal regained the cup.

Vachon watched from the bench for the entire play-offs as Dryden dazzled. Both the Canadiens and Vachon could see where the team's netminding future lay. After playing in only one period of one game—and letting in four goals—in the new season, Vachon went to general manager Sam Pollock that November and asked to be traded. In two days, he was on his way to L.A.

A trade to an inept expansion club was often hockey's death march to Bataan, but for Vachon it was a career-making move. He married his Montreal girlfriend, grew his hair long, sprouted a Fu Manchu moustache, and became the most beloved hockey figure in the history of the Kings, more beloved than even their latter-day saviour, Wayne Gretzky. He was named the Kings' most valuable player in 1973, 1974, 1975 and 1977, and was adored as much for his on-ice performances as for his charitable work away from the rink. His physical and emotional character was tailor-made for a warm California reception. Back in Montreal, his loss was mourned widely and unrelentingly. The Canadiens had the brilliant, lanky, cerebral Dryden, but a big part of the fans' hearts was still with the gnome-like Quebecer who had been poised to inherit Worsley's crease.

He defied the game's tradition of smaller goaltenders being the most acrobatic: he stayed on his feet and made up for his size by playing his angles carefully. Largely on the strength of his performances, the Kings became a much better team.

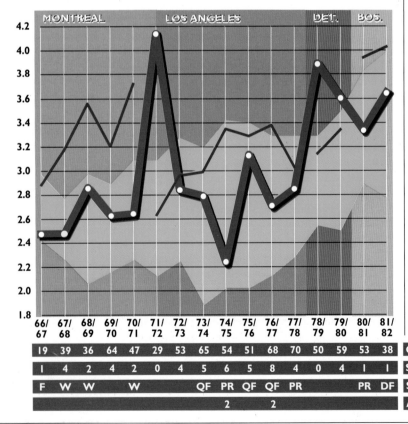

	66/67	67/68	68/69	69/70	70/71	71/72	72/73	73/74	74/75	75/76	76/77	77/78	78/79	79/80	80/81	81/82	
	19	39	36	64	47	29	53	65	54	51	68	70	50	59	53	38	GAMES
	1	4	2	4	2	0	4	5	6	5	8	4	0	4	1	1	SHUTOUTS
	F	W	W		W			QF	PR	QF	QF	PR			PR	DF	STANLEY CUP
							2			2							ALL STAR TEAM

The Kings were out of the playoffs from 1969/70 to 1972/73, made it as far as the quarterfinal in 1973/74, then turned it all around in one magnificent season.

Vachon launched the 1974/75 season by recording a GA of 1.41 in the first seventeen games; it was the best start since 1957/58, when Jacques Plante had managed a GA of 1.33 in his first fifteen games. The Kings won nine more games and amassed twenty-seven more points than in the previous season, and finished only eight points behind the league leaders. Vachon was touted as a Hart contender. Had he won it, he would have been the first goaltender since Plante to do so. But L.A. bowed out of the playoffs in the preliminary round and Bobby Clarke, who led the Flyers to their second straight Stanley Cup, edged Vachon in Hart voting. *Hockey News*, however, named Vachon the league's player of the year.

Jovial and big-hearted, in competition he was a focused terror. "Ounce for ounce, Rogie has to be one of the fiercest competitors in sport," said L.A. defenceman Terry Harper, who had followed Vachon to the coast from the Canadiens in 1972. "He gets mad when you beat him, in a scrimmage or a shooting session." Vachon explained: "When you lose, you want to die."

L.A. never did make it to a Stanley Cup final with Vachon. He made his most lasting mark in the international forum. In the 1976 Canada Cup, neither Bernie Parent nor Ken Dryden was available to play for Team Canada, and Vachon was one of several bright though less lauded netminders, including Glenn "Chico" Resch and Gerry Cheevers, who stepped into the void. They all understood that whoever started the tournament and stayed hot would play every game, and it happened that it was Vachon who caught fire, turning in one of goaltending's greatest performances. In the first six games of the tournament, he allowed only six goals; when it was over, and Team Canada had defeated Czechoslovakia in two straight games in the best-of-three final, Vachon was named the team's most valuable player. But the tournament's MVP award went to Bobby Orr, a sentimental favourite whose knee problems had kept him out of the 1972 Canada–Russia series. Vachon was vocally miffed. "I have to be honest," he said. "I thought I deserved the big award. Everyone said I would get it and I was disappointed when I did not."

After two more seasons in L.A., Vachon became a free agent, and surprised the sport by opting to go to Detroit, lured by a five-year, $1.9 million contract. He had two catastrophic seasons, and would come to blame himself for most of his woes. An arbitrator had ordered Detroit to give up Dale McCourt to L.A. as compensation, but McCourt balked, gaining a restraining order that allowed him to nix the move. Detroit fans were soured by the kerfuffle, and Vachon didn't help matters by playing poorly. For two seasons, his GA reached previously uncharted personal heights. Detroit marched him to doctors, suspecting he had double vision. By the end of the 1979/80 season, Detroit had him on waivers, his contract available to any other NHL team for just $3,500. Everyone passed, but then Boston took a chance on him—Gerry Cheevers had just retired from playing and was now coach—and traded away their very capable veteran netminder, Gilles Gilbert, to get him. Gilbert didn't fare any better in Detroit than Vachon had: his GA jumped by more than a goal and went over the 4.00 plateau. In Boston Vachon posted better than average GAs for two seasons before deciding to retire.

Vachon was sending out résumés in 1984, looking for work as a goaltending or assistant coach, when he received an extraordinary offer from his old team, the Kings: how would he like to be general manager? He took over that autumn, and in January 1985 his welcome back was pressed home by the retirement of his number. He retired in 1991/92, but then came back as assistant to the club president. When president Bruce McNall was indicted on fraud charges, Rogie put up the bail money. ◯

A BIG-HEARTED MAN AWAY FROM THE RINK, IN HIS CREASE VACHON WAS A FOCUSED TERROR: "WHEN YOU LOSE, YOU WANT TO DIE." IN 1975, HE JUST MISSED BECOMING THE FIRST GOALTENDER SINCE JACQUES PLANTE TO WIN THE HART TROPHY.

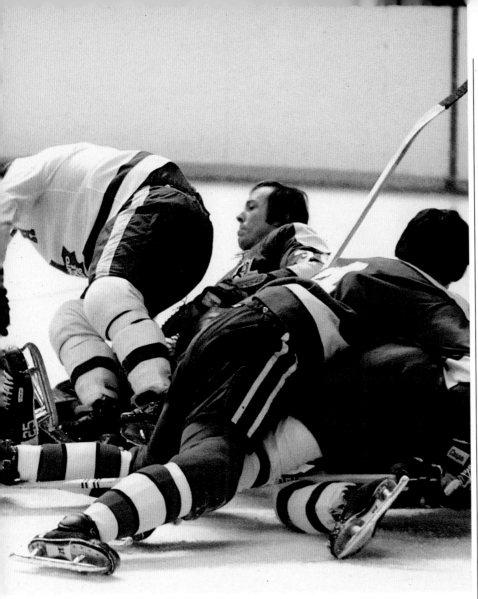

The last of the barefaced warriors: Andy Brown was still playing without a mask with the Pittsburgh Penguins (here in their original blue uniforms) in 1974.

Continued from page 136

were pelted by seventy-two shots at Boston Garden on December 10, 1970, and lost 8–2. The Bruins, with scoring stars like Phil Esposito, Bobby Orr, Ken Hodge and Johnny Bucyk, amassed 399 goals that season, 108 more than Montreal, the next-best offensive unit. They were the first team to have three forty-goal scorers (and two fifty-goal scorers), and with Eddie Johnston and Gerry Cheevers sharing the net, they were shoo-ins for a Stanley Cup. But when they met Montreal in the quarterfinal, they were stopped cold by Ken Dryden, who had only played six games for Montreal that season. The expansion years may have provided whipping boys for the best clubs, but they had not changed the paramount importance of goaltending in the playoffs. Dryden won the Conn Smythe as Montreal captured the cup, and Bernie Parent won it with Philadelphia in 1973/74 and 1974/75.

After 1974/75, the NHL governors seemed to forget about goaltenders for the next seven seasons of Smythe awards. Coincidentally, LGA continued to climb, reaching a record 4.0 in 1981/82, and Vezina GAs climbed with it. Even so, Ken Dryden, who won five Vezinas (the last three with Michel Larocque), was never far from his career GA of 2.24. League-leading GAs reached 2.90

with Montreal in 1980/81. In 1981/82, the New York Islanders won their third straight Stanley Cup that season, but they would have to win their fourth straight before goaltender Billy Smith was awarded the Conn Smythe, bringing to an end the long drought for goaltenders. During these years, goaltenders were also overlooked entirely in Calder voting. Ken Dryden won it in 1971/72, but no goaltending rookie would again be honoured until Buffalo's Tom Barrasso in 1983/84.

In the gold rush of professional hockey in the 1970s, goaltenders for the most part got left behind. The game celebrated its scoring stars as never before; the arrival of the fifty-goal men, and the bidding wars for their services between the NHL and WHA, created great divides between the top-dollar superstars and the journeymen. More often than not, the goaltenders, regardless of their skill levels, were lumped in with the journeymen. Despite the long-held maxim of hockey that a club couldn't win without goaltending, the goaltenders weren't attracting the sterling salaries being tossed in the direction of the big points-producers. Only in the last few years have goaltenders been able to secure salaries in line with their marquee status in the game. Ed Giacomin, looking for any way to get ahead, struck a deal with Champion spark plugs to carry an advertisement for them ("Spark with Eddie") right on his mask. Needless to say, the league vetoed the initiative.

It was an era when goaltenders attracted more abuse than admiration. The expansion years helped resuscitate the "great goaltender on a bad team" label, which hadn't been used much in the Original Six days (netminders like Gump Worsley and Chuck Rayner, who suffered with the Rangers of the 1950s and early 1960s excepted). Gilles Meloche was typical, spending all sixteen seasons of his NHL career with expansion clubs. He toiled thanklessly for the woeful Oakland Seals and their temporary incarnation, the Cleveland Barons. For his first three seasons as a Seal, he averaged more than four goals per game. He enjoyed a few seasons of success with Minnesota, but then ended his career on the pitiful Penguins. He played in 788 NHL games and won 270.

The greatest abuse a goaltender came to suffer in the expansion years came not at the hands of the opposition, but at the hands of his own team, in particular his coach and general manager. The "two dressed to play" rule of 1965/66 may have allowed goaltenders to play less than a full season, and so preserve their skills and sanity as the schedule moved toward eighty games and beyond, but it also laid the foundation for some new twists that undermined the goaltender's self-respect.

Before 1965/66, the goaltender's confidence was not to be messed with by his team. His play was not criticised by his teammates, and if he had an off night, then it was a given that the whole team had an off night. On psychologically healthy teams, an 8–0 blowout was something suffered by the team, not by the man between the posts alone. If a goaltender began to lose his edge, he could be replaced, but certainly never in mid-game. That

A BREED APART |

was as unthinkable as it was impossible, since no one else qualified was on hand to take his place. Normally it took a serious injury to remove a goaltender from the ice.

Punch Imlach, the Leaf coach and general manager who had paved the way for the two-goaltender rule by employing both Johnny Bower and Terry Sawchuk, did switch from one to the other during a game, but only between periods. The one and only time Bower was pulled right off the ice was in 1968/69, the last season of his career, when St. Louis scored on him three times in the first period and Imlach decided to play Bruce Gamble in his stead. It was a home game for the Leafs, and when Bower was summoned to the bench, the fans didn't quite know what to make of it. They responded by giving Bower an ovation.

The two-goaltender rule had made it possible to "pull the goalie"—yank him right out of the net during a stoppage in play and send in a replacement. (Some coaches experimented with using the second goaltender like a relief pitcher in baseball, sending him in to "close" a game.) Other players had this happen to them all the time. If they weren't playing well, they came off on a routine line change, rode the bench or saw minimal ice time. But nobody got removed from the ice quite like a

goaltender. It was a new, and supremely humiliating, experience in effect to be told by your coach, in front of all of your teammates, the opposing players and the crowd in the arena, that you were playing so badly that someone else was getting a turn. It was hard enough to summon the nerve just to play the position. Now the goaltender took up his station in the crease knowing that he could have his ego crushed in full public view if the martinet behind the bench felt the last goal had been on the soft side.

Not every coach was wont to pull the goaltender, but it came to happen enough that "Pull the goalie!" became a common refrain by frustrated home-ice fans. With another dressed-to-play goaltender handy on the bench, the goaltender on the ice could now serve as a scapegoat for whatever was going wrong in the game. A bad goal that was really the fault of the defencemen could get the crowd on the goaltender's back. Being stuck with the goat's role was particularly infuriating to goaltenders who still considered hockey a team sport, and who thought that the lack of backchecking by the big-salary forwards deserved at least some of the blame for the numbers on the score clock.

Continued on page 146

Continued on page 146

A CHORUS LINE: DALLAS SMITH IS BEATEN BY A LEAF SHOT, BUT GILLES GILBERT IS THERE TO COVER FOR HIM. GILBERT BECAME BOSTON'S MAIN NETMINDER WHEN GERRY CHEEVERS SWITCHED TO THE WHA.

GERRY CHEEVERS

THE GUY WHO NEVER WON A VEZINA OR MADE AN NHL ALL STAR TEAM WAS THE BEST TRETIAK HAS EVER SEEN

When it came to applying math to goaltending, the most important function to Gerry Cheevers was not division, but subtraction. "I don't care that much about my average," he wrote in 1971. "My philosophy's always been that the other team can fill the net on me as long as we get one more goal."

Cheevers' average wasn't ever shabby, but it wasn't ever good enough to earn him a Vezina based on the old standard of team GA. Other measurements could be applied to his game: he set a record for the longest undefeated streak for a goaltender—thirty-two games (twenty-four wins, eight ties) in 1971/72; and for the most consecutive playoff wins—ten, in 1969/1970. And his career win percentage of .676 was bested only by Ken Dryden's .758.

Incredibly, Cheevers never won any kind of award, major or minor, while in the NHL. His career got off to too tentative a start to attract a Calder. In his Stanley Cup victories with Boston, he was overshadowed by the likes of Phil Esposito and Bobby Orr, which ruled out a Conn Smythe. And he never made it onto an NHL All Star team. Cheevers' greatness wasn't etched in any piece of silver but the Stanley Cup. Yet teammates and opponents knew his worth. Vladislav Tretiak has called him the greatest goaltender he has ever seen.

With the exception of a two-and-a-half-season side-trip into the World Hockey Association, Cheevers spent his major-league professional career with the NHL's Bruins, and will always be remembered as the guy in the scarred mask with the great Boston teams of the early expansion years.

Growing up in St. Catharines, Ontario, "Cheesie" was scouted for the Leafs by his own dad, a star lacrosse player and minor hockey coach. The elder Cheevers engineered a scholarship for his son with the Leafs' Junior affiliate, the St. Michael's College Majors, and he was the goaltender on the last great St. Mike's team of 1960/61, which won the Memorial Cup.

As the property of the Leafs, Cheevers butted his head against a glass ceiling placed over his career by the existence of Johnny Bower and then Terry Sawchuk on the Leaf roster. Toronto tried him for two games in 1961/62, in which he gave up seven goals, and shipped him hither and yon—to Sault Ste. Marie and Sudbury in the Eastern Canadian Professional League, to the Rochester Americans in the American League. While with Rochester, he made the first All Star team of 1964/65 as the Americans won the league championship. But in the NHL intraleague draft that summer, the Leafs left Cheevers unprotected in favour of Bower and Sawchuk.

It was, in fact, the second straight season Cheevers had been left unprotected, and this time there was a taker. Boston signed him, paid the Leafs the requisite $30,000 fee, and shipped him to the Oklahoma City Blazers of the Central League. Joe Crozier, coach of the Rochester Americans, sensed that a big one had got away. "Cheevers is the most exciting goalie you'll ever see," he reportedly told the Bruins. "He'll have your fans on the edge of their seats all night."

He came up to Boston for seven games in 1965/66 and allowed thirty-four goals, but three of his games were shutouts. Harry Sinden was Oklahoma's player-coach, and when he was hired as the Bruins' coach the following season, he brought along Cheevers, who had been named the league's outstanding goaltender.

Cheevers' style was aggressive and instinctive. The only goaltender to accumulate more penalties than him during his time in the NHL was Billy Smith of the New York Islanders. Counting his WHA minutes, he became the all-time leader, with 304. Known for his enthusiasm in clearing his crease with his stick, he offered in 1970, "I'm not dirty, just aggressive," and added, "Fighter pilots have machine guns. I have only my mask and stick."

Cheevers was always good for a quote, which made him popular with scribes. But he never grandstanded, being known above all as a team player and, ultimately, a

CHEEVERS WAS THE MAN IN THE FRIGHT-NIGHT MASK, GUARDING THE BRUINS GOAL THROUGH A COMBINATION OF INSTINCT AND ACROBATICS. FEW GOALTENDERS HAVE BEEN MORE EXCITING TO WATCH.

clutch player. "He's the kind of guy you can count on to make the big saves that turn games around," Sinden said in 1970. "He'll let the odd softie in but he gets the big ones. You prefer that to having a guy who gets all the softies and misses the big ones."

Two of his greatest assets were his skating and stick-handling. He was the equivalent of a third defenceman, and his puck-handling had undoubtedly been helped by his lacrosse play, which he had given up in the 1960s for fear of an injury that would hamper his hockey career. At St. Mike's he had even played on left wing for a dozen games when the Leafs brought in prospect Dave Dryden to give him some Junior A exposure. It was the one and only time in his career that he had a breakaway on Roger Crozier. Crozier stopped him, and so did every other goaltender he skated in on.

The Bruins won two Stanley Cups with Cheevers in the early 1970s, and then lost him to the rogue WHA. He was the first big signing for the league after Bobby Hull, becoming a Cleveland Crusader with a seven-year, $1.4 million contract the autumn that followed Boston's 1971/72 Stanley Cup win.

At first everything seemed swell with Cheevers and the new league. He was its top goaltender in 1972/73, and in 1975 was named Cleveland's player-coach. In 1974, the WHA All Stars played the Soviet national team in an eight-game series. The pros lost, but with dignity, and Cheevers was critical to their respectable showing.

But the WHA experience soured for Cheevers. The Cleveland franchise began to run dry on funds. Pay cheques were bouncing; Cheevers was privately lending teammates money to tide them over. Then team manager Jack Vivian suspended Cheevers and fined him $1,000 in the middle of the 1975/76 season after a 4–2 loss to Indianapolis, saying "We haven't been getting $200,000 worth of goaltending out of him." Cheevers, incensed, said that Vivian had "accused me of not trying and not caring." He was released from his WHA contract and returned to Boston. In his first game back as a Bruin, he shut out Detroit 7–0.

Cheevers was part of the Team Canada training camp in 1976 that ultimately resulted in Rogie Vachon playing all the team's games. Watching Cheevers perform at camp, fellow netminder Glenn Resch paid tribute. "Gerry brings a lot of class to the position of goaltending. Everyone thinks of the goalie as the flake and the guy who is a bit weird. He defies all that. He doesn't have the best technique in certain instances but he's an intelligent guy, a thinking goalie. He reacts to situations better than others. He doesn't lose his angles and has excellent anticipation."

Harry Sinden summed him up more succinctly in 1969: "Gerry would throw his head in the way of the puck in order to stop a shot."

The Bruins he returned to were not the flashy squad of the early 1970s. These were the dedicated grinders of

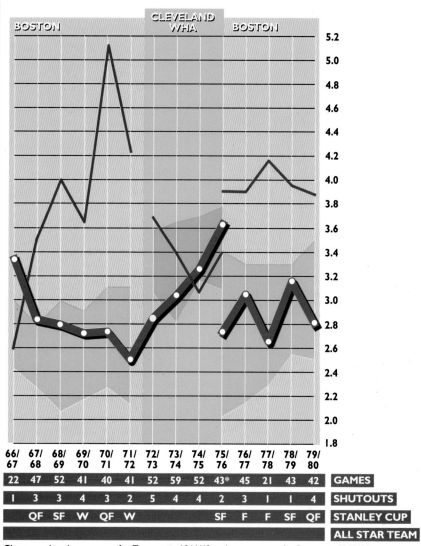

	66/ 67	67/ 68	68/ 69	69/ 70	70/ 71	71/ 72	72/ 73	73/ 74	74/ 75	75/ 76	76/ 77	77/ 78	78/ 79	79/ 80	
GAMES	22	47	52	41	40	41	52	59	52	43*	45	21	43	42	
SHUTOUTS	1	3	3	4	3	2	5	4	4	2	3	1	1	4	
STANLEY CUP	QF	SF	W	QF	W					SF	F	F	SF	QF	
ALL STAR TEAM															

Cheevers played two games for Toronto in 1961/62 and seven games for Boston in 1965/66.
*Cheevers played twenty-eight games (with one shutout) for Cleveland and fifteen games (with one shutout) for Boston in 1975/76.

coach Don Cherry, with Sinden as general manager, who couldn't quite win a Stanley Cup in two tries against the Canadiens. In 1978, in a Stanley Cup game against Montreal in the Forum, Cheevers turned in a performance that elicited every manner of sportswriting superlative, despite his being on the losing team.

Cheevers was plagued by knee problems through much of his career, and at the end of the 1979/80 season he could not continue. He had long had an interest in horse racing—Bobby Orr had been an investor with him in the Four-Thirty stable, named after their sweater numbers—but Cheevers had scarcely time to call himself retired from hockey before Sinden signed him right back on as the Bruins coach. He lasted four and a half seasons, with Boston finishing first or second in their division in the first four, before Sinden fired him in the middle of the 1984/85 season as the team struggled. He was inducted into the Hall of Fame before the year was out. His signature mask took up a place of honour on his living-room coffee table. ○

Continued from page 143

A whole new territory of mind games opened up. The idea that the team stood behind its goaltender was challenged. If the goaltender was having a bad second period, or perhaps a game or two, the team was supposed to bolster his confidence, get him back in the groove. But with another NHL-quality goaltender in the roster, reassurance was no longer so readily offered. Perhaps the team didn't feel like getting behind this goaltender any more. Perhaps they felt that a change would be good, and if a coach sensed that his team thought this way, he might change goaltenders, whether in the middle of the game or in the middle of a road trip, just to give them the psychological boost they craved. A hot goaltender could lift the team as a whole to a higher plane of performance. But just as easily, a struggling goaltender could drag them down. With two goaltenders on hand, it was far easier for the coach to cut loose a goaltender, however unfair this might be, to get his team back afloat.

Two-goaltender lineups have very rarely featured two players of equal or near-equal ability. The trend has long been to have a "starter" and a backup who plays when the starter is injured or needs a rest. Emile Francis, the former goaltender who coached and managed the Rangers in the 1960s and 1970s, firmly believes that a team has to have one main goaltender. Francis's Vezina-winning pairing of Gilles Villemure and Ed Giacomin worked, Giacomin feels, because Villemure was not hankering to play half the games. He was happy providing backup services, which left him time to indulge his passion for horse racing. (In the off-season, Villemure was a first-rate trotter driver.)

In rare instances, teams have used two goaltenders as alternating equals, as in the case of Boston's Gerry Cheevers and Eddie Johnston in the early 1970s, and Chuck Rayner and Jim Henry, the pioneering tag-team of the Rangers, in the late 1940s. Both pairings worked because the players got along and didn't feel particularly threatened that the other guy was going to take his job away. A Machiavel-lian coach or general manager could use this fear to wring a more concerted effort out of a goaltender—or think they could, when in fact all they were doing was destroying the player's self-esteem. While having two first-class goaltenders in the roster can push each of them to a higher level of play as they try to beat each other to the starting job, often the two (or even three) goaltender lineup has led to conflict between the goaltenders, or at least between the goaltender riding the bench and management. Someone ends up getting the bulk of the work, and even with two relative equals, a team will almost always go exclusively with whoever is judged "hot" once the playoffs start. In the 1980s, Andy Moog endured the frustrating experience of playing half or more of the Edmonton Oilers' regular-season games, only to have Grant Fuhr draw the starting assignment in the playoffs. After the 1986/87 season, Moog left the Oilers to play with Canada's Olympic team, then resumed his NHL career as the main goaltender for the Bruins.

O F MORE THAN FIFTY NUMBERS THAT HAVE BEEN RETIRED OR HONOURED BY LEAGUE TEAMS, NINE HAVE BEEN WORN BY A MAN IN THE NET. EVERY GOALTENDING NUMBER RETIREMENT CAME AFTER THE LEAGUE EXPANSION OF 1967. THE BOSTON BRUINS ARE CONSPICUOUS AMONG ORIGINAL SIX FRANCHISES IN NEVER HAVING RETIRED A GOALTENDER'S NUMBER, WHILE THE CHICAGO BLACKHAWKS HAVE RETIRED TWO.

HERE ARE THE LUCKY FEW:

35 TONY ESPOSITO, CHICAGO BLACKHAWKS
31 BILLY SMITH, NEW YORK ISLANDERS
30 ROGATIEN VACHON, LOS ANGELES KINGS
1 ED GIACOMIN, NEW YORK RANGERS
1 BERNIE PARENT, PHILADELPHIA FLYERS
1 GLENN HALL, CHICAGO BLACKHAWKS
1 TERRY SAWCHUK, DETROIT RED WINGS
1 JACQUES PLANTE, MONTREAL CANADIENS

IN ADDITION TO THESE, IN 1995 THE TORONTO MAPLE LEAFS PAID SPECIAL TRIBUTE TO THE "1" WORN BY JOHNNY BOWER AND TURK BRODA WITH A COMMEMORATIVE BANNER, FOLLOWING RECENT CLUB POLICY TO HONOUR RATHER THAN RETIRE NUMBERS.

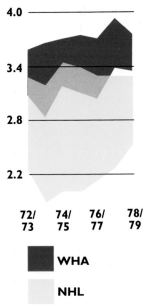

WHA

NHL

IN THE 1970S, GOALTENDING IN THE NHL WAS MARKED BY AN ENORMOUS SPREAD BETWEEN LGA AND VEZINA-WINNING PERFORMANCES, WHILE THE DIFFERENCE BETWEEN THE BEST GOALTENDING PERFORMANCES AND THE AVERAGE ONES WAS MUCH TIGHTER IN THE RIVAL WHA. THE BEST GA IN THE WHA WAS OFTEN AS HIGH AS, OR HIGHER THAN, THE LGA OF THE NHL, UNDOUBTEDLY BECAUSE THE WHA EMPLOYED OVERTIME IN REGULAR-SEASON GAMES.

I t was during the 1970s that goaltenders forged new personae for themselves. The arrival in force of the mask in the 1960s had robbed them of their identities. Their faces obscured, they lost the presence they had enjoyed with spectators in the game's barefaced days. One could not imagine a modern goaltender, sealed up inside his headgear, jabbering away at the opponents and teammates the way Chuck Gardiner had in Chicago in the 1930s.

Mind you, it added an aura of mystery to their personalities. At the end of a game, it became a treat for spectators to watch the goaltender lift away his mask, like a fencer, to reveal what sort of man lurked beneath all that equipment. If he won, he was pleased, his hair dripping with sweat, his animated features the antithesis of his mask's android stolidity. If he lost, he might not remove the mask at all, storming off the ice toward the dressing room with his inner self still firmly encased.

Gerry Cheevers was the first goaltender to exploit the expressive possibilities of the inexpressive mask. During a practice in 1967/68, the first season of the expansion era, Cheevers was hit on his new mask by a shot from Fred Stanfield. As a joke, the nick in the mask was painted in as stitches to represented the injury that might have been. By 1971, Cheevers had added 110 stitches to three different masks. The macabre visage turned the goaltending trade into a funhouse nightmare; it was entirely appropriate that when the *Friday the 13th* film series was launched, its principal nemesis, the psychopathic Jason, sported a goaltender's mask. The anonymity of the mask gave the chainsaw-wielding maniac the depth of character required.

As other players started to decorate their masks, they tended to stick to the safety of team logos. Cheevers' buddy Doug Favell added whimsy to the process by spray-painting his mask orange in honour of Halloween (that funhouse nightmare again). Masks became more adventurous, more stylised, more...outspoken. The most repressed players in the rink, restricted to one corner of the ice, buried under increasingly complex equipment, assaulted by 100-m.p.h. pieces of rubber, jerked from their creases by capricious coaches, began shouting back, not with their voices, but with their faces. They became a combination of samurai warrior, Kabuki actor, comic book superhero and professional wrestling weirdo. When confirmed eccentric Gilles Gratton had a startling lion's face painted on his mask (in honour of his astrological sign, Leo), the art of the mask reached its nadir, and so did the ability of the goaltender to transform himself into something other than the nerve-racked loner the public expected him to be. The goaltender became the most fascinating character in the game, if not in professional sport. He became the only professional athlete with an alter ego.

Vladislav Tretiak was puzzled by the North American game as he found it in the 1970s. He derided the style of some NHL players, who seemed to eschew the nifty playmaking of his comrades in favour of pure firepower. Opponents seemed to want to shoot the puck right through him rather than outsmart him. But he admired the goaltenders. "What first impressed me about Canadian goalkeepers was their amazing ability to come out of the net while under attack in order to cut down the angles," he has written.

Professional hockey in the late 1970s reached simultaneous highs and lows—there were more teams than ever before, and great concerns about the overall quality of play in the light of humiliations suffered at the hands of touring Soviet hockey teams, which culminated in the 8–1 defeat of Team Canada in the deciding game of the 1981 Canada Cup. Throughout it, the quality of goaltending was never questioned. And despite the tremendous expansion in total teams, the profession was almost completely dominated when it came time for accolades by Montreal's Ken Dryden. As the Canadiens won four straight Stanley Cups, Dryden won four straight Vezinas and was voted to the first All Star team four straight times. Others vied for attention—Don Edwards and Bob Sauve in Buffalo, Glenn "Chico" Resch and Billy Smith with the New York Islanders, Rogie Vachon in Los Angeles, Gerry Cheevers in Boston, Bernie Parent in Philadelphia, Eddie Giacomin in New York. When Dryden retired at the end of the 1978/79 season, a changing of the guard was again under way in the netminding ranks. Bernie Parent was forced to retire that season because of an eye injury. Eddie Giacomin had played his last nine games in 1977/78, and Gerry Cheevers, who had somehow had one of the NHL's great careers without ever winning a Vezina or landing on an All Star team, hung in for one more season following Dryden's retirement.

Dryden's retirement left a vacuum; he had been one of those goaltenders, like Benedict, Vezina, Brimsek, Durnan, Sawchuk, Plante and Hall, who were recognized as players whose greatness transcended their particular era. But even in Dryden's years, the game had come to take for granted the greatness of goaltending in a way it never had before. Goaltenders were there to stop pucks, and if the pucks didn't get stopped, you pulled them off the ice and sent in another one. It had become a shooter's game: they won the Harts and the Conn Smythes. Defencemen wanted to be Bobby Orr, and the discipline of allowing as a team a minimum of goals became a rare pursuit. When Dryden retired, LGA was at 3.30. Already nudging upward in the 1970s, it increased rapidly in his absence, and as four surviving teams of the great WHA experiment were folded into the NHL, it reached 4.0 in 1981/82. The four-goal barrier hadn't been broken since the free-for-all wartime season of 1943/44. Tony Esposito, who had recorded a 1.76 GA in 1971/72, saw his GA reach 4.52 in 1981/82. It would take another decade for the NHL to move away from the high-scoring game. Changes in basic game philosophy would help make it happen, but ultimately it was up to the goaltenders. And ten years after Dryden retired, the position had undergone a revolution in equipment and technique the likes of which had not been seen since the catching glove and the slapshot had transformed the goaltender's role in the first seasons of the Original Six. ◯

IN JANUARY 1975, KIM CROUCH, AN EIGHTEEN-YEAR-OLD GOALTENDER FOR THE MARKHAM WAXERS OF THE ONTARIO JUNIOR A, WAS WEARING THE MASK AT TOP WHEN A SKATE SLICED A SIX-INCH CUT IN HIS NECK, SEVERING HIS JUGULAR VEIN. KIM NEARLY BLED TO DEATH ON THE ICE; THE WOUND TOOK FORTY STITCHES TO CLOSE. KIM'S BRUSH WITH DEATH INSPIRED HIS FATHER ED, THE FIRE CHIEF OF WHITBY, ONTARIO, TO INVENT THE CROUCH COLLAR. INSIDE IS BALLISTIC NYLON, THE MATERIAL BUTCHERS USE TO PROTECT THEMSELVES. THE FIRST MODEL (MIDDLE) WAS PATENTED IN CANADA IN 1976. A REVISED MODEL (BOTTOM) RECEIVED A U.S. PATENT IN 1987.

BERNIE PARENT

THE SECOND COMING OF JACQUES PLANTE WAS THE GOALTENDER TO BEAT IN THE MID-SEVENTIES

The first time Bernie Parent ever played goal, he was scored on twenty times. His older brother was coaching a Pee Wee team in Long Pointe, a town outside of Montreal, in 1956, and the regular goaltender couldn't play. Eleven-year-old Bernie was pressed into service, and suffered a drubbing that only made him determined to learn how to stop pucks. He practised for a month, got another chance and won 5–3. He was almost twenty years away from winning two Stanley Cups, two Vezinas and two Conn Smythes, but he was on his way.

For two seasons in the mid-1970s, Bernie Parent was the biggest name in goaltending, at least in the NHL. As the last line of defence for the Philadelphia Flyers, he helped give the Broadstreet Bullies legitimacy as a champion hockey club. It may have been chock full of grinders and brawlers, but the first expansion club to win a Stanley Cup also had the second coming of Jacques Plante. Neither of the Flyers' back-to-back cup wins, the first against Boston, the second against Buffalo, would have been possible without Parent.

He came out of Junior hockey as championship material. Starting out with Rosemount of the Quebec Junior league in 1962/63, he moved over to the Niagara Falls Flyers of the OHA for two seasons. He was named the Ontario Junior A's top goaltender in both seasons. Paired with Doug Favell, a buddy of Gerry Cheevers' from St. Catharines (their dads played lacrosse together), he was a member of the Memorial Cup–winning Flyers team of 1965.

Signed by the Bruins, Parent was sent to Oklahoma City of the Central League for the 1965/66 and 1966/67 seasons. At the time the Bruins had a surfeit of goaltending prospects, including Cheevers, and had been confident enough to deal away the rights to Ken Dryden in 1964. Parent played fifty-seven games up in Boston over those two seasons, backing up Eddie Johnston, but he did not impress, and his $7,500 salary flew through his fingers. When expansion came in 1967, the Flyers claimed him in the draft, and picked Favell as well.

Parent logged three and a half solid seasons in Philadelphia before being dealt to Toronto on January 31, 1971, in a multi-player deal that included Maple Leaf netminder Bruce Gamble. Gamble lasted only another year before heart problems forced him from the game. For Parent, the trade was an unexpected trip to finishing school. Waiting for him in Toronto was that wily sage of the nets, Jacques Plante, in the twilight of his career but still capable of making the second All Star team that season. Looking at Parent in 1971, Cheevers noted, "He's probably got more natural ability than any goaltender in this league. I don't know too much about his desire, though... He's not the most enthusiastic goaler I can think of."

Parent had grown up watching Plante on "Hockey Night in Canada." Now taken under his hero's wing, Parent was turned into a Plante "carbon copy" (in Gump Worsley's words), right down to the way he threw his arms up in a V-for-victory after a win. Physically, they weren't much alike—Parent was a bit on the chunky side. As Cheevers put it, "He's sort of a fat Jacques Plante." In one important respect, their styles were far apart. Parent never developed Plante's nerve in roaming from the net. "It's like a kid who goes into the woods with his father," Parent explained. "As long as I'm close to the net, I figure I'm all right."

Plante trained him so well in Toronto that in 1972 the Flyers gave up a first-round draft choice and Favell to retrieve Parent, who was packaged with a second-round Toronto pick. But then the WHA came calling. The Flyers never got a

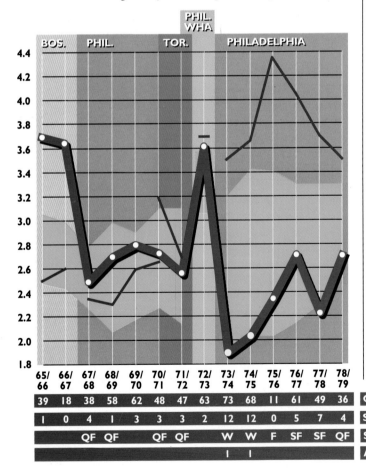

A STANLEY CUP–WINNING PARENT SKATE, AUTOGRAPHED BY THE FLYERS

	BOS.	PHIL.					TOR.	PHIL. WHA		PHILADELPHIA				
	65/66	66/67	67/68	68/69	69/70	70/71	71/72	72/73	73/74	74/75	75/76	76/77	77/78	78/79
GAMES	39	18	38	58	62	48	47	63	73	68	11	61	49	36
SHUTOUTS	1	0	4	1	3	3	2	12	12	0	5	7	4	
STANLEY CUP			QF	QF		QF	QF		W	W	F	SF	SF	QF
ALL STAR TEAM								I	I					

chance to put Parent back on the ice. The Miami Screaming Eagles of the new league signed him with a five-year, $750,000 deal that included a new boat, house and car every year. In his final season in Toronto, Parent had been making $40,000. When the Miami team failed to materialize for the first WHA season, 1972/73, Parent's contract was picked up by the league's Philadelphia Blazers club.

It was an unhappy experience. He broke his toe at the start of the season, played in front of crowds of 2,000, and allowed a goal a game more than he had in Toronto. When he refused to play after an overtime loss in the first game of the play-offs against the Cleveland Barons, who had Cheevers, teammates accused him of walking out on them; the Blazers, sans Parent, were swept four straight. But Parent said money was the issue: he had discovered that $400,000 of his salary package, which was supposed to be in escrow, wasn't. His WHA rights were transferred to the New York Golden Blades, which had no bearing on Parent's plans. He was going across town to the Flyers.

"I used to watch poor Bernie in a WHA game," said Fred Shero, the Flyers' coach. "And, hell, he had to stop forty-five shots a game. Rather than hurting him, the WHA made him a better goalie. He'd never seen so many shots in an NHL game."

In his first game back in the NHL, Parent let in seven goals in twelve minutes, and Shero pulled him. Opening-night jitters dispensed with, he grew his trademark moustache and turned into a brick wall, winning the Vezina with a GA of 1.89, leading the league with twelve shutouts and anchoring the Flyers' Stanley Cup win that spring with a 2.02 average and two shutouts in seventeen games.

"When Parent is out there," said Shero, "we know we can win games we have no business winning."

His pregame regimen was uncomplicated: half a dozen beers and eight hours of sleep. In 1974/75, he won another Vezina, another Stanley Cup and another Conn Smythe. "Bernie makes you feel like you can walk on water," said Flyers captain Bobby Clarke. In this fifteen-game playoff campaign, Parent's GA was 1.89, with four shutouts. No goaltender had a better GA or more

shutouts in the 1973/74 or 1974/75 playoffs.

A neck injury in 1975/76 reduced his season to eleven games; Wayne Stephenson played net for the Flyers as Montreal defeated them in the final to begin a four-cup winning streak. The injury also denied him the chance to play in the 1976 Canada Cup.

He always feared a serious injury, hoping to enjoy the kind of endless career Plante had, and he was fortunate that, apart from his neck problems, the game had been kind to him. But on February 17, 1979, in a home game against the Rangers, a stick to the eye ended his professional career at 671 regular-season games, with a lifetime NHL GA of 2.55.

"I feel bad about the whole thing," he said at the end of the season, when doctors told him there was no way he could return to play, "but all good things must come to an end sometime. I've got many pleasant memories, especially those two Stanley Cups." A religious man, Parent could be found giving motivational talks at schools and churches when he wasn't off bow hunting or deep-sea fishing. He stayed in the Flyers organization as a goaltending coach. The team retired his number, and in 1984 he was inducted into the Hockey Hall of Fame. ○

PARENT SCRAMBLES AGAINST HIS FORMER TEAM, THE TORONTO MAPLE LEAFS, WHERE FOR ONE AND A HALF SEASONS JACQUES PLANTE TAUGHT HIM EVERYTHING HE KNEW.

ED GIACOMIN

IN AN ARENA NOTORIOUS FOR TURNING ON ITS STARS, "FAST EDDIE" WAS ALWAYS A FAVOURITE OF RANGERS FANS

Frank Boucher's description of Chuck Rayner as "brilliantly aggressive" could be applied with equal confidence to Eddie Giacomin, who took charge of the New York Rangers goal more than a decade after Rayner's performances had earned him the Hart Trophy. But if there was an essential similarity in the attitude Rayner and Giacomin brought to the assignment of playing goal for New York, it was a quirk of history rather than a case of emulation on Giacomin's part. "Fast Eddie" Giacomin never saw Rayner play, and growing up in Sudbury, Ontario, his goaltending hero was Turk Broda, because Toronto was the team young boys like Giacomin followed devotedly on "Hockey Night in Canada."

Giacomin's success required enormous persistence. At fifteen he was cut at a tryout for the Hamilton Red Wings, Detroit's Junior affiliate; at eighteen, he was sent home from a Detroit tryout. A kitchen stove explosion severely burned his legs and feet and nearly claimed his ability to skate. After playing two seasons of industrial-league back in Sudbury, he got a break through his brother Rollie, five years older than him and an accomplished goaltender in his own right, who provided crucial

GIACOMIN TRIED TO CARRY A "SPARK WITH EDDIE" ADVERTISEMENT ON HIS MASK AT THE END OF HIS CAREER. THE LEAGUE WOULDN'T ALLOW IT, BUT THE SPARKING MOTIF HE'D HAD PREPARED SURVIVED IN HIS FINAL MASK, WORN AS A DETROIT RED WING.

tutorials to the young Eddie. Rollie had been invited to play for the Washington Presidents of the minor pro Eastern Hockey League, but couldn't go, and sent Eddie in his place. The younger Giacomin played so well that he was invited to the training camp of the American League's Providence Reds.

In refining his game, Giacomin took inspiration from the butterfly style of Glenn Hall and the wandering tendencies of Jacques Plante. He made his NHL debut in 1965/66 after five seasons in Providence. The Reds, which had no parent NHL club, were a struggling outfit, and Giacomin never did win the Holmes, the AHL's version of the Vezina. Nor did he ever make an AHL All Star team. But Rangers coach and GM Emile Francis, a former goaltender himself, knew talent when he saw it, and cut a deal for Giacomin. Much was made of Giacomin's arrival in New York, as Francis dealt away four players to the Reds to get him.

Giacomin had a disappointing rookie season: in thirty-six games his GA of 3.66 was more than half a goal above LGA. "I was so excited," says Giacomin. "I was twenty-six and I didn't think I was ever going to make it to the NHL. I forgot that I was there to stop pucks."

Fortunately for Giacomin and the Rangers, Francis gave him another chance, and made him the team's regular starter for 1966/67. Giacomin responded magnificently. In only his second season in the big league, he was named to his first professional All Star team—and onto the first team, no less, ahead of Glenn Hall. For five straight seasons, Giacomin was either a first or second team appointee. His GA dropped to 2.61 in his second season, and just kept getting better. By 1970/71, it was down to 2.16, and with his backup Gilles Villemure, Giacomin won the Vezina with a combined GA of 2.27.

The Rangers of Emile Francis and Eddie Giacomin were a true sporting dynasty. After the team had missed the playoffs in Giacomin's debut season, the Rangers were part of the "second season" for the next nine years. The peak of his career in New York came in 1971/72, when the Rangers reached the Stanley Cup final for the first time since Rayner and company in 1949/50. Like the Rangers more than thirty seasons before them, Giacomin's Rangers lost, this time to Boston.

"It was Eddie's ambition to score a goal," says Francis. Giacomin came awfully close twice on empty nets. In a game against the Maple Leafs, he nearly did it on a fluke clearing shot, flipping the puck off the glass and down the ice. The puck ran out of steam in the Toronto crease. Against the Canadiens in Montreal,

	65/66	66/67	67/68	68/69	69/70	70/71	71/72	72/73	73/74	74/75	75/76	76/77	77/78
GAMES	36	68	66	70	70	45	44	43	56	37	33	33	9
SHUTOUTS	0	9	8	7	6	8	1	4	5	1	2	3	0
STANLEY CUP		SF	QF	QF	QF	SF	F	SF	SF	PR			QF
ALL STAR TEAM		1	2	2	2	1							

Gump Worsley had just been pulled for an extra skater when Giacomin made a deliberate bid for a goal, taking aim at the empty Montreal net. He was so sure it was going in that he was celebrating his achievement when the puck glanced off the outside of the post.

Giacomin came perilously close to becoming the first goaltender ever to be scored on by another goaltender, when he came up against the ambitions of Gary "Suitcase" Smith. Smith would share the Vezina with Tony Esposito in Chicago in 1971/72, but from 1967/68 to 1970/71 Smith was toiling for the Oakland Seals. (He was called "Suitcase" because he played on eight different teams in his fifteen-season career.) During a near-fateful game between the Seals and the Rangers, Smith took it upon himself to get the Seals on the scoreboard, and took off for the Rangers end, crossing centre ice. "Rod Seiling was the last man back," Giacomin remembers. If Smith had managed to beat Seiling, there would have been a truly spectacular breakaway. The rules were later changed to forbid the goaltender from crossing centre ice. Giacomin has no idea why. "The goaltenders never make the rules," he says. "They're always changing the rules to make it worse for the goaltenders."

Growing up in Sudbury, Giacomin played a lot of three-on-three pick-up hockey, in which the goaltender often played as a forward as well, and this helped make Giacomin a particularly strong skater. He made for a dashing, handsome figure in the New York goal, with carefully groomed hair and an unmarked face. In his entire career, he was cut for about a dozen stitches, and only took to wearing a mask later in his career because of increasing concerns about eye injuries.

Giacomin's final seasons were marked by significant changes in professional hockey. The explosion of professional clubs through the arrival of the WHA and expansion in the NHL had made for a very different game on the ice. "There was more open ice," he says: a less disciplined style created more three-on-one rushes and breakaways, which helped boost LGA in the latter half of the 1970s. And he found the air travel wearying. That, more than anything, was the reason you needed a backup goaltender, says Giacomin. When he started out in the league, there was a seventy-game schedule; in four seasons from 1966/67 to 1969/70 he played all but six games, and from 1966/67 to 1968/69 led the league in

victories. But once teams started having to roam all over the continent, those seventy games, which increased to eighty by 1974/75, became a lot harder to play. "The time changes really got to you. You needed somebody else to take your place."

In 1975/76, John Ferguson replaced Emile Francis as the Rangers' general manager. Giacomin was thirty-six and, in Ferguson's book, yesterday's man. In November 1975, to the dismay of intensely loyal New York fans, Ferguson sold Giacomin to Detroit. When he made his first visit back to Madison Square Garden as a Red Wing, the ovation was deafening, and Detroit won 6–4. It was one of the few high points for Giacomin that season. The Red Wings logged their sixth spring without a playoff appearance, but the Rangers didn't make the playoffs, either. The Red Wings missed the playoffs again in 1976/77, and after playing only nine games in 1977/78, Giacomin retired.

The Rangers became one of only four NHL teams to retire a goaltender's number when they put aside his "1" for good. After a spell in the restaurant business in Michigan, Giacomin returned to New York to serve as a goaltending coach from 1986 to 1989 under GM Phil Esposito, who as a Bruin had taken the Stanley Cup away from him in 1972. He was elected to the Hockey Hall of Fame in 1987. Fast Eddie now lives in Florida. ○

GIACOMIN HAD A PONDEROUS RISE TO STARDOM, WHICH INCLUDED FIVE ANONYMOUS SEASONS IN THE AMERICAN LEAGUE. WHEN HE WAS ELECTED TO THE NHL'S FIRST ALL STAR TEAM IN HIS SECOND SEASON, IT WAS THE FIRST ALL STAR TEAM HE'D EVER MADE.

CHAPTER 8

INTERNATIONALE

GOALTENDING
STARS OF THE
INTERNATIONAL
AMATEUR GAME

The Czechoslovakian national team of the 1970s, which won world titles in 1972, 1976 and 1977, featured outstanding goaltending by Jiri Holecek *(spread)* and Vladimir Dzurilla *(inset)*. Dzurilla was a star of the 1976 Canada Cup, delivering Team Canada its only loss of the tournament, a 1–0 shutout.

When Vladislav Tretiak showed up in Montreal in September 1972 to face the cream of Canadian professionals, Canadian strategists thought he was the least of their worries. After all, the word on Tretiak (on Soviet goaltenders in general) was that they were the weak spot in the Russian ice machine. Back in 1957, for example, a team of Soviet selects played the Whitby Dunlops at Maple Leaf Gardens with a netminder named Erkin *(above left)*, and lost 7–2. Tretiak, of course, proved himself to be any-thing but a weak spot. And he was no fluke. The Russians had won big games before with great goaltending. Their goaltender when they won their first world championship, in 1954, was Nikolai Puchkov *(above right, with trophy)*, whose talent rivalled Tretiak's. A soccer player, he didn't even begin playing hockey until age twenty, four years before winning the world title. Puchkov stunned the Canadians by delivering them a 7–2 loss in the gold-medal game, and he went on to anchor a long string of Soviet international victories.

Every twenty years, the United States hosts a winter Olympics and stages a miracle on ice with some clutch goaltending. Jack McCartan did it in Squaw Valley in 1960 *(left)*, making thirty-nine saves in a 2–1 semifinal win over Canada on the way to a gold medal. In 1980 in Lake Placid, Jim Craig held off the Russians in a 4-3 semifinal victory that allowed the Americans to go on to win gold. Neither McCartan nor Craig were able to repeat their amateur successes in the professional arena. McCartan had an eight-game stint with the Rangers after the Olympics, then came back with the WHA's Minnesota Fighting Saints in 1972. Craig played twenty-three games with the Bruins after the Olympics, and three games with the Minnesota North Stars in 1983/84.

Women have been playing hockey just about as long as men, but it has taken high-profile victories by the Canadian women's team at the world championships to reaffirm the legitimacy of women's hockey. The team's goaltender Manon Rheaume *(left, at the 1994 worlds)* has been pursuing doggedly a professional career in a game otherwise dominated by men.

Goaltenders didn't get much better than Joe Sullivan, who decided professional hockey was no way to make a living. Sullivan was the netminder for the University of Toronto team that won the first Memorial Cup, the Canadian Junior hockey championship, in 1919. As a member of the superb University of Toronto Varsity Grads, which was managed by future Maple Leaf impresario Conn Smythe, Sullivan wore the maple leaf at the 1928 Olympics *(right and below)*. He was never scored on in the entire tournament as Canada struck gold. Returning home, he debated turning pro with Smythe's newly acquired Maple Leafs, but resolved that a career in medicine was the more prudent course. Sullivan became a leading surgeon specializing in hearing problems. Active in the Progressive Conservative party, he was appointed to the Canadian Senate in 1957. ◯

CHAPTER 9

TROIKA

IN THE 1970s, THE DOMINANT NAMES IN GOALTENDING WERE TRETIAK, DRYDEN AND ESPOSITO

Three goaltenders provided the dominant images of their profession in the 1970s. Others shared the limelight—Gerry Cheevers for one, Bernie Parent for another. But in Ken Dryden, Tony Esposito and Vladislav Tretiak the public found a troika of netminding stars. Their paths crossed and recrossed in some of the most exciting hockey ever played. Though they all burst upon the scene within a two-season span, there was a considerable spread in their ages: Esposito was born in 1943, Dryden in 1947, Tretiak in 1952. They were similar if only because they were so different from everyone else: each came from a background very different from the kind that customarily led to netminding excellence.

Ken Dryden is remembered, above all, for The Stance: hands atop his stick, chin atop his hands, one knee flexed, more contemplative of the spectacle of the game than the spectators on the other side of the boards. Goaltending, ultimately, is a reactive discipline, and it has been Ken Dryden's metier to react as arrestingly on the ice as off. For most of his little more than eight seasons in the NHL, he was the game's dominant goaltender. But in a discipline of outsiders, he was an outsider even among them.

He was so different as a character that the fact he was one of the best ever to wear a set of pads became almost secondary to his mystique. He is not usually cited as one of the all-time goaltending greats. Dryden himself, in his book, *The Game*, declared, "For me, the greatest goalies must always be Hall, Sawchuk, Plante and Bower." But greatness in the net certainly was the foundation of everything else that Dryden was and became.

Ken was overnight famous, his ambitions played out under a harsh public glare. He amazed and confounded observers by making a law degree as important a goal as winning Stanley Cups. His older brother Dave, also a professional goaltender, was methodically and successfully pursuing similar dreams of forging a professional life away from the rink. But Dave was able to do this beyond the limelight that held Ken. For the younger Dryden, any ambition to satisfy his personal goals had to defy notions of his obligations, real and imagined, to his country and to the greatest hockey team in the world.

Tony Esposito also had an older hockey brother, the celebrated Phil. The Espositos were much closer in age than the Drydens—Tony and Phil were separated by fourteen months, Ken and Dave by six years. But with the Espositos there was a sense of "younger" and "older" as strong as with the Drydens. Both Dave and Phil served as mentors and role models to their siblings.

And both sets of brothers had fathers in the construction industry. Patrick Esposito worked for Algoma Contracting in Sault Ste. Marie, Ontario; Murray Dryden sold bricks and building materials. Their parents were also, to varying measure, hockey parents. Murray Dryden paved the backyard of the family home in the Toronto suburb of Islington with red asphalt, turning it into a year-round road hockey arena. Windows were boarded over and barred to prevent breakage; some days Margaret Dryden felt as if she was living in prison. Patrick Esposito was absolutely devoted to minor hockey, making sure Algoma Contracting sponsored the teams his sons played on, and when he decided the Soo needed a Junior A hockey club, he pooled his resources and with several partners founded the Greyhounds.

Dryden played Junior B in Toronto, and was good enough to be selected in the NHL's draft of unsigned amateurs in June 1964, not yet seventeen. Dryden was picked third by Boston, fourteenth overall. Boston thereupon committed one of the greatest recruiting errors of that decade, rivalled only by the Toronto Maple Leafs' failure to secure the rights to Brad Park in 1966, when Park was playing right in the Toronto feeder system. (For that matter, Toronto had also overlooked Ken Dryden, even though he, too, was in their territory—they had even once held the contract of brother Dave.) Right after the draft, Boston traded its rights to Ken Dryden and Alex Campbell to Montreal in exchange for the rights to Guy Allen and Paul Reid. Of the four, only Dryden ever played professionally.

At the age Dryden was drafted, Tony Esposito wasn't close to sure he was going to play professional hockey. He grew up in the shadow of his supremely talented older brother, and the fact that he had to wear glasses when he played (with a cage protector) hampered his game. His parents invested money in contact lenses when he was about sixteen, a considerable investment then, and that probably saved his career. Even then, he showed much more promise as a football halfback than as a hockey player. He hung in as a Juvenile player until his final year of eligibility, at eighteen, and then dropped out of hockey in favour of football. He probably would never have played Junior A if his dad hadn't organized the Greyhounds and the team hadn't badgered him into joining.

His Junior career was brief, lasting only the 1962/63 season. At nineteen, he got a hockey scholarship to Michigan Tech, arranged for him by a Soo sporting goods dealer, Al Bumbacco. In three seasons between 1964 and 1967, he played in fifty-one games with a 2.60 average. Whatever equivocation he had shown about the game back in the Soo, at Michigan Tech he was a standout. Twice named an All American, in 1965 he led Tech to the

OPPOSITE: TONY ESPOSITO CAME OUT OF OBSCURITY TO WIN THE CALDER AND THE VEZINA WITH A RECORD FIFTEEN SHUTOUTS IN 1969/70. HE REGULARLY PLAYED THE BULK OF THE BLACKHAWKS SEASON UNTIL HIS RETIREMENT IN 1984.

BELOW: A PROGRAM FROM THE 1972 CANADA–RUSSIA SERIES, SAVED BY A CANADIAN FAN WHO MADE THE TRIP TO MOSCOW.

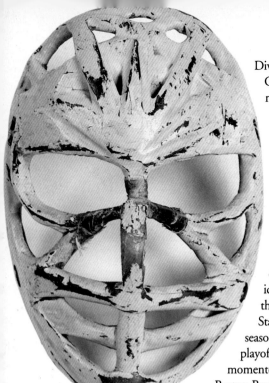

KEN DRYDEN WORE THIS MASK IN HIS COLLEGIATE DAYS AND IN HIS FIRST SEASONS AS A MONTREAL CANADIEN.

Division 1 championship. The Montreal Canadiens quietly placed him on their negotiating list.

Ken Dryden was concerned and fascinated with the idea of image in *The Game*. The image we have of him today is cerebral and academic; it has suffocated in the collective memory the Dryden the world was first introduced to: a brilliant, idealistic, even brash young man, a rangy talent who supposedly came out of nowhere—nowhere usually being identified as Cornell University—to lead the Montreal Canadiens to the 1970/71 Stanley Cup after playing only six regular-season games. His first act in those fabled playoffs was anchoring the Canadiens' momentous upset of the season's-champion Boston Bruins in the quarterfinal. Dryden came to understand that it was his performance in the 1970/71 Stanley Cup playoffs for which he will always be remembered. How he got there has been little appreciated, usually consigned to a convenient fog in favour of the out-of-nowhere myth. Dryden unquestionably burst upon the professional hockey scene in spectacular fashion, but he was not some longshot talent pulled off an unlikely shelf by the savvy Montreal management. Dryden had been promising stardom for some time. He simply wanted it on his terms.

Ken Dryden came into the professional hockey system just as it was undergoing its most significant change. After twenty-five seasons of stability as a six-team loop, the NHL expanded to twelve teams in 1967/68, and went on growing. At the same time, the old system of clubs securing the professional rights of amateurs through scouting systems, and then bringing those players up through affiliated amateur and minor professional teams, was dispensed with. A universal amateur draft, first held in 1969, divvied up talent in an ostensibly more equitable matter (for the professional teams), and sponsorships of amateur clubs were abolished. Ken's older brother Dave had come up through the old system, signed as an amateur by the Maple Leafs, playing his Junior hockey with the Leafs' affiliates, the St. Michael's College Majors and the Toronto Marlboros. Ken came in at the tail end of the old system, his amateur rights secured by Boston and then dealt to Montreal. But by the time his talent was sufficiently developed to make him a serious professional prospect, expansion had arrived and the lie of the land had changed entirely.

Montreal general manager Sam Pollock thought highly of the young Dryden, knew he wanted to get an education, and proposed that he play for the Peterborough Petes of the OHA Junior A and attend Trent University. Instead, Dryden accepted an athletic scholarship at Cornell University in upstate New York, home to a powerful Division 1 NCAA hockey program.

So it happened that the two most honoured NHL goaltenders of the 1970s, Ken Dryden and Tony Esposito, both matured in the U.S. college system while the property of the Montreal Canadiens; and their scholarships were accepted less as a ticket to NHL stardom than as a way to further their education. Young men who pursued a professional hockey career and a university degree were very rare. Some, like Maple Leafs Bob Pulford, Billy Harris and Dick Duff in the 1960s, got their degrees in the off-season. Dave Dryden made a concerted effort to get his degree while serving as Glenn Hall's backup in Chicago, taking time away from the game when necessary; today, he is a high school principal. The younger Ken always looked up to his brother—it was why he became a goaltender in the first place. And Dave's experiences and advice played an important role in Ken's decisions about his career path.

At Cornell, Ken earned a BA in history, with an eye to studying law, while amassing an outstanding collegiate hockey record. In three years at Cornell, he won seventy-one games, lost four and tied one, with a 1.65 GA. He was a three-time All American, as Cornell won the Division 1 title in 1967 and finished second in 1969. His first season of American college hockey was Tony Esposito's last.

The American collegiate system was not considered a serious route to the professional game; overwhelmingly, the Canadian Junior system was the dominant channel for young prospects. But Division 1 play was of a high quality, and as it happened, Montreal was in no great hurry to push Dryden into the professional ranks. The club's goaltending talent pool never looked better. In 1967/68, Montreal had Gump Worsley and his outstanding young backup, Rogatien Vachon; and out in British Columbia they had Tony Esposito. After graduating from Tech with a business degree in 1967, Esposito was assigned by the Canadiens to the Vancouver Canucks of the Western Hockey League. In sixty-one games he recorded a 3.20 GA; he would credit Vancouver coach Jim Gregory, who became general manager of the Maple Leafs, with giving him the opportunity to learn the goaltending trade.

Dryden, for his part, was in no hurry to turn pro. He wanted to begin his law studies. When Dryden graduated from Cornell in 1969, Sam Pollock had made a few adjustments to his goaltending pool. Worsley had suffered a nervous breakdown in November 1968, and was on his way out of Montreal. Vachon stepped into the void and played wonderfully, but when he hurt his hand Esposito had to be brought up from the Central League, where he was playing with the Houston Apollos. On December 5, he skated onto the ice of Boston Garden to face brother Phil, who after being traded away by Chicago in 1967 had turned into a scoring menace. Both brothers found the experience frightening; Phil found the chinks in Tony's armour and scored twice as the game ended 2–2. Tony was then given what should have been an easy game against the expansion Seals. "I fanned on two soft goals and let in the winner on a pretty easy backhander,"

Esposito would recall as the Seals won 5–4 and Montreal called up Ernie Wakely. But when Wakely lost 4–2 to New York, Esposito got another chance. "He makes fundamental errors one minute and a miraculous save the next," Montreal coach Claude Ruel would observe. Esposito played thirteen games for Montreal that season, but the Canadiens weren't sold on him. With Vachon back in fighting form, the Canadiens won the Stanley Cup. Esposito was a third wheel. Ken Dryden appeared to be the second.

Knowing that Dryden was determined to stay in school, and with Vachon doing so well, Pollock pulled some strings to get Dryden's career path on a course the Canadiens thought appropriate. Pollock brought Dryden to the attention of Canada's national team program.

In February 1969, Hockey Canada had been formed as a joint venture between the Canadian Amateur Hockey Association, the NHL, the NHL players' association and the Canadian government, its mandate to put Canada back on the international amateur hockey map after years of taking a back seat to the Russians, the Czechs, the Swedes, even the Americans. In the spring of 1969, with Vachon headed for a Stanley Cup and Esposito about to be left up for grabs in the June intraleague draft, Dryden was flown to Stockholm, where the world championships were under way and the Canadians had just been demolished by the Soviet Union 7–1. He played two games of what was a disastrous tournament for the amateur Canadians, although Dryden personally stood out, earning a 1–0 shutout against the Americans in the second round.

That same spring, a young goaltender's career on the other side of the Atlantic jumped onto the fast track. Vladislav Tretiak—Vladik to chums—was a seventeen-year-old who had just attended his second European Junior championships. He had been the team backup in 1968, when the Soviet team disappointed by finishing second. This time they won the title. When he returned home, the legendary Soviet coach Anatoly Tarasov brought him onto the Central Red Army team, the main source of players for the Soviet national team. Tarasov had resolved to fashion him into the world's best goaltender.

Tretiak was raised in the town of Dmitrovo, near Moscow, his father an armed forces pilot, his mother a gymnastics instructor and former field hockey player. Tretiak didn't reveal his father's occupation in his autobiography, noting only that he was very demanding, and that Vladik sometimes resented the pressure. His father was more concerned about academics than athletics; his mother plainly was the source of his sporting enthusiasm. He became interested in hockey fooling around with his mother's field hockey stick at home. For five years of his childhood, he attended summer sporting camps, every inch a product of the Soviet athletic development system. At ten, he made the cut of young boys who came to an open tryout session for midget hockey at the Central Army Children's Sports School; Tarasov was on the selection board. Tretiak was not yet a goaltender; he has said he decided to become one because all he really wanted was a team sweater, and if he tried out for the position he could have one. He trained for one and a half hours a day, three days a week. By the summer of 1967, at only fifteen, he was working out as a fourth goaltender with the Central Red Army team.

Tarasov's methods were brutal by Western standards. He worked his athletes relentlessly, on and off the ice, to the point of humiliation (and sometimes past it). He went after Tretiak for goals scored in practice, no matter how inconsequential. "My coach didn't want me to be indifferent to being scored on," Tretiak would explain. "He wanted me to feel that each puck in my net was a personal defeat."

The Soviets, in the course of winning every world and Olympic championship since 1962/63, had produced some great goaltenders, such as Nikolai Puchkov, Grigory Mkrtchan, and Viktor Konovalenko, who were idolized on their home ice. But the ultimate goaltender in Russian eyes was Jacques Plante. When the Soviets played an exhibition game against the Montreal Junior Canadiens in 1969, Plante, then forty, played goal for the Juniors, and the young Canadians won 2–1. Plante impressed Tarasov, who dissected his style, admired the way Plante moved out to challenge shooters, the way he studied his opponents. Tarasov added his own embellishments to the Plante style, and when he looked at the young Tretiak, he decided the young man could embody it. He had the height, the hands, the intelligence. In August 1969, Tretiak made his first trip to Sweden with Central Red Army, and while there attended a goaltending camp at Vasteras. On the personal insistence of Tarasov, Tretiak was added to the national team that autumn.

He was a model son of the Soviet system. He joined the team's Communist Youth League branch, and completed his entrance exams at the correspondence faculty of the Institute of Physical Education. "Of course, it wasn't easy to study," he would remember. "After practice, so tired that I could not even hold a book in my hands, I would force myself, with the help of coffee and cold showers, to get back to my studies. Homework, homework, and more homework. Five years later, I successfully completed the course."

When he returned home from the 1969 world championships, Dryden struggled with the options open to him. It was a very public debate; Dryden was not some anonymous amateur. He

PORTRAIT OF A GOALTENDER AS A YOUNG MAN. KEN DRYDEN AS A COLLEGIATE STAR AT CORNELL (BOTTOM); IN WASHINGTON, D.C. AS A NADER'S RAIDER THE SUMMER OF 1971, FOLLOWING HIS CONN SMYTHE–WINNING PERFORMANCE IN THE STANLEY CUP (TOP).

hired a New York agent, and he was reported to be seeking a multi-year contract from the Canadiens worth $100,000. The Canadiens wanted him to play for their new American League farm team, the Montreal Voyageurs, and study law at McGill. But he thought it was impossible to do both. Rapid developments on the international hockey front opened up an option. That summer, the newly formed Hockey Canada was able to wrest from the International Ice Hockey Federation a promise that Canada could use up to nine outright professional players on its team when it hosted the word championship the following March, provided they were not NHLers. Hockey Canada was now in a position to compensate players for their services; Canadians had been arguing for years that the Eastern Bloc players they faced at the Olympics and world championships were really paid professionals, in the case of players like Tretiak nothing more than hockey professionals given army rankings and pay (plus perks) and sent off to play hockey all year. Dryden opted for a three-year contract with the national team, which would pay him about $37,000, as opposed to about $50,000 a season with the Voyageurs. The national team program was based in Winnipeg, so Dryden could attend law school at the University of Manitoba. He was the first important signing for the national team under the new contractual program. The first universal amateur draft was held by the NHL that summer, and the national team program was in a lopsided competition for the hearts and skills of talented amateurs. Dryden was a high-profile example of an alternative development path open to young hockey players with scholastic ambition.

AN EARLY GLANCE AT GREATNESS: A SEVENTEEN-YEAR-OLD VLADISLAV TRETIAK FENDS OFF THE CANADIAN NATIONAL TEAM IN DECEMBER 1969, TWO AND A HALF YEARS BEFORE A SCOUTING REPORT PROMISED A MEDIOCRE PERFORMANCE FROM HIM IN THE 1972 CANADA–RUSSIA SERIES.

Dryden attended a tournament in Leningrad in late August, and wrote an article for *Sport Canada* magazine on his return. He had just turned twenty-two, and comes across as a typically bright postgraduate who has been touched by the social upheavals of the day. Encountering Soviet university students, he welcomes the opportunity to discuss pressing issues. Vietnam, for example, elicits Dryden's disapproval (the Cornell campus experienced antiwar rioting), as it naturally does theirs.

On matters of hockey, the Dryden article supplies interesting observations. The Canadians won the tournament, although Dryden was well aware that they were not playing the very best Soviet teams. Dryden had never played a Russian club before, and he came away from the Leningrad experience less impressed than puzzled by the Russian style. "They play a puck-control game, like ball-control in basketball," he wrote in *Sport Canada*. "Most players don't shoot very hard, but by passing it around until they find a player in a scoring position, they don't need to. However, for the number of times they find a man in a good scoring position, they score less often than they should."

Meanwhile, training camps for the NHL were being held. That summer, Sam Pollock had left Tony Esposito off his protected list, and on June 11, Chicago picked him up for the $30,000 draft fee due to Montreal. Esposito came into camp with two established netminders ahead of him: Denis DeJordy, who had won the Vezina with Glenn Hall in 1966/67 and was favoured to get the starter's job, and Dave Dryden, who had also served as Hall's backup between breaks to complete his university education.

At twenty-six, Esposito seized the opportunity, taking charge of the Blackhawks goal and playing sixty-three of seventy games. Dave Dryden took the year off to work on his education; DeJordy was dealt to Los Angeles. Little in Esposito's résumé foreshadowed the season that unfolded. He recorded a 2.17 average and won the Vezina. He also won the Calder, and was the only player other than Bobby Orr to be declared a unanimous selection for the first All Star team. Of 180 votes actually cast, Esposito attracted 178. He set a modern record of fifteen shutouts, a feat that turned his name into "Tony O" with Blackhawks fans. In his fifty-one games with Michigan Tech, he had only recorded two shutouts. He had managed four with the Canucks in sixty-one games, and one in nineteen games with the Houston Apollos. But his performance with Montreal the previous season, two

games. Boston and Chicago—the teams of the Esposito brothers—ended the season tied at ninety-nine points, but Chicago took first overall by having the most wins. It was all academic. In the playoffs, the Bruins took apart the Blackhawks. Brother Phil pumped goals past Tony, driving his playoff GA above 3.00. The hockey world was not yet convinced that Tony Esposito was the real thing.

Within six months of Dryden's signing a three-year contract with the national team, the program was in serious trouble. The Russians were unhappy with the IIHF decision to allow Canadian professionals at the 1970 worlds, and Avery Brundage, president of the International Olympic Committee, joined them in putting pressure on the IIHF to back out of the agreement.

The Soviet national team came to Canada in December 1969 for an eight-game tour, playing the Canadian team in different cities. Konovalenko was the starting goaltender for the Soviets, Wayne Stephenson the main netminder for Canada. (Stephenson would play more than nine seasons in the NHL, five of them in Philadelphia, and he and Dryden would meet in Montreal's four-game sweep of Philadelphia in the Stanley Cup final of 1975/76.) In the game in Vancouver, the backups took to the ice. More than 13,000 fans turned out to see the Soviets play a very different kind of game from the one Dryden had encountered in Leningrad. These Russians weren't just passing the puck around. They were shooting it. Forty-four of them found the Canadian net, and nine of them went in. Dryden would remember thinking in the midst of the barrage, "What am I doing here?" Tretiak, at the other end of the rink, allowed three goals. The next night, in Victoria, Stephenson was back in the net, and the Canadians repented with a 5–1 victory.

While the Canadians fared reasonably well in the series, splitting their four western games with the Soviets, it was all for naught. The IIHF was reneging on its promise about the eligibility of Canadian professionals. Canada pulled out of hosting the worlds, and the national team program was in disarray. Sam Pollock would call Dryden's spell with the national team "a wasted year."

Dryden was supposed to remain with the national team through to the 1972 Olympics, but the program's confused state following Canada's cancellation of the world championship clouded his future. Montreal could not have been confident he would actually leave the national team program, though. In June 1970, the Canadiens took the significant step of using one of their two first-round draft picks to secure a goaltender, Flin Flon's Ray Martiniuk. As it happened, Martiniuk never did make the professional ranks, and that summer Dryden decided to leave the national team. He was turning twenty-three, which meant he was getting on

shutouts in thirteen games, had hinted at the capability to blank the opposition.

He had his detractors. There was the matter of the complete rebuild of the Blackhawks philosophy that season. Gone was the shoot-em-up offence, and in its place was a newfound emphasis on tight defence. Bobby Hull was even converted (temporarily) from left wing to centre. A superb defence corps of Doug Jarrett, Keith Magnuson, Bill White and Pat Stapleton, along with some capable backchecking by the forwards, was given much of the credit for Esposito's performance.

Then there was the matter of style. Esposito had adopted the trademark butterfly style of Hall, and he had Hall's size, being an inch shorter at five-foot-eleven and about twenty pounds heavier, at 185 pounds. "I probably watched Glenn Hall more than any other netminder," Esposito would explain. "He is sort of an expedient type of a goalie, and I think that is my style. I just try to stop the puck."

But his mechanics scandalized the experts. He hung too far back in his net, they groused, making stops right on the goal crease. Conversely, others were ready to argue that he played too far *out* of the net. And he gave up big rebounds and didn't seem to know what to do with loose pucks at his feet. None of that mattered much to the Blackhawks. He got in the way of the puck. They won for a professional prospect.

"I had an agreement with Hockey Canada and I could have had a comfortable life, collecting my money from them and playing at the University of Toronto, but I've had enough college hockey," he explained. "I decided if I was going to continue playing, it would have to be with the pros." He was no longer so intimidated by the thought of playing in the American League and going to school. For the first part of the season he would concentrate on his law books at McGill, and then would start playing with the Voyageurs.

He played for the Canadiens in an exhibition game against the Bruins that fall, stopping forty-two shots as Montreal won 5–4. He was a standout of the game, and if he hadn't been set on law school he certainly could have begun playing regularly in the NHL that very autumn, though probably (at least initially) as a backup to Vachon. Only one thousand fans turned out to see him make his professional debut in a regular-season game, when his Voyageurs defeated the Quebec Aces 4–0 on December 12, 1970.

He played thirty-three games for the Voyageurs, recording three shutouts and a GA of 2.68. When Sam Pollock brought him up to the Canadiens at the end of the season, he knew exactly what he was getting: a tremendous talent he had been steering into a Canadiens uniform for almost seven years.

Montreal's main goaltender was Rogie Vachon, who was having an uncharacteristically uneven season and didn't have the faith of management that he could carry the team through the playoffs. The Canadiens turned to Dryden, who would come to see how shrewdly the club had prepared him for the playoffs, letting him get the feel of the NHL game against weak expansion teams in the last half-dozen games before subjecting him to the firepower of the Bruins in the opening round. In those six end-of-season games, he gave up only nine goals. On March 20, the Canadiens hosted one such expansion club, the Buffalo Sabres, at the Forum. The Sabres, who were in their first season, started the game with Joe Daley in the net. Montreal went with Vachon. When Vachon was injured, Montreal coach Al MacNeil sent out Dryden. Sitting on the Sabres bench was Ken's brother Dave, back from university. Sabres coach Punch Imlach could not resist giving history a helping hand. He pulled Daley and sent Dave out to play against Ken. Each allowed two goals as Montreal won 5–2. It was the first time the NHL had ever seen two netminding brothers confront each other. On the final weekend of the season, Dryden was held in reserve as the Bruins punished Montreal 7–2, their fifth victory in six encounters between the two clubs that season.

The Bruins were the first club in the NHL to have two 50-goal scorers in one season, Phil Esposito and Johnny Bucyk, and then there was Bobby Orr, who produced 19 more points than the 120 that won him the scoring crown of 1969/70, and still had to settle for second behind Esposito. The team's 399 goals for the season was 108 better than Montreal, the second-best offensive

unit. And with Gerry Cheevers and Eddie Johnston in goal, the Bruins had allowed nine fewer goals than the Canadiens.

Dryden did not shut down the Bruins easily. Montreal lost the opener 3–1, and were trailing the second game 5–1 before rallying in the third period to win 7–5. But Dryden was playing so well that, had he not been on the ice, both games could have been substantial Bruins victories. With the series tied 2–2, Dryden had held Phil Esposito to a single goal. "I'll solve that guy yet, even if I have to shorten his catching arm about a foot," Espo promised. As it happened, Dryden was staggered in game five, a 6–3 loss that allowed Boston to move within a game of advancing to the semifinal. But the Canadiens refused to switch to Vachon, and Dryden carried them through the two victories needed to topple the Bruins in seven games. "That guy Dryden, he was unbelievable," said Orr. "Fantastic. We called him the Octopus. That's exactly what he was like out there." In seven games, Boston had fired 260 shots at Dryden. He had stopped all but twenty-six.

Dryden's giant-killing performance in the quarterfinal had been charged with undetected irony. As a kid, he "always insisted on wearing a Bruins jersey," his mother Margaret would relate. "Boston was always Ken's team as a boy." And Boston had very nearly ended up being Ken's team, having selected him in the 1964 draft.

After dispensing with Boston, Montreal rolled over Minnesota and advanced to meet Chicago in the cup final. It is a seven-game series that hockey fans have all but forgotten. The Boston–Montreal match-up in the quarterfinal echoes down from the spring of 1971. Esposito, too, was overshadowed by this striking newcomer. Already he had been passed over in All Star voting in this, his sophomore season, the first-team selection going to Eddie Giacomin, the second-team to the ageless Plante, now with the Maple Leafs. He had only six shutouts in the season, but his 2.27 GA was very, very good—as good as the the Rangers' team GA, which won Giacomin and Gilles Villemure the Vezina. In eighteen playoff games, Esposito whittled his season GA down to 2.19, proving that he could excel in the post-season. But the final series against Montreal only served to put another annoying asterisk of doubt against his accomplishments. In the deciding game, with Chicago leading 2–0, Esposito surrendered three goals, including a sixty-footer by Jacques Lemaire. Montreal won the cup, and Ken Dryden took home the Conn Smythe.

Dryden and Esposito had both been collegiate goaltenders, but they could not have been more different people. Michigan Tech was not Cornell. Dryden's school was in the Ivy League loop, while Tech was stuck up in Houghton, in the copper belt at the tip of Michigan. It was, however, a longstanding hockey hotbed. In 1903, the world's first professional team, the Portage Lakers, had been formed in Houghton by a transplanted Canadian dentist and outfitted exclusively with Canadian stars. Tech was a place where

Esposito could play softball and be one of the guys. A base runner once ended up being stripped naked; Esposito got into trouble when he accidentally broke a glass of beer on the back of someone's head. Cornell was the sort of eastern American college in the late sixties where new ideas were in ferment, where an idealist drawn to activism could find inspiration. Dryden came from a devoted United Church family; his father had a Christmas tree farm whose proceeds he used to underwrite a charity, Sleeping Children Around the World, which supplied bedding for Third World children. In the summer of 1970, when Dryden dropped out of the national team program, he and his wife did the VW microbus camping tour of Europe.

In his first year at Cornell, Dryden had read Ralph Nader's damning indictment of the U.S. auto industry, *Unsafe at Any Speed*. The summer that followed his Stanley Cup victory, Dryden secured a summer job with Nader's Raiders in Washington, D.C., his assigned cause helping fishermen fight for clean water. He returned to the Canadiens that fall, a peculiar but captivating blend of netminding brilliance and social activism. He spoke of writing a book, to be called "Citizen Action in Canada," which would explore why people don't become involved in social issues. In November, he was appointed to the legal advisory committee of the Society to Overcome Pollution. He lamented the state of the St. Lawrence River. After sizing up the talent of this (by hockey standards) eccentric newcomer, Rogie Vachon asked to be traded, and went to Los Angeles.

Dryden's Stanley Cup heroics proved not to be a fluke. Technically, he was still a rookie, and he won the Calder in 1971/72; he also made the second All Star team. Tony Esposito earned the first-team selection. There was no miracle playoff performance, though. The Bruins, even more accomplished than in 1970/71, lost only three of fifteen post-season games as they drove over the rest of the league in pursuit of the Stanley Cup.

Dryden's attitude to the game was either a breath of fresh air or disturbingly indifferent, depending on the perspective applied. Those who thought that an NHL career should be the crowning glory of any young Canadian male's life were perturbed. He had difficulty seeing himself as a professional hockey player. In his first few seasons in Montreal, he wrote "law student" as his occupation on the green card he needed to play on the road in the U.S.

"I can't say I want to win the Stanley Cup for each of the next ten years," he said in December 1971. "Sure, I'd like to, but that's not what you think about. I just want to stop the next shot, win the next game. So far, I really like hockey and I'll continue to play it as long as I enjoy it. Or

as long as I enjoy it more than other things."

Esposito never enjoyed it. "It's a job, that's what it is, a job," he would say in 1972. "I have to do it. But it's tough. I don't like it. To be playing well as a goalkeeper, you have to be afraid. Not afraid that you'll get hurt, but afraid that they're going to score on you. Every time they come down the ice with that puck, I'm afraid the puck is going to go in."

After the Soviets won the world championship in the spring of 1971, the spring that introduced Dryden so abruptly to the fans of the professional game, Tretiak took over from Konovalenko as the national team's starter. In the winter of 1972, Tretiak played in his first Olympic Games, in Sapporo, Japan. The Soviets won the gold medal, the United States the silver, the Czechs (surprise world champions that year) the bronze.

The international amateur game was not taken seriously in North America. Sportswriters still routinely referred to the Stanley Cup winners as the world champions, as if the result of a contest with a foreign team would be a foregone conclusion. Come September, though, Canada was going to at last get a chance to prove what the stuffy regulations on amateur status would never allow it to prove at the world and Olympic level. A select squad of Canadian professionals (save players signing with the new World Hockey Association, made ineligible by litigation between the two professional leagues) were to meet the reigning Olympic champions of the Soviet Union in an eight-game series.

As the first- and second-team All Stars, Dryden and Esposito were natural choices as the two starting goaltenders for Team Canada. Because of the ineligibility of stars crossing over to the WHA, the Team Canada brain trust of Harry Sinden and John Ferguson had to scratch an important name, Gerry Cheevers, from their wish list. On the opposing team, twenty-year-old Vladislav Tretiak was expected to carry the entire series for the Soviets.

The Red Machine was not given much of a chance, and its goaltender was probably the Russian given the least chance of all. But the first sixty minutes of the tournament transformed Tretiak from an absolute unknown into a household name. It is difficult to understand today just how big an unknown Tretiak was, although his anonymity does underline the complete indifference North America displayed toward international amateur hockey. Tretiak was not a Ken Dryden brought into the last six games of the season and sprung on the Boston Bruins. He'd been the starting goaltender for the Soviets for about eighteen months, and had a world championship tournament and an Olympic Games to his credit. The story of the Canadian scouting faux pas made prior to the 1972 series has been oft told. Gerry McNamara took in a performance of Tretiak's with Central Red Army on August 22, shortly before the Soviet national team was due to leave for Montreal for the start of the series on September 6. Tretiak was a sieve, allowing nine goals. McNamara went home to report that goaltending was the least of the Canadians' worries. What McNamara didn't know was that Tretiak was getting married the very next morning, and was somewhat distracted as a result. Two days after his wedding, he was flying to Montreal. "I tell people I spent my honeymoon with Canadian players," he would say.

Before the opening game in Montreal, Tretiak received an extraordinary visit. Jacques Plante appeared with a translator. He had met the young Tretiak before, and in 1971 had given him a copy of his goaltending manual. "Steady strain," he told Tretiak in the Forum dressing room. "That is the fate of us goaltenders." He went to the dressing room's blackboard and proceeded to explain to Tretiak how to play the big Canadian guns. Tarasov (who had been replaced as the national team coach the previous spring) had always admired Plante's capacity to study and catalogue his adversaries. Now Plante was giving Tarasov's protégé an unmatchable tutorial on the moves of the likes of Mahovlich, Cournoyer and Phil Esposito. Mahovlich would unwittingly remark after the game that Tretiak had played him like he'd known Mahovlich since he was a kid.

"I'm still puzzled by what motivated him to do that," Tretiak would say of Plante's visit, fifteen years later. "He probably felt sorry for me, the little guy, in whom Esposito was going to shoot holes."

What transpired is now firmly cemented in sporting

lore. Dryden drew the opening assignment in Montreal, and suffered the most humiliating defeat of his career as the Soviets and Tretiak won 7–3.

Dryden personally suffered the consequences of the lack of preparation of an entire team that night. And while the loss cut all the Canadian superstars down a notch, none felt the cut more deeply than Dryden, who had to endure the loss in his own rink. Standing nearly six-foot-four and weighing about 210 pounds, Dryden covered a lot of net. His trademark was a lightning quick glove hand; his weak spot, if not in actual skill then in style, was that he tended to look bad on goals. With his size came an image of ungainliness when he was down on the ice. It didn't matter that he made some of his career's most spectacular saves when it appeared he had no hope at all. The ones that did get by him managed to make him look even more helpless than a smaller man. Dryden was conscious of this; he didn't like watching films of himself playing. In the Montreal Forum, on September 6, 1972, a substantial part of the nation watched him get stung for seven goals, three coming in the game's final six

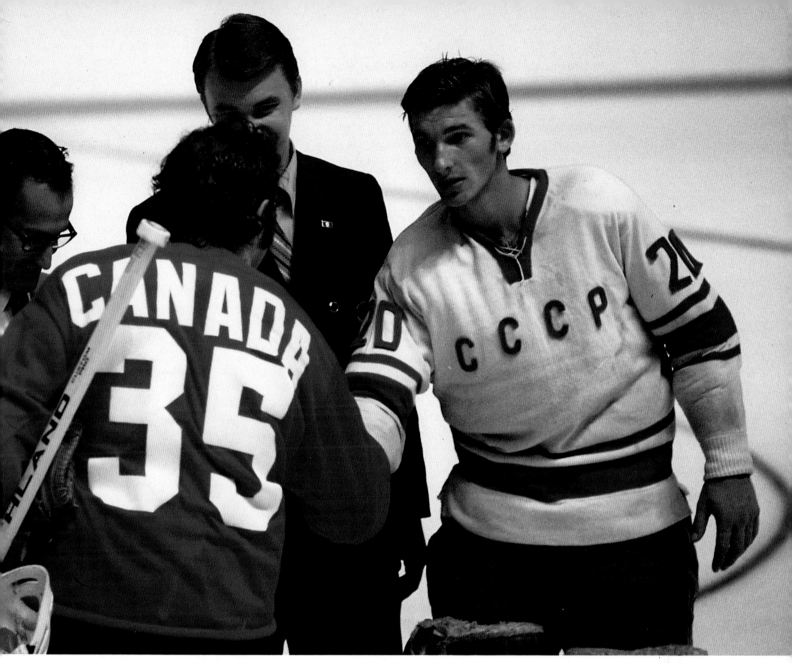

and a half minutes. While in later years the country would explain away the Canadian overconfidence by citing our professionals' unfamiliarity with the international game and its stars, Dryden had had at least some limited experience in that theatre in 1969 and 1970.

After the 7–3 blowout, the team lineup was overhauled; one of the most significant changes was the switch to the proven Chicago defensive ensemble of Tony Esposito, Pat Stapleton and Bill White. With Esposito in goal for the next two games, the Canadians came away with a 4–1 win and a 5–5 tie. Tretiak was not going to be relieved by anybody if he could help it—he was one of those goaltenders, like Esposito in the NHL, who was going to play every single game if his health permitted.

After three games, Canadian backup Eddie Johnston complimented the young Russian. "He's making the big saves, and I think he's still developing. He doesn't come out very far to cut down the angles. Don't get me wrong on this, though. There are just a couple of minor adjustments he could make and meanwhile he can stop the puck."

Remarkably, Tretiak *was* still learning even as he was turning away the best scorers in the Canadian game. Three years would pass before he was playing at what he felt was his peak. Tretiak would confess in his autobiography that in his early years in goal he was afraid to wander from the crease; it was a phobia that also gripped Bernie Parent, another goaltender who had been greatly influenced by Plante. Tretiak graduated from the Regional Institute of Physical Culture in Smolensk by writing a thesis entitled "A Research of Tactical Actions of a Hockey Goalkeeper." He would write in his memoirs: "For many years, my movements had been limited and bound by the goal crease. In no way could I overcome the fear of leaving the net to come forward and handle the puck." He would defeat this phobia by practising quick rushes and retreats to the faceoff circles: "I learned to find the net intuitively from anywhere on the ice."

When Dryden returned to the net in Vancouver for game three, the Canadians came up flat, and lost 5–3. The last time he had faced a Soviet team complete with Tretiak in Vancouver, he had surrendered nine goals. On this visit to Vancouver, he was one of the Canadian players who were the target of booing. In two games of the 1972 series, he surrendered twelve goals.

Two-thirds of the way through the opening game of the Soviet leg of the series, it appeared that it would be left to Esposito to provide the Canadian netminding heroics. He had already logged a win and a tie, allowing only six goals, back in Canada. Esposito was anchoring an impressive 4–1 lead for the Canadians in the third period when the Soviets came back and scored four unanswered goals to put their record at three wins, one loss and one tie. "We should have won it 7–0," series co-organizer Alan Eagleson told author Scott Young in *War on Ice.* "But Tony had a bad third period in goal... He just shook his head and said, 'I blew it. There was no way they should have got five goals in one period. I'm the one to blame. Goddamnit, we can beat them, and we would have tonight if I hadn't let you down.' "

Such unadorned humility was typical of Esposito. He was always, first and foremost, a team player. He did not point fingers when he had an off game. Esposito's apology provided a catharsis for the rest of the team. He gave them permission to break one of the game's taboos, to blame the goaltender. The team had played more than

AFTER HIS THIRTEEN-GAME TRYOUT WITH MONTREAL, TONY ESPOSITO SPENT HIS ENTIRE NHL CAREER WITH THE CHICAGO BLACKHAWKS.

well enough to win. Esposito helped make them recognize that the series was winnable. Eagleson came to see the Esposito apology as an important rallying point.

The door was left open for Dryden to redeem both himself and the Canadians. In game six he made sure the team came away with a critical 3–2 win, although both Dryden and Eagleson knew it should have been 3–3—a shot in the first period beat Dryden, caught a bit of net and dropped into Dryden's glove before the goal judge could see what happened.

And Esposito was not finished. He was in the net for the 4–3 win of game seven, and finished the tournament with the best GA and won–lost record of all three goaltenders. Tretiak, playing every Soviet game, won three, lost four and tied one, with a GA of 4.00. Esposito won two and lost two, with a GA of 3.50. Dryden won two and lost two, with a GA of 4.75. It was Dryden, in the net for the final game, shutting down the Soviets in the third period as his teammates rallied from a 5–3 deficit to win the game and the series, who would emerge as one of our most memorable players. But it was Tretiak, a thrilling novelty for Canadian fans whose enthusiasm for excellence did not recognize uniforms, who became the biggest goaltending star as a result of the Canadian win. The Henderson goal in the dying seconds of the game, the most famous goal ever scored in hockey, never made a scapegoat of Tretiak. "I will always count that goal as the most maddening of all goals scored on me in hockey," Tretiak would write. The game's fans put it out of their minds when estimating Tretiak, and waited eagerly to see him play again.

Dryden followed up his Team Canada success with another Stanley Cup, his first Vezina and a first-team All Star appearance. Now the professional game's most celebrated goaltender, he proceeded to do the least expected thing. He quit.

It should not have been entirely unexpected. Dryden had graduated from law school in early 1973, and he had to begin articling within two years. That would mean a full year of apprenticing at a law firm; playing NHL hockey at the same time would be out of the question. He was even interviewed at the time of his graduation about his immediate future. But when Dryden walked out on the Canadiens just before the start of training camp in September 1973, he made it clear at the press conference he called on September 15 that, articling aside, money had come between him and the team. He had signed a two-year contract after the 1971/72 season, but when his Team Canada stint was over in the fall of 1972 he had asked Montreal management if they would improve it. Management said nothing; Dryden seriously considered quitting right then, but decided to play. He couldn't have hoped for a better season, which was capped by the Canadiens defeating Tony Esposito and the Blackhawks in six games for the Stanley Cup. But over the course of the season Dryden watched the influence

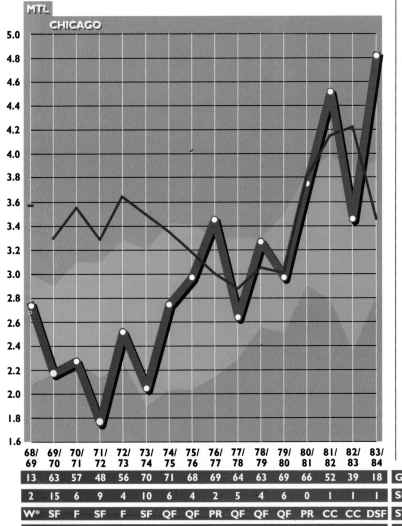

	68/69	69/70	70/71	71/72	72/73	73/74	74/75	75/76	76/77	77/78	78/79	79/80	80/81	81/82	82/83	83/84	
GAMES	13	63	57	48	56	70	71	68	69	64	63	69	66	52	39	18	
SHUTOUTS	2	15	6	9	4	10	6	4	2	5	4	6	0	1	1	1	
STANLEY CUP	W*	SF	F	SF	F	SF	QF	QF	PR	QF	QF	QF	PR	CC	CC	DSF	
ALL STAR TEAM		1			1	2	2						1				

ence of the World Hockey Association drive up player salaries, goaltenders included. Dryden was getting about $80,000 a year. Bernie Parent was lured to the WHA with a five-year deal worth $150,000 a year—and this before Parent had even established himself as a marquee netminder. "I can name six goaltenders who were higher paid than me," Dryden said at the press conference. "That bothers me and I can't see any reason why this should be the case."

He took flak. "We're in a sorry state when lawyers don't honour contracts," Leafs coach Red Kelly said. Gump Worsley, beginning his final NHL season in Minnesota, was disgusted. "I never understood why he quit the Canadiens," he would write. "Hell, he was president of the NHL Players' Association, and he had a contract he was supposed to honour. One day he'll find out that money isn't everything. As far as his comeback is concerned, I'll be sitting and watching, but I won't be rooting."

Dryden was exasperated with the criticism. He hadn't broken any contract. The contract only called on him to play for the Canadiens *if* he chose to play hockey. He chose not to play hockey. On September 17, he began articling at the Toronto law firm of Osler, Hoskin and Harcourt for $134 a week.

"I heard he's getting by on $125 a week while he's articling," said Montreal sniper Steve Shutt, "so I phoned him up and offered him $150 to chauffeur the 1956 Bentley I just bought."

Alan Eagleson, executive director of the players' association and a lawyer himself, simply could not believe that Dryden was serious about taking a year off hockey. "I can't see the best goalie in the game sitting out until his NHL contract expires next year." Eagleson (who didn't even represent Dryden) floated the idea of a trade to Toronto to allow him to keep playing while he continued to article. (Dryden couldn't article in Montreal because Quebec's civil law, based on French precedent, was entirely different from the English civil law in which Dryden was trained.)

Dryden stayed true to his word, plugging away at his articling, playing some industrial league hockey as a forward to keep in shape. Early in his articling, he had talks with the Toronto Toros of the WHA about playing with them when his contract with Montreal expired, but they came to nothing—as far as Dryden understood, Montreal would have first dibs on his professional services anyway. The season that followed Ken Dryden's year of articling, his brother Dave left Buffalo to play in the WHA, where he stayed for the life of the league.

While Ken Dryden was away from the game, Esposito shared the Vezina with Philadelphia's Bernie Parent (who had returned from an unhappy one-season stint in the WHA), and the Flyers won the Stanley Cup. And another summit series was organized, this one between the stars of the WHA and the Soviets. The Soviets won this time, but they didn't overwhelm the Canadians, who came to play with a more European-influenced style, and the series was a big boost for the rep-

utation of the WHA. Tretiak, for his part, was impressed with the Canadian goaltender, Gerry Cheevers. He is the only goaltender he faced in competition with the Canadians who elicited individual praise from him in his autobiography. He was "superb" in the opening game in Quebec City, a 3–3 tie. "I was fascinated by the goalie Gerry Cheevers. He was fearless, skillful and calm; a very good goalkeeper. As an individual he was one in a million. Before the game he would come over and hit me on the pads with his stick, his way of wishing me good luck. What I could not understand is that he smoked." Asked in 1984 who the best goaltender in the world was or is, he replied, "Of those I could see, unquestionably Gerry Cheevers. In 1974 he was outstanding." He made no mention of Esposito's skills in his autobiography. Of Dryden, he only noted cuttingly that the first time he had played against him, Dryden had given up nine goals.

A year later, the North American professionals and the Soviets were at it again, this time when the top Soviet clubs played an exhibition series against NHL teams. Tretiak and Central Red Army, boasting a lineup chock full of national team members, came to Montreal's Forum to play the Canadiens on New Year's Eve, 1975. It has been called the greatest hockey game ever played. In this Dryden–Tretiak showdown, Dryden played a tentative game, stopping only ten of thirteen shots he faced all night, although it has been noted that at least ten of those shots were solid scoring chances. Tretiak was the single largest factor in preventing a romp by the Canadiens, turning away thirty-five of thirty-eight shots as Montreal saw a 3–1 lead slide into a 3–3 tie. After the game, Tretiak posed with fellow game stars Yvon Cournoyer and Peter Mahovlich. It was as if he had become an honorary citizen of the Forum, a goaltender boasting as special a relationship with the venerable building as Dryden or Plante.

In fact, Tretiak wanted nothing more than Dryden had, which was a brilliant career in the NHL, above all with the Canadiens. All ups and downs in the international game aside, Dryden had established his rightful position in the pantheon of goaltending greats by performing superbly in hockey's most fabled environment, the NHL. "He reminds me of Glenn Hall," his coach, Scotty Bowman, had said back in 1971, invoking the same goaltending great that had inspired Esposito. "He

TEAMMATES: WHILE TONY ESPOSITO COMPILED THE BEST WON–LOST RECORD AND GA OF THE THREE GOALTENDERS WHO PLAYED IN THE 1972 CANADA–RUSSIA SERIES, IT WAS KEN DRYDEN'S PERFORMANCE IN THE FINAL PERIOD OF THE FINAL GAME, SHUTTING DOWN THE SOVIETS AS HIS TEAMMATES MOUNTED THE COMEBACK VICTORY, WHICH HAS LEFT THE MOST LASTING IMPRESSION.

can make the big save when you need it. He can give you the big period when you need it. His style is similar to Hall and so is his courage and ability to rise to the occasion."

When Dryden returned to the game in 1974/75 after a one-year hiatus, he absolutely dominated the position. In his first season back, the Flyers still ruled the league, and Bernie Parent won the Vezina and the first-team All Star berth, with Rogie Vachon second. But for the next four seasons, as Montreal won every Stanley Cup, the Vezina was Dryden's, and so was the first-team All Star spot. No goaltender had so lorded over both categories of awards since Jacques Plante had reigned supreme when the Canadiens owned the Stanley Cup in the late 1950s. And no team had ever experienced the scoring surplus of the Canadiens dynasty of the late 1970s; between the team's scoring and Dryden's netminding, the average Canadiens game came with a built-in cushion of two to three goals.

When the first Canada Cup tournament was held in 1976, Tretiak and Esposito were on hand, but not Dryden. Both he and Parent were sidelined by injuries. The goaltending job for the Canadian team fell exclusively to Vachon, who started the series hot and stayed in the net right through to the Canadian victory. Esposito never got on the ice. Tretiak was part of a Soviet national team in the process of rebuilding. Although they had won Olympic gold at Innsbruck, Austria, they finished second and third at the next two world championships as the Czechs took over. At the first Canada Cup, the Soviets didn't even make it out of the opening round.

Viktor Tikhonov took over the national team in 1977, and Tretiak chafed under his authoritarian style. His play suffered; he started taking sleeping pills to get a night's rest. His image back in North America remained that of an indomitable netminder, but the fans who saw him shine in the Forum weren't around to see him have a seven-goal game, or to see the occasional sixty-footer slip by him. It was Dryden's misfortune to have had his most vulnerable moments in front of a home crowd; Tretiak was struggling out of the North American limelight.

The Russian star recovered his form in 1979, when he and the Soviets returned to North America for the Challenge Cup, a three-game miniseries against the NHL All Stars at Madison Square Garden. Coach Scotty Bowman iced a team dominated by his Stanley Cup champion Canadiens, which meant Dryden was back to face Tretiak. The NHLers won the opening game 4–2, and were leading the second game 4–2 when the Soviets rebounded to win 5–4; with his typically blunt feelings with regard to Dryden, Tretiak wrote that the goaltender opposing him had "panicked." Dryden for his part described the Soviets of the Challenge series as "robot-like." He and Tretiak would never see eye to eye on the differences in the games their two systems played. To Dryden, the Soviets were too patterned and predictable, a squad of rote disciplinarians; to Tretiak, his countrymen played with a creative, balletic artistry. For the deciding game of the Challenge Cup series, the NHL team switched to Cheevers, whom Tretiak so admired. The Soviets tarred him 6–0.

At the end of the season, Ken Dryden retired. He was thirty-one years old. In eight NHL seasons, he had won the Vezina five times, made the first All Star team five times and the second team once, won the Conn Smythe once and the Stanley Cup six times. He had expe-

KEN DRYDEN STANDS GUARD BEHIND SERGE SAVARD AND GUY LAPOINTE. CANADIENS COACH SCOTTY BOWMAN ADMIRED DRYDEN'S COURAGE AND CONSISTENCY. HIS OUTSTANDING GA AND THE TEAM'S PROLIFIC SCORING PRODUCED A TWO- TO THREE-GOAL ADVANTAGE IN AN AVERAGE GAME.

MONTREAL

	70/71	71/72	72/73	73/74	74/75	75/76	76/77	77/78	78/79	
	6	64	54		56	62	56	52	47	GAMES
	0	8	6		4	8	10	5	5	SHUTOUTS
	W	QF	W		SF	W	W	W	W	STANLEY CUP
		2	1			1	1	1	1	ALL STAR TEAM

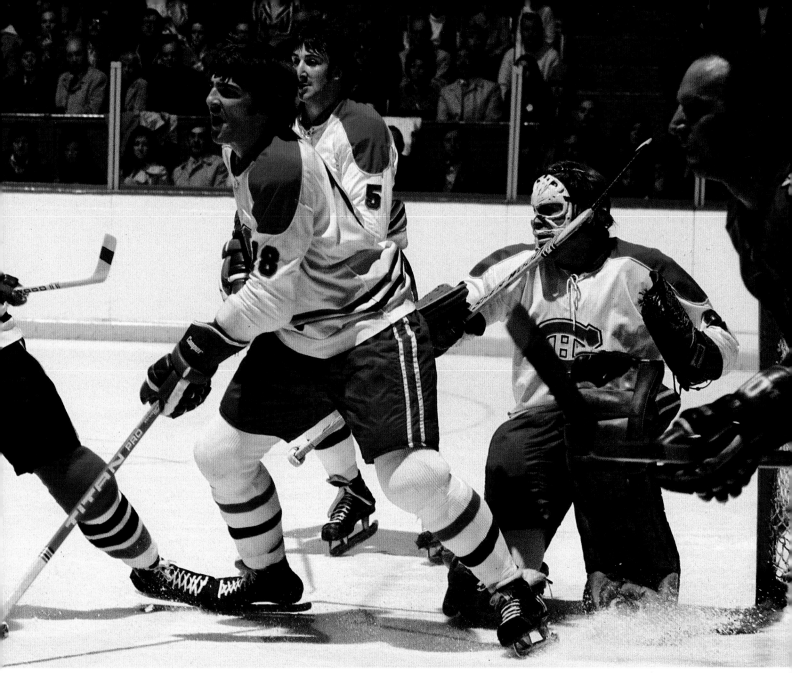

rienced a professional epiphany in a game against the struggling (and shortlived) Colorado Rockies. He let in some soft goals, but after every goal his teammates just went out and got another one, until the Canadiens finally won the game 6–5. It struck Dryden then that this team didn't need him any more to win.

It was an ironic turnabout for Dryden. In the first phase of his Montreal career, he had been the aloof intellectual. "Before my sabbatical season," he wrote, "I had little time for the team... I was young, and, in pre-dynasty times, better than the team. I had standards no one could meet. Those who didn't backcheck as often as I thought they should, those who drank too much, let *me* down. They had seemed more like opponents than teammates, lined up against me, keeping me from being what I wanted to be. And, silently, I raged at them."

When he came back, the team as a whole was better, and he felt more a part of it. Yet, he wrote, "It became less clear to others, finally to me, who needed whom."

The team won a record sixty of eighty games in

1976/77, fifty-nine in 1977/78. They were so powerful that Dryden pronounced the 1977/78 Stanley Cup playoffs a bore. With his wife and their two children, Dryden moved to Cambridge, England, to further his education, wrote *The Game*, and in the process created an entirely fresh perspective on his profession and the sport.

When the Soviets regained the world title from the Czechs in 1978 and defended it in 1979, with Tretiak named the championship's top goaltender, his career appeared to be back on track. But at the 1980 Olympics at Lake Placid Tretiak's career fell apart in front of the entire hockey world. In the semifinal game against the inspired U.S. team, which would decide who had a shot at the gold medal, Tretiak was stunned by a bizarre goal in the dying moments of the first period, with the Soviets ahead 2–1. As the seconds ticked away, Dave Christian fired a long shot at Tretiak, which he stopped. Almost everyone on the ice—everyone except Mark Johnson—was relaxing and getting

back in North America for the 1981 Canada Cup, he delivered the most emphatic demonstration of his excellence. In six games, he allowed only eight goals. In the Montreal Forum, in the deciding game against the Canadians of Wayne Gretzky, Tretiak was triumphant in an 8–1 mauling. Dryden, of course, was not there to face him. Nor was Cheevers, who had retired the previous season. Mike Liut of the St. Louis Blues suffered the shocking defeat, and Tretiak felt genuinely sorry for him, saying his teammates let him down. Tony Esposito was there, but as an American—he had secured his new citizenship just in time to play for the U.S. team, and lose 4–1 in his match against the Soviets.

Esposito had turned into one of the last great ironmen of the goaltending profession. While it was now routine for top goaltenders to be relieved for at least part of the season by an understudy or equal partner (Dryden shared his last three Vezinas with Michel Larocque, but appeared in all the playoff games), Esposito was almost singlehandedly guarding the Blackhawks net. Like Tretiak and Dryden, he would always be associated with one great team (in Tretiak's case Central Red Army, and for most international games, the Soviet national team). Having always worn a mask, he never had a serious injury. He played more than 4,000 minutes in five different seasons. The only other goaltender to play more than 4,000 minutes in a season at the time was Vachon in Los Angeles, and he did it once. "I get paid for eighty games," Esposito explained. "I think I play better when I play more."

"He's not as fast as many goalies," said his defenceman Dave Hutchison in 1981, "he doesn't play the puck as well as some, but he outsmarts most shooters."

Beginning in 1975/76, Esposito's GA had risen into the three-goal range as Chicago's scoring fell and LGA climbed. Esposito blamed the league's youth kick. "Teams are concentrating on young players and they're making more mistakes. They're learning their job and their inexperience is resulting in a lot of goals. You see a lot more three-on-twos and two-on-ones than there used to be."

He followed in Dryden's footsteps by becoming the president of the players' association, and was in the job when a new collective bargaining agreement was reached in 1982 that avoided a strike. His total games began to ease off. In 1983/84, approaching forty-one, he played only eighteen games. When he lost 4–3 to the Hartford Whalers on February 5, he had a 4.83 GA and a record of five wins, ten losses and three ties. It proved to be his last NHL game. He wanted to play for Minnesota the following season, but Chicago refused to release him; nor did they invite him to training camp. He retired, and served as a consultant to the players' association

ready to leave the ice. Johnson sensed the inattention of the Soviet defencemen, skated in behind them, jumped on the rebound, and put it behind Tretiak to tie the game.

The teams left the ice, but it turned out there was still one second left in the period. A furious Tikhonov refused to put Tretiak back on. His backup, Volodia Mishkin, was sent out in his place, and played the rest of the game. The Americans won 4–3, and went on to take the gold medal. Tretiak went home with a silver medal, his career all but ruined. He had never been pulled from a game before. He would insist, years later, that the Soviets could have won the game if he had played all of it. And for a year, he would say, he could not show his face on the street.

He was tired of the grind. He had never spent a New Year's with his family. Only twenty-eight, he was burning out. At the beginning of his career, he had been puzzled by the emphasis Jacques Plante put on the mental consequences of their trade in his goaltending manual. "It seemed to me at the time that he spent too much time on the psychological strains experienced by goalies," he said in 1984. "I paid no special attention to these lines, thinking Jacques Plante was merely exaggerating. Now I know how right he was."

Tretiak might have retired, had it not been for the disgrace of Lake Placid. He decided to stay another four years so that he could play in another Olympics and redeem himself—and the team.

He made a quick return to the top. He won back the starting job from Mishkin, and the next four world championships. At the 1981 and 1983 worlds, he was named the top goaltender for the third and fourth time. And

until 1988, when he was offered the general manager's job of the Pittsburgh Penguins. His brother Phil by then was GM of the Rangers; they formed the first front-office brothers pairing in the NHL since Muzz Patrick ran the Rangers and Lynn Patrick the Bruins back in the 1950s and 1960s. Tony lasted little more than a season before Craig Patrick took over. When Phil Esposito became the general manager of the new Tampa Bay Lightning franchise in 1992, he hired Tony as his director of hockey operations.

In 1984, Tretiak got his avenging gold medal in Sarajevo, and joined Tony Esposito in retiring from hockey, five years after Dryden had elected to leave the game while on top. Tretiak wrote an autobiography laced with contempt for "Canadian professionals" and their occasionally brutish game, and it was difficult to know when reading it where the real Tretiak lay. The book had originally been published in Russian for domestic consumption. Were his opinions tailored to the home audience, or were they genuine? The latter seemed likely. As the son of an army pilot and a gymnastics instructor in the Soviet sports bureaucracy, he was brought up to toe the company line. He had joined the Communist Youth Party at nineteen, and graduated from the Vladimir Ilyich Lenin Military-Political Academy. He was awarded the Order of Lenin in 1978. He was twice voted onto the central committee of the Young Communist League, and, as he wrote, "I saw my role not as a passive member of the Central Committee, but as an active one."

He lambasted those who "transform the noblest occupations into objects of profit." He wrote that "Athletes are, in fact, on the main line of the ideological fight of two social systems. Our athletes have to prove constantly that they are not only the strongest and most talented, but, more importantly, they must let the world know that behind them is the strength of Communist ideals, the all-triumphant truth of our Soviet morality."

In 1983, Tretiak had been the subject of a maelstrom of rumours that he was going to play for the Montreal Canadiens. Serge Savard, an opponent back in the 1972 series who was now general manager of the Canadiens, gave Tretiak a tour of the fabled Forum, out of which apparently came an expression of interest by Tretiak to play for the team. Savard took this interest seriously enough to secure Tretiak's rights in the 1983 draft, taking him 138th overall. Tretiak insisted he had been misquoted, or at least misunderstood. "There were several offers and the Canadiens were offering millions," he would recall telling an audience of fans in Russia. "But I think they understood this was pure science fiction. I am a Soviet athlete, interested only in defending the honour of my Motherland."

As glasnost and perestroika came to the Soviet Union, Tretiak's hardline resolve melted away. Perhaps there is a middle ground in comprehending his autobiography: perhaps he had been trapped in the mind-numbing rationalizing of the Soviet system, making every effort to excel within it even while the West tugged at him. Even as he was denouncing the professional game, there were leaks that he was in fact trying hard to make a buck from it. It was reported in 1988 that in August 1987 Tretiak—then managing the Central Army club—had sought out a goaltending coaching job with the Edmonton Oilers, the Stanley Cup champions. He wanted $250,000 for a job that normally paid $40,000 to $70,000. Oilers owner Peter Pocklington came back with a three-year offer worth $150,000, but no deal was made.

Tretiak then admitted that, in his denials of the draft controversy, "I was not telling the truth." In April 1994, he elaborated. "I wanted to play for the Canadiens and I had meetings with the Soviet Ice Hockey Federation, but I was told not to talk about it. I still don't want to talk about it."

In 1990, he was finally allowed to travel overseas as a goaltending consultant. He dismissed his Communist Youth Party membership, explaining that "Everyone had to join something." He established a string of hockey schools, and became a good friend of former NHL goaltender Phil Myre, who was the assistant coach of the Detroit Red Wings. Through Myre, it was learned that Tretiak had been ready to make a comeback in the NHL at thirty-six, in 1988.

He became the goaltending coach for Tony Esposito's old team, the Blackhawks. His first big assignment was rookie Ed Belfour. When Belfour won the Vezina, the Jennings and the Calder in 1990/91, Tretiak beamed. "I take a little credit for the success Ed Belfour had last year," he said in 1992. And, observing Russian stars like Sergei Federov who had been allowed to play in the NHL without having to defect, Tretiak confessed, "I'm a little jealous of them. I was ready to come here for so long and I think I could have done well. I've dedicated my whole life to hockey and I would have given playing one hundred fifty per cent."

One can look at the photo of Tretiak, arm in arm with Cournoyer and Mahovlich after the magnificent New Year's Eve game of 1975, and imagine them not as friendly rivals, but as teammates. One can easily imagine Tretiak having the same thought—at the peak of his game, adored by the Forum crowd. Ken Dryden is about to start his astonishing run of Vezinas, All Star appearances and Stanley Cup victories. Tretiak is about to experience some of the bleakest seasons of his career. One senses that his put-downs of Dryden—the recollection of the 9–3 victory in 1969, the silence over his skills, the observation that Dryden "panicked" in the second game of the 1979 Challenge series—were rooted at least partly in professional envy. What might have happened, had Tretiak been able to play for Montreal after the great New Year's Eve game, rather than being bound by the Soviet system and perhaps his own ideology to Central Red Army? Could he not just as easily have assumed the mantle of Canadiens greatness his mentor, Jacques Plante, had last worn?

"I would have loved to play in Montreal," he has said. "That is my city." ◯

CHAPTER 10

1981/82–1995

MODERN
Times

GOALTENDING IS IN ITS GLORY YEARS. BETTER EQUIPMENT IS DRIVING DOWN AVERAGES AND MAKING THE PROFESSION SAFER. THE EQUIPMENT IS ALSO BIGGER—SO IS THE CREASE AND SO ARE THE SALARIES

ANDY MOOG TURNS AWAY A BUFFALO SABRES SHOT WHILE IN GOAL FOR THE BOSTON BRUINS. MOOG MOVED ON TO BOSTON IN 1988 AFTER TOILING IN GRANT FUHR'S SHADOW IN EDMONTON SINCE 1981. HE COMPILED THE HIGHEST CAREER WIN PERCENTAGE AMONG ACTIVE GOAL-TENDERS WHILE WITH THE BRUINS, THEN WAS DEALT TO THE DALLAS STARS.

T hree factors have influenced the changing role and play-ing style of the goaltender: the rules, as they pertain both to the goaltender and the game as a whole; the equip-ment available to the goaltender; and the evolving scor-ing weapons of the offensive players. In the game's early years, changing rules, with some evolution in equipment, had the greatest impact on the goaltending trade. During the Original Six era, rules were far less important than the introduction of the slapshot and the curved stick, which begat corresponding innovations in goaltending equipment, from pads to gloves to the arrival of the functional mask. The era also saw important stylistic innovations: Sawchuk's gorilla crouch, Hall's butterfly and the more aggressive, wandering style pioneered by Rayner and Plante. The 1970s were most notable for the radical shift in the psychology of the profession, as two dressed-to-play goaltenders on each team led coaches to indulge in the tactic of switching goaltenders in mid-game when things were going badly. The mask also gained broad acceptance in the fraternity, and that helped change the way the goaltender faced down the shooter.

For more than a decade equipment has been over-whelmingly the major area of change in goaltending, serving as a catalyst for fresh changes in how the position is played. At the same time, coaching techniques have transformed the way the best goaltenders are shaped. In less than twenty years, goaltending has undergone its greatest transformation since the arrival of the slapshot in the early 1950s.

Gone are the days when equipment was made of felt, straw and leather, and soaked up water at a muscle-ebbing rate. Synthetic materials have made equipment light, truly protective and ready to wear into a game off the shelf.

A BREED APART

Bill Ranford has enjoyed success in both the NHL and the international game. Acquired by Edmonton from Boston in exchange for Andy Moog in March 1988, he filled in for the injured Grant Fuhr in the 1989/90 playoffs and won the Conn Smythe as the Oilers took the Stanley Cup. Playing for the victorious Team Canada, he was the top goaltender at the 1991 Canada Cup with a 1.75 GA. He was named the outstanding goaltender at the 1993 worlds, and in 1994 recorded a 1.17 GA as Canada won gold.

The modern mask is light-years removed from the first fibreglass model worn in a game by Jacques Plante in 1959. Despite undergoing steady changes in the 1970s, molded masks are things of the past, having been replaced by a mask/helmet hybrid with a wire cage providing facial protection. Eddie Giacomin is astounded by the size of the new contraptions—they make him think of a deep-sea diver's helmet—but they are very light. They also provide far greater protection than the masks worn in the 1970s.

Anyone who played goal in the Original Six era, or even as recently as the 1970s, can only marvel at the advances made on the goaltender's behalf in the last fifteen years. Not only is the equipment better—for the most part it is also bigger, allowing the modern goaltenders to cover more of the same old four-by-six net, getting in the way of the same old one-inch-by-three-inch rubber disk, simply by standing still. The catching glove in particular is enormous, a veritable peach basket compared to the baseball-style trappers that appeared in the late 1940s and prevailed through the Original Six. (See "Hands of Time," pages 96–97.)

The stick has also changed significantly. Sticks overall have grown longer with time, if only because players overall have grown taller. Once limited to a maximum length of fifty-three inches from heel to butt, they increased to fifty-five inches in 1965/66, fifty-eight inches in 1980/81 and sixty inches in 1986/87. For the goaltender, this has meant more range for poke checks. The goaltender's blade and paddle shaft widths remain at their historic 3.5 inches, but after limiting the paddle height to twenty-four inches from the heel in 1951/52, the league allowed the paddle to increase to twenty-six inches in 1975/76. The length of the blade has also changed. As short as 12.5 inches in 1965/66, it stretched to 15.5 inches in 1969/70. Thus, for more than twenty years, goaltenders have stopped pucks with a blade about 25 per cent larger than the one used in the Original Six era. The blade now also has a curve, which has given the goaltender more power when clearing the puck; Giacomin feels it may have made the difference between his failure to become the first goaltender to score in the NHL and Ron Hextall's success in 1987.

After sixty years of leg pads limited to ten inches in width, the NHL decided to permit an increase to twelve inches, which translates to an increase in area of 20 per cent. The increase was not absolute. For years, the league wrestled with the problem of the leather pads being wider than the prescribed ten inches. Goaltenders routinely bounced on them before the start of a game, to get them to flatten out and so become wider. In 1974/75, the NHL declared that league staff would measure pads before the start of the season. By 1989/90, with the advent of synthetic materials in pad construction, officials could be more confident of pads holding their true shape, and permitted a size increase that may not have been much of an increase at all. That

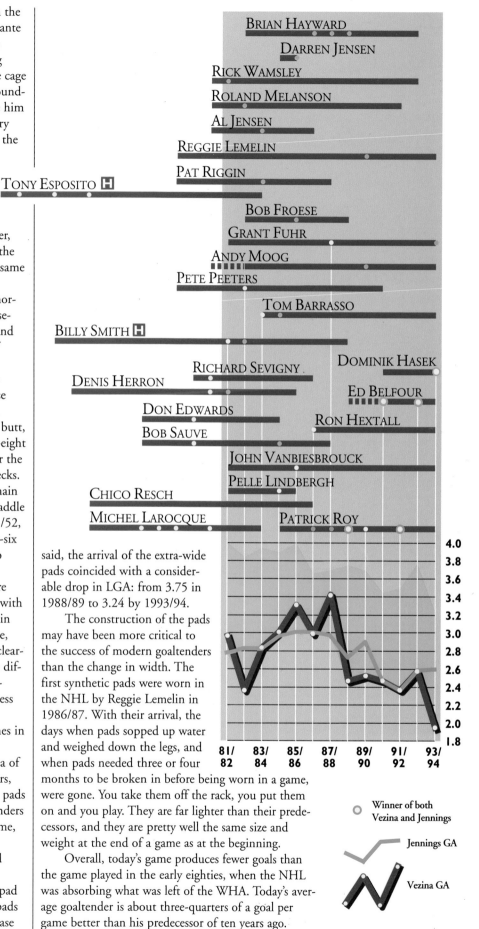

said, the arrival of the extra-wide pads coincided with a considerable drop in LGA: from 3.75 in 1988/89 to 3.24 by 1993/94.

The construction of the pads may have been more critical to the success of modern goaltenders than the change in width. The first synthetic pads were worn in the NHL by Reggie Lemelin in 1986/87. With their arrival, the days when pads sopped up water and weighed down the legs, and when pads needed three or four months to be broken in before being worn in a game, were gone. You take them off the rack, you put them on and you play. They are far lighter than their predecessors, and they are pretty well the same size and weight at the end of a game as at the beginning.

Overall, today's game produces fewer goals than the game played in the early eighties, when the NHL was absorbing what was left of the WHA. Today's average goaltender is about three-quarters of a goal per game better than his predecessor of ten years ago.

Continued on page 179

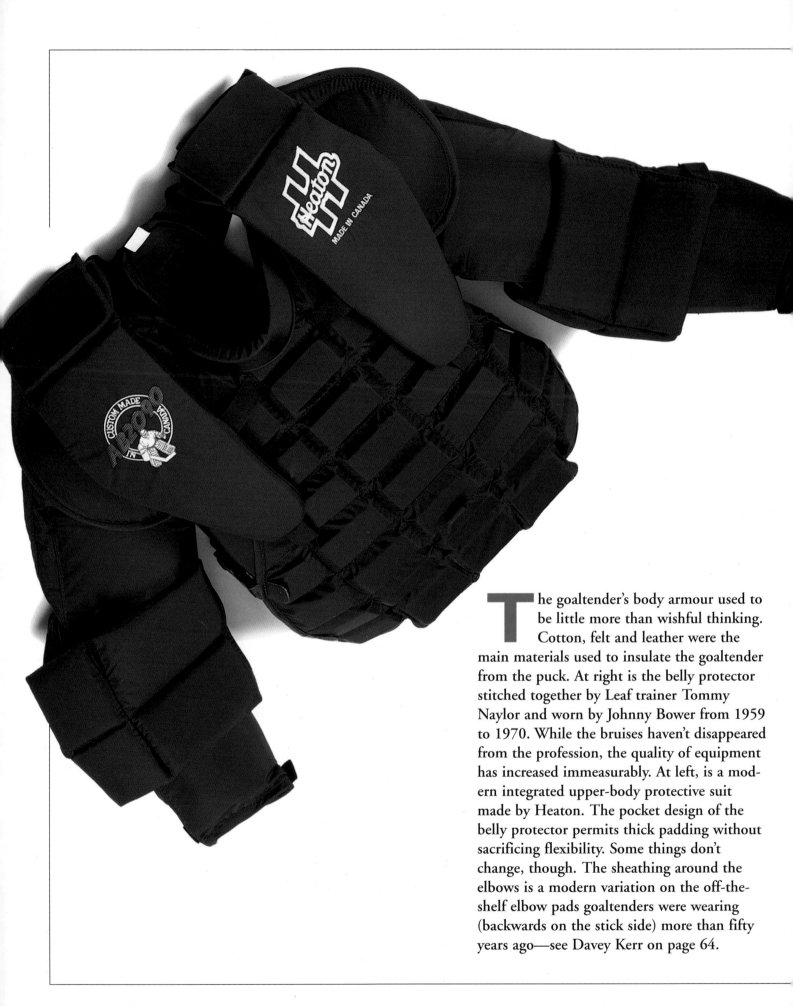

The goaltender's body armour used to be little more than wishful thinking. Cotton, felt and leather were the main materials used to insulate the goaltender from the puck. At right is the belly protector stitched together by Leaf trainer Tommy Naylor and worn by Johnny Bower from 1959 to 1970. While the bruises haven't disappeared from the profession, the quality of equipment has increased immeasurably. At left, is a modern integrated upper-body protective suit made by Heaton. The pocket design of the belly protector permits thick padding without sacrificing flexibility. Some things don't change, though. The sheathing around the elbows is a modern variation on the off-the-shelf elbow pads goaltenders were wearing (backwards on the stick side) more than fifty years ago—see Davey Kerr on page 64.

Continued from page 175

Or is he? Skill, as we have seen, is a difficult thing to assess using a measuring stick of raw numbers. If the goaltenders aren't better, they are assuredly different, and the game around them is different. The goaltender has never been more respected. Leaving aside the permissiveness in equipment, significant changes in the playing rules have also served to increase the goaltender's comfort zone. In 1987/88, the league introduced a dual crease—adding a six-foot semicircular crease as it prepared to phase out the old four-by-eight rectangle. In 1991/92, the rectangle disappeared, and penalties were conferred on attacking players infringing on the crease or making unnecessary contact with the goaltender. A goal would also be disallowed if an attacking player was standing on or inside the crease line, or had his stick inside it. At the same time, however, the NHL goaltender's job has been made more of a challenge in the NHL by the addition in 1990/91 of an extra foot of space between the back of the net and the end boards. With more room for attacking players to direct scoring chances from behind the net, it should be no surprise that goaltenders like Arturs Irbe and Dominik Hasek, at ease on the international amateur game's larger ice surface, have done so well in the NHL.

Not all goaltenders are cheering the general progress from which the latest members of the fraternity benefit. Frank Brimsek and Gerry McNeil watch modern goaltenders ply their trade and blanche at what they see. For one thing, they wander too much. "I don't like it now," Brimsek declares. "They have no business roaming. They get caught so badly, it's pathetic. They'd be wise to fine the guy $500 for every goal that got by. In my day, you could hit a goaltender. Once he left the crease, he was another player. You can't do that now.

"You just worried about the angles," adds Brimsek. "But I didn't come out like they do today. You'd lose the direction of the net. You wouldn't know where it is."

"There was a lot more passing then than now," says McNeil. "It's more bashing now. They come in and have to wind up and shoot. It used to have a little more finesse. If you went down, the guy would go to the other side of you."

Maybe, McNeil concedes, goaltenders today have adopted a style they have to play. For it is a different game entirely from the one he knew.

Three of the great stars of the Original Six and the expansion years, Glenn Hall, Johnny Bower and Eddie Giacomin, have gone on to coach the new generation. Glenn Hall is the goaltending coach for the Calgary Flames, Johnny Bower still runs his hockey camp, and Eddie Giacomin was the New York Rangers' goaltending coach under general manager Phil Esposito from

Continued on page 188

GERRY CHEEVERS SWORE A GOALTENDER WOULD HAVE BEEN KILLED IF THE MASK HADN'T BEEN INVENTED. IN THE 1993 NHL PLAYOFFS, THE VALUE OF THE MODERN GOALTENDER'S HELMET WAS REAFFIRMED WHEN A SLAPSHOT BY LEAF CAPTAIN WENDEL CLARK HIT ST. LOUIS GOALTENDER CURTIS JOSEPH WITH SUCH FORCE THAT HIS HELMET (*ABOVE*) WAS TORN OFF. JOSEPH IS ALIVE AND WELL AND PLAYING GOAL.

BILLY SMITH

"BATTLIN' BILLY" WAS THE ULTIMATE MONEY GOALIE AS THE ISLANDERS WON FOUR STANLEY CUPS

Some goaltenders are remembered for their unique style. Billy Smith is one of them, but it's not for the way he stopped pucks. It's for the way he sent people to the infirmary with his stick. Battlin' Billy was more tenacious in clearing his crease than Gerry Cheevers, and slightly less manic about it than Ron Hextall. He was a self-proclaimed goaltending goon, an agitator who stirred up trouble when the rest of his team didn't, and he thought they should. All hacking and slashing aside, though, Smith was one of goaltending's true greats, his career stretching from 1971 to 1989, with all but five games played as a New York Islander. In only two seasons was his GA higher than LGA—his first and his last, and in those seasons his team's scoring dipped below LGA as well.

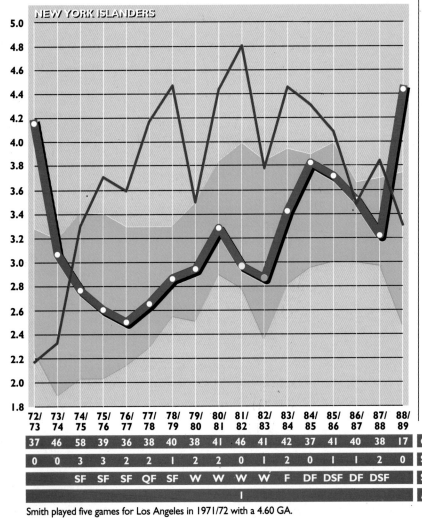

	72/ 73	73/ 74	74/ 75	75/ 76	76/ 77	77/ 78	78/ 79	79/ 80	80/ 81	81/ 82	82/ 83	83/ 84	84/ 85	85/ 86	86/ 87	87/ 88	88/ 89	
GAMES	37	46	58	39	36	38	40	38	41	46	41	42	37	41	40	38	17	
SHUTOUTS	0	0	3	3	2	2	1	2	2	0	1	2	0	1	1	2	0	
STANLEY CUP		SF	SF	SF	QF	SF	W	W	W	W	F	DF	DSF	DF	DSF			
ALL STAR TEAM										1								

Smith played five games for Los Angeles in 1971/72 with a 4.60 GA.

Like Jacques Plante, Smith was an iconoclast who went his own way. He warmed slowly to strangers, and told Islanders coach Al Arbour what he was and wasn't prepared to do. He was prepared to win games, big ones and small ones. He skipped team meetings. He avoided practices and training camp, arguing that he was only asking for an injury. But he wasn't lazy. Smith was a devoted tennis player, and believed that the game helped a goaltender with his footwork. He also swore by the ability of video games to hone hand–eye co-ordination. He played them at home with his kids; more seriously, he worked out on a machine developed by an ophthalmologist, Dr. Leon Revien, designed to "strengthen vision and reflexes." Old-time netminders like Davey Kerr, who avoided movies and wore sunglasses when he read to preserve his eyesight, would have been appalled by the sight of Smith parked in front of Dr. Revien's device, trying to stop a dot shooting across the screen at 250 miles an hour, or trying to identify fourteen digits flashed on the screen for 1/100th of a second. As odd as the training method was when Smith became an advocate in the early eighties, such tools are now a standard part of off-ice preparation for goaltenders.

Smith didn't keep a book on shooters like other goaltenders, because he said the best opponents changed their tactics. He paid attention to his GA, but if a game was going well he wasn't adverse to trying something unorthodox, since he didn't believe practice was the place to learn anything. Like Plante before him, he was able to go his own way because he won games. There was no way to argue with the fact that Smith knew what he was doing.

Smith grew up in the eastern Ontario town of Perth and played his Junior hockey in nearby Smith Falls and Cornwall. Drafted by the L.A. Kings in 1970, he was assigned to Springfield in the American league for two seasons, and won the league championship in 1970/71. He saw action in five games with L.A. in 1971/72, but when the Kings acquired Rogie Vachon from Montreal in November 1971, he was made expendable. The New York Islanders, a new franchise joining the league in 1972, picked him in the expansion draft. Ten years later, Smith would be the only original Islander left on the team.

That was no big surprise: the original team was pretty awful, winning only ten of seventy-eight games in its first season, thirteen in its second. Al Arbour was hired as coach for the second season, and with GM Bill Torrey he began to build a contender. Glenn "Chico" Resch, four years older than Smith, was made a tag-team netminding partner in 1974. They were an odd couple: Resch was far more gregarious, always ready to talk to the press. "Chico, he'd talk to the wall if it would listen," Smith reflected in 1979. Smith, on the other hand, mistrusted the press, at least early in his career, annoyed by misquotes. But they meshed well, playing tennis together and respecting each other's desire to play as many games as possible.

Resch attracted the most attention. For five straight seasons his GA was below 2.50 and he made the second All Star team in 1975/76 and 1978/79. Smith's one note of glory came in 1979, when the Colorado Rockies pulled their goaltender in favour of an extra attacker and accidentally put the puck in their own net with an errant pass. Because Smith was the last Islander to touch the puck, he was credited with the goal, a first for an NHL goaltender.

As the Islanders turned into a Stanley Cup contender, Smith began to attract attention too. Notwithstanding a very good GA, Smith was making headlines as a hatchet man. "I don't bother people unless they're bothering me," he said in 1982. "I just try to give myself a little working room. But if a guy bothers me, then I retaliate." It was a standard explanation by stick-wielding goaltenders (Davey Kerr would have agreed with him at least on this), but Smith also had a pugnacious streak to which he freely owned up. In the playoffs of 1977/78 and 1978/79, the Islanders had appeared ready to challenge Montreal's grip on the Stanley Cup, but never got the chance, bowing out to Toronto and the Rangers before they could reach the final. Smith, for one, felt the team had let itself be pushed around. He was determined to start pushing back.

Almost overnight, Smith was heralded as the game's greatest goaltender. Ken Dryden and Gerry Cheevers retired; Bernie Parent was forced out by an eye injury. The Islanders won the Stanley Cup in 1979/80, then Resch moved on to the expansion Colorado Rockies. And there was Smith, winning Stanley Cups—four in a row. He won the Vezina in 1981/82, the first season in which the trophy was put to a vote rather than being awarded to the goaltenders on the team with the lowest GA, now the domain of the Jennings. For good measure, Smith and his new partner, Rollie Melanson, won the Jennings in 1982/83. He was named to his first (and last) NHL All Star team in 1981/82. In 1983/84, when the Islanders' cup streak ended with a final-series loss to Edmonton, Smith broke Ken Dryden's record of eighty playoff wins.

"He may be the all-time money player," Torrey said in May 1983 after cup number four was in the bag and Smith had won the Conn Smythe. Indeed, money was a critical bottom line to him. He didn't believe in shaking hands with opponents after a playoff series loss because congratulations seemed a bit hypocritical when the other guy was picking up the bonus money.

His most lasting contribution to the game may have come through the injuries he inflicted on opponents. In the 1981/82 playoffs, Vancouver's Tiger Williams expressed the desire to "punch Smith in the esophagus so he has to eat out of a blender for six months." His slash of Glenn Anderson in the 1982/83 Stanley Cup brought calls from the Oilers for his suspension. In 1985, he broke the cheek and jaw of Blackhawk Curt Fraser, incurring a six-game suspension. "If they change the rules and make the crease bigger," he said at the time of the Fraser injury, "it would stop all this cheap stuff. I've been recommending that for ten years and it's like talking to a wall."

In 1987, the league finally listened, and introduced the six-foot semicircular crease. Smith enjoyed two seasons of NHL hockey with it before retiring at thirty-nine and becoming a goaltending coach. In 1993, Smith became the first goaltender who had his big wins in the 1980s to be inducted into the Hall of Fame. ○

LAST MAN BACK: SMITH WAS THE ONLY ORIGINAL ISLANDER LEFT WHEN THE TEAM WAS WINNING STANLEY CUPS, TEN YEARS AFTER IT ENTERED THE LEAGUE.

ED BELFOUR

INSPIRED BY ESPOSITO, TUTORED BY TRETIAK, HE HAS SHOT FROM OBSCURITY INTO GOALTENDING'S ELITE RANKS

Until Tom Barrasso came along in 1983, goaltenders flew in the face of accepted hockey recruiting wisdom. Taking them in the first round of the amateur draft was a waste of a pick because goaltenders rarely showed their true potential when they were still young amateurs. It was almost unheard of for a young amateur to come into the NHL and immediately cause a sensation. Those who did—Tony Esposito and Ken Dryden were two—had had some grooming in the American collegiate and minor pro system, and were at least true to form in not having been top draft picks.

When Barrasso was picked by Buffalo in the first round, and came into the NHL right out of a Boston high school at age eighteen to win the Calder and the Vezina, traditional wisdom was stood on its head. Three years later, Ron Hextall crashed into the league after a short minor pro stint and won just about all the goaltending marbles. In 1990, it was Ed Belfour's turn.

Belfour did not burst into the NHL with quite the suddenness of Barrasso, but it was an impressive arrival nonetheless. It was the standard "out of nowhere" tale, Ed Belfour's nowhere being Carman, Manitoba, population 3,500. "In grade three, I drew a couple pictures of Tony Esposito and I won first prize in an art show," he would relate; naturally, he developed an Esposito butterfly style.

The professional hockey world paid him scant attention. At twenty-one, he came to the University of North Dakota on a hockey scholarship. As with Esposito and Dryden (and Jon Casey, his predecessor at North Dakota), the U.S. collegiate system fed him into the NHL pipeline. North Dakota won the national title in Belfour's first season, 1986/87, as Belfour compiled a 29–4 record, with a GA of 2.43. His performance got him on the western collegiate first All Star team, but in the amateur draft that summer, every NHL club passed on him. In September, though, Chicago—Espo's team—signed him as a free agent.

Belfour was assigned to Saginaw of the International League, where he was named rookie of the year and a first-team All Star in 1987/88. His next season was split between Saginaw and the Blackhawks; in his twenty-three appearances for Chicago,

CHICAGO

	88/89	89/90	90/91	91/92	92/93	93/94	
GAMES	23	0*	74	52	71	70	
SHUTOUTS	0	0	4	5	7	7	
STANLEY CUP	CC	CC	DSF	F	DSF	QF	
ALL STAR TEAM			1		1		

*Belfour played nine games for Chicago in the 1989/90 playoffs, with a 2.49 GA.

his 3.87 average indicated a need for more minor-league seasoning. Chicago acquired Greg Millen from the Nordiques; with no ice time available, Belfour chose to make a detour into the Canadian Olympic team program. At the end of the season, though, the Blackhawks brought him up for the playoffs. They got as far as the conference championship, and Belfour's 4–2 record, with appearances in a total of nine games, produced a 2.49 average. For 1990/91, the starter's job was his.

A storybook season unfolded, abetted by the collapse of the Soviet Union, which permitted Vladislav Tretiak to venture overseas as a goaltending coach for the first time in 1990. Chicago hired him, and Belfour became his star pupil. Belfour led the league in games played (seventy-four), in wins (forty-three), in GA (2.47) and in save percentage (.910). Named to the first All Star team, he walked away from the league's annual awards presentation with just about everything there was for a goaltender to win: the Vezina, the Jennings and the Calder.

One cloud cast a shadow over his marvellous rookie season. The Blackhawks had been blown out of the playoffs by the upstart Minnesota North Stars; Belfour went 2–4 with a 4.07 GA. For many pundits, the true measure of a goaltender's greatness is not GA or save percentage, but whether or not he can deliver a championship. Having won every goaltending honour in his first full tour of duty in the NHL, Belfour now faced the task of proving himself as a netminder who can get the Stanley Cup into the Windy City, which had fallen short in every season since 1960/61.

He has at least shown himself to be the real thing, not a one-season wonder who fades quickly after a spectacularly showy debut. In his second season he became the third-highest-paid goaltender in the league at $925,000, behind Toronto's newly acquired Grant Fuhr ($1.6 million) and Montreal's Patrick Roy ($1.2 million). His second tour didn't bring any silverware, though he did lead the league with five shutouts and his playoff performance was solid: a league-leading 2.47 GA with twelve wins in eighteen starts. In their drive to a Stanley Cup appearance, the Blackhawks won a record eleven straight games. But then, so did the Pittsburgh Penguins, and when Chicago and Pittsburgh met in the final, it was no contest. The more experienced Tom Barrasso was exceptional as Belfour and the Blackhawks went down four straight.

In 1992/93, Belfour was back collecting prizes, winning the Vezina and the Jennings as well as making the first All Star team. But after another fine season, the Blackhawks made an early exit from the playoffs. That June, trade rumours swirled around Belfour. He was now twenty-eight; perhaps it was time the Blackhawks cashed him in with a lucrative trade. The team had been keeping another promising netminder, Jimmy Waite, in the wings since drafting him eighth overall in 1987. Chicago had already parted with Dominik Hasek

in August 1992, trading him to Buffalo. The Blackhawks had picked up the Czech star as a draft afterthought in 1983, taking him 199th in the fourth round. He was spectacular in the 1991 Canada Cup, and with the crumbling of the Eastern bloc, was ready to come to the professional game. Hasek would have an outstanding season in 1993/94, winning the Jennings and the Vezina and finishing runner-up in Hart voting.

Chicago general manager Bob Pulford chose to stick with Belfour, and Waite went to the new San Jose Sharks. The Blackhawks finished fifth of six in the Western Conference's very competitive central division and made a quick exit from the playoffs. It was a season when Belfour lived up to the temperamental reputation he'd had since his North Dakota days. In December

1993, Belfour's relatives had come out to see him play the Winnipeg Jets, but when he let in two goals on the first four shots, coach Darryl Sutter pulled him. Belfour boiled over at the humiliation, throwing his stick at the bench and delivering Sutter a public tongue-lashing. He also led the league in shutouts for the third straight season, and when no individual honours came his way, he made his displeasure known. Fan voting chose two other goaltenders from the central division, Curtis Joseph of St. Louis and Felix Potvin of Toronto, as starters in the All Star game. "They get a lot more coverage than I do," he complained. "Toronto's a big-time hockey market. I get tired of hearing all the time that Joseph stops the most shots. Anyone can stop shots from the red line." ○

AS A KID, BELFOUR WON AN ART CONTEST DRAWING PICTURES OF TONY ESPOSITO. HE NOW PLAYS FOR ESPOSITO'S OLD TEAM, WINNING GAMES WITH ESPOSITO'S STYLE.

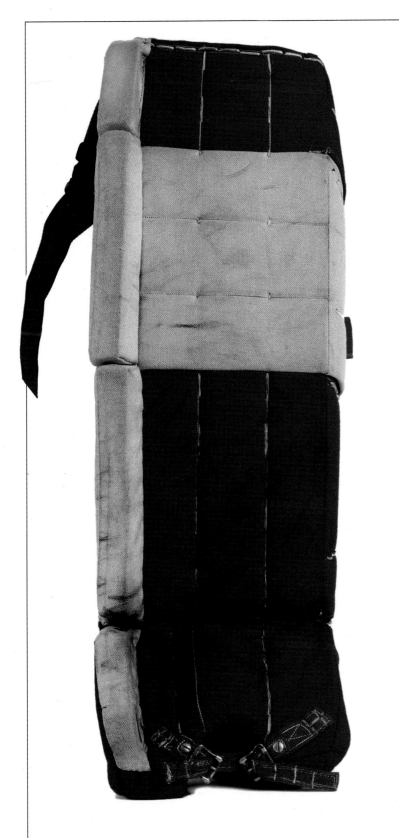
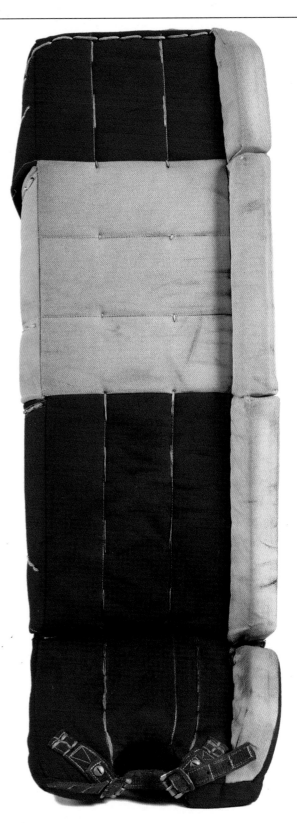

Early in the 1986/87 season, Calgary Flames goaltender Reggie Lemelin tried out this prototype set of synthetic leg pads made by inventor Jim Lowson. They were undersize, even by the old ten-inch width standard, and in the spring Lemelin got a new pair. The synthetic pads were one-third the weight of conventional ones. Lemelin found they took the strain off his back, and they helped revitalize his career.

Synthetic leg pads are now a standard part of the goaltender's inventory, but the look and feel of leather has not vanished. Modern pads with leather exteriors take advantage of new construction techniques and materials to solve the problems of deterioration and weight gain associated with their spongelike predecessors. This set was worn by Corey Hirsch, goaltender for Canada's silver medal team at the 1994 Olympics.

FELIX POTVIN

AFTER A FOUR-GAME TRYOUT IN 1991/92, THE CAT CAME BACK TO THE LEAF GOAL, A YEAR AHEAD OF SCHEDULE

The annual universal draft is a place old hockey hands are constantly telling young hopefuls to avoid. Don't go and sit in the arena, waiting for your name to be selected by one of the NHL teams. Stay home and wait for the news by telephone, if and when it comes. Because when you aren't selected, the sense of rejection, of failure, is excruciating.

Felix Potvin made the mistake of attending the 1989 draft at Minnesota's Met Center. He was told that if he was going to be picked, it would come in the first three rounds. When selections moved on to round four, and no one had chosen him, the eighteen-year-old goaltender for the Chicoutimi Sagueneens was left alone and in tears in the stands.

It was the only hiccup in Felix Potvin's rise to NHL stardom. He has come to take his place in goaltending's top ranks by following a steady, logical progression. In a profession in which the best consistently show up from the most unexpected avenues, Felix the Cat has come into the big city right down Main Street, in plain view the whole way.

Like Ron Hextall, he has hockey in his blood. His father, Pierre, was a centre in the Quebec Senior league who chose firefighting over the opportunity to turn pro in the Bruins system. Felix started out playing as a forward in the east end Montreal neighbourhood of Anjou, but the equipment the goaltenders got to wear intrigued him. As an Atom, he was enrolled in a goaltending school by his parents, and that fixed his future. Though he grew up in greater Montreal, he was not a Canadiens fan. He followed the Nordiques, and as a role model looked to the Islanders' Billy Smith.

After his rejection in the 1989 draft, Potvin went back to the Sagueneens and the Quebec Junior league and fine-tuned his game. His GA in the offence-minded Quebec league dropped from 4.66 to 3.99. And in the summer of 1990, the Toronto Maple Leafs spoke for him in the second round of the draft, taking him thirty-first overall. He returned to the Sagueneens for one more season, a superb one. His GA fell to 2.70 as he was named the top Junior goalie in Quebec and in Canada and placed on the first All Star team of the Quebec league and the Memorial Cup national Junior tournament. In 1991, he was the number two goaltender on the Canadian World Junior championship team.

For 1991/92, Toronto assigned him to their American League farm club, the St.

John's Maple Leafs. Toronto's development program had provided frustratingly few genuine talents over the years—trades were usually used to bring in new faces—so the Leafs were determined to bring Potvin along carefully, giving him two years in the American League before making an NHL starter out of him. As Potvin went to Newfoundland, the Leafs cut a deal with Edmonton for Grant Fuhr. The celebrated veteran could give the team solid netminding during the seasons Potvin's skills were maturing.

He took to the American League readily. In December 1991, St. John's coach Marc Crawford promised the media: "When Felix Potvin arrives in the NHL, it will be for good." He came up to the Leafs for four games, and while he was tagged for two losses and a tie, his GA was 2.29. Back in the American League, Potvin won its rookie of the year and top goaltender award and made the first All Star team.

At the start of the 1992/93 season, he was only twenty-one, but by his age Tom Barrasso had already been in the NHL three seasons. Although slated to spend another season in St. John's, injuries to both Fuhr and his backup, Rick Wamsley, meant he got the call-up. In nine games, he won six, tied one and lost two, with a 2.65 GA, the third best in the league. The trade rumours—which Leaf general manager Cliff Fletcher dismissed—began to swirl around Fuhr. And when Potvin hit a pre-Christmas slump, a disappointed young prospect was sent back to the minors as Fuhr took over again.

In the new year, though, another Fuhr injury brought Potvin back. That January, Potvin won seven of nine starts and attracted a player-of-the-week accolade from the league. Coach Pat Burns moved quickly to reconfigure his netminding lineup. An expansion draft was coming that summer, for the Anaheim Mighty Ducks and the Florida Panthers, and the Leafs were in danger of losing either Potvin or Fuhr. Burns named Potvin the Leafs' starting goaltender, a half-season ahead of schedule, and on February 2 Fletcher dealt Fuhr to Buffalo.

Potvin was named the league's rookie of the month for February, and became a strong candidate for the Calder, although ultimately the scoring binge of Teemu Selanne (who by the time he arrived in the NHL had spent four years in Finland's professional league) would land the rookie trophy for the Winnipeg right-winger. His season GA of 2.50 was the best individual GA in the league, and his 2.84 GA for twenty-one playoff games was outstanding, as the Leafs endured three series that went the full seven games, with Potvin playing in every one of them. And he was only making $145,000.

That summer, his agent, the former Canadiens enforcer Gilles Lupien, made an astounding contract demand: the Leafs were going to pay Potvin $2 million, or he wasn't going to play. Sixteen NHL goaltenders

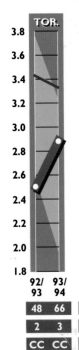

TOR.

3.8
3.6
3.4
3.2
3.0
2.8
2.6
2.4
2.2
2.0
1.8

92/93	93/94	
48	66	GAMES
2	3	SHUTOUTS
CC	CC	STANLEY CUP
		ALL STAR TEAM

Potvin played four games for Toronto in 1991/92, with a 2.29 GA.

were making more than $1 million a season. Fletcher, who initially offered $300,000 in return, was out-raged—he wasn't disposed to paying one of the highest goaltending salaries in the league to someone coming off a rookie season, and wasn't moved by the new deal Montreal struck with Patrick Roy that September, which would pay him a min-imum of $16 million over four years. An angry Fletcher explored the possibility of trading Potvin to the Nordiques, who were thrilled at the prospect. Potvin was a bit taken aback by all the brinkmanship—he took a less strident public stand than his agent, saying he only wanted the going rate, which wasn't necessarily $2 million. The quiet young man didn't seem to have an ounce of egotism in his soul, which saved him from becoming an outcast with Toronto fans.

Potvin and the Leafs finally settled at $1.2 million, and the season started in fine style. The Leafs set a league record by amassing ten con-secutive wins from the start of the season, and Potvin was named the league's player of the month for October as he won nine of those games, with a 2.20 GA and a save percentage of .934.

Then came the mid-sea-son slump. If Potvin has shown a weak spot, it is his streakiness. He is not—yet—a Ken Dryden who might lose the odd game, but almost never two in a row. Having already been voted by fans the starting goal-tender for the Western Conference in the All Star game, Potvin's play hit the skids. He was pulled three times in seven games in favour of Damian Rhodes, who had played with Potvin in St. John's. Burns then sat him out for a spell and he regained his form, but at the begin-ning of the playoffs it happened again. When the Leafs met the unheralded San Jose Sharks in the opening round, Potvin was initially swamped by soft goals. Leading 3–1 in one game, the Leafs fell behind as San Jose scored four times on eight shots; in the third peri-od, the Sharks scored three more on five shots. Potvin snapped out of his struggle with the shrinking puck and finished his eighteen-game playoff tour with a 2.46 GA.

He had showed himself to be a genuine major-league goaltender in his second season, but could not yet claim a place in the exclusive ranks of the elite reserved for Roy and Belfour and a handful of others. It was noted that fifteen other goaltenders who had played at least twenty-five games in 1993/94 had a better GA, and he was ninth overall on save percentage. As he him-self said in September 1994, "I think there are a lot of ways I can improve." ○

POTVIN IS A MODERN GOALTEND-ING RARITY, A TALENT CAREFULLY GROOMED BY AN NHL CLUB RATHER THAN ONE BURSTING ONTO THE SCENE FROM VIRTUAL OBSCURITY.

TAKE YOUR PICK

SINCE THE UNIVERSAL AMATEUR DRAFT WAS INTRODUCED BY THE NHL IN 1969, NO GOALTENDER HAS EVER BEEN PICKED FIRST OVERALL. BLAME THE RAY MARTINIUK SYNDROME: THE MONTREAL CANADIENS USED A FIRST-ROUND DRAFT PICK TO TAKE THE FLIN FLON JUNIOR FIFTH OVERALL IN 1970, THE SECOND UNIVERSAL AMATEUR DRAFT HELD BY THE LEAGUE, AND HE NEVER MADE IT TO THE PROS. TEAMS WERE THEREAFTER LEERY OF COMMITTING THEIR FIRST PICK TO THE UNPREDICTABLE TALENTS OF YOUNG NETMINDERS. EVEN SO, SEVEN NHL GOALTENDERS—TOM BARRASSO (ABOVE), MICHEL LAROCQUE, GRANT FUHR, JIMMY WAITE, JIM RUTHERFORD, BOB SAUVE AND MARTIN BRODEUR—HAVE BEEN SELECTED IN THE FIRST ROUND.

A NUMBER OF TOP GOALTENDERS WERE NEVER PICKED, INSTEAD BEING SIGNED AS FREE AGENTS AFTER MAKING THEIR MARK IN THE U.S. COLLEGE SYSTEM. THEY INCLUDE ED BELFOUR AND JON CASEY (BOTH UNIVERSITY OF NORTH DAKOTA), BRIAN HAYWARD (CORNELL), GLENN HEALY (WESTERN MICHIGAN), CURTIS JOSEPH (WISCONSIN) AND BOB MASON (MINNESOTA-DULUTH; U.S. OLYMPIC TEAM).

5th	Tom Barrasso, Buffalo, 1983
6th	Michel Larocque, Montreal, 1972
8th	Grant Fuhr, Edmonton, 1981 Jimmy Waite, Chicago, 1987
10th	Jim Rutherford, Detroit, 1969
17th	Bob Sauve, Buffalo, 1975
20th	Martin Brodeur, New Jersey, 1990
23rd	Craig Billington, New Jersey, 1984
24th	Sean Burke, New Jersey, 1985
28th	Mike Richter, New York Rangers, 1985 Curt Ridley, Boston, 1971
31st	Al Jensen, Detroit, 1978 Felix Potvin, Toronto, 1990
33rd	Pat Riggin, Atlanta, 1979
35th	Pelle Lindbergh, Philadelphia, 1979
37th	Don Beaupre, Minnesota, 1980
38th	Kelly Hrudey, New York Islanders, 1980
45th	Ken Wregget, Toronto, 1982
51st	Patrick Roy, Montreal, 1984
52nd	Bill Ranford, Boston, 1985
56th	Mike Liut, St. Louis, 1976 Mike Vernon, Calgary, 1981
58th	Rick Wamsley, Montreal, 1979
59th	Rollie Melanson, New York Islanders, 1979
64th	Tim Chevaldae, Detroit, 1986
72nd	John Vanbiesbrouck, New York Rangers, 19
107th	Kirk McLean, New Jersey, 1984
119th	Ron Hextall, Philadelphia, 1982
125th	Reggie Lemelin, Philadelphia, 1974
132nd	Andy Moog, Edmonton, 1980
138th	Vladislav Tretiak, Montreal, 1983
196th	Arturs Irbe, Minnesota, 1989
199th	Dominik Hasek, Chicago, 1983

Continued from page 179

1986 to 1989. They praise the new breed, above all for their reflexes, but they also express concerns about the way the position has come to be played. It used to be thought that the risk of serious injury hampered the effectiveness of the goaltender. Now, some of those goaltenders who once feared for their lives fear that goaltenders who no longer fear for their lives aren't as sharp or as attentive as they should be. Giacomin sees a strict positional game as devoted to angles as it ever was. The goaltender places himself in the predetermined place to cover off the net for a particular shooter, but now there is an important difference. With all the equipment a goaltender wears today, once in position he just has to hope the puck hits him, whether he sees it coming or not. If it hits him in the middle of the forehead, it's not fun, but he won't necessarily be going to the hospital. Back in the bad old days of goaltending, the netminder had to track the puck relentlessly, never losing sight of it. If he did, and he didn't know when or where it was coming from, it could take out all his teeth. Modern equipment has saved incalculable amounts of dental work, but at the same time Bower feels it has cost some goaltenders their powers of concentration. Being indestructible has made them to some degree inattentive. "They don't follow the puck as

much, with so much equipment on," he says. "When we didn't have the equipment, we were more cautious."

Dave Dryden sees a subtle but important change in the way goaltenders are playing high shots. In his day, when a shot came in at shoulder level, the goaltender threw up his shoulder and arm to block it, and instinctively leaned his head away from the shoulder that would take the shot. Today, he sees goaltenders leaning their helmeted heads *into* the shot, using the head as one more part of the body to stop the puck.

The strict positional game has undoubtedly been given more emphasis by the fact that, in today's NHL, it's all but impossible for a goaltender truly to know the moves of every shooter, the way goaltenders in the Original Six days did. Back then, a grand total of about seventy forwards were dressed to play in the league. Now there are more than three hundred. Some teams

A BREED APART

meet each other only a few times each season, and because goaltenders rarely play most of a season, they gain even less exposure to all the shooters. What's more, many big guns, such as Sergei Federov, Pavel Bure, Jeremy Roenick and Mark Recchi, have completed (as of the end of 1993/94) only about four seasons or less in the NHL. Facing them down are a new crop of goaltending stars who are also new faces in the league. It's a big change from the 1960s, when a goaltender like Johnny Bower, who had been playing professionally since 1949, was confronting the likes of Jean Beliveau, who had been playing professionally since 1950.

The size of the league, and the relative infrequency of play between particular teams, has placed a heightened emphasis on a goaltender's ability to perform in the playoffs. Thirty years ago, a playoff series was an extension of regular-season rivalries. When the Leafs played the Canadiens, they knew exactly who they were facing, and the goaltenders knew exactly whose scoring efforts they were trying to stymie. Today, goaltenders in playoff series find themselves playing opponents they scarcely know. Those who succeed manage to rise to the pressure of a series while proving a quick study of vaguely understood opponents. Today's playoff hockey may be the most demanding a goaltender has ever confronted.

It is less an art now than a science. Historically, goaltenders have broken every golden rule coaches have tried to impose on them. If they weren't supposed to wander, they wandered. If they were supposed play barefaced, they wore a mask. If the equipment they were given wasn't good enough, they made their own or told the manufacturer exactly what to make. They were individuals in every sense, alone in their role on the team, often as distinct in style from each other as a moat is from a brick wall. They came upon the best way to play the position largely on their own, watching other, more experienced goaltenders for clues to self-improvement. Sometimes they weren't technically perfect, but they made up for it in intelligence and tenacity. Now there are manuals, and video replays, and hand-eye co-ordination testing, and one-on-one coaching. A goaltender must be trained the way a fighter pilot is trained, and there is definitely a right way and a wrong way to fly this aircraft today.

Glenn Hall echoes the general concerns about the trade. He agrees that goaltending has become dominated by one particular style, an inverted-V modification of his original butterfly stance. "What bothers me is that they accept not seeing the puck," he says. "They accept the screen, which is unacceptable to accept."

Goaltending as exemplified by the professional North American game has undergone changes that are inextricably linked to the changes in the game as a whole. A much more diverse talent pool has emerged. Goaltenders are still coming out of the prairies and other far-flung quarters of the Canadian hinterland, but they are also coming out of Europe in record numbers as the NHL has filled its rosters with ever-more players from Scandinavia and eastern Europe. From 1969 to 1973, NHL teams chose one European in its annual draft. From 1974 to 1979, forty-six were selected. From 1980 to 1989, there were 457. Goaltenders drafted these days don't just come from places like Saskatoon. They come from Czech addresses like Pardubice (Dominik Hasek), Hradec Kralove (Robert Horyna) and Kladno (Milan Hnilicka). They also hail from Schaffhausen in Switzerland (Pauli Jaks); from Helsinki (Markus Ketterer, Timo Lehkonen, Sakari Lindfors), Uusikaupunki (Kari Takko) and Savonlinna (Jarmo Myllys) in Finland; from Dabrowa Bialostocka in Poland (Peter Sidorkiewicz); from Riga in Latvia (Arturs Irbe); and from Stockholm (Tommy Soderstrom, Pelle Lindbergh). The modern game has also seen the deepest American netminding talent since Mike Karakas and Frank Brimsek came from Minnesota to the NHL in the 1930s. Jon Casey, Bob Mason and Damian Rhodes are three recent Minnesota products. And three of the most accomplished goaltenders of the past decade are also Americans: Tom Barrasso was born in Boston, John Vanbiesbrouck in Detroit, Mike Richter in Philadelphia.

There is a sense that today's players are less recognizable as individuals, as true personalities, with all the marvellous quirks that go along with the territory (although this probably applies to all professional athletes, and not just to goaltenders). It is impossible to scan the ranks of modern goaltenders and pick out the equivalent of a Gump Worsley, a Gerry Cheevers, a Chuck Gardiner, a Jacques Plante. Who are they, besides superlative technicians? They have never been more anonymous. When goaltenders played barefaced, their individuality was obvious. The arrival of the mask at first obscured it, but then artistic impulses allowed the creation of colourfully painted alter egos. Today, the cage-style helmets have robbed them to some degree of this individuality. The face is dimly seen through wire, the paint restricted to the surrounding fibreglass. The helmets are colourful, but they are no longer masks in the traditional theatrical sense. The players have been swallowed up by their equipment.

And yet they are still unquestionably some of the game's great stars. They are what sets the sport apart from football and baseball and basketball. When the Stanley Cup is on the line, they are on their goal line. When New York met Vancouver in the 1993/94 final, one of the best in recent memory, the performances of Mike Richter for New York and Kirk McLean for Vancouver were front and centre. And as Vancouver pelted Richter with shots in the final moments of the final game, striving in vain to tie the score, Richter was the focus of all attention, on the ice, in the stands, on millions of televisions. He was doing what the goaltender has always done: making the difference between winning and losing. ○

HE *Shoots,*
HE *Scores!*

RON HEXTALL WAS NOT THE FIRST GOALTENDER TO HAVE AMBITIONS OF PUTTING

A LATE DRAFT PICK BY THE PHILADELPHIA FLYERS, HEXTALL WON THE VEZINA AND THE CONN SMYTHE AND MADE THE FIRST ALL STAR TEAM IN HIS ROOKIE NHL SEASON.

a puck in the opposing team's net. Eddie Giacomin had pursued the dream over a career stretching from 1965 to 1978, and came as close as hitting the post. Technically, the first goal had already been scored by an NHL goaltender when Ron Hextall came to the league in 1986. It belonged to Billy Smith, but it was really an artifice of scorekeeping. In a game on November 28, 1979, between Smith's New York Islanders and the Colorado Rockies, the trailing Rockies had pulled the goaltender in favour of an extra attacker. An errant Colorado pass in the Islanders' end went the length of the ice and into the Colorado net. Because Smith had been the last Islander to touch the puck, the goal was his.

But this wasn't the kind of goal that Giacomin had been trying to score. An audacious goaltender could try the most direct route, as Gary Smith did while in Oakland when he took off with the puck at Giacomin and got as far as centre ice before the last Ranger back prevented a breakaway. But the accepted way for the goaltender to score, if he ever were to, would be to wait for the other team to pull its goaltender, corral the puck and then fire it some 180 feet down the ice, hoping to hit the six-foot-wide net. In some seventy years of NHL hockey, no goaltender had ever managed this ice carnival feat.

Hextall was not going to wait passively for the opportunity. When he reached the NHL he made up to 300 rink-length shots in a day to hone his aim. He used a stick with a curved blade to give his shot more power. In practice, he could hit the far net five times out of ten. He was going to succeed. This was, after all, a Hextall.

Growing up on a farm near Brandon, Manitoba, Ron Hextall was blessed by some of the greatest hockey genes in the country. His grandfather Bryan had starred with the New York Rangers in the 1930s and 1940s, and had scored the winning goal in the 1939/40 Stanley Cup. His drop shot had been a goaltending terror. Ron's father, Bryan Jr., had also played for the Rangers—briefly, in 1962/63—before logging seven seasons from 1969 to 1976 mainly with Pittsburgh. And his uncle Dennis had played twelve seasons from 1968 to 1980, the first with the Rangers, the rest with Los Angeles, California, Minnesota, Detroit and Washington.

All of the preceding Hextalls had been forwards, and of modest dimensions—Bryan Sr. five-foot-ten, Bryan Jr. and Dennis five-foot-eleven. Ron towered at six-foot-three, and around age eight he decided he was going to be a goaltender.

Being a large man, and growing up in the glory days of Ken Dryden, he took the Canadiens netminder as a role model. He played three seasons on a nondescript Brandon Wheat Kings Junior team; his GA was as high as 5.77, but Ron proved himself to be a tenacious team player. In the league final one season, Hextall cut a cast off his broken ankle to play against Regina, losing in overtime.

He was not the hottest prospect around. Philadelphia drafted him 119th overall in the summer of 1982, after his first Brandon season. When he finished with the Wheat Kings in 1984, the Flyers sent him at first to Kalamazoo of the International League, and after nineteen games moved him up a notch to the Hershey Bears of the American League. Hershey is a Pennsylvania town not far from Philly, which made it easy for Flyers goaltending coach and netminding legend Bernie Parent to drop in on Hextall's games and practices and give him pointers. He was the first goaltending coach Hextall had ever had.

"His greatest strength is here," Parent would say, tapping his head. "He can allow a bad goal or have a bad period and put it out of his mind. He's on an even keel. A goalie has to be like that or he won't last."

Hextall didn't win the American League's top goaltender award, but in 1985/86 he won the rookie award, played more games than any other goaltender, led the league with five shutouts and was named to its first All Star team. The Flyers brought him into the 1986 training camp, and the rangy twenty-two-year-old was up against stiff competition for a job. The death of its star goaltender, Pelle Lindbergh, in an alcohol-related car accident in 1985, had left the club reeling, but Bob Froese and Darren Jensen had stepped into the gap and played well enough to win the Jennings in 1985/86. Hextall was so good in training camp and in exhibition games that Jensen's NHL career was effectively ended; Froese was traded to the Rangers to make way for the rookie.

Hextall was a classic overnight goaltending success. He came into the league that autumn and not only made a place for himself in the elite ranks, but showed an entirely new way for the position to be played.

Other goaltenders had been called "third defencemen" in their time for the way they handled the puck in

their own end. With Hextall, opposing players and coaches were ready to move him up onto a forward line. In Hextall's first month in the NHL, Leaf coach John Brophy said: "He shoots the puck so well he could play point on the power play." Other goaltenders, like Tom Barrasso, were very capable stickhandlers. Hextall took the goaltender's art of puck control to a new level. He wandered far and wide from the net to snare loose pucks, delivering pinpoint breakout passes that erased the effectiveness of dump-and-chase hockey; he was so effective that he could catch forecheckers badly out of position when one of his passes launched a Philadelphia counterattack. He came out of the minors to assume one of the most important roles on the Flyers team, serving as both a defensive and an offensive threat, as well as the emotional core to the team. He fused the size and quickness of Dryden, exceeded the puck-handling skills of Rayner, Hall, Plante and Giacomin (while wearing the cumbersome gloves of the modern game) and wrapped it all in a team-based perspective that was worthy of Cheevers.

His brilliance in his rookie season was such that, when it came time for the Edmonton Oilers to defend their Stanley Cup against the Flyers that spring, the main subject was Hextall. "We have to do anything possible to keep the puck away from Hextall," said Wayne Gretzky. "He's so good with the puck he's an added offensive threat. I've never seen anyone handle the puck like this kid." If you didn't know better, you would have thought Gretzky was talking about an opposing centre.

The Oilers' goaltender, Grant Fuhr, suggested Edmonton "bump him a bit. He's hot-headed. You can make him lose his concentration if he loses his temper."

There was that about him. Hextall had a very short fuse attached to a highly combustible stick hand. When he wasn't using his stick to let fly breakout passes, he was chopping and hacking at opposing players who wandered into his crease. Since the crease was introduced in 1934, the game's history has been peppered with goaltenders—Davey Kerr among the earliest, Gerry Cheevers and Billy Smith among the most recent—who vigorously defended their allotted territory. But no one has ever defended his domain with quite the menace of Hextall. His rookie season was the last before the NHL introduced the expanded semicircular crease, five seasons before the league would toughen up its interference rules with regard to goaltenders. "Running" the goaltender was part of the game, and Hextall was giving no quarter. In that first season, he logged 104 penalty minutes, a record for a goaltender, which meant that fifty-two of the power plays he faced were of his own making.

And even when he was within the rulebook's bounds, he was hyper-aggressive. In their Wales Conference series against Montreal, the defending Stanley Cup champions, Hextall's pregame warmup included clanging his stick resoundingly on both posts and charging the Montreal bench to whack the boards with his stick.

Against Edmonton in the final, Hextall laid out Kent Nilsson with a wicked slash to the back of his legs. There were long and loud calls for Hextall's suspension, and the league finally assessed an eight-game one—which would begin the next season, after the playoffs were through.

Edmonton built a 3–1 series lead, then watched Philadelphia fight back to force a deciding seventh game. The Oilers prevailed with a 3–1 win, but Hextall's performance (the Nilsson slash delicately overlooked) had been so fundamental to the Flyers' performance that he was given the Conn Smythe award as the series' MVP. More awards followed. He outpolled Mike Liut of Hartford 65–60 to win the Vezina, and just missed the Calder as Luc Robitaille of the Kings edged him 208–190.

With an eight-game suspension awaiting him at the start of the new season, Hextall's bad-boy reputation moved up a notch with an embarrassing incident at the August training camp for Team Canada, preparing for the Canada Cup in September. In a goalmouth scramble, Hextall caught left-winger Sylvain Turgeon with his stick, breaking his arm. Hextall swore it was an accident, but he received a stiff lecture from Team Canada coach Mike Keenan, who was his coach in Philadelphia.

Keenan was concerned enough about Hextall's temper that he had brought in Dr. Carl Botterill, a psychologist with the University of Manitoba, to work with Hextall to control his impulses. The new, larger crease, rather than giving him more security, gave him even more area of the ice in which to feel free to discipline opposing players. Notwithstanding Dr. Botterill's counselling, in his second tour of duty Hextall began collecting even more penalty minutes than he had in his rookie season.

He had been waiting for the right situation to try the shot: a pulled goaltender, a loose puck and at least a two-goal lead. He didn't want to jeopardise the team's lead by risking an icing call and a faceoff back in their own end if the margin was only a goal. In Philadelphia's Spectrum on December 8, 1987, the Boston Bruins provided the proper alignment of variables. At 18:11 of the third period, down 4–2, Bruins coach Terry O'Reilly pulled Reggie Lemelin in favour of an extra attacker. When the Bruins dumped the puck in the Flyers' end, Hextall considered trying the shot, then decided it was too risky. But on the next dump-in, he was ready. Bruins defenceman Gord Kluzak fired the puck wide of the net. Hextall moved out, laying his stick on the ice to prevent the puck from reaching the boards. With a powerful flick of his curved blade, he sent the puck spinning above everybody's head, not touching

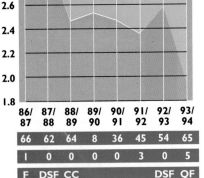

down until it was just outside the Bruins blueline. It slammed into the Boston net inside the right post. The Flyers bench emptied. The Spectrum erupted. Ron Hextall now had as many goals as shutouts in the NHL.

The Flyers were eliminated from Stanley Cup contention in the division semifinal in the spring of 1988, an exit that also brought about the firing of Mike Keenan, who moved on to Chicago. Hextall logged another season as the Flyers' main goaltender, and in the 1988/89 playoffs repeated his 1987 scoring miracle. On April 11, the Washington Capitals became the second team to make the mistake of pulling the goaltender when they were down by two goals and Ron Hextall was on the ice. In three tries to score a goal in the NHL, Hextall had succeeded twice. And he now had more goals than shutouts in the NHL.

He was now immortal, but he was about to become truly notorious. In the Conference Championship series against Montreal, Canadiens defenceman (and Norris winner) Chris Chelios caught Flyer Brian Propp with an elbow that knocked him unconscious but did not produce a penalty. Hextall, above all other Flyers, did not forget the incident. In the dying moments of game six, with the Flyers' elimination assured, Hextall dashed out some forty feet from his net and swung his stick at Chelios's head. Chelios saw him at the last moment, ducked and felt only the wrath of Hextall's blocker.

To many observers, Hextall was now at worst a maniac, at best an impetuous team player who didn't understand what was and was not appropriate in the name of honour. Was the near-decapitation of Chelios the act of someone Bernie Parent thought was on "an even keel"? Hextall's wife Diane, a former fifth-ranked Canadian figure skater, emphasised the essentially gentle nature of her husband. He doted on his family. He was not a guy who tore up bars. Writing in the Toronto *Sun* in February 1990, Bob Olver argued, "The team is an extension of his family. He'll react to protect a teammate with the same ferocity with which he would protect his wife, his children, his parents."

But in the fall of 1989, the team—at least the management—was no longer as close as family for Hextall. Unhappy with the multi-year contract he had signed at the end of his rookie season, he stayed put in Brandon, working out with his old Junior team for six weeks before at last reporting. The Flyers, who had Pete Peeters (the Vezina winner with Boston in 1982/83) and Ken Wregget(a fellow Brandon native), seemed to have plenty of goaltending talent on hand. Plagued by injuries, Hextall only played eight games that season.

His days as the Flyers' dominant goaltender were over. Coach Paul Holmgren, impressed with the Rangers' success with the tag-team of Mike Richter and John Vanbiesbrouck, opted for a similar strategy in Philadelphia, and Hextall divvied up the 1990/91 season with Peeters and Wregget. In exhibition play at the start of the 1991/92 season, Hextall's slash of Detroit Jim Cummins earned him a six-game suspension.

For the third straight season, Philadelphia missed the playoffs. That summer, the NHL turned into a bidding free-for-all as the Quebec Nordiques put their intransigent draftee Eric Lindros on the open market. Hextall was one of six players and two first draft choices Philadelphia traded to Quebec to get Lindros. Hextall played well for the high-scoring Nordiques, but after only one season he was on the move again. The league was holding an expansion draft to fill the rosters of the Anaheim Mighty Ducks and the Florida Panthers, and teams could lose a maximum of two players—one forward and one defencemen or goaltender. Teams deep in goaltending talent wanted to get the best price on the open market, rather than settle for expansion compensation. New York decided to move John Vanbiesbrouck; Toronto offloaded Grant Fuhr. Knowing Hextall would be vulnerable to the draft, the Nordiques traded him to the Islanders, pairing him with their 1993 first-round draft pick to get Mark Fitzpatrick and the Islanders' first-round 1993 draft pick .

He had a difficult season, culminating in a horrible playoff. On their way to their 1994 Stanley Cup victory, the Rangers knocked off Hextall and the Islanders in four straight in the preliminary round. Hextall was up for grabs again, and this time it was the Flyers who did the grabbing. Eight years after stunning the league with his rookie performance, Ron Hextall was starting all over in the city of brotherly love. O

AFTER SIX SEASONS IN PHILADELPHIA, HEXTALL WAS SHIPPED TO QUEBEC IN THE BLOCKBUSTER ERIC LINDROS TRADE OF 1992. THE NORDIQUES THEN TRADED HIM TO THE ISLANDERS RATHER THAN RISK LOSING HIM IN THE 1993 EXPANSION DRAFT. ONE SEASON LATER, HIS CAREER CAME FULL CIRCLE AS THE FLYERS REACQUIRED HIM FOR 1994/95.

HE SHOOTS, HE SCORES!

COLD FURY

AN UNWAVERING
PRESENCE IN
FOUR STANLEY
CUP VICTORIES,
GRANT FUHR
NEARLY
SUCCUMBED TO
PRESSURES
OF LIFE AWAY FROM THE RINK

"Grant never gets excited," said Grant Fuhr's teammate Wayne Gretzky in April 1985, as the Edmonton Oilers marched toward their second Stanley Cup.

The Edmonton Oilers gambled in the 1981 draft, using their first-round pick to secure Fuhr. The promising young Albertan was welcomed to the team at the draft by Wayne Gretzky.

"He never gets mad. He never gets happy. His attitude to anything is just, 'Oh well.' He's like a relief pitcher. Nothing gets him down. Nothing gets him up. He's a hard guy to describe."

By then Gretzky had been a teammate of Grant Fuhr's for four seasons, and it seems in retrospect that he, like many people, scarcely knew who Fuhr was. He was, it is now apparent, rock-steady on the ice, but off the ice a shy young man who for a half-dozen years turned to drugs and alcohol rather than confronting his problems. When he was "outed" as a cocaine user by his ex-wife Corrine at the start of the 1990/91 season, one of the greatest goaltending careers was almost irreparably derailed. That he has been able to recover from this scandal, and the humiliation and suspension that went with it, is a tribute to his quiet determination and the faith others have placed in it.

In his greatest years, he was the security blanket of a young, creative offensive machine, the Edmonton Oilers. Fuhr was often left on his own, as Gerry Cheevers had been by the Bruins of the early 1970s, to keep the score in Edmonton's favour. His GA, as with Cheevers', was irrelevant when it came to assessing his skill. And like Cheevers, the normal accolades regularly passed him by. Cheevers never made an NHL All Star team, while Fuhr, after being named to the second team in his rookie season, had to wait until he and the Oilers were on their way to winning their fourth Stanley Cup before he was named to an All Star team again.

He was raised in Spruce Grove, Alberta, twenty miles west of Edmonton, by white parents who adopted him when he was thirteen days old. When he arrived in the NHL, writers felt duty-bound to acknowledge his race, but he refused to make an issue of being black. "My colour doesn't matter much, does it?" he proposed to a scribe in January 1982, and that was pretty well the end of that subject.

He was fortunate to have been raised in a town only five miles from Stony Plain, where goaltending great Glenn Hall has his farm; as a result, Fuhr had Hall as a coach while in Pee Wee, and he came to play with a trademark Hall butterfly style. He was so good so young that in 1979, at seventeen, he was on his way to Victoria, B.C., to play for the Cougars in the Western Hockey League Junior A. He had also been sought out by the Calgary Wranglers, but Fuhr picked Victoria "because I'd never been there before and the weather was better than Calgary's."

In two seasons in Victoria, Fuhr racked up victories. He won thirty of forty-three games with a GA of 3.14 in 1979/80, forty-eight of fifty-nine games with a league-leading GA of 2.78 in 1980/81, and was a first-team All Star in the western league in both seasons. The Cougars won their league title in 1980/81, and the only knock anyone could come up with against Fuhr was that he was fairly ordinary in the playoffs, with a GA of 3.00. In his first season, scouts called him the best Junior prospect since Bernie Parent.

He would always be a three-goal-a-game goaltender, often higher, not often lower. He has never challenged the two-goal GA the way other greats have, and this has been mainly because of the kind of teams he has played on. Fuhr has always excelled as the last line of defence in the wide-open game.

The professional club most interested in him was his hometown team, the Edmonton Oilers. Their veteran netminder from the club's WHA days, Dave Dryden, had retired early in the 1979/80 season, moving into the assistant coach's job. Dryden set out to find his own replacement. "I spent two to three weeks scouting Juniors, scouting Fuhr and Moog. I really liked Moog." The Oilers took Andy Moog deep in the 1980 draft, 132nd overall. Like Fuhr, he was a product of the Western Junior A, and he played seven regular-season and nine playoff games for the Oilers in 1980/81, with another twenty-nine for Billings in the Central League.

While Moog showed well in the Oilers' playoff games, he had just turned twenty-one and the Oilers decided he needed more seasoning in Billings. To cover all their goaltending bases, Oilers scout Barry Fraser wanted to use Edmonton's 1981 first-round pick to get Fuhr. Coach and general manager Glen Sather agreed. "It was a big decision to take a goaltender in the first round," said Sather in 1982, "especially after the way Andy Moog played in the playoffs. But we discussed every angle and I always remember what Emile Francis told me years ago—that you can't have enough defence. Well, we figured we can't have enough good goaltenders."

Fuhr came into the Oilers' starting lineup that first season, and played wonderfully, losing only five of forty-eight games, but he was overlooked entirely in Calder voting, despite making the second All Star team. "He's a little like Tony Esposito," said Eddie Johnston, the former Bruins goaltender, who was coaching Pittsburgh that season. "He gets down like Tony O, but he covers a fair amount of the net. He also shuts you off very quick. I had heard he was going to be one helluva goaltender and he certainly has shown me that." Oilers assistant coach Billy Harris (Dave Dryden had moved on to coach Peterborough of the OHA Junior A), who played right wing for Toronto from 1955 to 1965, noted: "The only rookie goalie I've seen with as much poise, and as cool as this kid is, was Johnny Bower. But Johnny was in his thirties when he was a rookie and had been a pro a dozen years."

The Oilers went from fifteenth to second place in the league standings in one season, but in the first round of the playoffs were upset by Los Angeles, the last team to qualify for the post-season. The next season hit Fuhr with the traditional sophomore goaltending jinx. By January, Edmonton fans were booing him as his GA hit 4.28, and he was demoted to the Moncton Alpines of the American League for ten games. Ed Chadwick, Edmonton's goaltending coach, who had played for Toronto in the late 1950s and had groomed Chico Resch for the New York Islanders down in the Central League in the early 1970s, was assigned the task of smoothing out Fuhr's wrinkles. Andy Moog became the main Oilers netminder, carrying them to their first Stanley Cup appearance, against the reigning Islanders. The Islanders had struggled to sixth overall in the standings, but jelled in the playoffs as Billy Smith held the Oilers to only six goals in a four-game sweep and won the Conn Smythe.

In 1983/84, Fuhr was back, and in form, and Moog moved onto the Oilers back burner as the team started winning Stanley Cups. Moog would play half the regular season, sometimes filling in for Fuhr when injuries waylaid him, but when the playoffs rolled around, Moog would go back on the bench. In four seasons from 1983/84 to 1986/87, Moog appeared in only eleven playoff games.

In 1986/87, Fuhr appeared poised to win the Conn Smythe as the Oilers led the Philadelphia Flyers three games to one in the Stanley Cup final. But when Ron Hextall's goaltending got the Flyers back in the series,

forcing a deciding seventh game that Edmonton won, the Smythe went to Hextall.

The next season, 1987/88, Fuhr recorded his signature performance. Back in 1971, Gerry Cheevers had declared that "nobody can play seventy games plus nowadays. Nobody." Bernie Parent proved him wrong, logging seventy-three with Philadelphia in 1973/74. In 1987/88, Fuhr broke Parent's record, playing seventy-five regular-season games (leading the league with forty wins), as a frustrated Andy Moog quit the Oilers to play for the Canadian national and Olympic teams. Fuhr at last won the Vezina and made it onto the first All Star team; while he was touted for the Hart, it went to Mario Lemieux. In the playoffs, Fuhr won sixteen of nineteen games as the Oilers took their fourth Stanley Cup in five seasons.

The brutal pace of that season's games was an anomaly for Fuhr. He generally played about forty to forty-five games, his ice time cut down in part by injuries that constantly nagged him. A bad knee kept him out of the 1984 Canada Cup; he separated his shoulder in February

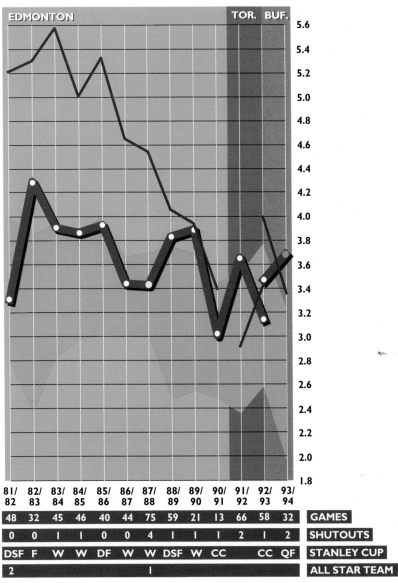

	81/82	82/83	83/84	84/85	85/86	86/87	87/88	88/89	89/90	90/91	91/92	92/93	93/94	
GAMES	48	32	45	46	40	44	75	59	21	13	66	58	32	
SHUTOUTS	0	0	1	1	0	4	4	1	1	1	2	1	2	
STANLEY CUP	DSF	F	W	W	DF	W	W	DSF	W	CC		CC	QF	
ALL STAR TEAM	2						1							

In 1992/93, Fuhr played twenty-nine games, with one shutout, for Toronto, and twenty-nine games for Buffalo.

| *COLD FURY*

1985 when he fell on his stick.

But he never made an issue of his injuries, or the bruises he nursed, or the way his teammates did or did not support him. "Nothing ever seems to bother Grant," Gretzky said in the 1984/85 playoffs, "or if it does he's able to keep it disguised. He never gets excited when things are going good or down in the dumps when they're bad. He just stays on a steady, even keel. No matter how many mistakes are made in front of him or how badly guys goof up on a play, he never blames anyone else for a goal against him."

After the glorious 1987/88 campaign, Fuhr's starting job could not have seemed more secure. On March 8, 1988, the Oilers traded away the frustrated, absent Moog to Boston for Bill Ranford. (In Boston, Moog shared the Jennings with Reggie Lemelin in 1989/90, and could boast the highest percentage of winning career games of any active goaltender.) Ranford filled in for six games for Fuhr at the end of the season, resting up the starter for the playoff drive. Ranford appeared destined to be another Moog, a talented understudy for the ever-reliable Fuhr.

But the Oilers were, in retrospect, the most insecure club in hockey even as they won their fourth cup. That August, club owner Peter Pocklington began cashing in his assets, dealing Wayne Gretzky, Mike Krushelnyski and Marty McSorley to Los Angeles. Fuhr had an uncharacteristically sub-par season in 1988/89, and Ranford stepped in for twenty-nine games. Fuhr took over in the playoffs again, and the first round paired Gretzky's Kings against his old teammates. The Oilers built a 3–1 series lead, only to have the Kings, with Kelly Hrudey holding its shooters to six goals, come back to take the series.

Fuhr appeared to lose control of his life in the summer of 1989. He filed his retirement papers that June, and talked about selling cars for a living. His agent, Rich Winter, suspected drug use, despite his many denials, and made him take a test. When it came out positive, Fuhr agreed to enter the Straight Center in St. Petersburg, Florida, in August. Gretzky had come close to the essence of Fuhr in these years when he noted in 1985 the possibility that Fuhr might be disguising his feelings. Since about 1983, Fuhr had been

seeking relief from the pressures of the game, and the pressures he placed on himself, in alcohol and then drugs. Although he would never specifically refer to cocaine (simply referring to a "substance"), and he would refute any suggestion that he had suffered from an addiction, as a self-described introvert he had taken to drugs to feel part of the "in crowd" (as he put it), and to avoid dealing with problems. A quality essential to his career as a superb goaltender—keeping his emotions in check—nearly ruined him. "I basically self-destructed," he said in January 1991.

His drug use came close to being exposed when *Sports Illustrated* ran a story in 1986 alleging cocaine use by several unnamed Oilers. Fuhr was confronted by Sather at this time about his use, as well as by the RCMP, and vigorously denied it. Sather himself then blasted the magazine for printing allegations the Oilers said were without foundation.

Despite the ongoing personal problems, Fuhr was ceaselessly feted as the most level-headed, unflappable of people. "Pressure has little effect on Fuhr," assured the Toronto *Sun* in February 1988, the month Fuhr signed a new eight-year deal worth $400,000 a season. "He doesn't get uptight about a lot of things," Sather said at the time. "He's very relaxed emotionally and he's a confident, level-headed guy. He's got the right attitude to play goal."

Fuhr himself contributed to the image of nonchalance. "Life is too short to get tense about anything," he offered in the spring of 1985. His lightning-fast hands were compared with those of Philadelphia netminder Pelle Lindbergh, a portentous choice, as Lindbergh was killed in the fall of 1985 driving his sports car at high speed under the influence of alcohol.

When he came out of the Straight Center in August 1989, Fuhr moved through a flurry of changes. He separated from Corrine, dropped both his retirement plans and Winter as his agent, and signed a new deal with Sather. But he was no longer the Oilers' starting goaltender. Ranford played fifty-six regular-season games and all twenty-two playoff games in 1989/90, winning the Conn Smythe that eluded Fuhr as the Oilers brought the Stanley Cup back to Edmonton.

Fuhr's personal problems might never have come to public light had Corrine not decided to tell all to the *Edmonton Journal* in September 1990, one week after Fuhr had remarried. Her story included the nightmare of drug dealers coming to the house during the 1983/84 playoffs, threatening to "kneecap" Fuhr if he didn't come up with drug debts. Fuhr was furious, and saw it as nothing more than spite on Corrine's part, despite her avowal that it was a move to make him confront his problems. Fuhr said he'd been clean since his visit to the Straight Center in August 1989, and that the exposé had proved especially hurtful to the eldest of his and Corrine's two daughters. Agreeing to be interviewed by the *Journal*, he explained, "I was trying to get my life straightened out. I wasn't happy."

Corrine's revelations and Fuhr's acknowledgment that he had been treated for substance abuse landed a hot

FUHR MADE THE SECOND ALL STAR TEAM IN HIS ROOKIE SEASON AND STEADILY EMERGED AS THE MAIN OILERS NETMINDER AHEAD OF ANDY MOOG.

potato in the lap of NHL president John Ziegler. The league had adopted a "zero tolerance" policy on drug use: if you were revealed to have used drugs, you were gone. Although Fuhr insisted the drug years were behind him, and that he was continuing to receive counselling to keep himself straight, the league's strict policy led Ziegler to banish Fuhr from the game for one year.

As much as the game had been a source of pressure, to Fuhr it was also his sanctuary, and he was not going to give it up easily. "Once I'm on the ice, I'm in my own little world and I enjoy it," he said in 1990. "I have fun when I'm on the ice and nobody can take it away from me."

Much outrage ensued. The Oilers were accused of having turned a blind eye to Fuhr's problems. Corrine insisted she had taken her concerns directly to Sather during her marriage to Fuhr, but that nothing had come of it. The league was berated for a draconian policy that would effectively punish any player who admitted to a drug problem and turned to his team for help. Rather than keeping drug users out of the league, it kept them secretly bottled up within it, with no way to get help without destroying their careers at the same time. Smarting under the attacks, the league commuted Fuhr's ban to sixty games. In February 1991, Fuhr returned to the ice to shut out the New Jersey Devils.

Fuhr appeared in twenty-one games in the last few months of the season, then played the majority of the playoff games, seventeen in all, as the Oilers struggled past Calgary and Los Angeles before bowing to the late-surging Minnesota North Stars.

While Sather had gone back to Fuhr as his starting goaltender after his suspension was over, the Oilers decided that henceforth Ranford was to be their starter. In September 1991, the Oilers traded Fuhr, along with Glenn Anderson and Craig Berube, to the Toronto Maple Leafs. "I think he's got a great psyche for a goalie," said Toronto coach Tom Watt. "He never gets excited about anything. You can drop a bomb beside him and he might turn his head." The Leafs made him the league's highest-paid goaltender with a $1.6 million salary, $350,000 ahead of Patrick Roy. It was a resounding expression of confidence in Fuhr as a franchise player. Whatever his problems might have been in the past, they were not now a part of his game or his life.

His new career in Toronto started shakily. He was injured, and not playing well, and when an unspecified family crisis arose in the first month of the season, Fuhr disappeared while the team was in Winnipeg. The incident blew over, but by December dissatisfied Leaf fans were booing him at home, which outraged him. As the Leafs found their form in the second half of the season, though, Fuhr was a key ingredient in the turnaround.

He might have lasted longer in Toronto had injuries not continuously sidelined him. While Fuhr was sitting out two such spells in 1991/92, Felix Potvin came up from the minors and proved he was ready for the NHL slightly ahead of schedule. Not wanting to lose Fuhr in the expansion draft that summer, in February 1992 the Leafs shipped him to Buffalo in a trade that bagged them three players in return, including Dave Andreychuk.

Fuhr was a solid performer in Buffalo, though the Sabres' goal became primarily the domain of Dominik Hasek, a veteran of the Czech national team who won the Vezina and shared the Jennings with Fuhr in 1993/94 and was a runner-up for the Hart. Hasek's GA was by far the more impressive of the Jennings pair: 1.95 compared to Fuhr's 3.68. Hasek appeared in all of the Sabres' 1993/94 playoff games, and the following summer was rewarded with a three-year $8-million contract. When Fuhr showed up for the lockout-shortened 1994/95 season, he was wearing generic white pads...a colour that could be worn while playing for any team. Fuhr was now thirty-three; Hasek was about to turn thirty. Though Hasek was no fresh-scrubbed rookie, Fuhr well understood who had the upper hand in securing the starting job. He began the season fully prepared for the trade he was sure would come. In February, it came. Wayne Gretzky's Kings got him. ○

AS THE GREAT OILERS TEAM OF THE 1980S WAS BROKEN UP BY OWNER PETER POCKLINGTON, FUHR CAME EAST TO PLAY FOR THE MAPLE LEAFS. WHEN FELIX POTVIN DEMONSTRATED MAJOR-LEAGUE TALENT AHEAD OF SCHEDULE, THE LEAFS DEALT FUHR TO BUFFALO.

KING OF THE HILL

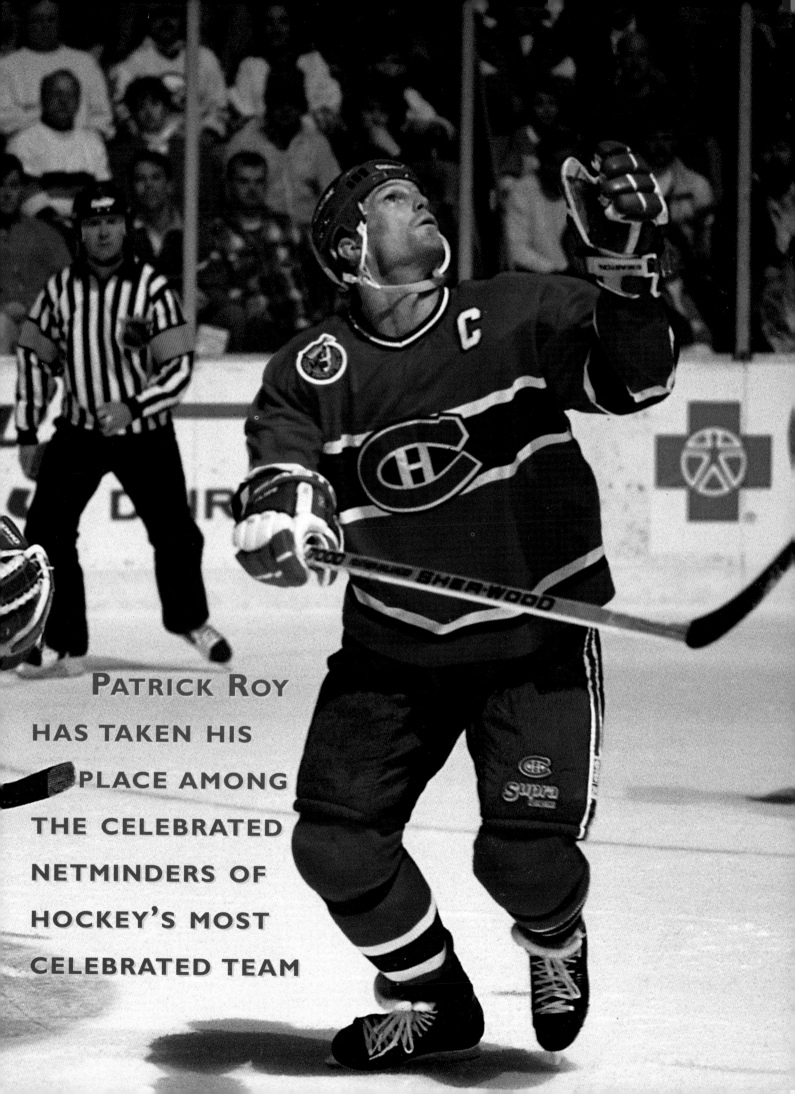

PATRICK ROY HAS TAKEN HIS PLACE AMONG THE CELEBRATED NETMINDERS OF HOCKEY'S MOST CELEBRATED TEAM

To PLAY GOAL, IT MIGHT BE ARGUED—TO REALLY PLAY GOAL—YOU MUST PLAY IT AS A MONTREAL CANADIEN. IF YOU CAN GUARD THE NET OF THE

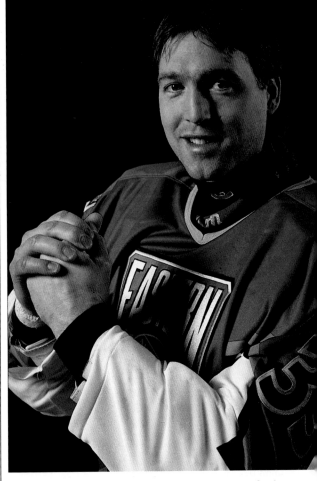

greatest team in the world, and win, you can take your place in an awesome pantheon of talent. Seated on the throne atop its Olympus is Georges Vezina himself, and surrounding him are Hainsworth, Durnan, Plante, Worsley and Dryden, as well as others who brought honour to the club and its city: Cude, McNeil, Hodge, Vachon, Larocque and Hayward.

Many others have attempted this ascent. Some got a running start and quickly ran out of steam. Some got thrown off the mountain. Others have pitched themselves from it. Just gaining a toehold on this chunk of rock is an accomplishment, but once there, you cannot simply cling to it; you move up or you move off. In 1986, a twenty-year-old prospect who had grown up rooting for the Canadiens' bitter rivals, the Quebec Nordiques, started the climb toward Vezina's right hand.

At times during Roy's first nine seasons in Montreal, opinions varied as to whether or not he deserved to remain on, or even to set foot on, this mountain. His initial success, it seemed, came too quickly for him. Some of his own teammates were initially inclined to shove him off. And many fans, after both cheering and enduring Roy for more than eight seasons, were ready to start an avalanche in his direction. But Roy, finally, has been allowed to stop climbing. He now has the nicest view the game can deliver.

IN NINE NHL SEASONS, ROY HAS APPEARED ON FIVE ALL STAR TEAMS, AND PICKED UP THREE VEZINA AND THREE JENNINGS TROPHIES ALONG THE WAY.

Fifteen years had passed since Ken Dryden had made his wondrous debut with the Canadiens in the spring of 1971, as a phenomenon who had played too few regular-season games to qualify even as a rookie, who carried the Canadiens to an unexpected Stanley Cup victory and won himself the Conn Smythe in the process. When Patrick Roy backstopped the Canadiens to an unexpected Stanley Cup victory in the spring of 1986 and won himself the Conn Smythe in the process, there were stirrings of déjà vu, although there were important differences in the circumstances of the two talents.

By the time Roy came along, Canadiens fans were impatient for the arrival of their next netminding great, as well as being impatient for another Stanley Cup. After Dryden's departure, the Canadiens suffered a disquieting string of playoff eliminations; from 1979/80 to 1982/83,

the Habs couldn't advance past their division semifinal. Like no other team, the Canadiens provided proof of the symbiotic relationship between outstanding goaltending and championship seasons.

Ever since Georges Vezina put on the bleu, blanc et rouge in 1910, the club had enjoyed a virtually unbroken string of star goaltenders. Dryden retired at the end of the 1978/79 season with no heir apparent. The Canadiens made three immediate goaltending acquisitions: they drafted Rick Wamsley, moved in twenty-two-year-old Richard Sevigny and acquired Denis Herron from Pittsburgh. Dryden's longstanding backup, Michel Larocque, with whom he shared the Vezina, had never been a playoff goaltender—that was Dryden's forte—and was traded to Toronto in 1980/81, though he got to share the Vezina with Sevigny and Herron that season. Wamsley and Herron won a Jennings together in 1981/82, but neither they nor Sevigny were judged to be franchise players as Montreal couldn't make any progress in the playoffs. Right after winning the Jennings, Herron was dealt back to Pittsburgh; Wamsley went to St. Louis and Sevigny to Quebec in 1984. In the 1985 playoffs, Montreal experienced its first Dryden déjà vu when newcomer Steve Penney played exceptionally well, but the following season his GA broke 4.00.

The Canadiens had another contender in the pipeline, a gangly six-footer named Patrick Roy, drafted in 1984. As the goaltender for the defensively obtuse Granby Bisons of the Quebec Junior league, Roy was accustomed to being peppered with fifty shots a game. "It was tough playing for them," he has recalled. "But I got a lot of work and it was a good experience. I learned to deal with the frustrations of losing and now I appreciate more the enjoyment of winning."

During 1984/85, Montreal brought him up from Granby to its new American League affiliate, the Sherbrooke Canadiens. He appeared in one regular-season game for the club, which played .500 hockey and had the second-highest goals-against in its division. He was scored on four times in that game, a better than average night for Roy, whose GA that season in Granby was 5.55—a season in which he only won sixteen of forty-four games but was still named the Quebec Junior league's top goaltender. He also got to play one period of hockey for Montreal, and he came away from it without being scored on.

When the 1984/85 American League playoffs began, Roy, who was brought in as a backup, got a break. Sherbrooke's regular starter, Paul Pageau, was off while his wife was giving birth. Then Greg Moffet had trouble with a leg pad strap, and Roy was hustled into the game. He stayed put, won ten of thirteen playoff games with a 2.89 GA, and Sherbrooke came from the middle of the league pack to win the championship. Another "out of nowhere" legend was rapidly gathering momentum.

He was moved up to the Montreal Canadiens that fall as the third-string netminder behind Doug Soetaert (acquired from Winnipeg in 1984) and Steve Penney. When both were injured, Roy was pressed into the starter's role. He had just turned twenty on October 5.

He was no shining saviour. At a time when top goaltenders were becoming technically indistinguishable, Roy was not a technician. For a tall goaltender, he went down on the ice a lot, probably too much. The Canadiens found him subsisting on a diet dominated by potato chips augmented by French fries (his nickname in Juniors, inspired by his favourite snack-food maker, was Humpty Dumpty), and had to get him to change his eating habits so that he didn't run out of energy. He added a traditional dose of eccentricity to the job by skating out to the blueline before a game, turning to face the net, and beaming telepathic thoughts at his goal posts. "I talk to my posts," he admitted. "It's a superstition. The forwards talk to each other. The defence is always close, but the goaltender is alone." He gave up soft goals, and some of his teammates, a focused defensive unit, were so dismayed by him that they went to the new coach, Jean Perron, and asked that he be replaced.

Demers stuck by him. Montreal finished second in the Adams division with a poor road record, and Roy recorded a mundane GA of 3.35.

Which brought on the playoffs. He dazzled, despite his shortcomings. "His gaffs are so extraordinary, and so obvious, that he can't even glare at the defenceman, an old goalie's ruse, to shift the blame," Rex McLeod observed that April in the *Toronto Star*.

Whatever mistakes he made, they didn't matter much. He led the league's goaltenders with fifteen playoff wins in twenty starts and a miserly GA of 1.92. The fact that he produced this GA with one shutout (the only one of the playoffs) underlines his remarkable consistency as the Canadiens, a team without the offensive stars that marked the Dryden years, overcame the heavily favoured Calgary Flames to win the cup. Roy was the obvious choice for the Conn Smythe. In Sherbrooke, and now in Montreal, Roy had demonstrated a quality that no manual and no amount of coaching or seasoning could instil: a gut instinct for winning the big game.

But was he just another Penney? The sceptics awaited Roy's sophomore campaign. Over the summer, Roy revelled in his stardom, getting a part-time job as a video jockey on the television show "Musique Plus." He was from a well-off family—his father was a vice-president of the Quebec auto insurance board—and a career in law had been contemplated for him, but now he was devoting himself exclusively to the net.

That September, Dryden, who had devoted himself to the net and to the law in equal measure, contributed his thoughts on the prospects for his long-awaited heir apparent. "When you're new," he noted, "anything you can provide a team is unexpected, special. So you can get judged as a prodigy, with people overlooking things about you that aren't so great. But eventually the fourteen-year-old becomes a seventeen-year-old and then a twenty-six-year-old, and you're not looking for the prodigy any more; you're looking for the artist. You have to grow and meet new standards. And the standards for a goalie are not occasional. It's not the spectacular game, but the routine good performances day after day."

Roy's new season got off to a shaky start when he showed up a day late for training camp. That summer, Montreal had traded Penney to Winnipeg and received Brian Hayward in return. Hayward played thirty-seven games in the ensuing season, Roy forty-six, but on balance it was Hayward's year. Roy was able to have his name inscribed along-

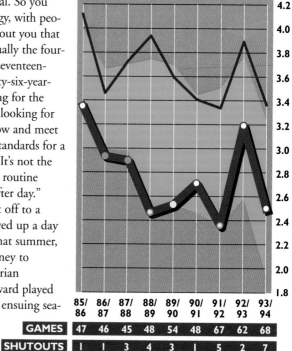

	85/86	86/87	87/88	88/89	89/90	90/91	91/92	92/93	93/94
GAMES	47	46	45	48	54	48	67	62	68
SHUTOUTS	1	1	3	4	3	1	5	2	7
STANLEY CUP	W	CC	DF	F	DF	DF	DF	W	QF
ALL STAR TEAM		2	1		1	2		1	

Roy appeared in one game with Montreal in 1984/85.

side Hayward's on the Jennings by producing a very good GA of 2.93, but Hayward's was better at 2.81, and neither of them would have won the award if Philadelphia hadn't fallen apart in its final game of the season, losing 9–5 to New York and allowing Roy and Hayward to move four goals ahead of Ron Hextall. In the playoffs, Roy could not repeat his sparkling performances of the past two post-seasons in the American and National leagues. Though he won four of the six games he played, his GA was 4.00, and it was Hayward who impressed. Appropriately, Hayward originally had been signed as a free agent by Winnipeg out of Cornell, Ken Dryden's alma mater.

For the next two seasons, Roy and Hayward were a netminding partnership, bringing their Jennings wins to three in a row. In 1987/88, the critics began to warm to Roy as a major talent; he was no longer simply a goaltender with brilliant moments, or one who benefited from the traditional defensive parsimony of the Canadiens. The season got off to a bad start when he skated out from his crease to lay a two-handed slash on the leg of Minnesota's Warren Babe, which earned him a major penalty. At the time, Ron Hextall was serving his eight-game suspension for slashing Kent Nilsson in the previous spring's playoffs. Roy received an eight-game suspension of his own. His first game back, he shut out Chicago 3–0. The season began a string of five straight All Star team appearances, and in 1988/89, when his GA plunged to 2.47, he won his first Vezina.

After that, Montreal essentially became a one-goalie town. In 1989/90, Roy played more than fifty games in one NHL season for the first time. He took the load in stride, winning another Vezina, leading all goaltenders with thirty-one wins, and was named to the first All Star team. After the season, Hayward was dealt to Minnesota.

As the personal honours were showered on Roy, Montreal fans longed for another successful post-season, something they hadn't experienced since Roy made his debut in 1986. In the ensuing years, the Stanley Cup went west, to Edmonton and Calgary, and then south to Pittsburgh. Pat Burns had taken over as coach from Perron in 1988/89, and after the 1991/92 campaign he decided to take his services to the Maple Leafs.

The 1991/92 playoffs were the first serious professional setback for Roy after his indifferent performance in the 1986/87 post-season. His 1991/92 season was probably his finest—a record sixty-seven games, with a league-leading five shutouts, a first-team All Star appearance, and both the Vezina and the Jennings. But in the post-season, Montreal struggled to get by Hartford, and were then swept in four by Boston as Roy won only four of eleven games. His poor play was blamed by some on burnout from the regular season. But a players' strike before the playoffs had given him some down time, and that summer, rumours circulated that Montreal was prepared to give up Roy to the Nordiques to get Eric Lindros, the sensational draft pick who was refusing to report to Quebec.

The trade didn't come, but the next season didn't hold up much promise of redemption for Roy. His GA began to climb, nearly a full goal above the previous season's. Roy-bashing became a new sport. Hartford players in the previous spring's playoffs had belittled Roy by saying he flopped around like formless jelly. Bruins general manager Harry Sinden swiped at both his goaltender, Andy Moog, and Roy in the new season by declaring that Moog was playing as badly as Roy had against Hartford.

Roy brushed aside the concerns about his three-plus GA. The new coach, Jacques Demers, was emphasising offence, he noted, and that meant less support for him back behind the blueline. Montreal indeed would score fifty-nine more goals in 1992/93 than in 1991/92, but would also allow seventy-three more as Roy's GA soared to 3.20. And although Roy led in fan voting for the starting role in the All Star game, he was not named to the first or second team, and critics wondered whether he really deserved to start the game ahead of netminders like Ed Belfour, Kirk McLean, Tom Barrasso, Jon Casey and Ron Hextall. The low point for Roy came in a radio phone-in poll held in Montreal over the Christmas holidays, in which more than half of the callers thought Roy should be traded.

All of it was put behind him in the 1992/93 playoffs. He recorded the most wins of any goaltender (sixteen of twenty games) and the lowest GA (2.13), and was second in save percentage to Curtis Joseph of St. Louis. His ten straight sudden-death wins set a record, and along the way he went ninety-six minutes and thirty-nine seconds without being scored on. Seven years after Roy last brought Montreal a Stanley Cup and himself the Conn Smythe, he did it again. The following September, Montreal made him the highest-paid goaltender in the league with a four-year contract worth a minimum of $16 million.

In 1993/94, Roy played sixty-eight games, the most in his career, led the league with seven shutouts and posted an enviable 2.50 GA. There was no repeat Stanley Cup or Conn Smythe—this would be New York's season. But Roy secured a place in Canadiens lore with a performance that exceeded in its heroics any cup-winning acrobatics. With Montreal trailing Boston in their playoff series 2–1, Roy was admitted to hospital with appendicitis. Refusing surgery, he opted for a dose of antibiotics and checked himself out of the hospital on the morning of game four. Less than twelve hours after he left the hospital, Roy stopped thirty-nine shots as Montreal won 5–2 to tie the series. The Canadiens were ultimately eliminated, but Roy's gesture left what might be the most lasting impression of all his accomplishments.

He has staked a legitimate claim to being the pre-eminent modern goaltender. Despite criticisms that he drops to the ice too much, that his stick work and glove hand are perfectly ordinary, Roy routinely stops more shots than anyone else, and he wins. In Montreal, that's the final measure of greatness. It has been more than enough to get him to the top of the biggest mountain in the game. ◯

ROY HAS STAKED A LEGITIMATE CLAIM TO BEING THE PRE-EMINENT MODERN GOALTENDER. HE IS NO TECHNICIAN. HE JUST WINS.

INDEX

CREDITS

IMAGES

All artifacts in this book are from the Hockey Hall of Fame collection. All photographs of artifacts and trophies are by Doug MacLellan/Hockey Hall of Fame.

Photographs not otherwise credited are from the general collection of the Hockey Hall of Fame

Imperial Oil/Turofsky/Hockey Hall of Fame
29, 38–39, 43, 47 (top), 62–63, 66, 72, 78, 79, 80–81, 84, 90, 91, 96 (Broda), 97 (Francis), 101, 102, 104–05, 108, 112, 114, 116–17, 121, 125, 125 (top and bottom), 154 (top left)

Frank Prazak/Hockey Hall of Fame
86–87, 93, 115, 134–35, 137, 146, 152, 152–53, 157, 159 (top)

Graphic Artists/Hockey Hall of Fame
99, 110–11, 138, 141, 142, 143, 144, 149, 151, 160–61, 163, 164–65, 167, 168–69

Miles Nadal/Hockey Hall of Fame
181, 196, 198

Doug MacLellan/Hockey Hall of Fame
155 (top), 172–73, 174, 178–79, 183, 187, 191, 193, 194–95, 199, 200–01, 202, 205

Glenbow Archives
Contents, 24, 96 (Tobin glove)

UPI/Bettmann
8–9, 32–33, 40, 43, 46, 49, 55, 79

Reuters/Bettmann/Peter Jones
10

The Bettmann Archive
52–53, 74–75

National Archives of Canada
18–19, Dept. of Interior Coll./NAC/PA–049739
21 (top), H.J. Woodside Coll./NAC/PA–016009
25, Eiji Kitagawa Coll./NAC/PA–117267
70, Gazette Coll./NAC/PA–108368

SOURCES

The author used the archives of the Hockey Hall of Fame as his main research tool, in addition to interviews noted in Acknowledgements. Files on individual players contain decades of news articles and published profiles, and from these the author has drawn quotes and facts that appear in this work. He also used the archive's microfiche records of *The Hockey News*. For his charts, he has drawn on statistical records of relevant leagues, and from them calculated figures such as league goals-against, team scoring averages, and in some cases individual goals-against records. He is particularly appreciative of the research on the Pacific Coast Hockey Association and affiliated leagues performed by Ron Boileau, which is available in the HHOF archives.

The number of books consulted in the course of writing and fact-checking this work are too numerous to mention, but several merit comment, having been either the source of quotes or facts or just a worthwhile read. These are *When the Rangers were Young*, by Frank Boucher (with Trent Frayne); *Lions in Winter*, by Chris Goyens and Allan Turowetz; *They Call Me Gump*, by Lorne Worsley (with Tim Moriarty); *Goaltender*, by Gerry Cheevers (with Trent Frayne); *Tretiak: The Legend*, by Vladislav Tretiak; *The Game*, by Ken Dryden; *If You Can't Beat Em In the Alley*, by Conn Smythe (with Scott Young); *War On Ice*, by Scott Young; *Hockey Night in Canada*, by Foster Hewitt; *The Glory Years*, by Billy Harris; *The Red Machine*, by Lawrence Martin; *The Trail of the Stanley Cup, Vol. 1 & 2*, published by the NHL; *The Montreal Canadiens*, by Claude Mouton; *The Chicago Blackhawks Story*, by George Vass; and *The Stanley Cup*, by D'Arcy Jenish.

In addition, the author relied on several volumes for league and player histories, including: *The Complete Encyclopedia of Hockey*, edited by Zander Hollander; *The National Hockey League Official Guide and Record Book; The American Hockey League Guide and Record Book;* and various historic editions of *Hendy's Who's Who in Hockey*, in particular a 1950 edition on loan to him from Sam Bettio.

ON MAKING THIS BOOK

Interior design, photo research, illustrations, black-and-white close-crops: Douglas Hunter
Jacket design: Martin Gould
Editor: Meg Masters
Copy editor: Jem Bates
Production director: Dianne Craig
Production editor: Lori Ledingham
Film work, printing and binding: New Interlitho Italia S.p.A. on acid neutral paper

A Breed Apart uses the typefaces Gill Sans and Adobe Garamond (thanks, Stuart) in the interior design. It was produced on a Mac platform using Quark XPress 3.3 for page design, Adobe Illustrator 5.5 for charts and illustrations, and Photoshop 2.5 for image position scanning and close cropping of final black-and-white images. A big thanks to Robin Brass of Robin Brass Studio for making available his transparency scanner, and a belated one to the fine arts department of McMaster University for teaching me how to see.